Living on the Edge

Living on the Edge

An American Generation's Journey
through the Twentieth Century

RICHARD A. SETTERSTEN JR.,
GLEN H. ELDER JR., AND LISA D. PEARCE

The University of Chicago Press
Chicago and London

The University of Chicago Press, Chicago 60637
The University of Chicago Press, Ltd., London
© 2021 by The University of Chicago
All rights reserved. No part of this book may be used or reproduced in any manner
whatsoever without written permission, except in the case of brief quotations in
critical articles and reviews. For more information, contact the University of Chicago Press,
1427 E. 60th St., Chicago, IL 60637.
Published 2021
Printed in the United States of America

30 29 28 27 26 25 24 23 22 21   1 2 3 4 5

ISBN-13: 978-0-226-74809-2 (cloth)
ISBN-13: 978-0-226-74812-2 (paper)
ISBN-13: 978-0-226-74826-9 (e-book)
DOI: https://doi.org/10.7208/chicago/9780226748269.001.0001

Library of Congress Cataloging-in-Publication Data

Names: Settersten, Richard A., Jr., 1964– author. | Elder, Glen H., Jr., author. |
    Pearce, Lisa D. (Lisa Deanne), 1971– author.
Title: Living on the edge : an American generation's journey through the twentieth
    century / Richard A. Settersten Jr., Glen H. Elder Jr., and Lisa D. Pearce.
Description: Chicago ; London : The University of Chicago Press, 2021. |
    Includes bibliographical references and index.
Identifiers: LCCN 2020022854 | ISBN 9780226748092 (cloth) | ISBN 9780226748122
    (paperback) | ISBN 9780226748269 (ebook)
Subjects: LCSH: Persons—California—Berkeley—Longitudinal studies. | Life cycle,
    Human—Social aspects—United States. | Social change—United States. |
    United States—Social conditions—20th century.
Classification: LCC HN57 .S47 2021 | DDC 306.0973/0904—dc23
LC record available at https://lccn.loc.gov/2020022854

♾ This paper meets the requirements of ANSI/NISO Z39.48-1992 (Permanence of Paper).

To Jean Walker Macfarlane,
pioneer in the longitudinal study of lives

Contents

PART ONE

Entering an Uncharted World

The year 1870 represented modern America at dawn. Over the subsequent six decades, every aspect of life experienced a revolution. By 1929, urban America was electrified and almost every urban dwelling was networked, connected to the outside world with electricity, natural gas, telephone, clean running water, and sewers. By 1929, the horse had almost vanished from urban streets, and the ratio of motor vehicles to the number of households reached 90 percent. By 1929, the household could enjoy entertainment options that were beyond the 1870 imagination, including phonograph music, radio, and motion pictures exhibited in ornate movie palaces.

ROBERT J. GORDON, *The Rise and Fall of American Growth*[1]

1

Americans in a New Century:
The 1900 Generation

> We today are probably living in one of the eras of greatest rapidity of change in the history of human institutions.
>
> ROBERT LYND AND HELEN LYND, *Middletown*, 1929

Americans born around the turn of the twentieth century experienced a rapidly modernizing world with disorienting effects that would alter their lives in unforeseen ways. On the eve of World War I, American writer and commentator Walter Lippmann, himself a member of this generation, wrote that "we are unsettled to the very roots of our being." This changing world is not "an illusion but a fact: we do actually move toward novelty, there is invention, and what has never been is created each day." We have "no precedents to guide us, no wisdom that wasn't made for a simpler age. We have changed our environment more quickly than we know how to change ourselves."[1] In what ways was the world of this generation changing more quickly than they knew how to change themselves? A large part of their life story involved mass immigration and migration across the country, the stunning growth of cities, and the revolutionary inventions of the late nineteenth and early twentieth centuries—electricity, telephones, motorized transportation, and the modernization of households.[2] The 1920s were especially transformative in the far west of the country, reflecting the torrid pace of urban growth. Over a century later, Lippmann's observations still ring true for contemporary generations of Americans who are living on the edge of change.

At the end of the 1920s, President Herbert Hoover came up with a plan for a team of leading social scientists to document "recent social trends."[3] At their first meeting in the autumn of 1929, Hoover spoke of "breathtaking transformations in traditional ways of life."[4] The scientists were impressed most of all by the dramatic cumulative impact of major inventions and the myriad social and economic forces that had hurried Americans "away from the days of the frontier into a whirl of modernisms which almost passes belief."[5] These elements of modernity extended to the emergence of giant corporations, mass merchandising, and the installment plan.

But a sense of well-being in society soon gave way to the storm clouds of a troubled economy, followed by its collapse in the Great Depression, with sharply rising unemployment that persisted across the decade among semi-skilled and unskilled workers. Nevertheless it later became clear that techni-cal breakthroughs brought a much brighter future and even what became "a great leap forward" from the 1920s to the 1970s.[6] This advance centered on the "production miracle" of the war years, fueled by an extraordinary level of federal wartime spending. Journalist and editor Carey McWilliams called this explosive growth the "'fabulous boom' in the 40s."[7] The level of spending rose to over four-fifths of the entire American economy by New Year's Eve 1939. Between 1939 and 1944—just five years—the real gross domestic product had nearly doubled, dramatically improving the well-being of workers and their families.[8]

The surging economy of the war years continued well into the postwar era as war-enforced savings and pent-up demand for consumer durables made such purchases possible. This demand soared as millions of veterans returned to civilian life with a generous endowment from the GI Bill that provided a financial bridge to higher education, job training, and homeownership.[9] A new wave of young families in the rapidly expanding middle class could now acquire a place of their own. Hard-won prosperity enabled both young and old to expect greater security in their later years.

As this historical record so clearly indicates, the 1900 generation's trajec-tory extended across an unparalleled series of socioeconomic ups and downs, all within Robert Gordon's "revolutionary century of economic growth" from the post–Civil War year of 1870 to the 1970s.[10] The century of change before 1870 was comparatively slow. For the 1900 generation, the great economic upsurges of the century were linked to dramatic collapse in the Great Depres-sion. Still, as we later show, not all families were uniformly deprived during such hard times. Indeed, some were largely spared the misfortune of job and income loss in the Depression, whereas others in the working class did not regain their 1929 level of income until the end of World War II.[11]

The Research Problem and Approach

How did this rapidly changing society influence the lives of middle-class and working-class Americans of the 1900 generation? How did they adapt to the disruptive and ever-changing world that included two world wars and the swings of great economic prosperity and depression? We address these questions by drawing on the remarkable data archive of a pioneering longitudinal project known as the Berkeley Guidance Study (hereafter the Berkeley study).

The study was launched during the late 1920s at the Berkeley Institute of Child Welfare by Jean Walker Macfarlane, a clinical psychologist in UC Berkeley's Department of Psychology.[12] The Institute eventually became the famous Berkeley Institute of Human Development, which developed an international reputation for its landmark studies that followed children from childhood and adolescence into their later adult years. The Berkeley study was no exception. Macfarlane directed her research program over four decades, following the lives of up to 420 members of the 1900 generation and their children. With birth dates concentrated from 1885 to 1908 in Europe and America, these men and women eventually settled in California, where they married and raised their families. By 1929 the study included over two hundred couples living in Berkeley, a city of approximately 40,000 residents across the Bay from San Francisco.

The couples who entered the Berkeley study each had a child born in 1928–29, when the sample of families was selected. The children and parents were followed in considerable detail across most of the twentieth century. Glen Elder discovered this trove of longitudinal records on the Berkeley study parents and children during a sabbatical year at the Institute (1972–73). It included qualitative life records comprising years of observation and interview notes stored in files. The study's breadth and richness of data collection on both the parents and the study children reflected the core scholarly interests and expertise of its founding director.[13] Macfarlane was clinically trained in family relationships and child development. To obtain information on the social origins of the Berkeley parents (the 1900 generation), she carried out retrospective life history interviews with them that included questions about their mothers' and fathers' social origins. These life histories place the 1900 generation in a social context and provide a valuable introduction to their own upbringing and migratory path to Berkeley.

Macfarlane's research team conducted open-ended interviews with the 1900 generation, among other methods of data collection, as a preferred way to understand the development and behavior problems in their children, an original focus of the study. These data were supplemented by questionnaires, staff ratings, and staff observations in the home and neighborhood. Periodic interview data were collected from these men and women from 1930 to 1947, and they were contacted again for data collection in 1969 and the early 1980s.[14] The combination of these rich data sources results in a relatively full picture of four generations: members of the 1900 generation, who anchor our inquiry and were born from 1885 to 1908; their parents, who were born in the wake of the Civil War; their children, who were born just before or during the Great Depression; and their grandchildren, all born after World War II. With its intergenerational and historical frame, the study provides a richly contextualized perspective on the 1900 generation as they experienced life's transitions, turning points, and pathways.

A framework for understanding the human life course, with its transitions and trajectories, emerged during the 1990s as a set of five paradigmatic principles that guide our study.[15] First, the life of every individual is related to others. With this interdependence in mind, the principle of "linked lives" views individuals as embedded in relationships with others and influenced by them. The second principle of "timing" concerns when people experience life events such as marriage, childbirth, and departure from the family. Variations in timing—whether such events occur early, on time, or late—have real consequences for the life course and relationships. Third, the principle of "historical time and place" directs attention to how people's lives are influenced by their economic, cultural, and social environments. Fourth, the principle of "human agency" is that people make choices and take actions that affect the direction and outcome of their lives. Last, the principle of "life span development" is that human development and aging are lifelong processes that are most fully understood from birth to death.

Basic features of this life course perspective and its project have much in common with a prominent early study of social change in families and lives: *The Polish Peasant in Europe and America* (1918–20), by William I. Thomas and Florian Znaniecki. They used retrospective life histories to depict individual lives, not longitudinal data records of parents and children over time, as in Macfarlane's Berkeley study. When life history information is gathered retrospectively, it is subject to the fallibility of a person's memory and the tendency to recall events selectively by "editing" one's life story to appear more coherent and orderly than it was. Nevertheless, *The Polish Peasant* drew on a wide variety of data, from life histories and letters to agency records and field observations. With its focus on the "Old World communities of immigrants" and their adaptation to a new world, this ambitious study is considered the "preeminent American sociological study of its era."[16] Moreover, it is noteworthy that one of the authors, William I. Thomas, recognized the limitations of retrospective life history studies during the 1920s and became an advocate for the direct observation of children as they develop from childhood through adolescence and young adulthood. At a 1930–31 seminar on social science methods at the Brookings Institution, Thomas argued for "development of the longitudinal approach" and for following "groups of individuals into the future, getting a continuous record of experiences as they occur."[17]

In our study we follow the lives of the Berkeley 1900 generation from their social origins through education, marriage and childbearing, and employment across the prosperous 1920s into the Great Depression of the 1930s, and from there to the mobilized home front of World War II and a long era of postwar prosperity for their later years, even into the 1980s and 1990s for the longest-surviving parents. We provide an intimate firsthand view of a group of individuals and families who experienced and talked about the distinctive historical times and places that had given shape and meaning to their lives.

In large part the Berkeley 1900 generation's life context makes this a California story, about a state that was a crucial player in America's history of pioneers, risk takers, and innovators: people seeking a better life. Some emigrated from Europe and others from the East Coast and the Midwest. The project builds on events that influenced how the western region developed, such as the establishment in the late 1860s of the University of California, Berkeley, as a public university, one that opened its doors to women in the early 1870s, well before many other land-grant institutions in the West. But their story will be much larger than California and both longer and wider in historical time as they become the forebears of those living more than a century later.

As a lifelong project, the Berkeley study enables us to follow individuals and their relationships over time. The men and women studied provided information on their own parents and on their marriage partners in 1929–31. We begin their life journey in chapter 2 by tracing the migratory paths the Berkeley 1900 generation followed to the San Francisco region (less than 20 percent were born there) and then across the young adulthood transitions of education and work, marriage and the birth of children up to the 1930s in the city of Berkeley (chapters 3 and 4). We turn to archival data on marriages, providing one of the earliest interactional accounts of how marriage partners viewed their relationship, whether harmonious and characterized by mutual understanding and by sharing experiences through conversation, or not (chapter 5). By the end of the 1920s, the couples had sorted themselves out on education, occupational role, and social class in ways that had major consequences for their vulnerability and resilience in hard times and periods of prosperity. Three out of five families were in the middle class in 1929.

As the Berkeley families entered the 1930s, they brought along whatever economic resources and social capital they had to weather what lay ahead. Within a year or two they would confront a faltering economy, which in the Bay Area hit bottom by 1933 when a quarter of the workforce was unemployed.

Not all middle-class and working-class families were exposed to hardship, though hard times became much more stressful when economic strain was coupled with marital conflict (chapters 6 and 7) and painful decisions about whether to have more children, given the circumstances and an uncertain future (chapter 8). In one-fourth of the households, tensions from the presence of an agitated elderly member of the older generation could quickly "throw a wet blanket" on the family mood, as one wife put it (chapter 9). Intergenerational households frequently spanned major differences in wealth, culture, and language, from peasant life in eastern Europe to the upper-class wealth of a San Francisco businessman.

By 1940 the 1900 generation and their families were in transition from a decade of "doing without" to a surging economy in which both men and women were recruited into the home front labor force to meet the ever-mounting demands for war matériel and civilian goods. Community life in Berkeley reflected the profound anxieties and pressures of wartime. Residents recount what it was like to live in a community whose fabric had been altered by the influx of southern whites and blacks and other outsiders searching for work in the shipyards, which would permanently change the composition of the Bay Area (chapter 10). They also recount what it was like to be in the shadow of the Japanese attack on Pearl Harbor, to see Japanese families in their communities vanish into internment, and to be in danger on California's coast as America went to war. Stressful change involved the mounting production pressure of war industries—with long hours and workweeks and a never-ending pace—which strained family life and compromised the emotional health of men, women, and children (chapters 10 and 11).

Longitudinal data enabled us to turn our lenses back to women's work before World War II, to earlier periods of prosperity and into the Depression years (chapter 11). Much research on the social history of women focuses on World War II as a powerful turning point in the work histories of American women. But we see that women in the 1900 generation, especially those from the working class, did not suddenly enter the labor market in wartime but in fact had work experience before they married or had supported their families financially during the Great Depression.

The war-mobilized culture and community created significant struggles for parents as their teenagers gained mobility and freedom and confronted many new temptations and risks in a rapidly changing world (chapter 12). So, too, was their parenting challenged by evolving ideas about gender—what it meant to be a man or a woman, husband or wife, father or mother—and what parents wanted for their sons and daughters as they entered adulthood. This generation parented as the scientific study of child and family development emerged, which left them more knowledgeable than previous generations. The story that unfolds, especially in the middle class, reveals a deep cultural turn in their commitment and approaches to parenting, paving the way for the intensive parenting of today.

In our closing chapter, we take a long view of the life course of the Berkeley men and women, viewed from the perspective of their later years (chapter 13), with emphasis on the personal legacies of Depression hard times and the stressful pressures of a world war. With interviews in hand, we piece together their reflections on lives lived across the radical ups and downs of the twentieth century, as well as the themes of their life experiences that have persisted, declined, or reappeared across successive generations, such as the security and insecurity of work and marriage.

The evolving lives of the Berkeley men and women over the twentieth century can be viewed in terms of cumulative advantage and disadvantage as they moved from comfortable or precarious childhoods to relatively prosperous young adulthoods in the San Francisco area of the 1920s.[18] Young adulthood was marked by the challenge of completing an education, finding a job and a mate, then starting a family. These transitions and achievements bear on their personal experience as they entered the 1930s and the Great Depression, steering them toward misfortune or opportunity. They carried these trajectories and disparities into the full employment economy and pressures of World War II, setting in motion potential turning points across the postwar years and subsequent pathways to old age.

The Analytic Framework

Two master concepts are central to this study: the generational status of the individual in the context of an extended family, and cohort membership in the context of historical time. As noted, the Berkeley study involves four sequential generations: the parents of the 1900 generation, the 1900 generation, their children, and their grandchildren. In the cycle of generational succession and interdependent lives, newborns are reared to maturity, give birth to the next generation, grow old, and eventually die. Differences in the average timing of births across the generations can notably alter their shared lifetimes.

This dynamic perspective draws attention to social ties among young and old within families and society, but it does not indicate when births and other events occur in lives and in historical time. This information comes from the age-graded life course; age provides an indication of individuals' life stage and their likely roles and responsibilities. In addition, all people born in a specific year or years are members of a specific birth cohort. As successive

cohorts encounter a social change, they are "distinctively marked by the career stage" they occupy.[19] By dividing the Berkeley parent generation at the
median birth year, we are better able to assess the historical implications of
social change, such as the career stage of families when exposed to hardship
in the Great Depression. With this approach, the 1900 generation forms two
potentially distinct "generational cohorts" of men and women—those born at
the end of the nineteenth century (before 1900) and those born in the beginning of the twentieth century (1900 and after).

Cohort membership in the 1900 generation (either younger or older) at
the turn of that century represented what sociologist Leonard Cain has described as a "historical hinge" separating the experiences of those who were
young adults in the 1920s from those of the earlier cohort.[20] It orients us to
the life stage when social change was encountered, such as the onset of World
War I for men. Only the older men in the nineteenth-century cohort were
likely subject to mobilization when America declared war on Germany in
World War I. On the other hand, at the beginning of World War II, most
men in both generational cohorts had passed the upper age limit for eligibil-
ity or were employed in essential occupations on the home front. For the
women, cohort membership mattered most in terms of how many children
they had. The younger cohort ended up with fewer children, in part owing to
the economic constraints of the Great Depression, and they were more likely
to marry when they were already sexually active, consistent with the liberated
image of young women in the 1920s.

Another conceptual distinction is important for interpreting generational
and cohort effects—that of status groups, such as social class, as well as gender, birthplace/descent, and religious affiliation. Gender is a major status differentiator within a birth cohort, since men's and women's lives come with
distinct expectations and opportunities. Social class, too, is a major source of
individual and family variation within birth cohorts, as revealed, for example,
by the study of Oakland children and families in the Great Depression.[21] Job
loss was concentrated in the working class, and unemployment continued
well into World War II for most of the fathers. Recovery from a heavy income
loss occurred more quickly for middle-class than working-class families.

The way these statuses intersect is highly relevant to how individuals adapt
to change, whether as deprivation or disruption. For example, the Oakland cohort of youth who grew up in the Great Depression experienced key elements
of drastic change and adaptation.[22] Change of this kind typically generated a
crisis in which conventional adaptations did not work effectively, perhaps in
part because of inflated expectations regarding personal skills or living standards. When options proved ineffective, people explored the effectiveness of

other strategies, such as greatly reducing expenditures or relying on multiple earners. This ineffectiveness illustrates Walter Lippmann's observation about Americans entering the twentieth century—that their environments were changing faster than they knew how to change.

Individual attributes that enable effective adaptations to social change include resourcefulness and resilience, personal qualities known to be acquired from successfully surmounting barriers and hardships. A prime element in mastering disadvantage and the demands of problem situations is being prepared to cope with challenging circumstances. Most important, the essential factor is whether adaptive experience brings success or failure. Studies indicate that mastery experiences across situations develop a repertoire of accomplishment, fostering skills that enable flexibility and resourcefulness. Developing these personal resources is relevant for the lives of the 1900 generation and their children, many of whom were born and reared in the stressful Depression years.

A longitudinal study like this one calls for an analytic model that links socioeconomic change to behavioral adaptations and subsequent outcomes across the life course. It also requires acute consideration of intersecting statuses that alter the influence of various changes. So, with an eye to how social change produces certain outcomes, we follow the lives and families of the Berkeley generation across the 1920s, 1930s, and 1940s up to their later years.

Berkeley: A University Town

A population headed westward was a central theme of America in the late nineteenth century with the continuing flow of immigrants from Europe, from rural to urban locales, and from east to west within the country in search of more abundant opportunities. The settlement of California vividly tells much of this story, as does the growth of San Francisco and the city of Berkeley along the eastern edge of San Francisco Bay. California's population doubled from 1900 to 1910. At that point a majority of California's residents had been born outside the state and sometimes outside the country. Chapter 2 tells the story of the varied paths the Berkeley 1900 generation followed to California. They typically traveled with others (parents, other family members, and friends) who were also likely to come from urban rather than rural areas of the Central Plains and Midwest. Only 20 percent were born overseas, but members of this population typically ended up in major urban centers of California.

Young people and families were drawn to the college town of Berkeley by the stature and accessibility of its distinguished state university and by the quality of its community life. The University of California, Berkeley (1868), became a reality after the Civil War when the private liberal arts college preparatory College of California merged with proposed Agricultural, Mining, and Mechanical Arts College as part of the federal land-grant provisions of the Morrill Act (1862) and its financial resources from land sales.[23] Leaders of the university movement named the town site surrounding the main university campus Berkeley in honor of George Berkeley, who had established the higher-education model for Columbia University. The university's medical school was eventually established in San Francisco and its school of agriculture on the outskirts of Davis, California.

During the 1870s the university most notably admitted women to the student body, and the number of women enrolled soon exceeded that of men, even though there were more university-aged men than women in the state. By 1900 the student body totaled more than three thousand. In the first two decades of the twentieth century, the university increased its prominence through its faculty's international distinction in teaching and research and through the generosity of philanthropists. By 1920 an impressive campus had grown up in the Berkeley hills, with neoclassical buildings in an attractive landscape. Jean Macfarlane, founder of the Berkeley study in 1928, had earned her doctorate in clinical psychology six years earlier from the University of California and became a pioneering female member of its Department of Psychology.

The university was established by the Board of Regents on the principle that admission and tuition would be free to all residents of the state. The only charge was for fees to cover the cost of student services such as health care. The institution's stature and minimal cost were a major attraction to families seeking a better life in the West. Also important were the city's reputation for having a low rate of infant deaths and its promise of first-rate medical care. Berkeley shared the benefits of California's history of opportunity.

The growth of the university's physical plant and its student body played a major role in the town's development, but at first faculty and students typically lived in the adjacent city of Oakland and commuted to campus by carriage. Residential development clustered first in the western section of Berkeley, which eventually became the industrial district (known as Ocean View along the Bay), followed some years later by the eastern section with the University of California campus. By 1900 urban development brought paved streets, post offices, schools, advances in transportation (e.g., street cars, trains along the Bay), a public library, and incorporation as a town with elected officials, public water supply, and fire control and police units.

California was and is still known for its earthquakes and fires. Two twentieth-century disasters played a notable role in the growth of population and housing in Berkeley during the first thirty years: the 1906 San Francisco earthquake and the Berkeley fire of 1923. Along with the earthquake's catastrophic destruction of residential and commercial buildings throughout San Francisco, firestorms from broken gas lines across the city leveled entire blocks and sections. Several hundred thousand residents were displaced, many ending up in the East Bay communities of Berkeley and Oakland. The *Oakland Tribune* vividly described trainloads of residents arriving on the day after the earthquake "with barely the clothes on their backs."[24] Hundreds of the refugees eventually became Berkeley residents, contributing to a tripling of its population between 1900 and 1910 and its establishment as a city in 1909.

The East Bay cities responded quickly to the crisis, establishing relief committees to manage the efforts and resources of churches, service groups, and individual volunteers. With the assistance of the military, seven tent camps were set up in the East Bay area. The Berkeley Welfare Society, which evolved from the charitable organization Society of Berkeley, was established to meet the needs of this tidal wave of humanity as people fled earthquake-ravaged San Francisco. Some members of the Berkeley 1900 generation families came from sections of San Francisco that had burned. One of these families had escaped the firestorms by taking refuge for several days on a rescue boat in San Francisco Bay. In addition to the displacement of population, the earthquake prompted some San Francisco industries to migrate to Berkeley's waterfront.

The second major disaster of the early twentieth century was the Berkeley fire of 1923. It swept down from the hills with strong winds, reaching the business district in the city's northwest area and destroying several thousand homes.[25] In large sections of this residential area, the only signs of houses were chimneys left standing here and there, reminiscent of the lonely remains on the battlefields of World War I France. The homes of over four thousand residents were destroyed, causing property losses of more than $10 million. Remarkably, the massive collective response enabled the city to recover within two years, an implausible rebirth after the fire's devastation. Few signs of the disaster were evident two years later except for the serious shortage of single-unit housing. Some families were forced to rent or purchase homes in adjacent communities.

Despite the catastrophic fire, the city's economy bounced back and flourished up to the 1930s. At this time nothing could have seemed less likely than the Great Depression and the prolonged economic crisis. Yet family income losses extended across the social classes, and working-class unemployment exceeded 25 percent. California and New York were among the states with the most unemployment and work relief during the decade, although the full brunt of hard times fell on the West Coast about six months later.[26] However, important advances also occurred during this decade, such as the completion of the Bay Bridge linking San Francisco to Berkeley and Oakland.

The severity of the Depression in this university town is vividly shown by the public role of the Berkeley Welfare Society, which had its origins in assisting refugees from the San Francisco earthquake. It handled all relief cases for the city of Berkeley up to the summer of 1935, when it reached the end of its resources. Only the passage of a $3 million city bond enabled this level of support. By the end of 1932, the number of families on relief had climbed to seven times the pre-Depression level for the city and its county, with approximately one out of ten Berkeley families dependent on a dwindling supply of public funds. The Berkeley Welfare Society became a private institution in 1935, specializing in supplementary family needs.[27] Federal and state work relief carried such support from this point on.

Few historical transitions have involved more of a turnaround than the transition from Depression times to the country's booming economy as it met the soaring military and civilian needs of World War II. The contractions and make-do adaptations of the Depression years were followed by the unparalleled mobilization for an "arsenal of democracy" in World War II.[28] The economic collapse of the 1930s economy and the isolationist perspective of the country had sharply reduced spending on education, health, the military, and infrastructure. The effect of this decline was keenly felt in the city of Berkeley, with drastic cutbacks in university support for students, faculty, and staff. But the gathering war clouds in Europe and Asia rapidly turned this decline around by fueling more federal spending for the reindustrialization of the country in World War II. By the end of the war, the university had received nearly $60 million for war-related projects.

The university's recovery from the Great Depression had much to do with the leadership and recruitment skill of its new president (appointed in 1930), Robert Gordon Sproul, a civil engineer. By the end of the 1930s, Berkeley faculty had advanced to the forefront of immense civil engineering projects, from the Bay Bridge to the grand achievement of Hoover Dam—now Boulder Dam. Ernest Lawrence pioneered the development of the first atom-smashing cyclotron and was awarded a Nobel Prize for his contribution. Other Berkeley scientists, led by Robert Oppenheimer, played a key role in the wartime effort to build an atomic bomb. After the war federal funds continued to flow into large scientific projects at Berkeley, prompted by the accomplishments of its faculty.

World War II also increased job opportunities for men and women in Berkeley and Oakland by enlisting draft-age workers from non-essential civilian jobs for military service. This also prompted the recruitment of workers from outside the state for new forms of urgent war production, such as the construction of shipyards along the coast of San Francisco Bay. Both white-collar and blue-collar workers were in demand for this new industry, but mass-production methods enabled it to hire workers with no shipbuilding experience or expertise.[29] Many of these workers were migrants from the most impoverished regions of the country, the South and lower Midwest. During the first year after America declared war on the Axis powers (Germany, Italy, and Japan), federal defense spending increased twelvefold, a dramatic reinvestment in the country's leading role throughout the Western world. Berkeley and the state of California continued to flourish across the 1950s to the end of postwar affluence in the mid-1970s.

Studying People "the Long Way"

When the Berkeley project was launched, the typical American study of individuals involved collecting data at one point in time. In the United States, fewer than a dozen studies of children were designed to record their development over time, and most were small, comparable to the Berkeley and Oakland studies at the Institute of Human Development. A major exception to the cross-sectional mode of study was Lewis Terman's longitudinal study at Stanford University of high-ability Californians—similarly born in the first two decades of the twentieth century—with a sample of more than a thousand males and females across waves of data collection.[30] Though not as large, the Berkeley study was distinguished by its unique design of following two generations, the study children and their parents, over their life course. It was also distinguished by its intensive data collection through open-ended interviews, household inventories, parent and child questionnaires, and annual record keeping on families.

Longitudinal studies launched at the time of the Berkeley study, unlike such projects today, lacked federal support. This limitation had major consequences, because studies of this kind were far more costly than single-wave surveys. The Framingham Cardiovascular Longitudinal Study was the first large-scale American study with a prospective design, and it was launched in 1948, two years after the National Institutes of Health were established. The NIH would eventually become a major source of funds for national longitudinal studies in the postwar era. Before then the Berkeley longitudinal study was supported in large measure by the Laura Spelman Rockefeller Memorial.

When people are studied over their whole lives, the sample can become very selective by late life because some members die or drop out, often leaving the participants who are most economically advantaged and healthiest.

The Macfarlane sample, drawn from "Old Berkeley," included families with children born in the late 1920s, and it understandably differs from what the composition of such a sample would have been if obtained in Berkeley after World War II. One of the most striking differences has to do with the city's growing and permanent racial diversity after the war, resulting from the mass in-migration of black families to wartime industries. The "Old Berkeley" sample of families in the 1920s included only a couple of black families, and it clearly became unrepresentative of postwar Berkeley. This is also true for Asian and Hispanic families. Social change is an integral feature of the world in which longitudinal studies are carried out, and the central task of this study of the 1900 generation is to investigate the lifelong effect of social change on the lives of the Berkeley men and women as members of this generation.

Families in Macfarlane's study were a representative sample of families experiencing a birth in Berkeley from January 1, 1928, to June 30, 1929. A total of 244 families were recruited for the study and randomly assigned to two subsamples: one with an intensive regime of data collection featuring parent interviews and observations, and one with a less intensive regime. In each subsample, two out of three families were middle class. The intensive regime of data collection was designed to provide ongoing guidance to parents as they encountered the challenges of rearing the children in the experimental group; hence the name of the original project, the Berkeley Guidance Study.[31]

Any study based on archival data inevitably encounters some tension between contemporary standards and what is possible with data that were collected for other purposes or with other procedures. The research task establishes requirements for suitable data, measurements, and research design, but an investigator's options are always shaped by the standards of the time when a project is launched. Consequently, secondary analysts of archival data must make the best of what we have.[32]

Fortunately the Berkeley archive's data collection offered a wide range of options and possibilities. Interviews and observations produced qualitative data, and systematic observational coding produced quantitative measures. Open-ended interviews and observations also gave us the opportunity to construct quantitative measures of concepts that represent a better match to our contemporary line of research. This feature proved essential for studying the life course, family patterns, and beliefs and values of the 1900 generation in a rapidly changing society.

For example, the Berkeley project was not designed to situate the study members and families in specified contexts, whether during the years of prosperity in the 1920s, during the hard times of the 1930s, or on the home front of World War II. Nevertheless its reliance on open-ended interviews let us design contextual measures of these historical times. Socioeconomic examples include worklife experiences and educational transitions during the 1920s, income levels and worklife changes during the 1930s, and incidents of changing work roles as well as upswings in earnings and work hours during World War II. Ideological examples in the 1920s involve educational goals and beliefs as well as worklife aspirations and beliefs regarding gender equality in marriage. The painfulness of income loss had much to do, for example, with the actual and preferred living standards of the Berkeley men and women.

We were fortunate to have a distinguished oral historian, Charles Morrissey, conduct oral histories in the 1970s with more than forty men and women from the Berkeley study.[33] They provided richly detailed accounts of the early years, from the 1920s to World War II and the postwar era. A case in point is a Berkeley woman's account of how during World War II her family held social gatherings in their home for servicemen from the navy and army. Another oral history told about the sorrowful separation when a family lost their Japanese gardener and his family to internment.

In the broadest sense, the research promise of this study owes much to the extraordinary temporal scope of the Berkeley data archive on lives and families across multiple generations. This lifelong accomplishment was inspired by Jean Macfarlane and her dedication to the goal of following the Berkeley children and their parents over many decades. However, no one could have imagined at the beginning of the project (about 1930) that the lives of the parents would eventually be documented and stored until the 1980s at the Berkeley Institute of Human Development. The detail and span of this data archive are without parallel for its historical time.

The plan for our study of the Berkeley 1900 generation emerged during Elder's year at the Institute (1972–73) when he first began to work with this rich and broad archive and the particular topics and historical times it covered. Most important, life history data were combined with essential historical details on experiences in the 1920s, 1930s, 1940s, and 1950s. The records probed the views of study members and contain their words. We see economic depressions, wars, and other historical and social changes interacting with the lives of these men and women and their families. This discovery led Elder to focus his year at the Institute on preparing data and creating an outline for a book on the Berkeley 1900 generation in the ever-changing world of the twentieth century. With this general framework in mind, the present book evolved over nearly half a century.

This book tells how a century of unparalleled growth in the standard of living (1870–1970), and the periods of great economic and social instability within it, left its mark on the men and women of the 1900 generation. They

were agents of their own lives and of social change itself, making a difference in the lives of their spouses, children, and elderly parents and in their
communities. Their life stories reveal an intricate process of adapting to such
change and managing its reverberations over time.

And yet the lives of the 1900 generation also foreshadow those of American generations born thereafter. Their stories are in some ways all our stories, since many aspects of contemporary life are rooted in the times they
navigated or the things they championed, and since generations of today and
tomorrow will easily relate to the profound and often paradoxical mix of experiences that come with living on the edge of an ever-changing world.

PART TWO

Making a Life: 1910–30

For men and women of the Berkeley 1900 generation, making a life in early adulthood during the first decades of the twentieth century involved two primary objectives: establishing themselves as individuals through education and self-support and building relationships leading to marriage. Their life stories often began far outside the Bay Area; most came from other parts of California and the United States or from Europe. Typically they made the journey with the help and company of friends and family (chapter 2). Migration stories tell of push and pull in the decision to seek a better life in this region.

The 1920s brought prosperity to Berkeley, with its industries and with the University of California, which welcomed young men and young women. Other local colleges and institutes provided additional options. Chapter 3 focuses on the educational and employment achievements of the men and highlights home-ownership as a core value. We ask whether men in the 1900 generation managed to use higher education as a path to middle-class employment. And what about the young Berkeley women in the emerging world of the white-collar worker so vividly described by C. Wright Mills in *White Collar: The American Middle Classes*?[1] Did they take advantage of access to higher education and the university's employment opportunities in the new middle class? In this era of expanding prospects for women beyond the household, chapter 4 considers how much the Berkeley women were broadening their life options through education, work, and community activities outside the household during a transformation of what was expected inside the home.

For men and women of the Berkeley 1900 generation, higher education was a potential route to wider chances and to personal development. Yet individual development of this kind could also bring marital conflict. As the worlds of work and family moved apart during the industrialization of the twentieth century, so did the lives of men and women. Following the insights of sociologist Ernest Burgess on family life in the 1920s and 1930s, chapter 5 investigates the quality of relations and communication in the Berkeley marriages. The workplace separation of husband and wife frequently became a major source of marital stress on the eve of the Great Depression. She, as homemaker, was eager to share her day when her husband came home from work. But he, as breadwinner, often didn't reciprocate. In economically threatening times, men often saw the act of sharing as a threat to their control and self-regard.

California, Here We Come!

My life divides itself into quite a few periods: the first when I left home, Kansas City, Missouri, in 1908; the second when I came to California in 1912.

BERKELEY MAN OF NORWEGIAN DESCENT

The course one follows in life cannot be understood apart from historical time and place. And so it is with the men and women of the Berkeley 1900 generation. Born around the turn of the twentieth century, they raised their children in worlds very different from those of their own childhoods. Fewer than one in ten were native to the San Francisco Bay region or to the city of Berkeley, where at least one of each couple's children was born in the late 1920s. Immigration and settling in the far west are significant elements in this generation's life history.

In this chapter we investigate their diverse paths to California and situate them within the larger history of westward migration. Changing residence is seen as a way to better one's chances. In the late nineteenth and twentieth centuries, America was viewed around the world as a land of extraordinary opportunity, especially the far west and California, with the city of Berkeley and its state university. The presumed closing of the western frontier in 1890 did not dampen the magnetism of California; it continued to lure people throughout the twentieth century. Early settlers passed on this good news to friends and families in the eastern states and Europe, creating continual waves of migration. This chapter shows how the Berkeley families were entangled in that story. It reveals important differences based on their birthplace, history, and descent, and it sets in motion the way their lives will unfold in this book.

Moving to California

A major impetus for California's growth in the late nineteenth century came from the transcontinental rail lines connecting Sacramento and Los Angeles to the East, and from their stiff competition for passengers. However, California's striking growth *after* the closing of the frontier in 1890 is more relevant to the westward movement of our Berkeley generation—slightly more than 60 percent were born elsewhere. In 1930 two out of three California residents listed birthplaces outside the state, and one in five were foreign-born.[1]

California's population more than tripled between 1900 and 1930, to 5.7 million, and approximately 80 percent of this growth was a net increase of those born outside the state.[2] Whether they were born in California or migrated to it, most people remained in California their whole lives.[3] More germane to our interest is that Berkeley's population more than tripled in the first decade of the twentieth century: from a small university community of 13,214 in 1900 to 40,434 in 1910, owing partly to the resettlement of large numbers of former San Franciscans after the great earthquake of 1906. The earthquake killed 3,000 people and displaced 300,000 through damage and fires; about half moved across the Bay to communities like Oakland or Berkeley, straining available housing.[4] In 1923 Berkeley would suffer a destructive fire that claimed 640 structures, including 584 homes, displacing more families and further straining housing.[5] From 1910 to 1930, the population of Berkeley would again see a massive increase, this time doubling to 82,109 just as economic conditions began to worsen.

The migration histories, or "trajectories," of the Berkeley men and women must be understood within the context of larger streams of people coming to California: their relation to economic conditions, their social origins, and their eventual places of settlement.[6] Generations of the Berkeley families were swept up in one or another of four waves of migration that generally parallel times of rapid economic improvement, not only in California but in the country as a whole.[7] The first occurred before the 1890 depression, one of the most severe downturns before the 1930s. Immigrants included large numbers of Chinese laborers headed for the mines and railroads and people from northwestern Europe—Ireland, England, Germany, and Scandinavia.[8]

The second wave of immigration to California, spurred by economic growth in agriculture, oil, shipping, and other industries, occurred after the 1890 collapse and lasted to about 1913, when the population increased by over 60 percent. Southern and eastern Europeans were most prominent among the immigrants who arrived at this time. Economic growth in this period included a series of major oil discoveries in the San Joaquin Valley and the Los Angeles region, brisk expansion of the electric power industry, and increasing reliance on electricity and oil as sources of industrial energy. There was another depression in 1914–15.

A third wave of migration occurred in the early 1920s, after the recession of 1921–22, and the fourth wave was during World War II, when manufacturing jobs in California increased over 75 percent, especially with the rapid expansion of shipbuilding and aircraft construction from the middle of 1942 to V-J Day (victory over Japan) on August 15, 1945.[9] The acceleration of in-migration sharply increased the demand for consumer goods and services, and especially housing.[10] Our Berkeley study families were living in California by 1929, but we show in later chapters how World War II transformed the Bay Area into a major defense hub and the local war industry brought new opportunities and challenges for the 1900 generation and their children.

These migration streams to California have been explained in studies of migration from outside and inside the United States.[11] Several motivators led people westward to California, including the hope for a permanently improved quality of life (the "California Dream"), temporary betterment (to make money and return home with more resources), desire for land (though this was more significant for settling the plains and the northwest than for California's growth), and nostalgia (the epic ideal of the pioneer and individualism).[12] California's overall picture shows an increase in migration after every depression beginning with the 1890 collapse, but the most pronounced spurts, as Margaret Gordon has noted, "have been associated with periods of unusually rapid economic development, when the rate of economic expansion of the state has exceeded that of the nation."[13]

Common images, both negative and positive, portray California's early twentieth-century migrants as coming from farms. On the negative side, the association of California with agriculture is most clearly seen in pictures of the rural poor fleeing destitution on the windblown, drought-afflicted plains during the Great Depression. On the positive side, "agricultural journalism" perpetuated the association of California with agriculture as it promoted the state's fertility and enviable agricultural attributes, paired with images of opportunity.[14]

These rural images reflected only part of California's landscape, which was equally urban. Even in 1900 most Californians lived in urban areas (52 percent), and from 1870 through 1930 the state ranked well above the US population on percentage urban. And yet over half of all native-born migrants to California from 1900 to 1940 had come from the agricultural states of the central region between 1900 and 1930, and the vast majority of these midwesterners were born in north-central states such as Iowa, Minnesota, and the Dakotas. During the catastrophic Dust Bowl era of the 1930s, places of origin shifted southward to include the west south-central states—Texas, Oklahoma,

Kansas—as well as urban centers.[15] Considering these migration patterns, rural midwesterners might seem to be a major component of California's urban growth. But, surprisingly, migrants to California during the 1930s typically came from and settled in urban areas. During this decade, only 24 percent of the migrants from states afflicted by drought came from rural areas, compared with 60 percent with urban origins.

Migration Stories

Some key factors of the migratory experiences of the Berkeley 1900 generation shaped their lives. Important considerations include "push" forces in migrants' place of origin that determine their need, desire, and means to move, as well as "pull" forces, such as economic opportunities, that orient them to a particular destination.[16] The Berkeley archives are replete with examples of push forces stemming from the precarious life experience of the 1900 generation: especially the high mortality and debilitating illnesses of parents, aunts and uncles, sisters and brothers caused by flu pandemics, tuberculosis, typhoid fever, pneumonia, or sepsis. Death and illness changed the terms of family life and functioning. Boys and girls who lost their mothers were sent to live with relatives, facing integration into a new family and competition with cousins for attention and resources. Widowers and widows quickly remarried, and young children were swept into new households with unknown and sometimes disliked stepmothers or stepfathers. The loss of jobs or political offices, or the bankruptcies of businesses, meant that families had to find new means of sustenance elsewhere and adjust to a lower standard of living.

Fires, floods, and earthquakes ravaged homes or farms, factories or shops, even entire villages or communities, causing the loss of material possessions, sources of livelihood, and personal relationships: A fire on the Great Plains claims the family farm. The son of a wagonmaker and blacksmith recalls that "three different times he got a shop built and a good business going and got out of debt, and then he'd be absolutely cleaned out by fire. All he'd ever do, though, was just turn around and start over again." These disasters could happen in the Bay Area too: many men and women recount living through the San Francisco earthquake of 1906 or through Berkeley's Great Fire of 1923, which displaced families to Berkeley, Oakland, or adjacent communities. Such events had a devastating effect on the infrastructure and social fabric of communities.

One Berkeley woman's story of her childhood brings this tumult to life: She and her mother were sleeping together in an old tin bed. The house shook dramatically and threw them on the floor. Her mother said, "Oh Jesus, Mary,

Joseph, save us, save us." They lived south of Market Street in San Francisco, and "all day long people were coming down with their parrots and dogs" to get on the ferries and flee to safety from the destruction and resulting fires. Together with three hundred other people, their family got on a "little sailing ship called the *Lizzy Dance*" and were out on the Bay for two weeks. She remembers "never being so hungry in my life" as they "slept with all the lumber down below with rats running over you." They returned to find their house standing, but everything else up and down the street was burned. Thereafter, sixteen people lived in their house, and they had to cook on the streets for months because stoves and chimneys in homes couldn't be used because there was no water in case of another fire. About a decade later she married and moved to Berkeley during World War I.

Common stories of pull forces also run through the migration experiences of the 1900 generation—especially assurances of work reported in personal letters from family or friends or in advertisements promoting prosperity and promising a better life in California. Other pull forces include the enticements of better schools and the progressive education of children that came with California's Compulsory School Act of 1903. This legislation featured the expansion of the University of California system and the growing visibility of UC Berkeley as its crown jewel.[17] The prospect of finding a desirable marriage partner within networks of trusted or similar others was also appealing. And let's not forget that, since its statehood in 1850, California had become a great symbol of the allure and mystique of the West. As one father raised on a Minnesota farm said, "I had always had my heart set on California, even when I was a little kid, and I used to read everything I could find out about it. I got more and more 'California fever' as I got older."

The attributes of a person or group also matter in setting migration into motion. It is one thing to feel the push or pull; it is another to alter the course of one's life, and the lives of others, by taking action. Such responses are not always a positive decision; they may be an unwelcome necessity. Although we cannot observe such attributes directly, the Berkeley cases are full of references to the personal characteristics of one or more family members that may have left them particularly open to moving: a father's willingness to take risks, a mother's hardy optimism that the family could manage anything in its path, a father's "yearning restlessness" and desire for change, another's openness to adventure and longing to travel, a mother's ability to envision a future for herself and her family in a new place, or another's unbounded trust in her husband to see that everything turned out fine. Individuals' characteristics might not just make them receptive to leaving but might *require* them to leave: a father's temper might lead to fights with coworkers and frequent moves to new locations.

What is overwhelmingly clear in the migration stories of the Berkeley generation is that social networks—"linked lives"—are the strongest pull drawing families westward. Social relationships propel families to California through what is known as a chain migration: the migration of a person or group becomes a lure and a base of economic and social support for the subsequent migration of kin or people from the same village or country.[18] Going *to* a person or a group fosters courage, brings comfort, and reduces the risk of making the leap. These later migrants have established knowledge and networks to help them get started. Their contacts are sometimes only distant relatives or family friends several times removed—names and addresses scribbled on scraps of paper.

Like most of life's transitions, migration is generally not undertaken alone but is interwoven with others. Social convoys of couples, parents and children, or other relatives (aunts, uncles, brothers, sisters) may move together or be otherwise involved in the process. These are often stories of a journey made together. A large proportion of overseas migrants—from Greece, Sweden, Italy, Russia, England, and other countries—came to California by rail or ship, without significant intermediate settlements other than temporary stops along the way to stay with family and friends.

Many families who made the journey within the United States, in contrast, took indirect routes to California, punctuated by longer stays in some places. These, too, often involved family members. For example, one of the older Berkeley women, born in a small farming community in South Dakota, traced her childhood journey westward first to her uncle's Oregon ranch, where she spent the first year of her life living in a covered wagon while her father worked on the Lincoln Highway. When she was eleven they settled in California's Mother Lode gold country, and from there she moved to Berkeley. There are many such stories of moves from America's heartland—originating in places like Minnesota, Indiana, Iowa, Kansas, Nebraska, Missouri, and Texas—where people made extended stays with relatives in Washington, Idaho, Oregon, and other western states before ultimately settling in California.

Networks at the point of origin can encourage or discourage a move. One can feel supported in leaving or be begged or ordered not to go. A woman born in Sweden remembered her father's parting words: "Remember, if you don't like it in America, we can somehow scrape up the money for you to come back here. But I know you're going to like it. Everyone I've known who's gone to America has loved it." One can also feel a strong or weak connection to a community or to land that makes it difficult or easy to leave—or to adjust to a new environment. A man born in Italy who emigrated to the Port of Richmond at age sixteen looked back with some resentment, feeling that the local Bay Area Italians who had come from his own district in Italy could have helped him get established. Instead they steered him wrong just for the fun of watching a greenhorn make mistakes. Social encounters during migration can bring supportive or destructive people into one's path: a stranger's kindness in offering leads for jobs or places to stay, or just in providing a warm meal, can be welcoming; a brawl on a factory floor or a city sidewalk can fuel a man's desire to flee.

Regardless of how migration comes about, it can be individuating, separating people from the past and from earlier customs and constraints. It can create a sense of loss in leaving old worlds to establish new ones, or it can create a sense of liberation from family and community controls but also leave people anchorless and adrift, at least temporarily. The migration patterns of the Berkeley generation are related to birthplace and descent, origins that continued to shape their lives as they grew up and grew older.

Birthplace and Family History

The Berkeley 1900 generation and their own parents span seventy or more years of American social and economic development, a period of large-scale immigration to American shores. One-fifth of their generation was foreign-born; two-thirds had at least one foreign-born parent. In their birthplace history and descent, they generally resembled those who had migrated within the nation and into the state during the preceding decades, a similarity that lets us place them within the ebb and flow of nationalities that distinguished this period. Cohort differences in birthplace and descent let us further refine these comparisons.

Very few members grew up on farms, and only 13 percent were born to farmers, consistent with their responses in later life to the question "Were you brought up mostly on a farm, in a town, in a small city, or in a large city?" Of the survivors who were surveyed in 1973, less than 20 percent responded that they were brought up "mostly on a farm." The foreign-born are slightly underrepresented among those with nonfarm backgrounds and slightly overrepresented in the small farmer and agricultural laborer classes, but these differences are not appreciable. Members of the second generation (born in the United States) are not different from those whose parents were native-born. In all respects, rural origin has minor significance in the life history of the Berkeley 1900 generation and bears little relation to foreign parentage.

Such underrepresentation of farm backgrounds reflects the type of opportunity available in the state at this time. Unlike the vast expanse of central and southwestern lands opened to settlement through the Homestead Act of 1862, California came to be dominated by large agricultural estates and offered little chance to buy land or acquire a small family farm. Especially after 1900, opportunity lay instead in the rapid growth of manufacturing and in expanding service, real estate, transportation, and construction sectors associated with the large-scale movement of people into the state. Despite the "closing" of the frontier in 1890, agricultural opportunities remained in other parts of the western region, such as the Northwest Territory, which emigrant farmers might have found more attractive than California. As we showed earlier, for many of the Berkeley 1900 generation who grew up in the rural Midwest, the route to California included brief stays in either Oregon or Washington, often to visit relatives.

An examination of birthplace history provides some details on their emigration and immigration. Table 2.1 shows that the older cohort, born before the turn of the century, is made up predominantly of persons who migrated to California; less than a third were born within the state, and only a sixth of this number were native to the Bay Area. Within the continental United States, the largest part of this older cohort emigrated out of the central sweep of states—the Great Plains and the Midwest; approximately one-fifth of these parents were foreign-born. In contrast the younger cohort, born after the turn of the century, includes a much larger proportion of native Californians: 48 percent of the women and 42 percent of their spouses were born within the state, with approximately one-fourth native to the Bay Area.

The most significant shift in origin between the two cohorts occurs within the younger group: a drop from approximately 20 percent foreign-born to 12 to 13 percent. Complementary analyses reveal that in the Berkeley 1900 generation the largest percentage of the foreign-born (37 percent) came from the United Kingdom (England, Northern Ireland, Scotland, Wales) or Canada, followed by Italy (20 percent) or Scandinavia (13 percent). Most foreign-born parents similarly came from the United Kingdom (37 percent), followed by Germany or Holland (17 percent), Ireland (13 percent), or Scandinavia (13 percent).

Overall, then, the Berkeley 1900 generation reflects the composition of groups migrating into California during this period. The greater proportion of native-born Californians among those born after the turn of the century almost surely reflects the substantial increase of migration into the state induced by the boom years of the early twentieth century.[19]

But what do these figures suggest about the types of communities the migrants came from? Our cases do not include direct or consistently gathered information on this. We know from other evidence that approximately

TABLE 2.1. Birthplaces of Berkeley women and men, by birth cohort

| | Percentage distribution | | | |
| | Women | | Men | |
Place of birth	Older	Younger	Older	Younger
San Francisco Bay Area	5	12	4	12
California: outside Bay Area	22	36	26	30
Northwest, mountain	9	9	9	7
Central, west, and east	33	13	22	23
South	4	7	5	7
Northeast (Mid-Atlantic, New England)	9	10	13	10
Foreign country	19	13	22	12
	100 (92)	100 (119)	100 (107)	100 (103)

Note: Ns in parentheses.

three-fourths of the native-born who came to California grew up west of the Mississippi.[20] Approximately half of these people might have characterized themselves as having been "brought up mostly" in a town or small city, with those of mixed native-born and foreign-born parentage more likely to have spent their childhoods in a large city. This evidence may reflect the intermediate position of the families of the native-born in the westward movement of the period. These members of the Berkeley generation most likely participated in the increasing urbanization, moving from the small towns and cities of the west and central plains to the rapidly developing metropolitan Bay Area.

Geography also structures the selection of marital partners. Whether or not they were native Californians, men in the Berkeley sample frequently married women from the general locale of their own birthplaces, reflecting a pattern of regional "homogamy" and the influence of early social ties in choosing mates.[21] Over half of the men born in California married women of similar origin; one-fifth selected brides from the midwestern region. Of the men born in the United States, only the New Englanders were more likely to have married women from outside their own region of origin; 43 percent married women who were California-born. This regional group, together with the foreign-born, includes a substantial number of men who moved to California as single young adults. Most wives of the foreign-born were native either to California (32 percent) or to the Old World (47 percent). In both cases the "match" generally occurred within a common nationality group, no doubt promoted through family- or friend-based matchmaking, shared networks, and social clubs in California that catered to particular nationalities.

Without more systematic information on the early years of the Berkeley 1900 generation, we cannot identify the relative frequency of various marital patterns: men who married local women before moving to California, unmarried immigrants who returned temporarily to their home community to marry, and immigrants who married women living in California who had emigrated from the same region. Nevertheless, we have examples of each pattern in the study: a couple from Minneapolis who moved in with relatives living in Oakland, an Italian immigrant who visited his native community to marry a local girl and brought her back to the Bay Area, and a young man who married the daughter of family friends who had emigrated from his place of origin in Kansas. In chapter 5 we address the selection of marital partners in greater depth. As we prepare to trace the lives of the men (chapter 3) and women (chapter 4) before they come together as husbands and wives, we ask how birthplace and descent might be related to differences in life chances and family experience.

Lifelong Influences

There may be culturally oriented distinctions between native-born Americans and those of more recent immigrant descent, as well as distinctions among immigrant groups themselves—concerns, values, and attitudes that may have had a substantial influence on families and their response to opportunity and deprivation. For example, American historian Stephan Thernstrom noted the attitude of American Irish and Italian families in Boston and Newburyport toward acquiring property rather than educating children.[22] Birthplace and descent might also bring advantages or disadvantages in educational and occupational attainment. The cultural aspect of descent is a complex mixture of situation and response as they relate to values and attitudes. At this point we focus on socioeconomic correlates of descent and birthplace because they define the social origins of the Berkeley generations and become a reference point for understanding the life paths and values of the study parents up to 1930.

The disadvantaged position of new immigrants in American society and the relative mobility of the second generation are recurring themes in social history. In the early twentieth century, this imagery was strong, as was a belief in social mobility as a central tenet of the American ideology of opportunity and individualistic industry.[23] Social judgment aside, the imagery was also largely accurate. Based on his analysis of census data for 1870 and 1880, E. P. Hutchinson, legislative historian of American immigration, noted that the "foreign-born were most typically employed in the factories, in the heavy industries, as manual laborers and domestic servants. Clerical, managerial, and official positions remained largely inaccessible to them."[24] Census information collected in 1890 on the occupations of the native-born children of immigrants enable some aggregate comparisons of the first and second generations: "Unlike the immigrant males who were in highest proportion among domestic and personal service workers, the second generation males were most numerous relatively among workers in trade and in transportation and manufacturing. . . . All together, the second generation conformed more closely to the occupational distribution of the entire white labor force than did the foreign-born."[25]

An immigrant in America who lacked a profession or a valued craft or industrial skill found the range of opportunity beyond that of unskilled laborer highly restricted. Sons of immigrants were disadvantaged both by their initial low position in the occupational structure and by the family's lack of money for the education that was becoming increasingly important for moving out of the manual classes, if not into the dominant American culture. It seems, however, that sons of immigrants may have been no more disadvantaged than sons of the native-born lower and working classes and, in some contexts, may even have been more successful, at least in moving into certain skilled trades and the lower white-collar positions.[26] The critical point, then, appears to have been not immigrant status or ethnic background but the father's occupation and his ability or desire to provide an education for his son. Despite some evidence that Anglo-Saxon Protestant groups enjoyed a slight advantage in the job market, it is difficult to establish whether other immigrant groups suffered from job discrimination or whether they were more challenged by the lack of language skills and their different cultural backgrounds.[27]

How do birthplace and family history of the parents of the Berkeley 1900 generation relate to occupational position? Table 2.2 allows some rough comparisons, despite the imprecision of generations, placing the Berkeley men in historical time, as well as tracing the shift in the occupational composition of immigrant nationality groups over this period.[28] A simple comparison of the number of people in the descent categories gives some indication of the changing composition between native-born and foreign-born and of the shift of immigration from the British Isles to Scandinavia and eastern and southern Europe. Most important, native-born men in the parent generation held fewer unskilled positions and more middle-class and upper-class jobs than the foreign-born. Country of descent aside, 30 percent of the native-born were categorized as "professional or managerial" and 30 percent as "farm" or "manual," while the comparable figures for the foreign-born are 14 percent and 43 percent. The pattern of birthplace and occupational distribution within descent groups is complex, and the small sample sizes make conclusions difficult.

Three patterns are worth noting. First, in the two cases where there are sufficient numbers in both the native-born and foreign-born generations to warrant comparison ("United Kingdom, Canada" and "Northern Europe," which are "old" immigrant zones), the foreign-born are concentrated more in manual and white-collar jobs than the native-born. Second, if we examine those descent groups with a small number of individuals (native-born Scandinavians, native-born southern and eastern Europeans, foreign-born Irish), we are in effect observing immigration during periods of relatively small emigration flows from a given area. In these cases we observe what the literature suggests: that immigration during such periods tended to be selective of relatively advantaged classes who were more likely to have idiosyncratic

TABLE 2.2. Occupations of fathers of the Berkeley 1900 generation, by descent and nativity (percentages)

Grandfathers' occupation by nativity	Percentage distribution of grandfathers by descent[a]				
	US, UK, Canada	Ireland	Northern Europe	Scandinavia	S.&E. Europe, Middle East
Native-born					
Professional-managerial	39	27	29	33	40
White-collar	32	33	38	67	40
Manual	15	20	21	—	—
Farm	14	20	13	—	20
	100 (74)	100 (15)	100 (24)	100 (3)	100 (5)
Foreign-born					
Professional-managerial	22	67	10	10	—
White-collar	33	—	60	35	42
Manual	28	17	25	40	37
Farm	17	17	5	15	21
	100 (18)	100 (6)	100 (20)	100 (20)	100 (19)

Note: Ns in parentheses. Information available in the grandparental generation was obtained from interviews with the parents in 1930 and 1931 and is restricted to the core sample of 112 families.

[a] Both grandfathers were included in the analysis.

motivations and who had the resources to make the move.[29] Third, the disadvantaged position of southern and eastern European foreign-born immigrants is clearly shown by their relative concentration in the manual and farm classes and by their absence from managerial and professional positions. This table cautions us not to hastily assume that being first or second generation is uniformly equated with low occupational placement. We also need to recognize the considerable variation in the occupational composition of the various groups.

Besides occupational position, how might birthplace and descent be linked to other characteristics of early family life of the 1900 generation? The information available allows us to examine two such aspects of family life—financial hardship and family size—that are important to family support and life chances, largely apart from ethnic differences in values. The evidence on hardship is based on recollections in later life (the 1973 interviews with surviving parents), and it reinforces the importance of viewing birthplace in relation to the intervening influence of socioeconomic position. Members of the 1900 generation were asked, "Did your parents have a hard time financially in raising a family or were they comfortable or well-to-do?"[30] The foreign-born were more likely to remember a childhood of some hardship than the native-born of either native or foreign descent and less likely to remember being comfortable. Here the differences are relatively small (approximately a 10 percent difference for both comparisons). But more striking differences appear in the relation between hardship and their fathers' occupational status. The proportion of the 1900 generation who described their own parents as "well-off" declined from more than two-thirds in the professional and managerial class to one-fourth in the farm class, while the proportion that experienced "some hardship" or being "very hard-pressed" rose from less than a third to more than three-fourths between the two categories.

The size of one's family of origin is more strongly related to foreign birth than are the 1900 generation's recollections of hardship in childhood. Across descent groups, foreign-born mothers consistently had more children than the native-born (averages of 5.4 versus 4.2). Fertility variations by descent generally correspond with the proportion of Catholics and thus may largely reflect the influence of Catholicism. For example, Catholic affiliation was most common among mothers who traced their descent to southern and eastern Europe (69 percent), followed at a distance by women of Irish and northern European stock (4 percent). Less than 10 percent of the women of Scandinavian and English heritage were Catholic.

The fertility differences of women across descent groups may also reflect differences in socioeconomic origin. To clarify the relative influence of cultural and economic factors in fertility, we analyzed six characteristics of the women's mothers: descent, whether foreign-born or native-born, religious affiliation (Catholic or Protestant), level of education, family's socioeconomic position, and whether the husband worked in a farm or nonfarm occupation.

Not surprisingly, Catholic affiliation has the strongest influence on fertility among these women, though descent makes a significant independent contribution as well, an effect that is comparable to that of foreign birth and socioeconomic status. Neither education nor agricultural employment adds much to this picture. Two general outcomes are worth noting. First, mothers of southern and eastern European origin tended to have the most children and those of Scandinavian origin the least, even apart from the influence of Catholicism, low socioeconomic status, and foreign birth. Second, differences in family size across socioeconomic strata provided some evidence of fertility control, especially in the middle classes. While limiting family size may have had little to do with economic considerations among the affluent, this adaptation was an economic decision among lower middle-class families committed to improving lifestyle and educational opportunity for their offspring.

For members of the 1900 generation who grew up in rural areas of the Old World, a large family often meant poverty in childhood and a hard life ahead. Such conditions influenced the decision to immigrate to America, as seen in the early life history of a young man who left his rural home in northern Italy at age sixteen. His family of seven brothers and four sisters farmed in the Piedmont region on the outskirts of Turin. Though relatively prosperous and productive compared with other landholdings in the area, the farm could not meet the needs of the large family and was too small to provide adequate holdings for each son after the father's death. Both of these factors influenced the young man's decision to immigrate to California in 1907, following his older sister. Some twenty years later he received a letter from his father asking about the portion of land that rightfully belonged to him. Having achieved some economic security, he urged that his land be distributed among the other sons: "I am never going back. There is nothing that I want—and even without the land I will be better able to provide for my family in this country than my brothers will. So, I want them to have it all."

Homes broken by death or separation were a common childhood experience in the 1900 generation—more than a fifth came from such homes—even more for those from more economically disadvantaged backgrounds. But whatever the strain and tensions associated with adaptations in the New World, we find no corresponding evidence on the incidence of broken families or even emotional climate. Closeness of parent-child relations and marital conflict were unrelated to foreign birth or parentage.[31]

Conclusion

The Berkeley 1900 generation, with its parents and its children to come, spanned a period of striking social and economic change. This chapter has looked at the massive flows of immigration into and across the United States, often in stages. By exploring their origin and migration stories, we have established a foundation from which to trace their experiences as they make their way into adulthood, then come together as husbands and wives, fathers and mothers.

These early stories of immigration and emigration powerfully illustrate the interaction between changing worlds and changing people. The resulting pathways reveal how the cultural and socioeconomic attributes of one generation carry legacies for subsequent generations, both constraining and opening life pathways amid the rapidly changing historical conditions these generations faced. New social conditions altered opportunities and expectations for these men and women relative to their parents. But as we also see, in giving shape and a cultural mix to the Berkeley generation, these experiences generated circumstances ripe for friction and conflict across the generations.

Most members of the 1900 generation moved to California and Berkeley with their own parents or as young adults and came of age in nonfarm or urban settings. They were subject to a variety of push forces that launched a migration, especially the precariousness of life for their parents, as well as the pull of forces that lured people to California with the promise of a better life. Perhaps most important is the central role that social relationships played in propelling individuals, families, and whole social convoys along migration pathways. Migration is rarely an individual experience. Many people are swept up in such motion, and their lives—and the lives of subsequent generations—are altered.

Foreign birth stood out as the most pervasive cultural feature of the couples' family backgrounds; only one-third of the Berkeley generation were offspring of native-born parents. Foreign birth frequently entailed some disadvantage in the family's social class and size, especially among those descended from southern and eastern Europeans. Cultural and socioeconomic patterns also exerted an independent influence on the family background of the 1900 generation. Large families, for example, were associated with low socioeconomic status, foreign birth, and Catholic heritage. As we follow the lives of the 1900 generation up to World War II, both cultural and socioeconomic influences will emerge as significant determinants of their position on the eve of the Great Depression and of how they weathered the subsequent years. But before we turn to that historical period, we need to follow the imprint of their social origin on their work, education, marriage, and childbearing through the 1920s.

3

Men on Their Way

You are never really secure until you feel insecure enough to work hard.
BERKELEY MAN

At the close of World War I, the Berkeley men were busily engaged in completing their education, establishing a career with financial security, and starting families. Some members of the older cohort, born toward the end of the nineteenth century, had served in the Great War and were now completing their education and getting rewarding jobs. Relative to the younger cohort born at the start of the twentieth century, during the 1920s members of the older cohort were more advanced in their worklives and earnings—a difference that would have notable consequences for their experiences in the Great Depression. This chapter examines the role of family origin and education in the socioeconomic careers of the Berkeley men, then compares the 1929 income, savings, and investments of the middle class and working class in the two cohorts of the 1900 generation.

Social and cultural changes in the 1920s shaped the times in which the Berkeley men launched their worklives. We begin with these themes and then turn to ways of making a living in the twentieth century: from acquiring education and particular work experience to income and living standards, which involve owning homes and cars and acquiring other investments, savings, and securities. Not only were these important symbols of social mobility and financial investment, especially in the working class, they also provided psychological rewards and meaning.

Central Themes in the 1920s

Rising affluence, unequal access to opportunity, and consumer incentives widened the gap between aspiration and reality for many Americans in the 1920s. Real wages increased substantially and family living standards rose, but the gains proved greatest for the middle class and those in the business world. From 1923 to 1929, corporation profits increased six times as fast as wages.[1] Commercial institutions enabled families without surplus income to acquire material goods associated with "the good life" through mortgaging their future income by purchasing on the installment plan. And yet these very same families steadfastly resisted social insurance that might have secured their survival during crises of illness and unemployment.[2] By the end of the decade, the distribution of income among American families told a vivid story of inequality, giving "much too much to persons at the top of the income scale and too little to those at the bottom."[3]

The Berkeley men grew up in a cultural era that provided a rationale for such inequality: the imperatives of social Darwinism expressed the ethos and operating principles of capitalism through hard work, initiative, and self-discipline in a free and competitive marketplace.[4] William Graham Sumner, the foremost apostle of this social philosophy, posited that in the struggle for survival, the strongest or fittest man is the self-controlled, thrifty, and industrious worker. Just as survival is ensured by strength, the pathway to material success is ensured by moral virtue amid unrestricted economic activity. Capital is formed through self-denial, and a competitive marketplace yields deserved outcomes, good or bad. Whereas one might assume that the hard work of men on the low end of the social order might bring them social mobility, this philosophy suggested that the family is the medium for transmitting these moral virtues and accrued advantages in wealth to offspring—and therefore that these men could never be equal to better-positioned men in their nature, opportunity, or outcomes.

Changes that threatened this social Darwinist philosophy were well underway by the time the Berkeley men assumed the responsibilities of marriage and family.[5] The growth of mass merchandising and advertising encouraged families to spend rather than save, and financial arrangements such as installment buying let them spend money they hadn't yet earned. A mentality of abundance fostered lifestyles within the middle class that placed a premium on automobiles and leisure spending.[6] Definitions of economic needs and aspirations shifted: need "came to mean anything that a particular family was unwilling to go without."[7] Rising material aspirations and expectations meant more families sought standards of living incompatible with sacrifice or self-denial.[8] Last, the debate over social insurance ("welfare") raised critical questions about an economic system that judged a man's character too much by his economic fortunes.

From what we know about the early adult years of the Berkeley men, some elements of the social Darwinist philosophy recur in their views of self and others. One man remembered his father's generation as "having a lot of get-up-and-go. They worked long hours and they worked hard. Now the whole idea seems to be to get out of work. It's the childish attitude of hollering for as many holidays as possible." From the perspective of middle age and the New Deal of the 1930s, another man complained about "the loss of freedom and enterprise. Everything is in the hands of corporations or else is checked by the government." Whether through rigorous discipline and goal setting in the home or through poverty, a number of Berkeley men cited "the school of hard knocks" as putting them on the track to worldly accomplishments. A successful professional attributed his "drive" to a sense of deprivation that "rankled in me all my early life. It can make me get up at five in the morning and work till 12 at night."

The virtues of self-denial and industry did not depend on growing up in a privileged home. As one man put it, "When you get by easy, you sort of get into the way of thinking that everything is going to be all right, and you have a tendency to just let things slide." Another man, who had been raised in one of the two wealthiest families in his midwestern hometown, looked back and saw many disadvantages: "I think it is very bad for a young boy [to have such privilege] because you are never really secure until you feel insecure enough to work hard. That's probably the main difference between my father and myself. He started out without any money and had an awful lot of drive and ambition, whereas I started out in a very comfortable home and never seemed to have as much energy to get out and make my way." An observation like this may not generalize to all the Berkeley men, but it does have much in common with the conception of workingmen in a social Darwinist age. The American dream of "making it big," as the rhetoric of the time reinforced, could happen through individual sacrifice and hard work despite family circumstances. And yet the reality, as we will see, is that for many of these men, life outcomes were not about effort and control but were instead about family advantage and disadvantage and about the historical events and changes of their times.

By the 1920s, a high school diploma had become a requirement for some jobs in clerical and managerial fields. For men born during the early to middle twentieth century, studies have consistently identified formal education as the primary path between a man's family of origin and his occupational status.[9] The main influence of family background occurs indirectly through education, especially in relation to career beginnings. Accordingly, our point of departure for examining the early careers of the Berkeley men is the educational legacy of their family history.

The imprint of class origin could be seen at all rungs of the educational ladder, from entry into secondary school to completion of high school and college matriculation. Low income and a large family, coupled with anti-intellectual values in the home, made college a dim prospect for urban youth of the 1910s and 1920s, though some of this disadvantage may have been countered for the Berkeley men by the unusual chance for higher education in California.[10] A first question, then, concerns how the varied socioeconomic and cultural origins of these men are reflected in education and thus in occupational standing and lifestyle before the economic collapse of the 1930s.

Another question concerns the material returns on investment in schooling and work, especially as gauged by earnings and the quality of home and neighborhood. If family background influenced a man's job opportunities and achieved status through education, this connection would presumably also ensure greater prospects of economic and psychological well-being through more rewarding jobs. The sequence from family origin to education, from education to occupational position, and from occupational position to earnings and lifestyle consumption thus shaped a man's ability to control life outcomes as he approached the Great Depression. Income is the most consequential factor in men's ability to secure a desired standard of living while also setting aside resources to safeguard family welfare in an age of economic uncertainty.

In the face of high standards of living and the pressing needs of a growing family, there were some options for augmenting economic resources. First of all, the male breadwinner might seek better-paid employment or take on a second job. Second, income might be supplemented by the wages of an eldest child or an employed wife, or by taking in boarders or lodgers.[11] At the end of the 1920s, however, the normative climate of American family life discouraged these secondary options, especially wives' employment. Despite the economic squeeze for many families, women seldom went to work because they were charged with the care of children, backed by strong community resistance to the employment of mothers.

The choices families made during the 1920s affected their responses to changes in financial position. The family that overspent its income—buying on credit and letting debt accumulate—would find its money committed as soon as it was earned. But commercial pressures whetted the appetite for immediate gratification and dulled the traditional conscience of thrift, prudence, and saving. As historian William Leuchtenburg observed, "Abandoning the notion of saving income or goods or capital over time, the country insisted on immediate consumption, a demand which became institutionalized in the installment plan."[12] Most automobiles, furniture, and radios were purchased on credit.

Overconsumption, however, had different meaning for families in different economic circumstances. Families that lived on the margin of low income (less than $1,000 a year in 1929) experienced chronic disparity between needs and resources. In Stephan Thernstrom's words, only those who adopted "ruthless underconsumption" could make ends meet with a modest sum left over.[13] Moreover, they were less likely to be assessed as a good risk for loans and credit than were established families from the middle class with skilled jobs. Financial dependence on friends, kin, and public agencies especially described life in the lower classes.

Armed with these themes, we examine pathways to adult status and the role of social origin in the lives of Berkeley men. We turn first to acquiring education and work experience and then to income, economic standards, and the use of family resources.

Acquiring Education and Work Experience

The Berkeley men came of age at the beginning of a new era in education. Although in 1910 only 9 percent of eighteen-year-olds in the United States completed secondary education, high school enrollment spiked sharply to about 35 percent nationwide by 1920,[14] which increased national median levels of education to ten years of formal schooling by 1930.[15] Riding the coattails of the Progressive movement, California prioritized the education of its young citizens by passing the Compulsory School Act in 1903, which required youth under eighteen to enroll in school and penalized the parents and employers of minors who did not.[16]

These and other social forces are at least partly the reason that nearly 60 percent of Berkeley men managed to complete high school, twice the national average at the time.[17] And at the upper end, fully one-third of the men graduated from a college or university, with UC Berkeley, Stanford, Dartmouth, and the University of Michigan among them. At the same time, fully one-quarter (26 percent) had a ninth-grade education or less. These gross differences in education, with such significant clustering at both extremes, would polarize the life pathways of the Berkeley men. While information about men's military service is not recorded in the early archives, we estimate that it also marked the lives of about 35 percent of the Berkeley men, likely in World War I (16 percent stateside and 19 percent overseas)—but probably for much shorter periods than their sons' service in late World War II or Korea.[18]

Two influences shaped men's pathways into education and, later, into work: socioeconomic status and cultural background. The importance of social class has already been described, but immigration in the family histories of the Berkeley men also brought both hope for a better life and a measure of disadvantage. Foreign-born fathers had much lower occupational attainment than native-born fathers, especially if they were of southern or eastern European origin. These differences were underscored by a corresponding inequality in their formal education. Moreover, foreign or Catholic parentage was generally coupled with having large families, which might also limit education. These educational disadvantages could stem from socioeconomic conditions or from cultural patterns that assigned lower priority to the education of sons than to the economic welfare of the family unit.[19]

What were the effects of economic origin and family size on men's educational attainment? And were the educational prospects less promising if the men's parents were foreign-born, Catholic, or both? Whether born in the nineteenth or the twentieth century, the sons of well-to-do parents had the greatest opportunity for education through high school. Over four-fifths of men from middle- and high-income families at least completed high school, compared with less than two-fifths of men from lower economic origins. In larger families, too, young men attained less education. Parents' birthplace adds little to an understanding of sons' schooling. But neither humble beginnings nor the economic pressures of a large family completely account for the persistent educational disadvantage of growing up Catholic at the turn of the century.[20]

Men's formal education represents a strong link in the transmission of occupational status across the generations. Lower socioeconomic status, a large family, and Catholic parents who were born in the Old World severely restricted prospects for advanced education and, consequently, chances for entering careers in the middle class by the end of the 1920s. But these dimensions of family origin have little or no direct effect on men's occupational attainment; they became powerful in shaping occupational attainment *through* education. Education affected occupational attainment by way of certification, access to placement services, the development of technical skills and values, and social intelligence.[21]

By the end of the 1920s, nearly 30 percent of the Berkeley men were in the professional or managerial ranks (such as physicians, professors, lawyers, designers, ministers, or chemists), and another 7 percent ran businesses of their own (such as stores or contracting firms). Other sizable groups (28 percent) were office or sales workers such as real estate agents, postal workers, or traveling salesmen; were in skilled crafts or trades (20 percent); worked as foremen; or engaged in mechanical work such as inspectors at industrial plants, carpenters, window installers, or tilers. Fewer men were service workers or doing unskilled or semiskilled work (7 percent each). Of course, the late 1920s naturally found the younger Berkeley men at an earlier stage of career building and with lower occupational status than the older men—but younger and older men did not differ in their overall levels of educational attainment.

The expense, effort, and sacrifice that enabled many men to enter professional or managerial ranks seem to be balanced by the benefits they gained: the extrinsic rewards of job security and relatively high income as well as the intrinsic values of the work experience itself (autonomy, responsibility, scope for self-expression). At the end of the 1920s, two-thirds of the professional and managerial men felt strongly committed to their jobs compared with less than 15 percent of other white-collar workers and an even lower percentage of manual workers. Lower occupational status is also associated with greater job dissatisfaction as indexed by interviewer ratings of 1930–31. Issues that mattered most to laborers—job protections, regular work, good wages—were mostly lacking in their work situations.

Earning a Living and Being Resourceful

For men, pathways to work are also intimately connected to the ability to form and support a family. By 1929 all of the Berkeley men had married and had at least one child. About half had married by age twenty-five, with the older men having married significantly later (median age twenty-nine) than the younger men (median age twenty-four). Having some college was associated with an "average" timing of marriage (ages twenty-two to twenty-five), but having less than a high school education was associated with both early (before age twenty-two) and late marriage (after age twenty-five). The high percentage of men with low education who married late (53 percent) may have been limited by their resources, since educational attainment was firmly linked to occupation and social class, and these in turn were firmly linked to men's resources.[22]

With social class as a core theme of this chapter, it is important to provide some detail on the measure in the Berkeley archive and our corresponding terminology. Social class (as of 1929) is measured by the August Hollingshead index, which is based on a man's occupational and educational status, using seven-point scales. Occupation is weighted by a factor of seven and education by a factor of four. The total range of scores was divided into five status groups. "Upper middle class" refers to professionals and managers (groups 1 and 2); "lower middle class" to administrators and white-collar workers (group 3); "working class" to skilled manual workers (group 4); and "lower class" to semiskilled and unskilled workers (group 5). To enable comparisons between middle-class and working-class families, we sometimes combine the first three groups as "middle class" and the last two groups as "working class."

The social class of men in 1929 is strongly related to their family income, which tells us much about their standard of living.[23] Figure 3.1 shows total family income by social class in 1929, by men's birth cohort. Economic resources in 1929 varied sharply by men's occupation, but each class also included men who were more advanced in their careers than others, as reflected in the difference between the older and younger cohorts.

As expected, the older men occupied more prestigious occupations at the time, which would ensure some advantage in earnings and assets. Presumably, with more time in the labor market, the advantage of older men would also apply to younger workers on the same occupational level. Comparisons of this sort let us view the family economy in ways sensitive to the changing economic careers and pressure points of families across the class structure. Manual workers, for instance, tend to reach their peak earnings early, when their children are young, whereas professionals attain their income peak much later, during or after the time their children leave home. These differences will bear on decisions about expenditures and investments.

The distribution of average family income by social class points to older men as having the greatest range of expenditure and investment options in 1929. From the younger to the older men, the economic gap between professional workers on the top and the unskilled workers on the bottom more than *doubles*—with most of this change occurring in the middle class. The age trend is toward much greater differentiation between families in the upper classes and those of lower status. Family income is related to the age of Berkeley men in the working class, but their gains fall well short of those experienced by the families of professionals and managers. Economic pressure was the common lot of young Berkeley families at the end of the 1920s, but the main burden among older men was found in the lower middle class and working class.

One consequence of these economic differences is suggested by number of children. Most of the younger families had only one child at the time, with the largest families concentrated among the working classes—an average of 1.7. Average family size was at least 2.2 across all classes of older men, with the poorest families again showing the highest number (3.2). If measured solely in terms of family size, the demand for income increased more than its supply by men's age among these lower-status families; only families in the upper classes show a modest gain in per capita family income by men's age.

From all accounts, the families of older men with high social position enjoyed substantial discretionary income, and some of their wives took ad-

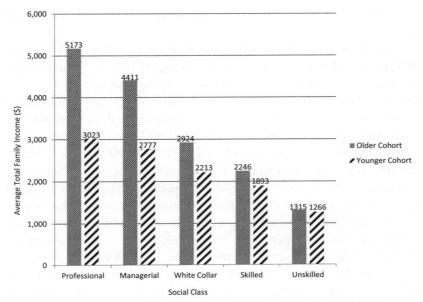

FIGURE 3.1. Average total family income by social class in 1929, by men's birth cohort.

vantage of it by hiring domestic help. Two out of five reported having some paid help with household chores, in contrast to none of the working-class families. Lifestyle preferences no doubt influenced this expenditure decision, because a third of the younger families in the upper middle class also claimed to have domestic help.

Families at the bottom of the class structure, whether headed by older or by younger men, faced painful choices. They lived on the margin of subsistence and had unmet needs that made hard living even harder. Glimpses of economic hardship in this class and the struggle to survive from day to day tell a story that has more in common with events to come in the 1930s than with those of the 1920s.

Whether men used their socioeconomic advantage, education, or self-employment to reach the higher classes, their economic values generally matched their accomplishments. Four subjective economic standards were identified from interviews with the Berkeley men in 1930–31: high, above average, average, and simple wants or needs. Each step up the occupational ladder, from the unskilled worker to the professional, comes with increased preference for an affluent lifestyle. On this measure, managers did not embrace higher standards than the professionals. A similar picture emerges from value orientations on the importance of upward mobility and making money.[24]

Overall, these data underscore the upper classes' desire for material goods, but they do not tell us about particular spending priorities or about strategies for making use of family income. Which occupational groups led the way in savings and security investments, in homeownership and home quality, and in financial and residential independence? Different goals or priorities may lead to strikingly varied patterns of saving and expenditure over time.[25]

We do not have information on financial plans among the Berkeley families, though a large percentage of men probably had no such plans in any explicit sense. Nevertheless, particular life situations favor certain goals and lines of action. With outstanding debts for postgraduate education and career establishment, young professional families may not have had the same options for saving and spending as the families of men in business management, quite apart from values. Likewise, big families and small incomes, plus uncertainty about stable work, would place heavy constraints on the saving of laborers, greater than those experienced by skilled workers. We begin with expenditures on housing, then turn to savings, securities, and life insurance.

TO OWN ONE'S OWN HOME

Few aspirations were more basic to the dreams of Berkeley couples—and Americans at large—than the desire to own their homes. In the words of President Herbert Hoover in a 1931 conference on home building and homeownership, "The desire to possess one's own home is the hope and ambition of almost every individual in the country."[26] As the largest financial commitment most families ever make, a home is both a source of status in the community and an investment for the later years of life. Homeownership connotes respectability and stability, a sense of worth and accomplishment. For some Berkeley families it also represented a degree of social mobility more attainable in a lifetime than significant occupational advancement.

Ownership and quality of residence are distinct bases for a man's satisfaction with his home. Ownership directly taps the achievement of residential independence and is a path to greater control over life outcomes. Quality of residence taps independent considerations of prestige, comfort, and assets. Especially in the lower classes, a man's pride in owning a two-bedroom cottage on a tiny lot may exceed the gratification he would gain by moving into a brand-new rental of similar size in a better neighborhood. The distinction between homeownership and quality thus brings to bear important issues concerning the meaning of a home to Berkeley men and women.

Residential histories and social evaluations of people who rent and own suggest a "normal" course for how families should evolve in terms of residence: from renting an apartment and possibly moving to better-quality rentals during the early years of singleness, childless marriage, or the arrival of children, to owning a home during the child-rearing stage with the goal of investing and integrating into one's community and providing stability in family life.

Homeownership among the Berkeley families generally followed this pattern. In 1929 most of the younger men and their families were either renting or living with relatives. Only one in four had assumed mortgage payments or owned their home, with an unusually high percentage being in the managerial class.[27] In direct contrast, three in five families headed by older men had mortgage payments or owned a home, with an especially high concentration in the professional and skilled classes.[28] For most families the dominant form of "other property" was a car (70 percent), followed by lots, vacation cabins, or other homes in the city (20 percent).

The success of older skilled men in acquiring a home was achieved on a very modest scale, as one might expect. The average value of their homes in 1929 was $5,681, well above estimates for the unskilled ($3,875) but much lower than for families in the upper middle class (which averaged $9,305 to $9,857).[29] Nevertheless, the statement of one skilled worker that "all our savings have been invested in our home" captures well the home orientation of such men. Only a small number owned "other property." This mode of proprietorship is restricted to the lower and upper middle class in both age groups, perhaps owing in part to family gifts and inheritance.

Regardless of age, men who entered the propertied class through homeownership were clearly the most satisfied with their living conditions. On a five-point scale using interviews in 1930–31, the homeowners ranked well above other men on pride and interest in their homes. A new home meant a higher standard of living for the Berkeley families, compared with the living conditions of renters or men living with parents. This change alone could account for homeowners' residential satisfaction. Aspirations for a home of one's own are thus part of gaining a higher standard of living; ownership is a means to this end, and it also contributes psychologically through a sense of independence, security, and respect. Homeownership most certainly reflected well on a man's stature and ability to provide for his family within the individualistic culture of the 1920s. Considering all these benefits, owning a home—no matter its quality—likely had its own effect on a man's satisfaction.

We therefore examined the direct link between homeownership and satisfaction with home, as well as standard of living as an intervening link, for the rewards of ownership may also be expressed through a family's standard of living.[30] We also took account of age (as a measure of one's cohort and career stage) and total family income in 1929. Ownership was the most important factor fueling a man's enthusiasm for his home. Living conditions represented a relatively weak connection between a family's income and homeownership and men's sentiment regarding their place of residence. No matter how modest the home, it had special value if a man held title to it, for it then became an extension of himself. Possession of the home and its neat appearance told the community something important about the man and his family, a presentation of self that hard times were soon to threaten. From his professional experience, an urban specialist noted, "People will go to great lengths to display to the public that they, in fact, own that house, even though it may not be much of a house. They'll put up fences and they'll plant flowers and they'll paint the front of the house even if they don't paint the rest of it in order to display the fact that they are independent."[31] This independence came with age (or career advancement) among the Berkeley men, as expressed through higher earnings that made homeownership and a better standard of living more possible.

We can gain perspective on the meaning of homeownership by comparing older and younger men. Younger homeowners occupied a position of psychological or social advantage in that they were "on time" or ahead of their age peers on homeownership. As such, the gratification of owning a home may have had less to do with material considerations than with the value of independence and pride of accomplishment. However, for both older and younger men, satisfaction with home is more strongly linked to ownership than to living standards, and this is especially so for younger men.

Level of income tells us more about a man's standard of living than about whether he owned the place where he lived, yet it is ownership that is central to the home satisfaction of the Berkeley men. Both objectively and subjectively, satisfied homeowners had a stake in their homes that would ensure greater residential stability, whereas dissatisfied men, especially among the renters, were prime candidates for residential change.[32] As the Berkeley men approached the end of the 1920s and the onset of the Great Depression, living arrangements and feelings about their residences offered important insight into their adjustment to hardship.

Besides homeownership, the automobile assumed an important status among aspirations. Only two in five Berkeley families were homeowners in 1929, but two in three had an automobile. The Sunday drive was a popular family ritual at the time. Owning one's home and car exemplified the cultural ideal of family privacy and control over its environment,[33] two values that would be sorely tested in the 1930s.

SAVING AND SECURITIES

At the end of the 1920s, less than a third of the Berkeley men reported having savings or investments in stocks and bonds and, overall, these were slightly more common among the older families. Class is at work again. For example, younger families in the managerial and skilled classes ranked below the average income of professional families, but they were over twice as likely to report a savings account. The low rate of saving among professional families suggests that they were spending more on material goods than on investments and paying off educational and other debts. The correspondingly low level of saving among white-collar families may reflect short-term priorities that arise from the pressures of aspirations matching those of the upper middle class but resources more similar to the lower classes. Given the extreme pressures experienced by families at the bottom of the socioeconomic ladder, it's not surprising that they also ranked low on savings. Among the savers, one suspects that few were able to put away enough to cover the loss of earnings for a single month. The older group in each occupational class, however, is better positioned—which is perhaps not surprising since older men had had more time not only to work and build experience, but also to save.

Families' savings behavior may also be connected to the desire for a place of one's own. Material achievement and life control are likely to have been priority issues among these families.[34] In the 1920s, as during the years following World War II, virtues of thrift were associated with homeownership. Workers who managed to save enough to make a down payment on a home could lay claim to the middle-class ethos of respectability and independence. Indeed, the pattern of saving among younger men corresponds with their homeownership. Families in the managerial class led the way on saving (and we've already seen that they also stand out on homeownership), and the professional and unskilled groups ranked lowest on saving (and occupy the same position on homeownership, though both are markedly higher on ownership in the older age category). Only the younger families of skilled workers were more likely to save than to own a home, a disparity that may reflect the time it took to achieve good credit and save the down payment on a relatively low income. In fact, homeownership is higher among skilled workers' families in the older age group than in any other social class; four out of five reported ownership, compared with three-fifths of the managerial group and little more than one-third of the unskilled.

Securities show a different pattern by class and career stage, with professionals leading the way among younger men on the possession of stocks and

bonds. Their unique prominence likely stems from intergenerational transfers, though we do not have systematic evidence of this in the archive. Only in
the managerial class does the prevalence and age trend on stocks and bonds
suggest a career-related propensity toward long-term investments.

While the upper-middle-class families may have been favored in securities at the end of the 1920s, securities also made them vulnerable in a declining economy. Families that sprinted ahead on stock market investments took
on additional risk. As one Berkeley executive recalled, the 1929 crash marked
the end of his dream of becoming rich by playing the stock market—and, he
added, "It also gave the Mrs. a stiff sock in the eye."

At the end of the 1920s, the most common form of economic security
was life insurance. Nearly nine out of ten families reported some insurance.
Younger families led the way on insurance coverage, reflecting the historical trend on commercial insurance during the first quarter of the twentieth
century.[35] The prevalence of life insurance policies across age groups and
class, however, implies a generalized consensus on private insurance as an
essential mode of protection against the uncertainties of the future. No provision against economic disaster was more characteristic of the era than private
life insurance. It did not, of course, protect workers from the everyday risks
of losing jobs or earnings, and policies may not have been large enough to
do more than shield families from the most immediate costs of a breadwinner's death. But life insurance was at least a modest step toward control over
life circumstances and gave a sense of security. With only one exception, the
younger men in each class surpassed the older men in the proportion holding policies, a slight difference that parallels Reuben Hill's observation of
progressively earlier investment in insurance across three generations in the
Minneapolis–St. Paul area.[36] The exception is the lowest class, where from
half of the older workers to all of the younger workers held policies, reflecting
their common vulnerability in economic standing.

The absolute value of insurance policies corresponds with family income
by men's age and social class. Families with the smallest incomes generally
invested least, while those with the largest incomes invested most. Older
families in the professional and managerial classes, for example, held policies
valued at approximately three times their income, compared with ratios of
one and a half to two times the average income of families at the bottom of
the class structure.

The overall picture on securities, then, is a familiar one in which affluent
families are best able to control their destiny, while those in the lower classes
were more dependent on kin and community.

DEPENDENCE ON KIN AND COMMUNITY

Rapid population growth and the Great Fire of 1923 made single-unit dwellings scarce and more costly within the city, reinforcing the expansion of apartment buildings and delaying the time when young singles and married couples separated from their parents. The year 1929 found two out of five families in the Berkeley study living with relatives. As might be expected, this arrangement was most common among younger men (54 percent versus 32 percent of older men): 45 percent of younger couples were guests of the wife's parents, as were 20 percent of older couples. This residential bias may be due to the westward migration of single men, the extension of households through the mother's side, the male imperative on independence from parents, and the shared interests of mother and daughter versus in-law tensions among women.

Berkeley men who owned their homes were seldom part of this intergenerational pattern. Only 15 percent shared their household with a parent or sibling, regardless of the man's age. For them the decision to buy a first home involved far more than a shift in contractual obligation from landlord to mortgage. It meant physical separation from parents and other relatives. In contrast, two-thirds of the renters occupied a residence that *included* parents or other relatives. Rental payments typically went to the wife's parents, who exercised more direct and intrusive control over the men's family life than any landlord did. If we assume that most homeowners also lived with in-laws or parents at one time, their first home marked a profoundly important step toward social and economic independence. The decision affirmed a man's ability to support a family and to function as its head. It's little wonder men cherished homes of their own.

Living with the wife's parents proved painful for some young men struggling to get started in work and married life. This was especially true of men with limited skills and success who married into higher-status families. Living with in-laws made such husbands easy prey for criticism and placed wives in the stressful role of intermediary. When conflicts occurred, no position women took could satisfy both sides. The following case of a young Berkeley family illustrates this point, as described by a fieldworker:

> A child was born (1928) some three years after she [wife] and her husband moved to Berkeley, following her parents down here. She says that her husband was as willing to come as she, but their relationship was never the same after they lived with her parents for a while and then moved into an apartment right across the street from them. That was a very uneasy period because her

husband felt that she was more attached to her family than to him. But she was torn and he was hurt, and she didn't have enough sense, as she later realized, to move out and away from them.

A number of older men lagged behind the residential expectations of their life stage. A fifth of the men in professional and managerial occupations were still living in parents' households at the time, a percentage not much below that of laborers of comparable age (29 percent). This form of dependence among older men tells us something about their economic careers. In the middle class and working class, older men who lived with kin generally had lower earnings than other men, reporting family incomes below the median in each class. Residential patterns among those at the bottom of the class structure reflect in unmistakable terms the interdependence of low-income families and the need to pool resources. Half of these families reported receiving financial aid from kin, and two-thirds were living in relatives' households, 18 percent higher than for skilled workers.

The greatest concentration of nuclear households appears not among the older middle-class families, as one might expect, but among the families of older skilled workers. Nearly nine out of ten lived in their own households, apart from relatives. Their residential separation does not tell us anything about the broader network of kin exchange and interaction, of course, but it does document a remarkable pattern of family success in achieving an independent domestic unit on incomes well below those of families in the upper middle class. The household structure of these skilled workers could not produce a more striking contrast with the domestic arrangements of older laborers, where half were doubled up with kin and nearly 30 percent lived under the roof and rule of in-laws. These dynamics are related to dependence on kin and community in the 1920s and, for some of these families, will foreshadow enduring themes as they move into the 1930s.

Conclusion

At the end of the 1920s, the Berkeley men found themselves on different rungs of the socioeconomic ladder, with very different prospects for controlling life circumstances. The privileges of birth, upbringing, talent, and ambition enabled some men to start their careers in advantaged positions. Men who had known the comforts of wealth in childhood generally followed the high road through advanced education and career beginnings in business, science, and the professions.

For other men, family destitution and misfortune charted a course of hardship marked by leaving school early and working in jobs that offered few chances for advancement. But the transition to young adulthood also provided many options for disproving predictions based on family position, especially through schooling in an era of rapidly expanding educational opportunity or through the diligent use of head, heart, and hands. The social position and career stage of these men tell us much about their family income and living standards, though income bore an uncertain relation to its use. Families on the same economic level frequently followed different strategies in their use of income, variations we have described in relation to their class position as of 1929.

Professional men could expect a prolonged growth of income over their careers, yet the Berkeley men starting out in the professions faced the heavy expense of advanced training and establishing careers, such as travel to conferences and research sites. They may have also felt the most pressure for conspicuous consumption. As a result, they tend to resemble the most disadvantaged men in the working class in their low level of savings and homeownership, despite much higher income. Life insurance stands out as their distinctive mode of investment. Intergenerational transfers (gifts of securities or property) were most evident during their early years. Being older and more advanced in their careers, most professionals owned a home and car, and a larger percentage had a savings account as well as securities of some kind. By comparison, younger men in managerial occupations appeared distinctive in their strategy of acquiring personal wealth and a material lifestyle. They resembled professionals in their economic positions but were more likely to save and acquire a home at an early age. Among all men in the study, they experienced perhaps the smallest trade-off between consumption and investment during the years of family expansion.

Lower-middle-class men, with incomes only slightly higher than skilled workers', were less oriented toward savings and homeownership than toward other forms of "middle-class" lifestyle consumption. The precise nature of this consumption is unclear, but these men showed much less evidence of homeownership as a path to social advancement than skilled workers did. Property mobility was most descriptive of the career of men in the skilled group, but it was mobility by owning a home, not by acquiring other forms of property. In both age groups, skilled men and their families led the way in owning a home, a status that offered a number of rewards: psychological security and autonomy; a means of gaining independence from kin; and a higher standard of living than was available for the same rental dollar. Control over life circumstances and security are important themes in their lives.

The deprivation of men at the bottom of the class structure in Berkeley is an important and neglected side of life in the prosperous 1920s. The good times made their hard times more difficult to bear. They had more children and less to live on than other Berkeley families. Setbacks in work, health, and marriage undoubtedly came more frequently to these men and their families, and they had less in reserve. The unfairness of life has left a deep imprint on their life records, from poverty and misfortune in childhood to more of the same in the adult years. Some came from families of higher standing but failed in education, drank heavily, or had health problems. A better life was still possible for the younger men as they approached the 1930s, but the prospects seem dim.

In the next chapter we turn to the women with whom they established homes and families. Their lives span a noteworthy period of change in women's options and preferences—in their chances for higher education, political participation, fulfillment in marriage, child rearing, and paid work. Up to 1930 these changes appear primarily within the middle class, but they had profound consequences for the lives of the Berkeley women, and thus for the homelife of their husbands and children.

4

Becoming Women

Women today are decidedly different from previous generations—wider education, much
broader outlook, opportunity and training to be more capable.

BERKELEY WOMAN

Most women of the Berkeley 1900 generation were raised by mothers with little education who spent much time and energy on home-based production—
sewing, cooking, gardening, and cleaning—in addition to caring for children
and husbands. However, they encountered new models of family life with
radically expanded educational, economic, and political opportunities. Such
change included optimism about the rising status of women, but also a reluctance to discard the ways of their mothers and grandmothers. Historical
circumstances may have been different for other generations of women, but
the core issues were the same: How does one form an identity, with suitable
paths forward, amid contradictory ideas about how to live one's life and amid
social forces that ease or block those pursuits?

The lives of the Berkeley 1900 women provide a rich occasion for understanding this question. In this chapter we trace their paths to young adulthood. These women had settled in Berkeley before the late 1920s, eventually
marrying the men described in the previous chapter. Some of these men had
completed college and launched promising careers; others did not finish high
school and were faced with unstable jobs and accepting occasional aid from
the Berkeley Welfare Society. They typically married between World War I
(1914–18) and 1926, and the next chapter explores these relationships in detail.
To better understand the women of the 1900 generation, we begin with their
routes into marriage and parenthood.

Education was very important in determining when and whom the women
married. To show how this dynamic unfolded, we begin with their education and their work experiences before marriage, revealing the influence of
family origins. From there we look at how they viewed their economic circumstances and their family, work, and civic roles early in married life. This

chapter thus provides a unique window into a generation of women who embraced new opportunities outside the home before and during marriage yet typically clung to the widely held notion that married women should rank service to husbands and children above any nonfamily pursuits.

Educational Pathways

Moving up the educational ladder was a primary source of life change for women at the time. The mothers of only two participants are known to have completed college, compared with one-fifth of the women themselves. Indeed, as chapter 2 makes clear, one of the motivational themes for migrating to California, and to Berkeley in particular, was a compelling desire for higher education. The University of California, Berkeley, opened its doors and provided free tuition to all qualified students in the state, male and female. Educational advancement was a well-known gateway to opportunity through self-improvement and occupational training. It also gave women access to well-educated potential husbands. Figure 4.1 shows the proportion of women achieving different levels of education.[1] Half the women (54 percent) had graduated from high school, and fully 38 percent had at least some college. In the nation and in California, women born from 1890 to 1899 and 1900 to 1910—the same years as the Berkeley women—averaged only a ninth- and tenth-grade education, respectively.[2]

A majority of the Berkeley women who went to college or obtained some other form of postsecondary training did so in Berkeley or nearby.[3] A fifth of the women attended UC Berkeley, many of them graduating at the end of four years and taking a fifth year to be certified as teachers. Some moved to Berkeley after attending educational institutions around the country, including the Universities of Washington, Nebraska, and Michigan. Others sought training as teachers at "normal schools" (teaching colleges) or attended women's colleges or convents such as the College of the Holy Names on the shores of Lake Merritt in Oakland. Next to teaching in appeal was business or commercial school, where women learned white-collar skills such as stenography and bookkeeping or were otherwise prepared to be secretaries. As historian Carl Degler points out, "The twenties witnessed the emergence of the white-collar class and women were a large part of it."[4] With families increasingly willing to invest in their children's well-being and success, and with the rise of white-collar jobs requiring skills obtained at college, education became increasingly valued and sought by women and men alike.[5]

During the early decades of the twentieth century, the educational enrollment of both women and men increased dramatically. Overall rates for

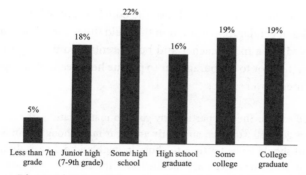

FIGURE 4.1. Educational attainment for women of the Berkeley 1900 generation (percentages).

five- to nineteen-year-olds rose from 51 percent in 1900 to 75 percent in 1940, and the proportion of college students among eighteen- to twenty-four-year-olds rose from 2 percent to 7 percent, but great variance remained in educational attainment.[6] Not surprisingly, the socioeconomic status of a woman's family of origin was highly predictive of her eventual level of education.[7] The better off a woman's family was economically, the more years of education she attained. Being Catholic and immigrating to the United States with parents were negatively related to educational attainment. Most Catholic parents had come from eastern and southern Europe, and they strongly believed their daughters should concentrate on domestic and family matters rather than going far in school.

The Berkeley women who attended college generally entered the 1930s with positive memories of their experiences. Some reported that college had broadened their thinking and values. Some women warmly reminisced about their social lives in college. It was typical for women who went to college to express such positive feelings about this time of life, praising the support and encouragement they received for their scholarship and their freedom and opportunity to socialize with other young people.[8] As we will see, the years between leaving home and getting married—whether or not women attended college—were years when they felt the greatest freedom and ability to pursue their own preferences and happiness.

Several women, however, were critical of the way their generation had been channeled into teaching, nursing, arts, or languages. For some the focus on general homemaking or liberal arts became a disappointment later on. As one woman put it, "I regret that my education has been wasted. I had no professional training and the education I had in college did not lead to anything useful."

A few women who did not achieve the education they hoped for singled out examples of gender discrimination that held them back. For example, one woman described a male teacher and her parents as unwilling to recognize her talent in math or to encourage her to pursue her dream of college. According to the interviewer's notes:

> She loved school. She was particularly good in mathematics—the best in the class. Her geometry teacher, an elderly and sour man, thought it inexcusable that a girl should be better than the boys in math and did everything to decrease the distance between her and the rest of the class. On one examination she recalls that she had completed all the ten problems long before the other students. The teacher then asked how many students had done each of the problems and didn't count beyond the number which several of the brighter boys had completed. She had planned to go to the University of Chicago and major in mathematics in preparation to teach school, but her parents considered post-secondary education unnecessary for a girl, and she never continued her education farther.

Although she reported that a female teacher encouraged her to go to college, this was ultimately not enough to outweigh the discouragement from her parents and the male teacher. Other women describe family economics or health crises that led them to drop out of school and pitch in at home despite their desire to continue their education.

Berkeley women who did not go to college, for whatever reasons, often regretted it, saying in interviews that it was one thing they would change about their lives. Some realized there would have been greater security in knowing they could support themselves or contribute to the household economy if needed. Even more often, they thought education would have made them more enlightened and better informed, saying they felt "handicapped," "inadequate," or "dumb" because they lacked it.

Paychecks and Some Autonomy

Whatever their level of education, it was not uncommon for the Berkeley women to work for pay before marriage. Almost half (48 percent) described holding paying jobs before marrying or having children. Another 18 percent mentioned jobs they held early in marriage but did not specify whether they started working before marriage, although they likely did. Only a third of the women made no mention of working before the birth of their children.[9]

During the postwar decade of the 1920s, the most dramatic change in women's work was a shift in the types of jobs they held, specifically the decline in agricultural and domestic work and the increase in sales, clerical, and service jobs.[10] However a woman might choose to use her education, she found she could work in a variety of these occupations—jobs without appreciable career potential, but that were easily entered and left at will or need. Most of the women who attended college for any length of time studied to become teachers and usually taught school for a year or two before marrying. Some taught longer if they had not yet married, and some never began teaching because they married before or soon after graduation. Women who had studied music often gave private lessons rather than working at a school. Other women were trained in nursing, went to business college, or took commercial courses to become advanced clerical workers and bookkeepers.

Regardless of training or years in school, almost all college-educated women quit working just before marriage or shortly thereafter. One woman, who was so committed to her college education that she enrolled again after each of two family moves and completed her art degree at UC Berkeley, gave up an interior design job after just a few days because her husband objected to her coming home so tired at night. Another woman, asked whether she continued to teach after getting married, replied, "No, my mother-in-law persuaded me to quit. She said, 'No, you quit. You get used to living on one salary and then it won't be so hard to cut back when you have a family.'" Stories like these convey the inevitability and power of social norms or cultural schemas suggesting that women shouldn't hold jobs after marriage.

Women who did not go to college were slightly more likely to work before marriage than those who did. These women held a wide variety of jobs, often switching from one to another. Some worked in canneries, mills, or factories. Others operated telephone switchboards, performed clerical tasks in offices, or were cashiers. Women also held jobs as domestic helpers, cooking, cleaning, or sewing, or cared for children in their homes.

These work experiences before marriage gave women a sense of autonomy and accomplishment and provided financial resources. Women also sometimes met their husbands at work. For most, work was understood as temporary and secondary to what society most expected of them—to become good wives and mothers. However, these early work experiences were formative and memorable. Some women reentered the labor force later on. We elaborate on these choices and experiences in subsequent chapters.

Then Comes Marriage

While these women were going to school and working, they were meeting potential husbands. Marriage happened at various times and in diverse ways, but it was universal for the Berkeley women and nearly universal for American women born in the same years. According to the US Census, nine out of ten women born from 1891 to 1910 married at least once during their lives. Their family background, educational attainment, and occupation were related to when and how they met their future husbands.

The dominant cultural script assumed a woman would complete her education and then marry, as all but a few of the Berkeley women did.[11] Yet marriage and childbearing, not a prolonged education and career, were the normative aspirations for this cohort of women. Continued education—at least at the bachelor's level—generally implied postponing marriage, a strategy that promised more options and somewhat more control over their life before marriage and childbearing.[12] For some women, postponing marriage was intended to give them time to finish a degree and possibly gain work experience. However, this was a risky strategy because, given the tendency for women to marry older men, unmarried women in their late twenties and early thirties encountered a greatly restricted pool of single men with comparable education. Especially high levels of education before marriage could diminish prospects for marrying a man with a similar level of education. Among college-educated women in this generation, the late teens and early to middle twenties were a time of waiting for a potential husband, whether or not they had already met, to complete his education and get a long-term job that could support a family.[13]

One of the Berkeley women called this waiting period her "in between time." She helped care for her ill father and worked as a bookkeeper and a telephone operator. Women's marital timing, continued education, and work experience are highly interrelated. The age when a woman marries not only has a significant effect on her life thereafter, but it can also be thought of as an outcome in itself. That is, it reflects women's own long-standing desire to accomplish certain goals before marriage as well as other people's expectations. Nevertheless, the relation between level of education and timing of first marriage for these women is strong. Those who married before age twenty-two largely had less than a high school education, and those who married at twenty-two or older were most likely to have acquired at least some college. Though both socioeconomic and cultural origins are significant factors in the education of the Berkeley women, they had little effect on the timing of marriage other than through education.

Some family influences, including family stability and paternal attention, work through education to affect the timing of marriage.[14] Insights regarding this early family environment come from evidence of family interactions and a retrospective measure of paternal lack of interest obtained in 1930–31.

Women who married early were most likely to have experienced their parents' separation or divorce and most likely to report (as young adults) that their fathers had little interest in them when they were young.[15] Children derive their initial sense of personal worth partially from their parents' positive attention, so this may explain why fathers' negativity is associated with precocious girls' involvement with older men.[16]

The greater the emotional deprivation, the greater the risk for such involvement, as the following woman's marital history illustrates. She explained, "I think the reason I married at fifteen-and-a-half was that my father was extremely strict about who I should have as friends. I was mature, and I craved affection and social life. I married the first boyfriend I had." This woman and a few others who described marrying the first man who paid attention to them mostly ended up regretting those marriages. Their first husbands were unfaithful, were sent to prison, or were abusive, compounding the adversity they faced in marrying young. The influence of both family structure and emotional climate was insignificant once women's education was taken into account, suggesting that education was an important mechanism through which household structure and family process affected women's age at marriage.

Sociologists Ernest Burgess and Paul Wallin describe a shift in mate selection priorities occurring in this era, from matching on family social status to an increasing focus on personal fulfillment.[17] In fact, when women and their husbands told how they met, they were largely sentimental and focused on the physical and emotional attraction that quickly drew them together, even if it took several years for marriage to come about. However, in the background of the stories—regardless of age, social background, or education—were usually strong family, peer, and community networks that set up meetings, vouched for each to the other, and encouraged assortative mating practices.

In general, women who came from lower-status backgrounds, and therefore had less education, tended to meet and marry men of lower occupational status. Couples often grew up in the same neighborhood and met as children or adolescents. One couple said they were "childhood sweethearts" and that he'd ridden her home from school on his bike each day. Another woman, who had immigrated to Berkeley from Portugal at age fifteen, noticed her husband-to-be when he passed her home each day going to a carpentry job from his home in the same neighborhood. Others were introduced by relatives or friends when they were in their late teens, getting to know each other through social outings like dances at the local Italian lodge. The few women who married men of higher education and more privileged socioeconomic backgrounds described meeting their husbands-to-be in their workplaces (e.g., a cashier in a pharmacy who married the pharmacist) or through female friends who worked in the same places as these men (e.g., when a stenographer introduced a friend to her boss).

Women with advantaged backgrounds and at least some college education tended to marry more educated men of higher occupational standing. For the most part the oral histories, combined with fieldworkers' notes, suggest that these couples met in college or soon thereafter. Several stories describe meeting through siblings, cousins, roommates, or friends of friends on group social occasions such as dinners, fraternity dances, house parties, or hiking trips. One woman met her husband through her cousin who was on the same debate team. After dating for a year, they were secretly engaged for three more years because, she reported, it would have been unacceptable to get engaged during college when he didn't yet have a permanent job.

Although most of these initial meetings are described as blind dates or serendipitous connections to a relative stranger, it is hard to miss the strong social and family networks operating behind the scenes. These networks provided potential spouses and vetted them as good prospects. The partnerships result from a long history of families' preferring that their children marry into families like them and the increasing age and class segregation produced by higher education and the labor force. Regardless of their similar backgrounds, almost all these couples report establishing and sustaining their liaisons through their physical and emotional attraction. They worked to develop a relationship that fulfilled their shared desire to love and be loved. This style of mating reflects a historical shift away from institutional marriages and toward more companionate marriages.[18]

Home and Lifestyle

Once they married, the daily lives of the Berkeley women changed a great deal. Rather than relying on support from their families of origin plus their own earning ability, they relied on their husbands to provide financially. If women worked for pay outside the home, it was to supplement their husbands' earnings. Marriage signaled their transition to focusing on "house, husband, and eventually children." One may question how women accepted this transition to the domestic sphere after securing the right to vote and gaining greater access to education and job opportunities. Why would young women of this generation, like generations of women before them, largely surrender nonfamily pursuits when they married? They accepted this gendered separation of work and family spheres because they did not experience it as a retreat to the past.

The general model of adulthood, and of household organization, remained highly gendered, driven by what was understood as the "naturalness" of husbands' working outside the home and wives' making homes and raising children. Rather than entering the labor force in large numbers, they chose to redefine models of wifedom, motherhood, and public engagement.[19] Outside the home, redefinition was found in the freedom of a small group of women to pursue careers, or civic and community engagement that let some women apply the aptitudes they had developed. Of course, how particular women redefined their lives depended on their resources.

Attending college enabled many women to share the social standing and material rewards of their husbands' jobs, including both higher income and the lifestyle it permitted. A third of the women had worked during marriage, mostly in the lower economic strata, and their contribution to the family economy was minor compared with their husbands'. In all strata, the Berkeley women derived their material lifestyle primarily from their mates' earnings.

A wife's satisfaction with her husband's job before the Great Depression reflected both her own sense of position, as derived from his occupation in 1929, and the economic benefits of his employment, as indexed by total family income. The higher the family income, the greater the likelihood of homeownership and a high standard of living—a standard expressed in the quality of the house, including its furnishings, accommodations, and location. Both homeownership and a relatively high standard of living (in 1929) were the primary sources of the wife's home satisfaction. The higher the husband's occupational status, the greater the material rewards of marriage (as measured by income, homeownership, and standard of living) and the greater women's satisfaction with their homes and their spouses' jobs.[20]

Most women, regardless of education or household income, were satisfied with their family's economic situation, though women with more education were likely to marry men with higher earning potential. However, the women most satisfied with their financial situations were those who had a high school degree or less and whose per capita household income was highest ($1,000 or greater).[21] In other words, women who became upwardly mobile through marriage were least likely to be critical of their homes or their husbands' jobs. Marriage had indeed brought them a good material life.

As we noted in chapter 3, owning a home meant a great deal to the women's husbands—even more than the quality of the house and its neighborhood. However, as homemakers the women had more at stake in their living conditions, and these were more important than ownership itself in determining how women regarded their homes. The assessed quality of home and neighborhood was the most significant determinant of how women felt, followed at a distance by whether they owned the home. Still, no matter how humble the structure or tiny the lot, property ownership amounted to a substantial accomplishment for families at the bottom of the economic ladder, requiring stringent underconsumption and prolonged sacrifice.

Evidence suggests that homeownership was more important to couples with low income than small variations in their living standard. Ownership was more important to home satisfaction for manual workers than it was for middle-class men (see chapter 3). Among relatively affluent families, ownership was generally regarded as a financial investment, and status distinctions depended more on the quality of the house. Compared with homeowners in the Berkeley working class, with their three- or four-room stucco and wooden structures in the Flats, well-established families in the upper middle class generally owned large homes in the hills. Status differentiation within the upper middle class centered on the size, furnishings, and location of the house. One of the most lavishly furnished homes was described by the interviewer as "a modern two-story, nine room structure—beautiful view of the Bay, flooded with sunshine, large rooms and abundant yard space for children, interior attractively furnished with fine carved furniture, draperies."

These socioeconomic differences also exist in the conditions that enhanced home satisfaction for the wives. In low-income families, women were most likely to take pleasure in their home if they owned it: differences in their standard of living were of little consequence. Qualities of the house mattered more than ownership for women who enjoyed a substantial advantage in family income. Assuming that prosperity fosters even higher material aspirations, this may account for the pronounced discontent of wives who were relatively young and well educated. Whatever their ownership status or living standards, they were less content with their homes than older, less educated women.

These findings further reveal how far women internalized having an impressive-appearing home as a reflection of their own abilities as wives and mothers. While men's status rested on providing a home, women's status relied more on showcasing the home, furnishings, and appliances, which signaled both having the money to afford these markers of status and their personal success in homemaking.

Changing Opportunities and Identities

Especially in the middle class, educational gains among women and changes in mode of family organization gave the 1900 generation women room to expand their activities and interests beyond the household,[22] perhaps leading more women, especially married women and mothers, to join the labor force. However, cultural resistance to wives' and mothers' working for pay outside the home ensured that society's acceptance of the women's increasing education would mainly entail revising expectations for wives and mothers *inside* the home and community, not in the sphere of paid work.[23] Even if it seemed that women were restricted to the domestic sphere, much like their grandmothers and mothers, they were rewriting cultural scripts for marriage, child rearing, and civic involvement, paving the way for future generations to make greater gains outside the domestic sphere. Thus it is important to outline the societal changes these women experienced and how they are reflected in the ways they viewed themselves and their roles inside and outside the home.

SHIFTING POSSIBILITIES

Household production and maintenance were less demanding for women who married between World War I and the Great Depression than for their mothers. By 1930, production within the household economy—preserving and preparing food, making clothing, cultivating kitchen gardens—had largely disappeared from the typical urban middle-class home. Declining family size during the late nineteenth century and into the early decades of the twentieth, coupled with increasing life expectancy, meant a shorter period of childbearing and a longer life after the last child left home.[24]

The women of the Berkeley 1900 generation started having children soon after marriage: 43 percent gave birth within one year of marriage, and 65 percent had a child within two years. Their average age at first birth was twenty-six. This is higher than the national average of twenty-three at first birth for women born in 1910 and is to be expected given the more urban setting and higher levels of education in Berkeley.[25]

These changes in household responsibilities did not go unnoticed. Considering only the disengagement of women from household labor, sociologist Edward Ross concluded at the beginning of the 1920s that "apart from motherhood, her role is chiefly ornamental."[26] Other observers, such as William Ogburn at the University of Chicago, saw more clearly the shift in family function from production to consumption and the transformation of mutual economic dependence within the household into a dependence based on interpersonal bonds and mutual gratification.[27] The image of middle-class marriage emerging in the 1920s emphasized members' emotional rather than economic needs—companionship and partnership.[28]

In the 1901–5 US birth cohort, college-educated wives gave birth to an average of 1.4 children, compared with 3.4 for women with a grade school education; a third of all college-educated wives remained childless.[29] Women of the Berkeley 1900 generation had, on average, 2.7 children (18 percent had one child, 36 percent had two children, 27 percent had three, and the remaining 19 percent had more than three). This matches closely the average completed fertility rate for US women born from 1891 to 1910: 2.6 children.[30] According to opinion surveys on college campuses in the 1920s, most female students by far expected to marry, but for a sizable number marriage was a matter of choice rather than a necessity—a choice that did not entail long years of childbearing and homebound domesticity.[31]

Smaller families and less home production changed homemaking for middle-class women in the postwar decade (1918–28), when four out of five women of the Berkeley 1900 generation first married. This did not mean homemaking was any less valued. As some tasks declined, other spousal or maternal roles were created or emphasized. For example, women were increasingly expected to demonstrate a family's wealth by consumption, engage in intensive mothering, and maintain their appearance for their husbands.[32] Also, stemming from increases in educational attainment and paid work experience in young adulthood, women at this time made dramatic gains in their social prerogatives, particularly occupational and civic.[33]

From 1920 to 1940, 25 percent of American women held paid jobs, but most of them were young and not married. In 1930, just 12 percent of married white women aged twenty-five to thirty-four were employed. A high proportion of these lived in households below the poverty line.[34] The constraints of motherhood and the negative connotations of married women's employment were aligned against a woman's using her education and work experience to continue a career after marriage. Arranging for children's care so she could work implied that a mother was neglecting her responsibilities to them and her husband. During this era, the likelihood that a married woman would work for pay was highly related to having a husband who was unemployed or poorly paid.[35] In fact, a woman's working for income implied that she had to do so, which reflected unfavorably on her husband's ability as a provider.

In the 1920s no more than one in ten of the Berkeley women held full-time or part-time jobs after marriage, and most of those working explained their economic role as meeting the family's basic needs, saving money, educating children, or paying debts.[36] As expected, work after marriage was most common for those whose per capita family income was less than $500 a year and who were among the least educated. Women in the highest category of per capita income ($1,000 or more a year) were least likely to work, and in this group it was those with the least education (a high school degree or less) who were more likely to have worked since marriage. Only 11 percent of women with some college in this highest income category worked in the first few years after marriage. Most of them report working only until the birth of their first child. The women who worked before marriage or only shortly thereafter and quit to be homemakers expressed few regrets, largely supporting the view of the time that wives or mothers should prefer housework and child care to work outside the home. Looking back at her child-rearing years, a middle-class, college-educated Berkeley woman said, "I wouldn't have wanted anything else. And a lot of the women around me felt the same. They were there to raise their families, and bring up good kids, and feed them correctly. I never saw any unhappiness at all; everybody was family conscious. They weren't looking for jobs and disrupting things. We thought we were lucky to have the [right to] vote."

In fact, regardless of education or income, in the early 1930s many of the Berkeley women identified strongly with homemaking. The only skepticism came from a few well-educated women in the higher income category. Many of the college-educated women reflected positively on the decision to leave the workforce on marriage or childbearing, but their narratives also reveal a sentiment expressed by the then president of Smith College: "The outstanding problem confronting women is how to reconcile a normal life of marriage and motherhood with intellectual activity such as her college education has fitted her for."[37]

College-educated women who could afford to pay others for help with housework and child care often turned to altruistic, unpaid work outside the home, such as being active in civic organizations like the League of Women Voters and the Salvation Army, religious institutions, or special-interest clubs (e.g., sewing, studying china or glassware). Several served as officers in these organizations, such as treasurer or secretary. Some also pursued arts such as painting or music. Among women in households with per capita income of $1,000 or higher, 65 percent said they were interested or involved in community or civic activities. The interest of women with less education or lower per capita income was much less. Therefore, although avenues for women to become involved in activities and organizations outside the home increased, they remained most feasible for women whose household incomes were high, and they were mainly altruistic, civic, or arts related.

Education and social class were reflected in women's preferences regarding homemaking, community, and work roles before the Great Depression and in orientations toward the emerging ideal of companionate marriage and an expanded social sphere. Educational advancement favored companionate marriage in that it reduced fertility, increased motivation for roles outside the family, and promoted a broader base of sharing between partners in family and community activities, fostering common worlds of experience between husbands and wives. Among the college-educated in particular, a desire for social contacts and organizational outlets outside the home may have reflected a discontent with the limitations of homemaking.

In view of the cultural climate of the 1920s, gainful employment was most likely to interest women who were facing economic pressures and those who were dissatisfied with living on a single income or whose husbands could not provide basic necessities. The educational level of the Berkeley women thus bears on their interest in two of the three domains—marriage and community—while socioeconomic circumstances in marriage most affect their attitude toward gainful employment.

Only slowly over the decades of the twentieth century did the changes and options in the pre-Depression world of middle-class women filter down to the life situations of women in the working class. Historically, a working-class origin indexed a traditional image of women's life and work, an image that also had roots in the Old World. Up to the 1930s, the change from production to consumption occurred more gradually among working-class households than among the middle class. Working-class and immigrant women who worked outside the home had little choice; they were generally forced to work by misfortunes that deprived them of adequate support from a husband. If they lacked education and social skills, these women had few options beyond the low-paying and often physically demanding work of the factory or domestic service. In the 1920s, as in the Depression decade that followed, public disapproval of employed married women weighed as heavily on the women of this disadvantaged class as it did on the wives of middle-class men.

DEFINING IDENTITIES

Several social roles were available to women at this time, in varying degrees: companionate wife, engaged mother, productive employee, and involved resident of the larger community. How did the Berkeley women combine these roles? Like women across time, they negotiated competing expectations, their own and others'. To find out, we use a statistical method called latent class analysis, a technique that uses data to identify key subgroups in a population—in this case to detect unique profiles of women based on responses to indicators of identification with marriage, motherhood, homemaking, employment, and community involvement.[38] This analysis reveals a set of common identity configurations held by women of the Berkeley 1900 generation in the late 1920s and early 1930s: companionate homemakers, mothers primarily, working mothers, and balancers.[39]

Most Berkeley women (56 percent) were classified in the identity configuration we call "companionate homemakers." These women found both marriage and raising children to be primary sources of gratification. They were also strongly inclined toward the ideal of mutuality in marriage. They liked homemaking and found marriage, child rearing, and housework central themes of their lives. These women generally had very little interest or experience in working for pay outside the home or in community activities of a civic or social nature. They appear to accept societal norms about women's singular focus on the redefined consumption-oriented style of homemaking.

We call the second type of identity configuration "mothers primarily" (28 percent of the Berkeley women). Similar to the companionate homemakers, these women found their children a major source of gratification and were very likely to see homemaking as a central role. They also had little interest in working outside the home or in community involvement. However, unlike the companionate homemakers, marriage was not as likely to be a source of gratification for them, and mutuality in marriage was not an ideal. In other words, these women are distinguished by a singular focus on their role as stay-at-home mothers. The women who were mothers primarily varied demographically from the companionate homemakers in being older, marrying later, and having fewer children. It seems likely that the younger cohort were more apt to embrace the companionate marriage model than those born earlier.

The first of the two smaller identity configurations, "working mothers" (6 percent of the Berkeley women), are very similar to the "mothers primarily" group but are unique in their greater interest or experience in working outside the home. These women were interested in working but were also more heavily focused on being mothers than on being wives. These women came from the most economically disadvantaged backgrounds, but they were also more likely to have had some college education than the companionate homemakers or the mothers primarily.

We call the final identity configuration the "balancers" (10 percent of the Berkeley women) because they expressed interest in and connection to all these roles. In effect, they balanced the old and the new. They were not as likely to report that marriage or childbearing was a *main* source of gratification in their lives, presumably because they also put career, community involvement, or both high on their list of interests. They themselves did not have a strong affinity for homemaking, but about a third of them nonetheless saw homemaking as central to women's roles. The balancers experienced the least financial strain in their families of origin, and most had at least some college education, so it is clear that greater resources and higher social status make balancing this set of roles more feasible.

Conclusion

The experiences and voices of the Berkeley women reflect the universal and constant interplay that people face between cultural schemata regarding how one should live life, the structured contexts of life that promote or prevent one's pursuing them, and the personal agency to implement these lifeways. When we note that these forces change across one's lifetime, we realize the complexity of becoming a woman in any particular time and place.

In the early 1900s, women encountered an expanding range of educational and civic opportunities and a contraction of home-based production for the family, especially in middle and higher social classes. Such changes could have opened doors to greater workforce participation and career development among women, but the prevailing culture opposed the idea of married women working, so those doors were only slightly ajar. Instead, women of this era seem to have found greater freedom and independence before marriage and motherhood and in expanding roles at home and in the local community afterward. This change included investing in the new model of companionate marriage, which raised expectations for communication and bonding, more intensive mothering, and, when resources allowed, involvement in civic organizations.

Some social observers of this era comment that the progress of women apparently stalled until what most identify as the sexual revolution of the 1970s and beyond. However, interpreting this "stall" as women's retreat to the conventions of their mothers and grandmothers misses important changes, even seeds of more obvious revolutions. To sociologist Alice Rossi, seeming periods of quiescence like this were not necessarily signs of retreat but "periods of rest during which new ideas are woven into the fabric of private lives."[40]

Historian Christina Simmons points out that the companionate marriage of the early 1900s, with its more democratic structure and greater incorporation of romantic and sexual love, redefined women as less submissive and maternal and more independent and sexual within the home, paving the way for greater advances outside.[41] Simmons draws on passages from Floyd Dell's 1923 novel *Janet March*, which nicely characterize women of these times.[42] Though Dell focuses on women who had gone to college, some of the same freedom and independence came to those with less education who worked outside the home.

> Wives had a common bond in having desired something more than the conventional lot of womankind. College had been, to each of them, part of a youthful program of rebellion, emancipation, self-realization. And they had

this in common, too, that they had given up their plans for careers and economic independence, and become happily married. . . . But if they had given
up without much regret their defiant early hopes, it had not been an abject
renunciation of their principles; their surrender was to love and not to convention, for the men they married had been men who sympathized with their
rebellion, perhaps loved them for it.[43]

Women of the 1900 generation became invested in a more loving marital bond and engaged civic life when possible, exerting their agency in these
more easily accessible arenas. Understanding these women and their husbands independently, and considering their experiences before they met, lays
important groundwork for the chapters to come. Knowing how their families
of origin shaped their educational or work experiences, and how newly married men and women came to see their personal and family circumstances
and possibilities, is important for situating their lives as they adapted to the
Great Depression and World War II as married couples.

Together and Apart in Marriage

*In place of the old comes a new kind of companionship between man and woman, re-
flecting the rise in status of the young wife and children.*
MICHAEL YOUNG AND PETER WILMOTT, *Family and Kinship in East London*

The Berkeley couples brought a mixture of old and new to their post–World
War I marriages. The old appears in a gendered division of labor with husbands as providers and wives as homemakers, the new in marital ideals of
mutuality, companionship, and greater equality. But these ideals often conflicted with changes in their lives, such as the worklife pressures of urban-
industrial growth for men and sentiments that favored a broader social sphere
for women. Couples felt drawn toward the values of companionship just as
their lives had become more spatially separate.[1] Men were working farther
from the home while their wives were more centered inside it, although some
women worked for pay out of necessity or engaged in civic activity.

The women of the 1900 generation had achieved notably higher levels of
education than their mothers, which opened up their worlds beyond homemaking.[2] In the postwar years, observers of family life described this shift as
"one of the great transformations of our time."[3] Women who had some college
were especially critical of a life focused solely on housekeeping, rejecting the
belief that a woman's place should be only in the home. They also wanted social and civic roles in the community and, sometimes, gainful employment—
though paid work was typically motivated more by economic necessity than
by a desire for self-fulfillment and autonomy, especially in the lower socioeconomic strata. Middle-class men began to support this broader conceptualization of women's lives after World War I, yet they were less likely than
women to favor equality in marriage.[4]

These considerations are especially relevant to the marriages of the Berkeley couples on the eve of the Great Depression. We view their marriages from
the perspectives of both husband and wife, comparing their responses. At the
University of Chicago in the 1930s, sociologists Ernest Burgess and Leonard

Cottrell had become pioneers in viewing marriages from this interactional perspective. They asserted that "any study of marital accommodation and integration must take into account how the two persons interact with each other, both as persons with specific characteristics and as unified personalities."[5] Reciprocating closeness and affection, as well as sharing of experiences, is an important feature of this interaction.[6]

What is less visible in the dyadic focus of the Chicago study is the profound change in marital households since the late 1890s, from the spatial integration of a couple's activities to their increasing separation. At the turn of the century, half of all families in the United States were still farming, a family business involving husband, wife, and even children. And a large percentage of small businesses were also family enterprises. By the 1920s, rapid industrial and commercial development had drawn rural populations to cities and pulled men to workplaces some distance from the household.[7]

In the context of the increasing spatial separation of husbands' and wives' daily activities during the 1920s, marital communication and sharing became more important in fostering a common foundation of trust, understanding, and meaning.[8] As one of the 1900 generation men noted, "When a husband and wife are separated a lot, as usually happens nowadays because of the nature of the husband's work, they tend to grow apart." During his childhood in a small community, he recalled that "men mostly worked on their own small farms or in little shops, and husbands and wives were always in each other's company." For the 1900 generation couples, when men's jobs took them away from their wives and children each day, a husband's failure to share his experiences could become a source of marital discord and increase "the tendency to grow apart." His unwillingness to share could reflect the painful circumstances of job loss and mounting economic problems. Women tend to disclose unpleasant feelings and experiences to a spouse more freely than men do.[9]

Marital compatibility varies among young couples and bears directly on a family's adaptation to life's strains. Sources of this variation include differences in how couples interact and in the life history of each partner. The dynamics of marriage reflect both harmony and conflict in areas such as finances, sexual relations, the discipline of children, and relations with kin. Some domains are more central to marriage than others. Financial disputes have particular relevance because they can lead the husband to withdraw and keep work and economic problems to himself.

Most of the Berkeley men and women fell in love with and married spouses who closely matched them on social characteristics (such as religion and socioeconomic origins) and thus were likely to enter marriage with relatively similar expectations and interests. However, a significant number of the couples differed in age and family origin. Age differences increased according to when women married—the younger the woman, the larger the age difference. A large age difference may also reflect the historical era of each partner, as well as their different life stages, their activity levels, and their interests. We will explore these different meanings.

Another perspective on differing life histories concerns the specific nature of a difference in age or socioeconomic origin. Does it matter, for example, whether the husband is younger or older than his wife or whether a man marries down or up in terms of family background? Another relevant aspect of social origin is place of birth, whether native-born or not. Nearly a third of the Berkeley generation were born overseas, including a good many from less developed countries in eastern and southern Europe. Some ended up with marriage partners born in the United States. The cultural conflict of such a pairing would presumably be greatest if it included an American woman from a middle-class family.[10] Corresponding educational differences would undoubtedly magnify the risk of such a marriage. Though a marital pairing of this kind seems improbable, there were such couples in the Berkeley 1900 generation.

Continuing in the spirit of the interactional approach of Burgess and Cottrell, we conclude with the role orientations of husband and wife regarding equality in marriage.[11] We ask how these orientations are expressed in patterns that are egalitarian, transitional, and asymmetric as well as in marital compatibility. In a rewarding marriage, do the husband's perceptions and attributes play a more influential role than his wife's, a marital pattern that Burgess and Cottrell observed among middle-class marriages in Chicago during the 1930s?

Burgess and Cottrell's distinctive contribution to an understanding of the Berkeley marriages stems from their concept of marriage as a social-psychological interactive process. In theory, this concept encapsulates the perspectives of both husband and wife, but their Chicago study of middle-class marriages drew primarily on the reports of one spouse, usually the wife.[12] To more fully capture the relational dynamic of marriage, we benefit from the family-based perspective of Jean Macfarlane, director of the Berkeley study, and her clinically trained staff who collected such rich data from and about both husbands and wives. Information on these marriages comes from the intensively studied families of the Berkeley 1900 wives and husbands.[13] Jean Macfarlane's Early Family Ratings were based on both observational and interview materials from the early 1930s.[14]

From the available battery of ratings, we focus on two general measures of the marital bond: adjustment in marriage and marital compatibility, which includes ratings of friendliness, hostility, and closeness of each partner toward the other, as well as sexual adjustment. We sometimes examine these aspects separately and sometimes use a summary index. When we turn to larger life history variations and marital role patterns, we use the summary index to provide a more holistic view of marital relations.

The Interior World of Marriage

A "good marriage" is a matter of perspective, and for some Berkeley husbands it entailed little more than the security and comfort of a home. But if we think of marriage as a companionate relationship, this judgment would imply closeness, affection, and a caring attitude. Such qualities were frequently mentioned when the Berkeley wives were asked about the ingredients of a happy marriage in the early 1940s:

> "Love and affection come first, and then consideration of one another and of each other's needs."

> "Respect and especially companionship."

> "Satisfactions come from understanding, sympathy, and affection."

> "A growing companionship that makes possible coping with life's situations."

> "Sharing confidences and being open with each other."

In addition, several wives stressed the importance of tolerance in the "give and take" of married life as well as a sense of humor, especially "when times are difficult."

The closeness and friendliness of husband and wife in the 1900 generation were elements of their overall adjustment in marriage, as suggested by our analysis of marital compatibility. However, partners sometimes differed in their feelings.[15] In most cases wives were slightly more attached to their husbands than husbands were to their wives (on both dimensions), but husbands' investment carried greater weight in marital adjustment. A husband's closeness to his wife was slightly more predictive of a couple's adjustment in marriage than was the wife's apparent sentiment.

The missing element in this conceptualization of the marital bond is the emotional ambivalence of intimate relations. As Freud once observed, "[When] hostility is directed against people who are otherwise loved, we describe it as ambivalence of feeling."[16] This sentiment in marriage is only suggested by case materials, such as a middle-class wife's sarcastic observation of the role her husband preferred for her: "He would be much more content to have me stay home, do big washings and be generally domestic—or at least he thinks he would."

Although husband-wife differences in marital sentiment tell us very little about specific aspects of a marriage, such as problem solving, we can think of the adjustment process in marriage as collaboration that may or may not produce mutually acceptable decisions on pressing issues. At the Institute, Jean Macfarlane viewed the Berkeley marriages in terms of whether couples were successful in addressing issues and resolving differences across family domains in ways acceptable to both. Three of the ratings focused on topics known for causing problems in families: finances (size of income and expenditures), sexual relations, and the discipline of children.

Certain aspects of marriage mattered more than others for couples' closeness or overall adjustment. Whether the Berkeley couples were in their first marriages did not influence marital closeness or adjustment (9 percent of the men and women were in second marriages), nor did the duration of marriage. Disputes over finances, sexual relations, and child discipline were most indicative of a troubled marriage with minimal adjustment, followed by a lack of shared general interests, and at a distance came conflict over culture, kin, and religion (see appendix table A5.1). Well-adjusted couples experienced little friction over such issues or were able to resolve disputes as they arose. They also tended to share social, recreational, and educational interests. The prominent role of financial conflict in a dysfunctional marriage has special relevance for understanding the vulnerabilities of couples just before the Great Depression. Such conflict tended to be associated with unresolved differences in other areas of family life—especially sexual relations, child discipline, and relations with kin—and represents a strong potential link between hardship and family trauma.

If couples did not get along on financial matters, they were even more likely to be estranged in their sexual relationship. Sexual issues are more closely linked to social-emotional distance in marriage than any other source of conflict. Problems associated with marital sexuality reflect a legacy of ignorance, myths, and emotional inhibitions at a time of increasing sexual liberality.[17] In the Berkeley sample, couples frequently embarked on married life with conflicting orientations toward sex (e.g., a husband's strong desire for physical gratification coupled with a wife's deep-seated fear of it). A number of the wives described their initial response to sexual intercourse as one of "fear" or "horror." As one wife noted, "Sex was the most dismal thing in the world for both of us." Whether they were from middle- or lower-status families, wives generally claimed they had not received sex instruction from their mothers. As a whole, middle-class marriages reveal all the tensions one might expect in a generation that occupies a transitional stage between the Victorian age and the post–World War II era.

We turn now to a process that bears directly on the likelihood of satisfying or dysfunctional marriages—marital communication as indicated by expressing affection and sharing experiences and opinions. The five-point rating on expression of affection extends from "very demonstrative" to "never demonstrative." The rating of sharing behavior varies from "wants all experiences and ideas shared" to "keeps things to oneself."

A compatible marriage implies mutual satisfaction of each partner's desire for affection, but we find little evidence of such mutuality in demonstrations of affection between husbands and wives. Variations in husbands' expressiveness are not related to the wives' expressiveness. In most marriages, wives are more demonstrative than their mates, and their tendency toward expressiveness is negatively associated with marital adjustment. In other words, women in less well-adjusted marriages are typically more expressive. The expressiveness could be a cause or a consequence of marital difficulties. Despite the independence of husbands' and wives' expressiveness, the association with marital adjustment is similar for men and women. Nevertheless, many wives with inexpressive husbands knew they were loved. As one explained, "My husband has always had difficulty in expressing his love, but I know just the same how deeply he feels about me."

Sharing experiences is part of a conversational process that makes marriage rewarding. As a woman from the middle class observed, "The sharing of confidences and being open with one another" seems essential to "making a marriage work smoothly." In marriages with a shared reality for husband and wife, ongoing conversation feeds on "nearly all they individually or jointly experience."[18] Indeed, experience may not be completely real until it has been "talked through." Talking through has particular significance for the Berkeley marriages, since husbands and wives were typically separated by their major responsibilities at work and at home. The husband's willingness to discuss his everyday experiences at work or in the community thus was a crucial link between the two worlds.

Couples who frequently expressed affection for each other tended to share their individual experiences as well, but differences in sharing far exceeded differences in expressed affection. This largely reflected the tendency for men of this generation to keep things to themselves. Other studies have found that wives are more likely than husbands to disclose unpleasant experiences to their spouses.[19] The Berkeley men who were unhappy with their jobs in 1930–31 were also not inclined to share experiences and thoughts with their wives, especially men in the working class. The link between economic problems and "an incommunicative husband" clearly had significant implications for these marriages as they moved into the hard times of the Depression.

Additional evidence on the relation between marital problems and an uncommunicative husband comes from these marital differences. Men's unwillingness to share thoughts and experiences with wives is most pronounced concerning finances, sexual relations, and child discipline, especially when the mates had differing interests, such as engaging as a couple in recreational and social pastimes. By contrast, wives' tendency to share their thinking did not indicate how they responded to these areas of conflict, except that they tended to avoid discussing sexual problems. In the sexual realm, conflict often led both partners to back away from solving the problems. Thus the conditions that influenced husbands' sharing behavior were most relevant to marital adjustment in the Berkeley generation. As mothers of young children, the wives were occupied with homemaking at the time (about 1930); few held paid jobs outside the home, and when they did, the jobs were usually part-time. Though a number of wives were involved in community activities, most were dependent on marital conversation and friends for contact with life outside the home. When men failed to share their day with wives, they seriously impaired prospects for marital companionship.

Wives' higher expectations about shared experience are most likely a key factor in the negative effect of an uncommunicative husband on their marital harmony.[20] In the postwar era, Komarovsky found that wives expected more than husbands and were more dissatisfied with their spouses' listening and conversational role: "They certainly want their husbands to be better listeners . . . to share for its [own] sake, or for reassurance, counsel, appreciation, and encouragement."[21] In more recent times, too, Wilcox and Nock found that men's emotional work is a key determinant of women's reports of marital quality.[22]

Large marital differences in expressiveness and sharing point to unfulfilled needs and a host of problems in family affairs. Whatever the source, the most common pattern of sharing—with the wife sharing much more than the husband—points to coping and defense tactics that contribute to the breakdown of marriage. As pressing issues arose, how did the Berkeley wives cope with withdrawn, unresponsive husbands? Did they respond aggressively and press their husbands for needed answers? How were disputes resolved when their husbands refused to discuss the matter? Using family ratings from 1930, we find that husbands who kept things to themselves generally refused to discuss disagreements with their wives, while their wives tended to respond with some form of verbal aggression, such as nagging, name-calling, or casting blame, depicting a pattern of mutual aggravation.

A striking example emerges from a comparison of husband-wife relations on closeness and sharing in marriages that are grouped by above- and below-average scores on the index of marital adjustment. The most significant difference between couples in the two groups comes not from the responses of individuals but from the degree of pair similarity on common dimensions. Feelings of closeness decline from high to low adjustment, especially among husbands, but more significant is the lack of commonality among poorly adjusted couples. Husbands and wives in this group differ markedly in their sense of closeness to each other and in their sharing of experiences, feelings, and thoughts.

The interior world of these marriages reveals wide variations in couples' potential for coping with deteriorating life conditions. To better understand these variations, we turn next to the social differences the Berkeley men and women brought to their marriages. We know that some came to marriage early in life and others much later. They were born into families of means as well as families burdened by scarce resources. Some were born into farming families, while others grew up in the country and moved to the city. Close to a third were born overseas and migrated to the United States.

Despite these differences, most marriages in the Berkeley 1900 generation were between people with similar backgrounds. This is what sociologists call the "homogamy" principle of mate selection: the greater the difference between potential partners on a variety of social attributes, the less likely they are to get together or stay together. But what are the marital consequences when people of different backgrounds do marry? We turn now to this question and focus primarily on three types of social differences—in age, socioeconomic origin, and birthplace.[23]

Different Lives: Together and Troubled

When the Berkeley couples were interviewed about the most important ingredients of a happy marriage, they often mentioned having a common background. Perhaps influenced by their own lives, they felt that a young man and woman who entered marriage with a common background would have the advantage of shared interests and values. They would be more likely to approach problems with similar expectations, maintaining congenial relations with both sides of the family. Religion, economic background, and education were singled out in most of the replies.

When social differences were noted, dominance was mentioned as a risk to domestic tranquility and stability. Consider the cases of a woman who married a younger and less educated man and a woman who married into a lower-status family. Drawing from personal observations, one of the wives felt that a woman is likely to "hold it over her husband if he has less education than she has, even if he makes good money." A skilled worker made a similar argument on age: if a "woman is older she might think she's got something on the man." Differences like these may create troublesome gaps in the social and intellectual interests of husbands and wives.

Nearly two-thirds of the Berkeley marriages conform to the traditional mating gradient in which the husband is older than his wife. In half of these marriages, this age difference does not exceed five years, and in only 4 percent is the husband more than twelve years older. Large differences of this sort are concentrated among older men and among those who married relatively late. Age similarity was the next most common marital pattern (28 percent), followed at a distance by couples in which the wife was older. Only 9 percent of the wives were older than their mates, and the age spread is greater than three years in only three cases.

Does a substantial age difference have a significant negative effect on marital compatibility, apart from the age of each partner and their class positions? Statistically, any age difference is a function of the relation between the ages of the spouses, so it is not possible to solve an equation that includes all three measures. However, the wife's age can easily be excluded, since it shows no meaningful relation to marital compatibility. When the influence of husband's age and class position is taken into account, we find that there is a strong negative impact on compatibility when husbands are older than their wives, especially when the difference is four years or more.

The strength of this effect is noteworthy, especially in view of the inconclusive outcomes in more contemporary studies and the finding of no effect in Burgess and Cottrell's nearly contemporaneous study.[24] This very likely reflects the pace of social change at the time in beliefs regarding family relationships, particularly marriage. From a cohort perspective, rapid change would likely widen the social gap associated with an age difference.[25] Older husbands tended to hold more traditional, asymmetric concepts about marriage and women's roles than younger men. If these men were married to much younger women, their customary social dominance was likely to be a major source of marital tension and conflict. Husbands who were much older than their wives were also likely to be first- or second-generation Americans, although generational status per se is not a key factor in marital compatibility, as we shall see.

The marital implications of a substantial age difference are most clearly seen in areas of social interaction and interests. Age differences between husbands and wives are significantly correlated with conflict over finances, sexual matters, and child discipline, as well as with differences concerning general interests. The greater the age difference, the less partners had in common and the more likely they were to have discrepant positions on key issues in their marriage. One such issue is companionship. Wives with markedly older husbands invariably complained about the lack of shared interests, activities, and friends. One said she had few friends in common with her husband, then noted, "in fact, no friends" were shared. Another observed that she is "still anxious to go out and do things, whereas he would rather stay home." Wives who talked about the clash of temperaments frequently expressed this complaint. Their self-perceptions as lively, energetic, enthusiastic, and outgoing contrasted with characterizations of their husbands as quiet, inexpressive, slow, and retiring. As one wife some fifteen years younger than her spouse explained, "we seem to be a generation apart" with such dissimilar ideas about earning and allocating family income and about raising their children.

In fact, marital differences in interests and expectations completely account for the negative effect of age "heterogamy" on marital compatibility.[26] An age gap between husband and wife had no consequence for their conjugal relationship apart from their differing interests and points of view. As we noted earlier, the effects of substantial age differences in the Berkeley marriages most likely reflected the rapid pace of social change in the lives of each spouse and provided insights regarding the marital consequences of the husband's greater age, such as wide differences between husbands and wives along the path of aging.

Another social difference with potential consequences for marriage is the socioeconomic origin of each partner. The Berkeley women acquired their husbands' social positions through marriage, but they frequently came from different socioeconomic backgrounds. Approximately a fourth of the women married men of lower socioeconomic status, and the same proportion married men from higher-status families. Such change is likely to influence how husband and wife evaluate themselves and their partners. For example, the upper-middle-class women who married down in social status may transfer the high economic standards of childhood to their new marriages and impose them on their husbands' accomplishments and economic careers. The more advantaged families of these women had little to gain from this interclass marriage—in contrast to the disadvantaged families, whose young people's marital success nonetheless brought the risk of wounded pride and greater pressure to be economically successful. Archival records provide examples of this kind of marital purgatory for the more disadvantaged partner in the marriage.

The daughter of a prominent industrialist expressed great unhappiness with her husband's salary in a managerial career, although it was above average at the time. Since she married, she had felt humiliated by having to adjust to a standard of living far below what she was accustomed to. Another man who could not satisfy his wife's material desires asked her, "Why have I worked so hard?" then replied, "To earn money to give you the things I thought you wanted. Money is not important to me, but it was to your family." In other cases a father showered material goods on a newly married daughter, further devaluing her husband who had "married up"; another husband's efforts to save enough to buy his wife a car were nullified when his wealthy father-in-law stepped in to offer the young couple a more expensive model as a gift, leaving him feeling belittled.

These archival materials on the Berkeley families provide a suggestive account of the costs and benefits of marriage between young people with different socioeconomic backgrounds. How are the differences and tensions they carried into marriage expressed in their relationship? Having different socioeconomic backgrounds has a significant negative effect on marital compatibility, with family origin and class position in 1929 controlled. What issues account for this effect? Consistent with earlier results, the key sources of disputes were financial matters, sexual relations, child discipline, and the lack of shared social and recreational interests. All show statistically significant negative effects on marital compatibility from a couple's differing socioeconomic backgrounds.

This leads to a final status distinction that has relevance as a social difference some Berkeley couples brought to their marriage—birthplace history. In well over half of the Berkeley marriages, the husband or wife came from a family in which at least one parent was born outside the United States, most frequently in a non-English-speaking country. Such early experience increased exposure to the strain between the Old World and the adaptive requirements of a new land, between parents still wedded to the past and their children's interest in new ways and in the future. Relationships between immigrant parents and their native-born offspring, with their tensions and misunderstandings, resemble relationships between husbands and wives who have roots in different cultures.

The most likely clash between culture and marital roles appears in the contrast between two groups of couples in the Berkeley middle class—the foreign-born wives of native-born husbands, who actually rank highest on marital compatibility (mean value 59 out of 100), and the native-born wives of foreign-born husbands, who end up with a much lower level of compatibility (mean value 45 out of 100). However, each group includes only half a dozen cases, and in the working class, only the group of native-born wives with foreign-born husbands includes any cases. One of the ratings on marital differences focuses on cultural conflict, and it shows that the two sets of middle-class couples are virtually at opposite ends of this dimension of family life. The marital history of the most contentious marriage is marked by explosive incidents and temporary separations.

As we noted, the Berkeley men and women arrived at their marriages by pathways that have brought compatibility and conflict to their relationships. Most found mates who resembled them on age and historical time, socioeconomic origin and education, and nativity or place of birth, but a significant number found mates who differed in important ways. Some men came to marriage much older than their spouses, and this difference played a role in the harmony or conflict of their marriages. Others found partners from the same social class or ended up marrying into a higher-status family. Last, over a third of the Berkeley men and women were born in another country and immigrated to the United States. Most of them found mates similar to themselves, but some did not. Life course differences bring consequences that can influence the quality of marriage.

Marital Roles and Family Patterns

The married lives of the Berkeley couples had much to do with how they got along, apart from the differences and conflict we have noted. We examine issues of dominance and equality by asking about the social quality and inequality of marital relations. An egalitarian, or symmetric, pattern refers to a relationship in which husband and wife share responsibilities and decision making. Inequality or asymmetry depicts a marital structure of social dominance, most likely male dominance.

With these two types of marital structure in mind, we reviewed observational and interview materials on the couples for evidence of marital inequality or equality in family behavior and culture. Three out of five marriages either clearly demonstrated "asymmetry" in relations or could be considered "toward symmetry"—about 30 percent in each category. The remaining cases displayed mixed patterns and were assigned to a residual category that we defined as "transitional." Assuming that the three types are grounded in marital behavior, we expected to find male dominance characteristic of asymmetric marriages. While no direct measure of overall dominance is available, we find that the dominance of either partner in financial management is most pronounced among marriages characterized by inequality, followed at a distance by marriages in the transitional and egalitarian categories.

These types of family structure bear some resemblance to those identified in sociologist Lee Rainwater's postwar study of family planning, contraceptive use, and fertility—segregated, intermediate, and joint conjugal relationships.[27] The segregated structure refers to "relationships in which the predominant pattern of marital life involves activities of husband and wife that are separate and different but fitted together to form a functioning unit, or are carried out separately by husband and wife with a minimum of day-to-day articulation of the activity of each to the other."[28] In marriages defined by a joint relationship, husbands and wives stressed the value of shared experience; each couple tended to undertake a range of activities with a "minimum of task differentiation and separation of interest. The more segregated the relationship, the less the husband correctly perceived and responded to the wife's affectional and sexual needs; in fact, only in segregated relationships did wives voice complaints about their husbands' inconsiderateness in sex relations."[29]

Similar differences emerge from a comparison of the Berkeley marriages by family type. Sexual relations turn out to be the only domain in which we find significant differences between the family types and conflict. Disputes over sexual issues increased consistently from the symmetric to the transitional and asymmetric marriages. Differing interests, as well as a lack of marital sharing, followed a similar trend, though less pronounced. The general implications of such variations are most clearly reflected in our composite index of marital compatibility: the more equal (symmetric) the marriage, the higher the couple's compatibility. The link between marital compatibility and egalitarian marriages applies to both the middle-class and the working-class families.

Middle-class couples clearly favor more symmetry in their roles within marriage than working-class couples do; almost half of middle-class couples are involved in such a relationship. By contrast, three out of five working-class couples' marriages are characterized as relatively unequal. The preferred marital structure, then, whether toward symmetry, transitional, or asymmetric, defines a major indirect link between social class and marital compatibility. But the evidence does not show a direct connection between a couple's class position and the quality of their marriage. For example, egalitarian marital relationships in the middle class and working class are comparable on marital compatibility. One might expect marital inequality to have more negative consequences in the middle class, where equality is more preferred. The data tend to support this expectation, though only six middle-class couples are

characterized by inequality compared with twenty-four marriages in the working class (see appendix table A5.2).

Role preferences (introduced in chapter 4) are closely aligned in conceptualization, with variations across family types on equality, and they provide
additional insight on conjugal relations. Two aspects of role preferences we
examine are the concept that a woman's central role is as a homemaker, and
husband-wife mutuality in affection and communication. Archival data used
in coding marriages on these dimensions reveal that in over half of the "toward symmetry" marriages, both the husband and the wife favored mutuality
in marriage. By contrast, both husband and wife valued mutuality in only a
quarter of the asymmetric marriages. The belief that a woman's place is in the
home best describes the outlook of asymmetric couples, while a broader conception of women's role and the ideal of mutuality are mainly concentrated
among couples who have more egalitarian relations (see appendix table A5.3).

Husband-wife differences in attitude on equality within each family type
tend to show the value of viewing marriage in terms of role orientations. A
substantial number of marital pairs in each category of equality are divided
on the issue of mutuality and woman's role, and in most cases it is the wife
who subscribes to the more companionate image of marriage, lending support to Groves's suggestion that men of these times preferred wives who emu-
lated the family roles of their mothers while women strove to embody ideals
of the new womanhood, including increased social and family influence.[30]
The implications of such differences hinge in large part on the relative weight
of each partner's attitude in adjustment to each other. Were women's orientations more or less consequential for the marital relationship than their husbands'? Burgess and Cottrell's study of middle-class families concluded that
the "new mores emphasizing equality of the sexes in marriage have not as yet
entirely displaced the old attitude that the husband should be more dominant."[31] They refer to culturally patterned behavior traits—male dominance
and female submission—as a plausible explanation for the continued potency
of the husband in shaping marriage.

To determine the relative influence of husband's and wife's behavior on
marital adjustment, we asked whether measures of marital adjustment and satisfaction were more aligned with the husband's attitudes or the wife's. The egalitarian marital orientation of men is strongly related to their marital satisfaction
and that of their wives, but the egalitarian orientation of the wife has no reliable
association with either her own or her husband's marital satisfaction. A similar
gender difference occurs when we focus on the general measure of "adjustment
to each other." The husband's role orientation is over three times as predictive of
marital adjustment as the wife's. These results and others suggest that marriages

in which the husband favored a more egalitarian image of marriage offered a more positive environment for wives to fulfill their aspirations and ideals.[32]

Marriage before the Great Depression

An important implication to be drawn from men's leading role in shaping their marriages pertains to gender relations. In a study of family systems around the globe, William Goode concluded that "it is the changing position of women with respect to men in the larger society that has changed women's position within the family."[33] And, as we have noted, the changing position of women in relation to men in society owes much to their own educational advancement. These Berkeley women typically surpassed their mothers in formal education, especially among the native-born who grew up in a middle- to high-status family.

Better-educated women expressed greater interest in intellectual matters and community roles than other women and were more inclined to favor equality in marriage and a lifestyle that included social options outside the home. Gainful employment represents another important development in women's lives, but interest among the Berkeley women largely stemmed from economic discontent and pressure. There is little evidence that paid work outside the home was more than an extension of domestic responsibilities.

Higher education clearly stands out as a primary source of women's aspirations for equality between the sexes. For those who married, higher education enhanced their chances of finding a mate who also favored equality and mutuality. These years of rising ambition had a downside in Émile Durkheim's "malady of infinite aspiration" as applied to marital relations in the middle class and the material aspects of life. The French sociologist coined this phase to refer to material conditions of life in which the more one has, the more one wants, so that unbridled aspirations can never be satisfied.[34] But in the San Francisco region of the 1920s, this malady also seems to apply to marital relationships, especially in the growing middle class.

Middle-class wives, in particular, expected much from their marriages, including a high standard of living. Economic misfortune thus posed a unique threat to the lifestyle of middle-class couples, whereas lower-status families faced a prolonged economic struggle with unemployment. The burden of meeting expectations for family support fell most heavily on men in each case. With few exceptions, men were the exclusive breadwinners for their families. All these considerations suggest that economic loss and unemployment would have a severe impact on marriages across the social classes, although economic survival was undoubtedly most precarious in working-class families.

To date, historical studies of family change have paid little attention to how changes in men's lives have affected marriage, especially changes in the structure and expectations of the work domain.[35] Our findings reinforce the fact that changes in the organization of daily life and societal expectations for both men and women had significant implications for the form and function of marriage, and vice versa. Education and the increasing "nuclearization" of family life called for greater companionship between husband and wife. This was countered by a growing spatial separation of the family and work spheres that pulled spouses apart, limiting their shared experience.

The resolution of these tensions in the coming years of economic depression has much to do with what we have called "the interior of marriage." The communication and sharing of experiences played an important role in fostering trust, understanding, and affection between husbands and wives who were living much of their day in different worlds. This "talking through" would enhance problem solving at a time when couples had many differences to resolve—in family economics, sexual relations, and child rearing. Would hard times encourage more understanding or drive couples further apart?

PART THREE

The Depression Years: The Worst and Best of Times

Differing life experiences in the Great Depression are one of the period's most distinctive features. Glen Elder's 1974 book *Children of the Great Depression* revealed that in the East Bay city of Oakland a great many families managed to recover from heavy income and job losses by the end of the 1930s. Most families in the middle class and working class lost over half their family income by 1933, but those in the middle class recovered from this loss more quickly and completely than families in the working class.

Are there comparable results for families in the neighboring city of Berkeley, as reported in chapter 6? Did the greater resources, such as education and work skills, that middle-class families carried into the Depression years enable them to make up their socioeconomic losses more rapidly than families in the working class? And how did job and income loss affect health? Chapter 7 takes up this question by focusing on both the initial quality of the Berkeley marriages and the emotional health of husbands and wives before the Great Depression. Marital happiness provided support during stressful times, and good health was a key inner resource for coping with the hardships of Depression life.

The bleakest time of the Great Depression occurred during the Berkeley couples' childbearing years. Did they postpone childbearing until the economy improved? Older children could help with household chores and perhaps contribute earnings from part-time jobs. However, boys from deprived families were also likely exposed to punishment by depressed and angry fathers. We explore these issues in chapter 8, then turn in chapter 9 to the ways that relatives helped each other. Older men and those from privileged, nondeprived families had a major resource advantage during the Depression. In what ways did they use it to help needy relatives in the middle class and working class, including taking an older parent into their household?

6

Misfortune and Privilege

My father's income took a tumble in 1929. They've been living under the concept that they're poor ever since.

SON OF BERKELEY COUPLE

Prosperity and hard times clashed in ways that made the Great Depression a searing experience for many families in Berkeley. California's economic growth in the 1920s brought appreciable gains to all but the lowest social classes, along with a buoyant appetite for material goods. For the Berkeley families this was a time of launching careers, expanding families, and building security; by 1929 annual family income averaged $2,300 and all but a few of the men were fully employed. Some three years later, in the depth of the Great Depression, annual family income had declined by 30 percent, as was true for California families in general. One out of five of the Berkeley men had lost their jobs, and an even larger number were working a short week. Between 1929 and the low point of the Depression, the number of Berkeley families at the bottom of the economic ladder (less than $1,500 in annual income) more than tripled. The Great Depression had become the new reality for many who had known only good times.

Middle-class families benefited from the prosperity of the 1920s, but this good fortune meant they had much to lose as the economy turned downward in the early 1930s—property and securities, social reputation, and standard of living. Quick and dramatic gains accompanied by ever-rising aspirations magnified the threat of economic misfortune. In the neighboring city of Oakland, heavy income losses produced strong feelings of personal loss and failure within the middle class.[1] But the most severe hardship afflicted the working class. Studies of earlier industrial depressions show that large income reductions and perceived loss of status were typically the most common type of family deprivation in the middle class, while unemployment was the central feature of family hardship in the working class.

This chapter traces the effects of the Great Depression through the socio-economic careers of the Berkeley men, middle class and working class, from 1929 and the Depression era to the onset of World War II. "Socioeconomic careers" refer to the course of economic conditions and worklife, based on the employment status, roles, and earnings of the household head. The economic collapse of the early 1930s and the subsequent uneven course of recovery pose questions regarding initial family deprivation, its overall pattern and sources of variation, and the way deprivation persisted up to World War II.

We begin our journey through the Depression years by describing socioeconomic change up to the mid-1930s among families positioned in the middle class and working class at the end of the 1920s, giving particular attention to economic change and the extent of economic recovery. For men who lost income and especially jobs, recovery prospects were undermined by inflationary trends, the slump of 1937–38, and a flurry of strikes and plant shutdowns between 1934 and the war years. Some families were able to maintain their standard of living throughout the 1930s, but others suffered the full extremity of hardship. To explain such diversity, we turn to the assets and liabilities men brought to the Depression decade, such as their education, skills, and work experience in vulnerable sectors of the labor market. We conclude by asking how some hard-pressed families managed to regain their former economic standing by the end of the decade while others were less fortunate.

Economic Deprivation and Family Hardship

The general economic picture in Berkeley over the first half of the 1930s shows the Depression bottoming out by the middle of 1933. But can we assume that this year was also the lowest point in the families' economic careers? Did the economic cycle of some families differ markedly from that of the local community? According to annual records of the intensively studied families, the Berkeley families were most likely to reach the bottom of their economic descent in 1933.[2] Economic changes between the three lowest years (1932, 1933, and 1934) were relatively minor. Family income declined by a fourth up to 1933 and by 30 percent by the lowest year of family income.

For our purposes, we rely on the lowest-year figure of family income because it provides the most accurate estimate of maximum change. In social implications and meaning, percentage change in total family income does not represent a continuum with equal intervals. In terms of objective hardship, the difference between a 20 percent loss and a 30 percent loss is considerably greater for a low-income family than for a family in a high income bracket. But the same cannot be said for the subjective effect of this loss. Any

income loss is likely to be a threat when the stakes are a middle-class reputation and way of life: high-status families are more inclined to exaggerate
the status consequences of economic change than are those in the working
class. This also applies to blue-collar families "whose previous standard of
living had been relatively high, who had a concept of themselves as a 'high-
class family—maintaining standards, codes, and responsibilities appropriate
to the status.'"[3] Class position before hard times thus represents an essential
context for assessing the course, meaning, and consequences of economic
change. Middle-class families entered the Depression with resources, expectations, and vested interests that differed in important respects from those of
working-class families.

LOWER INCOME AND COST OF LIVING

Two factors were influential in identifying families that were truly economically deprived: change in the cost of living and loss of family income. Four
out of five Berkeley families lost some income in the Depression, but in many
cases the loss of income was surprisingly less than the decrease in the cost of
living. Data assembled by the US Bureau of Labor Statistics indicate that the
cost of living among Bay Area communities declined by at least 23 percent
between 1930 and the spring of 1933, with the first hundred days of the Roosevelt administration.[4] The greatest drop occurred in food, clothing, and rent.

Based on this trend, economic losses up to one-fourth of pre-Depression
income could not qualify as hardship, though a smaller cut (20 percent) was
announced as such by the city manager, who voluntarily slashed his own income to "conform to conditions."[5] Two of the Berkeley women interviewed
in 1932–33 cited the much lower cost of living as the main reason for their
families' well-being in the face of salary cuts amounting to nearly a quarter
of their 1929 income. With some truth and some exaggeration, one of these
women reported years later, "We didn't know a depression was on." Her husband didn't lose his job and, she explained, "Everything you wanted to buy
got cheaper."

Substantial deprivation of one kind or another generally occurred as income loss exceeded one-third of the 1929 figure. These deprivations include
both general and severe budgetary restrictions (e.g., moving to a cheaper
rental), rapidly mounting indebtedness, exhaustion of savings and credit, and
loss of assets, from insurance policies to furniture, the family car, and a home.
Among the Berkeley families we find repeated references to the pileup of debt
(as one of the wives said to a fieldworker, "I could lose my mind if I let myself
think about it!") and to anticipated or actual losses (one family report noted

that the "family can't pay even the interest on mortgage, fears loss of home"). Similar effects were observed in a Depression study of middle-class and working-class families in Oakland: in both the middle class and the working class, families with an income loss of 34 percent and higher were classified as economically deprived.[6] From the evidence at hand, this division between the relatively nondeprived and deprived appears equally appropriate for the Berkeley families.

At the end of the 1920s, on the eve of the Great Depression, there is no major income difference between the families that go on to become deprived and those that do not; the major contrast at this time is by social class. After the economy collapsed in 1932–33, the economic decline of deprived families increased by four times that of the nondeprived in the middle class and by three times that of the working class. These changes both reduced and increased the relative economic advantages of some middle-class families relative to economic sectors of the working class. The reduction for the intensively studied families is shown by the sharp decline of the deprived middle class to an economic level below that of the nondeprived working class (see fig. 6.1).

Extremes on economic welfare are represented by the relatively stable middle class, which includes some families that reported "good years" in 1932–33 and a growing savings account ("since we are living cheaper, we really have more"), and the hard-pressed working class. Median annual income in the Depression ranged from above $2,000 to an average figure of $645 that meant destitution for some families, in which the bare necessities of life were in doubt from one day to the next. A brief entry by a fieldworker in the summer of 1933 concerning a machinist's family with four children reveals the harshness of this economic situation:

> With father mostly unemployed, family attempts to survive on less than one dollar a day. Inability to pay utility bills has left the small bungalow without electricity for lights and gas for heating and cooking. Parents and children gather wood to do the cooking, raise rabbits and chickens for meat, vegetables from garden. Clothes and food provided by the Berkeley Welfare Society.[7]

The economic situation was even more desperate for the family of a skilled worker who had lost his job in 1930 after some twenty years of stable employment. He obtained another job but was soon laid off for three years. By 1933 their annual income was only $60, and the family was on public assistance. Asset losses included their car and insurance. Case records for the winter of 1933 describe the family as "heavily in debt for milk, groceries, fuel; unable to make payments on the house. Relatives have exhausted their ability to help

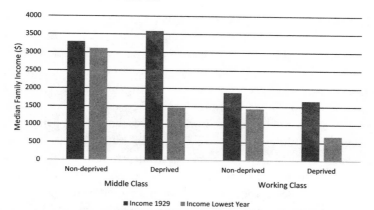

FIGURE 6.1. Median family income for 1929 and lowest year during the Great Depression, by economic deprivation and social class (in dollars).

out. Parents and children need medical care but can't afford it. Father terribly discouraged and anxious to find work."

Economic change among the Berkeley families generally corresponds to that observed among families in Oakland.[8] However, economic loss was greater in the Oakland middle class than in the Berkeley middle class, a difference that reflects variations in the composition of the middle class in the two samples. Small businessmen were more common within the Oakland middle class, and they were particularly vulnerable to heavy income losses. The Berkeley middle class had more professionals (educators, lawyers, CPAs), who generally managed to get by with minor cutbacks in family income.

The degree of economic loss among families in the Berkeley 1900 generation could indicate both a decline in men's earnings and family efforts to generate alternative sources of income. But having small children restricted wives' employment. Only about one out of ten women were employed in 1933–34, and most of them worked only part-time. Thus the economic change we observe among families is due to income change among the men. Family efforts to create alternative sources of income are best viewed as part of the recovery process during the late 1930s and especially the war years, a time when a large number of married women with children entered the workforce.

WORKLIFE PATTERNS

Worklife instability among the Berkeley men reflects class variations in the source of family deprivation. Occupational status was less stable from 1929

to 1934 among economically deprived men, and a large share of this instability is associated with unemployment. From 1930 to 1936, job loss was almost
entirely concentrated in the work histories of economically deprived men, especially those in the working class. Only 5 percent of the men in nondeprived
middle-class families were ever out of work during this time, compared with a
full third of those in the deprived middle class. By contrast, joblessness was virtually a way of life among deprived working-class families (65 percent, versus
25 percent among the nondeprived). The annual rate of spells of unemployment reached a peak in 1931–32 for men in the deprived working class (55 percent) and a year or so later for the deprived middle class (1933, 32 percent).

Changes also altered the worklife of men who retained their jobs. Some
firms cut back the workweek, and thus the paycheck, a practice that most often affected working-class men with skilled and unskilled jobs. In the middle
class, men could often choose to work "unpaid overtime hours" to improve
their chances for keeping their jobs amid growing unemployment, even at
their own workplaces. This strategy was also a major option for the self-
employed seeking to improve their prospects for making it through a rough
patch. To an unusual extent, men in the working class were also subject to a
shorter workweek. To reduce labor costs or to "spread the work," many firms
in the Bay Area put their employees on a shortened workweek—from six or
five and a half days to three or even two days.[9] These cuts brought severe
hardship to families that had little in reserve for calamities. Study notes reveal that one woman married to a longshoreman working a three-day week
in September 1931 was "extremely worried because all of the savings are used
up" and "wondering how we will get through winter."

In some cases a short week was only one step away from unemployment.
A kiln worker experienced this graduated loss of earning power and social
role; his family had exhausted their credit before the layoff and soon drained
all their savings and were borrowing from relatives and against insurance.
A quarter of the Berkeley working-class men were employed on a reduced
schedule in 1932; with the underemployed and unemployed combined, three
out of four men in the deprived working class did not have full-time jobs
in 1932.

In striking contrast, less than 10 percent of the Berkeley middle-class men
(deprived and nondeprived) were on reduced work schedules during the
early 1930s, a cutback so modest, as a rule, that it amounted to a blessing in
disguise for the formerly well-to-do. Instead of putting in the same amount
of time or more for less income, upper-middle-class men who lost a day of
work gained time for family and leisure without an appreciable cost to their
standard of living. A case in point is the hardworking executive for a local

power company who received his cut of 9 percent by getting Saturday off and ended up with a growing savings account (because of the lower cost of living), less exhaustion from a curtailed round of formal entertaining, and renewed fellowship with friends and family.

Such families may have been in the mind of the newspaper editor quoted in the Middletown study, who wrote, "This Depression Has Its Points. . . . Nerves are not so jaded. Bodies are better rested, and though fine foods are not so plentiful, digestion is better."[10] Even in the face of a soaring "relief" burden placed on local resources, the *Berkeley Gazette* chose to advance this perspective in an editorial titled the "Case for Thanksgiving," November 24, 1932: "We are a year nearer prosperity than we were last Thanksgiving and most of us, while we have less money than we had a year ago, owe less now than then, and are really more accustomed to the new social order and therefore happier. So, altogether, this is no occasion for lamentation."

In response to rapidly mounting layoffs, some men used "overtime" in a personal campaign to save their jobs; they extended their workday without additional pay, trying to increase their value to the company. The wife of a young oil company salesman explained to a visitor that her husband was working evenings "in an effort to not lose his job since many men had been laid off." Other examples of this tactic are documented in detailed notes in the archives, especially among middle-class men who were still relatively unscathed by the economy: they feared the worst but hadn't yet experienced it.

"Long hours" were virtually synonymous with the Depression lifestyle of the struggling proprietor who was doing all he could to save the business. In this category we find both men who entered the Depression with a business and those who tried self-employment as a way out of their economic predicament. From 1930 to the middle of the Depression, the notation "unusually long hours" appears mainly in the records of hard-pressed businessmen. "Much work, long hours [from sunrise to midnight in one case], heavy responsibilities, and low income" tell a harsh story of declining business.

The persistence of economic adversity throughout the Depression decade made recovery a slow, torturous process for many Berkeley families. Local conditions had improved markedly by 1937, but this year still found a third of the families in the deprived middle class below their pre-Depression economic level, and fully half of all families in the deprived working class were in the same predicament. To account for persistent hardship, we must first explain why some men lost their jobs and income and others did not. Were men who had existing worklife problems in 1929 more apt to lose their jobs and income during the Depression? If so, continuity suggests a pattern of disability that might persist even after an upswing in the economy.

Sources of Family Misfortune

The overall picture of the Depression experience is highly variable. Some families' economic losses far exceeded the decline in cost of living, while others experienced minimal hardship and a few even improved their economic well-being. To explain these differences, it is helpful to consider the stage of the family and the breadwinner's career before the Depression. What elements of the Berkeley families' pre-Depression environment increased or decreased the likelihood of economic loss and unemployment? Two general types of antecedent conditions bear on workers' economic security in the 1930s. First was the worker's sector of the economy and its vulnerability to the economic cycle and stagnation, as indexed by a general industry classification of men's work in 1929: construction, finance, manufacturing, and the like. Second was the worker's market value—characteristics that indicate employability under different market conditions: age, education level, and occupational skills in 1929.[11] Other considerations include the pre-Depression dependencies of the worker and family, such as assisting kin and indebtedness.

From the days of the Poor Laws and entrenched individualism to the welfare state provisions of the post-Depression era, Americans with power and privilege have been inclined to attribute workers' misfortunes to their lack of character, stamina, or intelligence.[12] Inequality of rewards is thereby thought to be justified; workers get what they deserve. While massive dependency in the 1930s would eventually make the Depression an exception to this interpretation in the minds of Americans who lived through it, these explanations were nonetheless commonplace in the middle class at the time.

DIFFERENCES BY INDUSTRIAL SECTOR

Types of industry that generally correspond to work roles provide a clear example of structural factors that shape men's socioeconomic fate during hard times.[13] From one valley in the economic cycle to another, historical statistics document the uneven impact of economic decline on workers in different industries and occupations. In the depression of 1920–21, the percentage of unemployed increased markedly in manufacturing while remaining low in the public service sector.[14] In the Great Depression, too, manufacturing and construction similarly stand out on measures of economic decline and unemployment.[15]

Though most evidence on worker status by industry in hard times relates to the unemployment of manual workers, we applied this comparison to relative income loss. Men were assigned to industry categories based on their 1929 occupation, then compared by their social class at the time. In the working class, industry sector did not account for differences in income loss, but it made a significant difference in the middle class. Four industry sectors tend to rank high on economic risk in hard times: manufacturing, finance, services (personal and professional), and construction. The first three also rank high on risk of heavy income loss in the 1930s, with an average loss of 49 percent. Interestingly, construction is more than 20 percent lower. This sector is generally one of the first to feel the effects of a depressed market-place, but we see no evidence of this vulnerability in the middle class, most of whom were self-employed. Nevertheless, high risk clearly applies to the skilled and semiskilled workers, as seen in the lives of men in carpentry:

> Yes, the Depression was very bad for people in my line of work. . . . We did get by finally but I was out of work most of the time for about four years and had to take work on relief. . . . I used to walk many miles a day looking for work because we didn't have a car. I remember the first job I got when the Depression began to lift. The contractor said he hadn't been able to find many carpenters because, though there were a lot of them out of work, they had all given up looking for jobs, and I was the first one who had come along and asked him.

Time out of work was much the same for another carpenter, though it occurred at an earlier stage of life, just after he had achieved journeyman status:

> While I was still an apprentice, we got married and settled down in Berkeley. I stayed with this contractor for a good many years, but during the Depression there was just no building, and we almost starved to death. I've never been fired for not doing a job . . . but I was laid off a lot, and from about '31 to '33, I don't think I worked five months.

If we think of a man's work role in terms of options for adapting to hard times, it is useful to distinguish between the economic position of a self-employed businessman and that of a salaried worker. A great many small firms collapsed in the Depression, but the self-employed had some adaptive advantages over white-collar workers and wage earners (see chapter 3), including the greater autonomy, control, and flexibility that helped them find solutions to their economic problems. To keep the business solvent and save their jobs they could reduce overhead and replace nonfamily employees with family members.

A WORKER'S VALUE IN HARD TIMES

Workers are ordered in a job queue according to their "employability" or market value at the time, as determined by employers.[16] During hard times, the least skilled and older workers are generally the first to lose their jobs and the last to find new ones. They are the dispensable workers, the least "employable" based on skills and liabilities. We used the age, educational status, and occupational skills of the Berkeley men as indicators of their relative market value in the Depression labor force. Studies have consistently found these factors to be among the best predictors of both job and income loss.

During the Great Depression, the risk of job loss among male workers in the United States was greatest among older men, followed at a distance by workers under age twenty-five. The rate of unemployment increased sharply among men over forty-five and reached its highest level among workers who were over fifty-five; once unemployed, older men tended to remain out of work longer than their younger counterparts.[17] Comparable results have been reported by studies of the postwar years: age discrimination is applied with a heavier hand when jobs are scarce and business is poor.[18] Employers preferred established younger men to older workers because of their better training, adaptability to new situations, and years of productivity before retirement.

In the 1930s, a number of companies set a maximum age for new employees, sometimes as low as forty.[19] Seniority or length of work experience was of little value in protecting the jobs of older workers, although the lack of such experience accounts in part for the high rate of joblessness among the youngest men. Unemployment was twice the average rate among fifteen- to nineteen-year-olds, and about one-third greater among men in their early twenties.[20] In view of these unemployment patterns, the Berkeley men occupied a favorable position in the age structure of the working population. With few exceptions, they were between twenty-five and forty-five in 1930 and thus escaped the high-risk categories, especially those in the middle class. But this age pattern was an advantage only for continuously employed middle-class men. In the working class, the risk of unemployment and economic deprivation increased steadily by age quartile. And both language skills and formal education tended to follow the same gradient.

Men who lack work skills and formal education occupy the bottom rung on employability, and their disadvantage is significantly greater in hard times.[21] The historical record shows that the unskilled and semiskilled suffered higher rates of unemployment than skilled workers in the 1930s. The unskilled made up 27 percent of the male labor force but 42 percent of all unemployed male workers.[22] Likewise, Thernstrom's analysis of Boston men from the 1900–1909 cohort shows that the Depression most adversely influenced the worklife of men with semiskilled and unskilled jobs before 1930.[23]

This low-skill category also stands out among the Berkeley families on hardship; over half of the semiskilled or unskilled were unemployed at some

point from 1930 to 1935, over twice the rate in any other occupational category. The prevalence of job loss is relatively similar among skilled manual
workers and lower-level white-collar workers—from 20 to 26 percent—then
drops abruptly among higher-status men.

If the percentage out of work gives a relatively accurate picture of hardship among men at the bottom of the occupational ladder, it fails to do so in
the lives of middle-class men generally. This observation is worthy of special
note given the tendency to rely on unemployment figures for estimates of
economic hardship. With few exceptions, the college educated in the middle
class did not experience spells of unemployment and, as a group, were in a
much better financial position than men with less education. Men who entered college but did not complete a degree program had no advantage over
those who never enrolled. The lower level of education for working-class men
is less of an asset for job security than occupational skill. Men with less than
a high school education were more likely to lose their jobs in the Depression
than better-educated workers, but this very modest effect is overshadowed by
the much greater disability of being unskilled or semiskilled.

Different antecedent conditions influenced the worklife and economic
status of men who entered the Depression from the middle class and working
class. Industrial sector of occupation in 1929 and education are most prominent in the Depression experience of middle-class men, especially in relation
to economic loss, with age and occupational skills most influential in the experience of working-class men. This brings us to an overview of the resources
and problems that men and their families carried into the Depression.

LEGACIES OF RESOURCES AND PROBLEMS

The Berkeley families came to the hard times of the 1930s with a set of resources and problems, some with many more than others. These differences
influenced their experiences during the Depression years. Both unemployment and heavy income loss were more prevalent in the working class than
in the middle class, though a substantial number of families in both classes
survived the initial impact of the Depression without either setback. To explain this, we turn to pre-Depression factors that provide insight on class and
family differences among men who ended up economically deprived or were
spared such misfortune.

We focus initially on the "position of the worker in the economy and its
vulnerability to a downswing in the economy," indexed by the industrial sector of the worker's occupation. Sectors that were relatively invulnerable to economic adversity included education and transportation. To this perspective

we contrasted the worker's problematic market value in a depressed economy, as defined by advanced age, limited education, and lack of job skills. The family situation of the workers represented another important legacy that has not been addressed—the resources and problems of socioeconomic dependence and independence. In 1929, on the eve of the Great Depression, some families had to deal with unemployment and the ever-present risk of indebtedness. A number of these families turned for help to relatives and to the local Berkeley Welfare Society. Workers' families were defined as "dependent" if any one of these conditions applied to them. All types of dependence were most prevalent in the working class, but the index was a significant predictor of economic deprivation in both social strata.

Dependencies of this kind bring to mind a number of plausible links to economic deprivation in the 1930s, including an erratic or unstable pattern of work by the breadwinner. In the middle class, indebtedness and dependence on outside economic support may reflect poor financial management, with its implications for uncertain economic aid. From a career perspective, one might expect dependence to be most common among the younger men who needed to establish themselves in a line of work that paid enough to meet family needs. Though Depression hardship is associated with economic dependence before the 1930s, it is a modest association, suggesting that many families that were not already dependent experienced such hardship. However, knowing that existing dependence placed families at somewhat greater risk of deprivation in the 1930s provides valuable insight on family economic circumstances.

The risk of heavy income loss was highest among middle-class men in the sectors of finance, manufacturing, and service, in categories below a college education, and in families classified as "dependent" in 1929 (see appendix table A6.1). A low level of education increased the prospects of joblessness in the 1920s and 1930s, as did employment in a high-risk sector of the economy. Neither men's ages nor their occupations were as predictive of a heavy loss of income as these factors, but there is still much to be explained. A good many of the men who were vulnerable to the economic downturn by reason of lower education, a high-risk occupational sector, and socioeconomic dependence avoided a heavy loss of earnings, whereas a substantial number of workers who occupied a relatively secure position before the stock market crash experienced such losses. All in all, the Depression appears to have been remarkably indifferent to the varied backgrounds and attributes that middle-class men carried into the 1930s. In the words of Robert and Helen Lynd, describing the city of "Middletown," Indiana, in the Great Depression, "The great knife of the depression had cut down impartially through the entire population, cleaving open the lives and hopes of rich as well as poor."[24]

Among working-class men, the chances for economic loss were both relatively high and uniform across industries, low skill categories, and educational levels (see appendix table A6.2). From the standpoint of economic loss, older men and socioeconomic dependence before the 1930s emerged as most predictive of income loss apart from the loss of a job in the Depression. These factors do not take us as far as we expected in explaining the varied economic fortunes of working-class men, but they must be seen in terms of their consequences for unemployment. Economic depressions and recessions have typically been harshest on families at the very bottom of the social ladder.

In Berkeley these families were headed by men with semiskilled and unskilled jobs, limited formal education, and meager earnings that too often fell short of meeting the most basic human needs. A large percentage of these families entered the Depression with a history of economic dependence and soon encountered a severe test of their survival prospects when the breadwinner lost his job and faced dismal chances for reemployment. The relation between socioeconomic problems before and during the Great Depression supports a "continuity thesis" on economic misfortune. That is, men who were least able to provide adequate family support before the Depression were more likely than the self-sufficient to experience greater problems as economic conditions declined sharply in the 1930s.

The concentration of unemployment in the lower occupational classes strikingly illustrates the uneven impact of hard times, and the long-term consequences of unemployment for these workers tend to be even more significant than its prevalence. In view of their competitive disadvantage in a depressed economy, it is not surprising that these men often remained out of work for a lengthy period or were able to obtain only part-time jobs. This effect of job loss brings us to the long-term consequences of the Depression on worklife and family status from the early 1930s to the beginning of World War II.

Pathways through the Great Depression

We have told the story of the Berkeley men's work and earnings up to the midpoint of the Great Depression, but there is more to cover during the second half of the decade. These years were marked by a second economic crash in 1937–38, briefer but nonetheless severe, and a surge of labor-management strife. Within the Berkeley-Oakland region, both skilled workers and the unskilled and semiskilled were laid off in substantial numbers during strikes and this second economic shock, which placed the newly reemployed blue-collar workers in greatest jeopardy.

After the heavy income losses and unemployment spells of the early 1930s, persistence through hardship and efforts at recovery defined the second half of the decade for the Berkeley men and their families. Why did some men in the middle and working classes remain mired in hardship while others managed to rise above their misfortune? As we noted earlier in relation to education and skills, the lasting consequences of job loss before 1935 were likely to be more extreme among working-class men than among men of higher status before the economic crash.

Mounting economic pressures among the stably employed in the lower middle class and working class may have prompted them to change jobs after 1934 for more income to meet family needs. Potential changes included finding a higher-paying job in the same line of work, launching a new business, or shifting to a different line of work, such as from bank clerk to car salesman. However, the structure of work in the middle class made such shifts costly and risky. Entering a new line of skilled work usually required retraining, with an initial loss of earning power. Attractive job changes out of an established career path were always a potential source of continuing disadvantage for men in the deprived middle class.

In both social classes, we assessed the effect of unemployment and income loss before 1935 on four types of worklife patterns: a succession of jobs and employers, including the transition to self-employment; the instability of worklife through ups and downs in occupational status and changes in line of work; evidence of continuing hardship—unemployment, public assistance, and low income through 1939; and the post-Depression occupational status of the household head. Initial losses of jobs and income are likely to generate worklife instability.

MULTIPLE JOBS AND EMPLOYERS

By the end of the 1930s, over half of the Berkeley men had held more than one job and worked for more than one employer. A quarter of the men had made four or more changes of this kind. A succession of jobs by itself does not usually tell much about a man's worklife, but changing jobs and employers during the Depression decade tended to be more an indication of structured disruptions than of choice among attractive options. In the absence of viable alternatives, the specter of unemployment could enhance the appeal of even the most dead-end, low-wage job. Thus a foundry worker in the Berkeley sample wanted to move into something better, but his wife noted that he "felt that he had to hang onto anything at the time." But he eventually ended up jobless and looking for work anyway.

This logic may have been widely shared among employed men, especially those blessed with a fairly stable job with adequate income. Indeed, nine out of ten nondeprived men in both the middle class and working class had a work history with only one job. In stark contrast, over three-fourths of the men in the deprived middle class reported having more than one job and employer, and the percentage was even greater among men in the deprived working class. As we might expect, the longest array of jobs and employers occurred among deprived men who were also unemployed during the early years of the Depression, especially in the working class. This pattern corresponds with the dismal prospects for stable reemployment among manual workers. Their unemployment forecasts a future of odd jobs, short weeks, and layoffs until the beginning of industrial mobilization for World War II.

A precise understanding of changes of jobs and employers during the 1930s is best achieved by specifying work situations as a mode of adaptation to scarce employment. Consider the transition from employee to proprietor. Among the Berkeley men, the ranks of the self-employed more than doubled from 14 percent in 1929 to 30 percent by 1940. A number of low-status men started small businesses "in the hope of supporting themselves."[25] As economic conditions worsened, owning a small business provided a measure of control in charting survival. No longer at the mercy of a self-interested employer, the new proprietor could apply his resourcefulness to achieving economic success.

New businesses were invariably linked to previous lines of work. Thus Berkeley men who had worked for employers in the following areas launched comparable enterprises, though on a much smaller scale: auto finance, ice and fuel, photography, mining machinery, and weed control. They took the entrepreneurial step before they had completely depleted their savings and property. Friends and kin were helpful in some cases, and several men pooled resources with a partner to make it through the "knothole" of the early years. Two-thirds of the new businesses remained in operation at least four years, even in the working class. Families had to sacrifice as profits were plowed back into the business.

UNSTABLE WORK AS ADAPTATION

The important point of assessing number of jobs and employers is to see whether they portray a stable progression of work or a truly unstable pattern of employment, with its discontinuities and inconsistencies, breaks in line of work, and status ups and downs—a worklife in which jobs are not linked in a sequence that follows a predictable course in status, expertise, and earnings. In this category, for example, we find a displaced electrical engineer and a salesman for a wholesaler. The engineer got a temporary job as a book salesman and eventually found employment as a construction supervisor by 1939. He managed to return to his original line of work during World War II. The salesman lost his job in 1931 and remained out of work until 1935, when he got a part-time job as a recreation director. This work ended in 1937 and initiated another round of unemployment, followed by a brief return to sales and then steady employment as a warehouseman for a shipyard at the onset of industrial mobilization for World War II. Though seemingly chaotic, these worklives have elements of effective adaptation to difficult circumstances.

Three defining aspects of worklife instability are illustrated by these two cases—a change in line of work, minimal persistence in a line of work, and an up-and-down pattern of status change. The engineer managed to find work and earnings to help support his family over a decade when he held a job outside his training and career path. His worklife was adaptive in what was a desperate time for many families, but it presumably offered little enhancement of his career prospects. The full-employment years of World War II let him return to his original line of work. The salesman experienced a more disruptive and deprivational path across the 1930s, marked by long spells of unemployment, and he seems to have accepted any available job to support his family, producing an erratic sequence of employment and joblessness.

By contrast, consider an example of worklife stability in the life of a printer for the *Berkeley Gazette*, the local newspaper. He rose from advertising sales in 1929–30 to production manager as the decade came to an end. The printer's work history is defined by the convergence of three features of stability: income stability (if not growth) over the 1930s, a successful career move into the middle class, and an advanced career stage when the Great Crash occurred.

To measure worklife instability with our data, we assigned scores of one to each of the following: any job change that departed from a functional line of work during the 1930s; less than twelve years in the same line of work from 1929 to World War II; and one or more "up and down" changes in status of work. Scores across these interrelated items were summed to form an index with values ranging from zero (stable worklife) to three (highly unstable worklife).

Men who avoided a heavy income loss typically gained the security benefits of a stable worklife throughout the 1930s, regardless of initial class position (see appendix table A6.3). Among the nondeprived in both social classes, most of the men followed stable career paths across the 1930s. By comparison, less than half of the men from the deprived middle class ended up with a stable career, and the percentage is even smaller for the deprived working class. The most unstable work pattern (scores of 2–3) ranged from less than 6 percent of the nondeprived to 27 percent of the deprived middle class and 49 percent of the deprived blue-collar workers.

Men entered the Depression at varying career stages, a difference with major implications for their worklife in the 1930s. Some had accumulated twenty years or more in the labor force, whereas others faced economic stagnation at an early stage of their career. In ordinary times, career switching and other forms of a disorderly worklife are more characteristic of young workers in the trial and establishment phase of their career than of older, well-established men. However, here we find just the opposite: younger nondeprived men in the Depression labor market were far less likely to have an unstable career than those who were older. This may reflect an attachment to their work role and an unwillingness to experiment and risk what they have, however little that might be. Of course, this interpretation assumes that the worker had some room for choice at a time when social forces were a major source of worklife instability.

WORKLIFE CONTINUITY AND CHANGE

An unstable worklife is a prominent legacy of Depression hardship and implies a continuing pattern of deprivation up to World War II or at least a troubled path to economic recovery. What kind of picture do we find of the socioeconomic well-being of men and their families as the decade came to an end? In lieu of systematic income records for the late 1930s, our best estimates of economic status at this time must rely on a variety of socioeconomic information—men's occupational status, unemployment, low income, and public assistance.

All Berkeley families in one of the following categories were defined as "hard-pressed" during the late 1930s: lack of economic recovery (not regaining 1929 income level) by 1939 or low income (below $1,200 annually) from 1936 to 1939; head of household lost job during 1936 to 1939; and family was on public assistance in 1936 to 1939. Whatever the Depression's initial impact, working-class families were more likely than middle-class families to end up in the hard-pressed category, though continuing hardship is linked to economic loss in both social classes. For the middle class, at least one aspect of hardship applies to 8 percent of the nondeprived and 35 percent of the deprived families. But for the working class these figures are 35 percent of the nondeprived and fully 78 percent of the deprived families. The history of continuing hardship is clearly shaped by Depression unemployment and an unstable worklife.

Worklife instability and unemployment are strongly predictive of persistent hardship among men in the middle class, followed at a distance by income loss. In combination these factors account for approximately two-thirds of the variation in post-Depression hardship. Among men in the working class, the important factor is unemployment; as a correlate it ranks well above economic loss and worklife instability. Loss of job in the early 1930s tells us as much about the path to hard times in the 1939 working class as all three of the factors combined.

The profound trauma of long-term unemployment in the Great Depression can be fully grasped only from a detailed life record, as presented in the account of a skilled worker written by a Berkeley fieldworker during the 1930s. Walter Herbst (pseudonym) had worked as a patternmaker for twenty years when he was laid off by his East Bay company in the winter of 1930, along with two-thirds of the company's employees. He learned after months of job seeking that his many years of skilled experience did not generalize to another trade. Over the next five years he tried in vain to obtain employment as the family struggled to pay bills by borrowing from relatives. During the entire year of 1933, his short-term odd jobs provided only $60. His wife, Helen, described their income decline as 99 percent. They worried about paying for everything from basic groceries to the medical care they could not afford. The family borrowed against insurance policies and ended up owing $2,000 by the summer of 1934, when they could no longer make payments on their mortgage and car loan. They had exhausted all the resources in the family's network. Ineligible for State Emergency Relief Aid, the family received county assistance with groceries and clothing disbursed by the Berkeley Welfare Society.

In fall 1934, a Civil Works Administration project hired Walter for six weeks on construction of an amphitheater at a local park. By the winter of 1935, the family finally received very good news—that Walter could have his old job back as a patternmaker. His wage was 10 percent lower than in 1930, but its purchasing power was greater because of the decline in the cost of living. With several more years of thrifty living and saving, the family was able to pay off their worrisome debt.

Inequality and the Depression Experience: A Closing Note

The Great Depression's legacy of persistent hardship into the war years underscores the importance of noting the class position of individuals and families at multiple points in this dramatic, historic era of change. The varied experiences of the Berkeley men and their families through the 1930s lead back to their socioeconomic position at the end of the 1920s. Our evidence depicts class differences in the nature of Depression hardship as well as in its antecedents and consequences.

Heavy economic loss is more prevalent among men who began the period in the working class than among those who were in the middle class, and so are loss of a job and a reduced workweek. The risk of income loss was greatest for middle-class men if they had less than a college education, worked in particular industrial sectors (such as finance, service, and manufacturing), and had trouble supporting themselves and their families before the Depression decade. Men in the working class experienced the greatest risk of loss if they were older than most workers in 1929 and also if they were "dependent"—on public assistance, unemployed, heavily in debt, or receiving financial aid from relatives. Dependence and lack of work skills (unskilled or semiskilled) are characteristics that stood out among the antecedents of Depression unemployment.

Social standing before the 1930s also made a difference in the consequences of Depression hardship, from worklife patterns to enduring deprivation and disadvantage. Multiple jobs and employers, shifts in line of work, and status fluctuations—these are common elements in the socioeconomic histories of deprived men and families, especially in the working-class men of 1929. Persistent hardship during the late 1930s (loss of job, public aid, low income, or lack of recovery) also appears mainly in the deprived working class, and its concentration owes much to the prevalence and disruptive impact of unemployment up to then. Men who lost their jobs in the worst phase of the Depression generally experienced more episodes of this kind before the 1940s. Such episodes were virtually nonexistent in the middle class.

Hard times and recovery are familiar themes in the Depression history of men and their families. Less recognized is the well-being, if not affluence, of many families and their male heads. Within the nondeprived portions of the middle class and working class, we find a socioeconomic history that bears little resemblance to popular images of the Great Depression, a history of continuous employment in a line of work (often for the same firm), status advancement without status fluctuations, and relative prosperity during the post-Depression 1930s. This way of life generated a comfortable living for the middle class—even considerable wealth—a way of life that brought undeserved self-satisfaction at a time when so many workers had failed through no fault of their own. Privilege and misfortune are notable contrasts in the Great Depression careers of the Berkeley men and families.

7

Hard Times Turned Bad

During this difficult time, I have nagged and only made him more tense.
BERKELEY WOMAN

When families experienced heavy income loss, their social standing in the community became more ambiguous or insecure. Inconsistencies emerged in the educational, occupational, and income status of families before and during the Depression. Some college-educated men ended up with jobs and family income more appropriate to the skill level and credentials of a man who did not complete high school. In the upper middle class, the education of men who suffered heavy losses of income bore little relation to their embarrassing and even traumatic economic plight. The significance of such incongruent statuses is partly expressed in the conflicting images they presented to both the individual and the community: Were a family's social standing and prerogatives to be based on the husband's superior education or on his joblessness and low income?

The unevenness of status change in the Great Depression is an essential observation for understanding family adaptations, especially in the middle class. To maintain the facade of social stability, families employed a variety of tactics in trying to present themselves as though nothing had happened: curtailing home entertaining, avoiding social contacts, painting the house, dressing children well for school and for the neighbors. Some men even delayed public judgment by traveling to and from work at the usual time, even though no business had been transacted for months, or saying, "I must hurry back," to a job that didn't exist. In *Middletown*, Robert and Helen Lynd refer to such efforts as "a brave social front that local canons of respectable competence require a family to present to its neighbors."[1] Economic standards of living and canons of respectable competence are essential guides for understanding the link between social position and family adaptations, social and emotional.

In this chapter we ask how families' social standards shaped the meaning of economic loss in different classes. Such standards are known to be especially demanding in the middle class, and we give particular attention to class differences in the psychological effects of losing income, employment, and social standing, as expressed in feelings of economic insecurity, dissatisfaction with living conditions, and marital quarrels over expenditures. We conclude by examining how the consequences of economic hardship for men and women during the 1930s varied by emotional health before the Depression and by marital support.

The Meaning of Economic Decline

For many Berkeley families the early 1930s marked the beginning of an extraordinary period of economic decline and hardship that clashed with their customary world and reputation. The usual advantage of these middle-class families in resources and social prestige before hard times also entailed a substantial status risk. Economic loss posed a more severe threat to their community standing than it did to families in the lower classes. With high standards and expectations, middle-class families were likely to regard income loss and unemployment as stressful and "to overestimate the hardship that they define as threats to their social position and the aspirations of their children."[2]

A family's sense of social position, with its preferred image and commitments, can be viewed as a cultural bridge between its objective status before change and its interpretation of the new situation. The more rapid and drastic the change, the more family members are likely to perceive and respond in terms of old realities. In the case of economic decline, the higher the status and lifestyle before the Great Crash, the stronger the likely resistance to the realities of lower income and social standing. In the words of economist E. Wight Bakke, families "whose previous standard of living had been relatively high, who had a concept of themselves as a 'high class family'—fought most energetically to postpone any departure from that status."[3] With mounting economic pressures, adherence to standards better suited to the past generated more frustration and despair, prolonging readjustment to the essential requirements of survival.

Assuming that adaptations to new circumstances are influenced by such frames of reference, we examine the association between the social standards of the Berkeley couples, their social class before Depression hardship, and their responses to economic decline. From the vantage point of the postwar era, sociologist Joseph Kahl identified two social standards as most central to an understanding of the American system of social classes: the "economic standards" of upward mobility and material possessions, and "a standard of respectability" with its lifestyle investments in homeownership, churchgoing, and children's education.[4] Kahl linked the economic standards orientation to the upper middle class and a standard of respectability to families in the "middle" class (the lower middle class and working class). These two groups of families commonly aspire to a better life, with its lofty economic standards, and seek to differentiate themselves from people lower down (the unskilled, etc.) as having greater perceived respectability.

When the Berkeley couples were first interviewed about 1930, they were not asked about their class identification or ideology, though such issues were very much a part of their lives and outlook. Indeed, vivid reflections concerning a sense of social position within the community emerged from evaluations of family background and life situation. Especially informative were preferences regarding contact with and avoidance of coworkers, neighborhood families, and kin. These considerations directed our attention to evaluative frameworks and the distinctive meaning they gave to class-based environments. To better parse differences among the "middle class," we separated these families into two classes based on husband's occupational and educational status in 1929: the upper middle class of professionals and managers (groups 1 and 2); and the lower middle class of administrators and white-collar workers (group 3).[5]

Families' residential area, whether in the Berkeley hills or in the Flats below San Pablo Avenue, was one of the most visible aspects of social standing. On the eve of hard times, where families lived, the quality of their residences, and whether they owned their homes offered no reliable clues to the economic course their lives would take in the Great Depression. But these pre-Depression aspects of residence were affected by economic misfortune, as revealed by a general index based on an interviewer's rating of house exterior and interior for 1933–34, the only such measure for the 1930s. Family economic deprivation lowered the standard of living across social classes, even with adjustment for husband's age. Living conditions declined as expected with economic loss, suggesting both the loss of material possessions and a lower standard of living. Interviewers' notes also revealed evictions and mortgage foreclosures and moves to more crowded and less desirable quarters. Case studies suggest that the pain of losing status when economic hardship demanded adjustments that resulted in a public *déclassement* was especially intense among "fallen" upper-middle-class families.

A vivid illustration of the pain of the fallen was a middle-aged man who owned a successful insurance agency that provided his family with an upper-middle-class income of slightly more than $5,000 a year. His wife candidly noted that during the good times, when their cost of living totaled about $400 a month, they had no savings account "because for years I bled him unmercifully for nice things." As if to symbolize their prosperity, her husband had just purchased an expensive new house in the Berkeley hills that offered an excellent view of San Francisco Bay. This year of 1931, an acceptable if not superior year by material standards, was followed by the worst year to date—the bottom dropped out of the insurance business. Monthly income for the family declined to little more than $100, and the couple could not afford the mortgage payments and taxes on the new house. By 1933 he had sold the house and moved to a "less desirable location." A visitor to the family described him as "feeling defeated and humiliated."

Economic standards were assessed based on interviews with the Berkeley couples and the fieldworkers' observations during periodic home visits. Levels of economic standards were identified by a question that asked whether the wife evaluated herself and others in terms of economic standards that were high, just above average, average, or plain. The same question was asked of husbands. Nine out of ten people in the upper middle class held standards that coders considered well above average.[6] The prevalence of these standards dropped to little more than half of the couples in the lower middle class. Above-average economic standards disappeared in the working class, while "plain" standards were the dominant perspective of families on the lowest rung of the socioeconomic ladder.

Most husbands and wives in the upper middle class held similar economic standards. The same was not true in the lower middle class, where one-third of the wives embraced higher economic standards than their mates. During the economic decline of the 1930s, this disparity was especially troublesome when wives were inflexible in their standard of living.

We then coded the presence or absence of economic flexibility during the 1930s among all families with "above-average standards" (because flexibility should matter most when standards are high) and discovered that rigid adherence to previous high standards was concentrated among lower-middle-class couples, and the wives.[7] Nearly two out of three of these women were inflexibly committed to their economic standards, compared with two out of five of the men. Inflexibility was uncommon among women and men in the upper middle class—less than one-third of women and one-fifth of men held this perspective. One colorful example of such flexibility is seen in the attitude of the wife of a real estate broker. With some amusement, she reported that "we swim when we have lots of money and we economize when we don't. We are born gamblers . . . ideals and standards are too high anyhow and since I can't have what I would really like to have, it doesn't make much difference if my husband earns $100 or $200 a month."

In the midst of hard times, these families were at risk of marital conflict over expenditures—whether to spend money and, if so, what to spend it on. Why were such marital differences concentrated in the lower middle class? This question has several answers. Women at this level were more engaged than their husbands in the lifestyle of their home, however modest, and no doubt they felt the ever-present threat of losing what they'd gained. Most likely they had family, friends, and relatives who had recently experienced hard times and so may have been sensitized to loss. Differing backgrounds could also contribute to divergent marital perspectives. For example, middle-class men were three times more likely to hold high economic standards when they married women from a lower-class background (43 versus 15 percent). Marriage to a woman from a lower-status group may well have increased a man's need to meet the higher standards of his own better-off family, an aspiration that appears to be supported by their wives' inflexible standards. Upwardly mobile married women tended to value the economic standards of their husbands' background, and most were established in the upper middle class as the 1920s came to an end.

Berkeley couples in the lower middle class who valued high economic standards from their perceived position "in the middle" were oriented toward the living standards of the upper middle class while holding firm to the living standard they had achieved. Unyielding economic standards among the wives of white-collar workers and craftsmen likely reflect their aspirations and the frustrations of making ends meet. Caught between higher- and lower-status families, they support their insecure position by "affirming who they are" as families that support education for their children and are proud of the small homes they own (see chapter 3). They lay claim to a life of respectability.

A third of the Berkeley couples, both men and women, endorsed a life of respectability—as reflected in observations about whether each wife and husband gave the impression of valuing moral character, such as integrity and trustworthiness, and of evaluating self and others in these terms.[8] A standard of "respectability" is very different from aspirations for a high standard of living.[9] More of these couples are in the lower middle class and working class than in the higher and lower classes. Interestingly, working-class couples rank highest on embracing a standard of respectability, with four out of ten endorsing this concept of self and family, in contrast to about three out of ten couples in the lower middle class and slightly less in the upper middle class. Joseph Kahl observed that all people in the middle are "on the fence; they are more conscious of being in between than are any other group. They cannot cling too strongly to career as a focus of their lives, for their jobs do not lead continuously upward. Instead they tend to emphasize the respectability of their jobs and their styles of life, for it is respectability that makes them superior" to people at the bottom.[10]

When Hardship Turns into Bad Times

FINANCIAL SECURITY, EXPENDITURES, AND
MARITAL CONFLICT

Hard times became bad times for families in the 1930s when marriages lost their mutual supportiveness in the midst of worsening economic conditions.[11] Spouses' economic standards and expectations contributed to this erosion of support. During the bleak winter of 1932, with countless men out of work and income, Jane Addams noted that the "stage is set for one of the most cruel and futile of our undertakings—one human being punishing another in order to reform his character."[12] Two indicators shed light on this scenario. Across the decade, Institute staff drew on a variety of sources (for example, observations and interviews) each year to assess with five-point scales the financial security or strain in the lives of the Berkeley couples as well as their consensus on financial matters.[13] The first assessment occurred in 1930–31, and we averaged all available ratings for the three worst years, 1932–34.

Ratings of financial security on all deprived families clearly show an economic decline in the early 1930s. But it is in the worst years of the Great Depression (1932–34) that differences in the security of deprived versus nondeprived families were particularly acute in both the middle class and the working class (in the middle class, average security for nondeprived families was 3.25, and for deprived families it was 2.28; in the working class these averages were 2.92 and 1.94). During this period of hardship, a number of middle-class families (as of 1929) had dropped to the insecure level of the stable working-class families that were spared significant hardship. The social class of families in 1929 represented a major source of their financial security or strain, but this effect did not come close to matching the more powerful effect of family economic losses during 1932–34.

Middle-class families were considerably more sensitive to the status implications of heavy economic loss than were families in the working class. The ratings suggest that the upswing of financial insecurity between 1930–31 and 1932–34 among deprived families was more than twice as great in the middle class as in the working class. If a sense of security closely reflects absolute income as the objective situation, we would expect a similar perception between the deprived middle class and the nondeprived working class. Their median incomes during the worst years of the Depression differed by only

$200. But the feeling of financial insecurity in the deprived middle-class family was much greater than in the stable working-class family.

Because economic hardship is a well-known determinant of marital instability, we expected conflict over spending to follow a pattern over time that parallels financial insecurity. The data concur. Such conflict increased as family income plummeted to its lowest point in the Great Depression, and harmony gradually returned as economic conditions improved. Consensus on spending in the deprived middle class declined more strikingly by 1932–34 than in the deprived working class (from averages of 3.17 to 2.15 compared with 2.77 to 2.21). However, consensus in deprived families was especially threatened in the depth of the Depression (averages of 2.15 and 2.21 for deprived families in the middle class and working class, but 3.31 and 2.82 in nondeprived families in the middle class and working class, respectively). It is at the lowest point of the Depression that we find the strongest relation between financial insecurity and disagreement on spending decisions.[14]

Mounting financial insecurity intensified the issue of how to spend scarce money. Before the depth of hardship, these family processes identify marriages that were least likely to be conflicted over expenditures. Among families that escaped the harsh deprivations of the 1930s (the nondeprived), financially secure couples were most likely to work out money issues amicably during the early 1930s. Among families with hard times in their future, couples with a history of consensus on expenditures tended to carry this practice into the trials of the Great Depression.

THE HIGH ECONOMIC STANDARDS OF WIVES

The evidence up to this point supports the hypothesis that heavy economic loss produced greater financial insecurity and marital conflict over spending money in the middle class than among families of lower status. This difference is based on measures of the marital unit, not of individuals, but corresponding evidence comes from the Berkeley women who were interviewed earlier, in 1931–32. The most relevant measure on status considerations is a seven-point rating of "dissatisfaction with lot"—a high score indicated that conditions in the woman's home failed to measure up to her expectations. In the middle class, women with substantial economic loss scored highest on discontent, significantly higher than women from this social class who were spared such income losses as well as women from the working class, whether economically deprived or not.[15] For many of these women the target is the inadequacy of the husband's job, which relates back to resentment and even anger over insufficient income for family needs.

But how are family needs determined? They reflect what people value in terms of standard of living, and they are expressed in part through what we have termed "class-related expectations and standards." To what extent did they account for the greater psychic impact of economic loss in the middle class? High economic standards, and inflexible adherence to these standards, were mainly found in the lower middle class, but we have not as yet examined whether they increased emotional distress and financial insecurity. To investigate this question, we focus on the economic standards of wives in nondeprived and deprived middle-class families. As we noted earlier, the standards of husband and wife are highly interrelated, and no advantage is gained by using a general family index. Because we want to know whether economic standards made a difference in subjective responses to hardship (1932–34) apart from actual living conditions, we made adjustments for yearly income.

The most striking connection between economic standards and subjective responses to hardship appears in the life dissatisfaction of middle-class women in hard-pressed families: the higher and more inflexible their economic claims, the greater their discontent (see appendix table A7.1). During the worst years of the Depression, women with such claims were also more likely than other women to experience financial strain and marital conflict over spending family income. However, a substantial result involves the psychic costs of an inflexible commitment to high living standards among middle-class women who were spared major losses. "Losing a little" while neighbors and friends were losing a lot could well have reinforced the importance of holding on to what they had. With much to lose, these women most likely feared what could happen to their way of life. Their lives were marked by a sense of financial insecurity and much quarreling over spending money.

Because the codes for economic standards are based primarily on interviews with the women in 1930–31, some adjustment to economic reality may have occurred among those who encountered heavy losses but had a rigid attachment to an affluent standard of living. If such change did occur, we might expect a negative relation between inflexibility and financial security as of 1930–31. The data show such a relation among women in the deprived middle class, but it is modest at best concerning both financial security and marital conflict over expenditure. Overall, the data provide at least tentative support for the hypothesized effects of economic standards during the early 1930s.

In case material, we find that women with an inflexible commitment to high economic standards frequently made disparaging statements about their husbands, and some compared them unfavorably with their fathers. One-quarter of the inflexible women expressed such sentiments, compared with only one woman with flexible or low standards. The reciprocal relation between financial strain and marital tensions frequently flared up in shouting matches, threats, and physical violence. Shortly after a man's consulting firm collapsed in 1931, for example, a visitor described the man's wife as hectic, irritable, and keenly sensitive to any mention of finances. Later in the year her husband appeared depressed and haggard, was having trouble sleeping, and "[sat] for hours at a time with his head in his hands." A family report goes on to say that "he has become so upset by his wife's 'explosions' that every time he goes out, she fears that he will take his life."

RESPECTABILITY AND "SAVING FACE"

Some of the wives in very difficult economic situations tried to put the best face on matters by lying to the interviewer about their socioeconomic facts. In reviewing annual records on families during the 1930s, we identified women who gave false reports (12 percent of the entire sample). Multiple sources of information over time enabled us to identify disparities between the wife's report about self and family and the actual record. Such misrepresentations included false statements about the husband's work, income level for a particular year, and receiving public assistance. Misrepresentations of this sort were most common among women with an inflexible commitment to high economic standards (25 percent, as opposed to 10 percent of the women with flexible or low standards). As a defensive strategy, other women closed their eyes to the real hardships of their world. In a 1934 visit to a woman who had made "an extraordinary adjustment to a very difficult situation," the interviewer reported that "she is trying desperately to fool herself and for the most part succeeds."

A standard of respectability is most compelling when family appearances become a problem, increasing sensitivity to the judgments of others and to social uncertainty. As we noted earlier, respectability mattered to some men and women in all classes, even the unskilled, but it was most important among white-collar and skilled manual workers. In view of this class distribution, we examined its correlation with financial security and marital consensus on expenditures among women in both the middle class and the working class. We excluded women's life dissatisfaction because it is relevant to economic standards but not to respectable conduct.

Not surprisingly, a standard of respectability appears to be most predictive of financial insecurity and strain in economically deprived families where reputations were at stake. In the middle class, this standard is relevant to financial security and to the choices made on spending money. A commitment to this standard increased couples' financial insecurity and their disputes over spending money. In the working class, people who valued respectability were less likely to feel financially secure, but it mattered less for marital consensus on spending.

The driving force of respectability as a standard of evaluation is expressed in the life of a bricklayer in the Berkeley sample. After two years of joblessness, by the early months of 1932 the family had exhausted all alternatives except public assistance, but the husband absolutely refused to go to the Berkeley Welfare Society, claiming he would "starve first and let his family starve." A fieldworker on the Berkeley project visited the home at the time and found the wife crying and depressed, utterly overwhelmed by the needs of her children and her husband's "black mood." He had threatened to hang himself if he didn't soon find a job. By 1935 the wife admitted she couldn't see anything in the marriage to salvage. "Isn't it terrible that I've lost all feelings for him?"

Such cases are not representative of all Berkeley marriages in deprived circumstances, but they do illustrate the experience of severe financial strain, its emotional pain, and the disintegration of marital ties. In other hard-pressed families, the marriage remained a bright spot of human courage and understanding in an otherwise bleak situation, though economic strains and marital tensions typically reinforced each other in families with spells of unemployment and heavy income loss. A substantial economic loss directly affected men's status, personal worth, and identity because they, not their wives, were the primary earners. Consistent with the individualistic values of the era, men commonly viewed the loss of jobs and income as a symptom of personal inadequacy.[16] Though often faced with extraordinary pressures and hardships, women could find significance and meaning in their family roles.

Gender, Marriage, and Emotional Health

When men lost jobs and income, they lost important social roles and saw their daily routines disrupted. The social roles of women, in contrast, tended to expand and become more complex. In *Middletown*, the Lynds observed that "it is the world of male roles that has been under most pressure."[17] And in Jack Weller's account of rural Appalachia in *Yesterday's People*, an interviewer's account of a rural couple in the 1930s vividly captured the drama of their gendered life: "Thus bit by bit, as her husband's role has decreased and as his life has lost meaning, her life has taken on new meaning in the community or at work."[18]

Do we find such gender differences between husbands and wives in the Berkeley families? To explore this question, we focus on their marital bond and social class before the Depression, their emotional health before and across the Depression years, and their exposure to substantial income loss.[19] Gender, health, social class, and the marital bond have special relevance for understanding how Depression hardship influenced health. To determine whether the effects of hardship varied between husbands and wives, we designed analyses that focused on initial health, then on social class and the marital relationship itself. Did strong marriages insulate men from the adverse health effects of substantial income loss?

The most essential resource for coping in hard times is good emotional health. Healthy and resourceful people typically are able to cope effectively regardless of adversity unless the strain is overwhelming. Among the least resourceful, economic pressures are likely to accentuate maladaptive behaviors, such as irritability and explosiveness, that may be manageable in less stressful situations. Stable people such as the "ego resilient" are better equipped to weather misfortune, as suggested by the concept of stamina: "the physical or moral strength to resist or withstand disease, fatigue, or hardship."[20] Lacking such adaptive strength, the economically deprived would be at higher risk of poor health outcomes.

In keeping with this concept of ego resilience, we assume that qualities of emotional stability reflect and enhance resourceful adaptation. The best available measure of this personal characteristic across the 1930s is a seven-point scale of emotional stability (consistent with the language of the time, this is labeled "nervous stability" in the archive). High scorers are described as "exceptionally stable" even in the "face of trying circumstances." Low scorers tended to be highly "erratic," such as a semiskilled worker who was described as quarrelsome and moody on the job, irritable and unpredictable at home, and a general threat to the well-being of his wife and children. The ratings for 1930–31 and across the 1930s were based on fieldworkers' interviews with wives and observations of the home. To maximize the number of cases, we averaged the annual ratings for two periods in the 1930s: 1933–35 and 1936–38.

Evidence suggests that resilient adaptation is likely under conditions of stable, positive emotional health and a strong, nurturing marriage. The support of an understanding and compassionate spouse can mobilize a partner's inner strength for effective coping.[21] Marital support generates emotional resources through bonds of understanding, acceptance, and confidence; tangible assistance in time, energy, and money; and advice and knowledge. These elements of marital support tend to buffer the stress of economic hardship. Accordingly, we hypothesize that the weaker the marriage among the Berkeley couples before hard times, the lower their marital support in deprived circumstances and the higher the health risk from such economic change. The buffering effect of marital support should be most evident among these men.

We measured marital quality with a composite of interrelated five-point ratings that represent the average judgment of an interviewer and a home visitor:
closeness of each spouse to the other, friendliness of husband and wife toward
each other, and adjustment to each other. These ratings were used in chapter 5 to
characterize the marital relationship of the Berkeley couples before hard times
in the 1930s. At the Depression's outset, the severity of hardship among men,
especially in the working class, combined with marital discord and the handicap
of poor emotional health to maximize men's health risk by the end of the decade.
Conversely, healthy men in strong marriages were well equipped to weather the
economic crisis. Correlation coefficients show that an irritable, explosive, worrisome style of interaction is characteristic of the emotionally unstable.

What then is the big picture on heavy economic loss and emotional stability? First of all, we note that drastic income loss does not have a general effect
on emotional health in the Depression years that applies across men and their
wives, whatever their initial health, marital quality, and class position in 1929.
But emotional stability at the outset of the Great Depression represents the
very best predictor of health across the decade. One-third of the variation in
emotional health across the decade reflects the state of men's health before the
economic collapse.

The significance of one's initial state of emotional health is most clearly
and simply shown by dividing men at the median of emotional stability in
1930. The adverse health effects of economic deprivation are almost exclusively observed among men with below-average health before economic misfortune. Less than 10 percent of initially stable men in economically deprived
families were judged unstable in 1933–35 (scores of 5 to 7). Among initially
unstable men, this percentage increases to 40 percent of the nondeprived and
to nearly 90 percent of the deprived. This comparison tells us little about the
emotional well-being of deprived women in the 1930s, except that those who
were initially healthy were likely to cope effectively with family hardship.

A more precise account of the effects of economic deprivation on emotional stability in 1933–35 by gender and initial health comes from a series of
multiple regressions. In figure 7.1, the graphed values for the effects of economic deprivation by gender and initial health represent standardized regression coefficients. Heavy income loss entailed substantial health costs for
men who entered the 1930s with below-average health, but there was no negative outcome for women in this vulnerable state. Indeed, among the initially
healthy, income loss is associated with modest health gains for women, in
contrast to the effects on men. The results suggest personal growth for many
women in hard-pressed families, possibly through the effort they exerted and
the strategies they used to manage the challenges of family life.

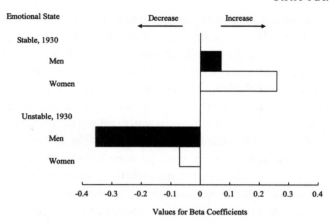

FIGURE 7.1. Hardship effects on emotional stability (1930–35), by pre-Depression stability (1930). *Source*: Glen H. Elder, Jeffrey K. Liker, and Bernard J. Jaworski, "Hardship in Lives: Depression Influences from the 1930s to Old Age in Postwar America," in *Life-Span Developmental Psychology: Historical and Generational Effects*, ed. Kathleen McCluskey and Hayne Reese (New York: Academic Press, 1984), fig. 5, 191.

Did a strong marriage enhance the protective benefits of initially good emotional health on men's well-being during the worst times of economic hardship? We find that a wife's emotional support improved men's health prospects when they ranked below average in health at the outset of the Depression era. However, a strong marriage did not come close to matching the protective role of good health before the economic crisis. For women, a stable marriage made a notable positive difference in their well-being during the stressful years of 1933–35 if they entered the 1930s with below-average emotional well-being.

To sum up, the most adverse effects of Depression hardship on emotional health appear for men who entered the Depression decade in relatively poor health. If we focus on this vulnerable group across the 1930s, what factors are likely to be important to their emotional health? This at-risk group varied widely in well-being during the early 1930s, and this variation made a significant difference in men's health by the 1940s. The higher their rating on initial emotional health, the better their chances for health as the decade ended. A supportive marriage in 1930 may also have enhanced men's emotional health across the 1930s. For the less skilled who suffered economic losses during the early 1930s, hard times continued; they were likely to experience periods of unemployment up to the war years. A stable worklife thus was an important contingency of men's emotional health as the Great Depression came to an end.

Last, what about the men who were most vulnerable on emotional health during this extraordinary extended period of hardship? Hardship over the Depression decade only heightened the economic instability of initially unstable men. This was especially true when economic troubles continued into the war years. Men who were still down socioeconomically by the late 1930s include a disproportionate number of the unskilled and semiskilled. These persistent troubles made it even more likely that relatively poor emotional health would continue into World War II. The Depression experience differed significantly for the Berkeley men and women who had emotional health and stamina before drastic income loss in the early 1930s and for those who lacked this resource. Consistent with the process of cumulative advantage and disadvantage, those who were well positioned going into the Great Depression managed to retain their health across the 1930s, whereas those who entered these years disadvantaged generally saw their disadvantage grow over time. However, the truly hard times of prolonged unemployment sorely tested even families that seemed well equipped to cope effectively, with good emotional health and strong marriages. A case in point is again Walter Herbst, the patternmaker who experienced over five years of joblessness (see chapter 6).

Before losing his job in 1930, Walter was described by an interviewer as an "unusually cheerful and self-reliant person," energetically involved in various projects at home. But his wife, Helen, noted that after a year of joblessness, her husband had become "fretful and irritable with the children under the strain." Constant stress over paying bills and an inability to find permanent work weighed heavily on him as his unemployment persisted, and he began to change from a "cheerful, relaxed outlook to an irritable belligerence, resentful of bill collectors, hostile toward the Berkeley Welfare Society, surly and full of suspicion." She observed that he had become less and less active during the daytime, often sleeping through the day after lying awake at night, and had "built up a defensive belligerence and a shrug of the shoulders at his past standards and values."

Helen was the family's emotional bulwark and understood her husband's discouragement, but the strain had been too costly for her health and appearance. An Institute observer noted that the stress had seemed to age her by ten to fifteen years, turning her hair gray. And yet she also noted that the exceptional strength of their marriage continued through years of struggle. In reflecting on this family time, she observed that "people aren't given happy marriages, they develop them. It's a matter of give and take, and consideration of the other person, knowing in turn that they will be considerate of you." This perspective had much to do with Walter's returning to some of his "old self," with a more cheerful outlook and renewed interest in family activities. His company flourished with the surge of military orders during World War II and his earnings steadily increased, but the personal damage of "his unemployed years" was apparent to his wife. "You know," she said, "he has never really lived down the humiliation of his unemployment."[22]

Walter's humiliation from years of joblessness no doubt owes much to his public loss of self-support through accepting social welfare. In the 1930s the personal shame of such aid stemmed in large part from its being "unearned"; receiving such assistance violated a widely shared belief regarding the notion of "just returns." Families that couldn't afford payments on their mortgages were supported by neighbors because they were committed to making such payments, and many lending agencies gave these families more time to pay. Walter received more time to make the overdue payments, but he also was pushed to the point of asking for help in feeding and clothing his family.

We do not know Walter's emotional struggle over making such a request, but a staff worker's notes on another unemployed worker tell such a story. "After running out of funds, he reluctantly made up his mind to apply for aid, although this was terribly humiliating for him. On the day when he went to register, he walked around the block several times, hating to enter the office. It took a supreme effort for him to pull together and go in."

We don't know Walter's experience with the Berkeley Welfare Society, but other men and women in the Berkeley study referred to the degrading experience of "qualification interviews," the condescending attitudes of agency workers, and the distrustful intrusion of agency surveillance. As a working-class woman observed, welfare people "are so sassy you hate to go to them." Another complained about home visitors, "Those snippy little welfare girls coming in and telling you how to run things. I just had to tell them to get the hell out. What did they know about running a family?" A craftsman, who had been out of work for over a year, told the interviewer he would not submit himself and his family to the humiliation of public assistance.

Among working-class families, welfare regulations imposed dysfunctional budgetary reductions through the qualification interview. If families satisfied the Berkeley Welfare Society's standard of destitution, they were still not eligible for aid if they had a car and intended to use it while on public assistance (even if just to find employment); if they had a telephone and couldn't prove it was used only for job contacts; and if they had life insurance. Some families borrowed from insurance dividends to pay expenses, as the Herbst family did.

Whether atypical or not, these experiences underscore an important theme concerning relief status during the 1930s: accepting public aid was foreign to the vast majority of the Berkeley families who entered the welfare category at some point during the 1930s. Using records from the project file, we find that only 4 percent of the Berkeley families had any experience with such aid in 1929, but by the end of the decade this figure climbed to 25 percent, almost exclusively in the working class. Only one out of ten middle-class families ever received such aid, compared with 48 percent of the working-class families. During the second half of the 1930s, two out of five working-class families had received public aid, and all were in the economically deprived group, consistent with our portrait of hard-pressed working-class families at the very end of the 1930s. The coming of World War II put an end to their Depression hard times.

On Making Bad Times Worse

Many families lost heavily in the Great Depression yet succeeded in making the best of their situation. Other equally hard-pressed families turned angry emotions on each other, making their life even more painful. This chapter has examined the family dynamics that made hard times even worse. One response was an inflexible adherence to previous living standards despite a real need to lower them. This was particularly true of families in the lower and upper middle class and for wives who worried about shame and rejection and feared the loss of social ties. This inflexibility often entailed marital quarreling and "blaming the other" for reduced earnings and expenditures. The lack of marital support in trying times is a general expression of this dynamic. Insufficient coping resources also became a major source of emotional health problems when men suffered job and income losses. Some families were resilient and coped effectively with their hardships. Class-based economic and social standards shaped the meaning of abrupt economic decline. The economic success of the upper middle class fostered a higher standard of living. Women were most heavily invested in maintaining this standard, and inflexibility made them especially vulnerable. This outlook was especially common among the lower middle class. Families aspired to affluence and feared losing their "respectable" separation from the families below them. Consistent with class-based standards, economic loss led to a steeper decline of financial security and less consensus on expenditures in the middle class than among working-class families. These conditions were also associated with inflexible economic standards among couples who had not as yet lost their employment or had substantial income losses. The more invested they were in their lifestyle, the greater their apprehensiveness.

As the primary earners in most families, men were most exposed to the social and emotional costs of Depression hardship. Consequently, gender played a major role in determining the mental health costs of unemployment and heavy income loss. Men who entered the 1930s in good emotional health were most likely to retain their well-being despite unemployment and a substantial income loss, especially with emotional support from their wives. However, poor health at the outset enmeshed them in an avalanche of disadvantage, even with marital support. By contrast, Depression hardship often brought greater significance and meaning to women as their relationships and responsibilities in family and community increased and the pressures of hard times made them more resourceful and resilient.

From young adult lives in the 1920s to the end of the 1930s, the Berkeley men and their wives contributed to markedly different marital outcomes for each other. The men determined the initial quality of marriages more than their wives did, whether negatively or positively, and as the primary earners in their families they also brought home the Depression's economic deprivation through loss of jobs, income, and well-being. Men were more often the casualties of this hardship than their wives, who—as we shall see in subsequent chapters—played an essential role in helping their families adapt.

8

Having Children in Troubled Times

The only thing I regret is that we had only one youngster. I know this was the greatest disappointment in my wife's life.

BERKELEY MAN

The economic collapse of 1929 caught the Berkeley couples in the midst of having their children. Faced by the economic uncertainties of the time, some had doubts about having another child at that time. By the second year of the decade, such questions had become more urgent for many marriages. Institute staff who regularly interacted with the families mentioned observing conflicts between couples on this subject and often hearing a reluctant conclusion: "We just can't manage another child."

Whenever hard times have followed a season of prosperity, analysts have noted a slowdown in the formation of American families: fewer people get married and fewer couples have children. Both changes occurred in the 1930s. In coping with economic setbacks, the least consequential response—postponing marriage—becomes the first action undertaken.[1] Sociologists Robert and Helen Lynd found evidence of this Depression strategy in their study of "Middletown," Indiana, where the marriage rate dropped by 41 percent between 1929 and 1933, compared with a reduction of 16 percent in the birthrate.

The Berkeley women in our study were already wives and mothers by 1929. For them the crucial decision now centered on childbearing—whether to have another child in the 1930s, to postpone doing so, or to settle for the present family size. It could mean simply adding one child to a single-child family among middle-class couples, whether deprived or not, or it could mean adding more than one child to an already sizable family, reflecting both a cultural preference for large families and a resistance to contraception. Having more children would increase the burden on family resources, though older siblings could help with household tasks and take on paid jobs, as they did in a good many deprived families in a sister study of older children in Oakland. The older boys in these families helped out by earning money from odd jobs in the community. By the late 1930s, the Berkeley children were old enough to help their families, and we explore their contribution and that of their older siblings using family case histories.

Children in hard-pressed families were likely to be exposed to disruptions and stresses in their parents' lives—their depression and anger and explosive emotions. We know from previous chapters that parents carried their vulnerabilities and strained resources into family life. A primary example linked the depressed economy to a father's job loss and his arbitrary violence toward the family. Some hard times became bad times when parents blamed each other in shouting matches and struggled with poor emotional health and dysfunctional marriages. These experiences suggest how parents may have passed their problems on to their children. Did this transmission occur mainly through fathers and their absence or through both parents? We know that the quality of the marriages had more to do with the behavior of fathers than of mothers.

Whether to Have More Children

The Berkeley couples occupied very different life stages when the economy collapsed at the end of the 1920s. Half had just started their families and had one child; one-fourth had two children; the rest had three or more. For most of those with a single child, fertility desires were clearly not yet fulfilled. But the economic standing of these families was also more vulnerable because younger workers were more likely to suddenly lose job and income.

We investigated these expectations by comparing the Depression fertility (1930–39) of women by number of children (1929) in nondeprived and deprived situations. To take into account other relevant factors, we adjusted the percentage of women who had one or more births during the Depression decade by influences on fertility—women's education, age, social class in 1929, and religion/ethnicity (Catholic, foreign-born, African American). With adjustments for income loss, none of these factors made a significant difference. (Owing to the small sample sizes, we were unable to confidently examine how fertility varied by these factors.) The results show that economic deprivation significantly reduced Depression fertility only among women who had just one child in 1929. However, these women were more likely to have another child than women who had two or more children in 1929 (see appendix table A8.1).

Life in the fortunate, nondeprived sector of the middle class produced a uniquely favorable situation for childbearing among women who entered the 1930s with a child. After adjustments for age, education, and ethnicity, we find that more than four out of five of these women gave birth to a second child during the 1930s. This percentage declined by half among middle-class women in families that lost over a third of their 1929 income. Whether hard-pressed or not, working-class women who had one child in 1929 were less likely than middle-class women to have another one during the 1930s, but the percentage who did was higher in the nondeprived group, as expected. About half of the nondeprived working-class women had another child during the 1930s compared with one-third of the deprived working-class women.

Middle-class women who were spared hardship were nearly two and a half times as likely to give birth to a Depression child as women in the deprived working class. The full significance of this contrast appears in lifetime fertility. With few exceptions, the mothers who did not bear a second child during the 1930s had made a decision that permanently shaped their families. They entered the postwar era and old age with only one child. In larger pre-Depression families, the middle-class mothers in deprived circumstances were more likely to avoid having a Depression child than their working-class counterparts. This difference suggests more use of birth control in the middle class. Indeed, the likelihood of a Depression birth in hard-pressed families dropped sharply for middle-class women who had one versus two or more offspring in 1929 (51 versus 16 percent), but it remained stable in the working class at 34 to 35 percent.

In our small sample of families, we view births in the 1930s as Depression children. But larger population statistics show much change in the economy and the birthrate across the decade. By about by 1934–35, some reversal of the fertility decline seems to have occurred in the middle class.[2] This paralleled the differential timing of family recovery among the Berkeley families by social class. Though most Depression births among the couples occurred before 1935, the national trend and theory point to a difference in the timing of births by social class, with deprived couples more likely to delay until 1934 or later.

Although monthly income data were not available for the Berkeley families, we explored the question of timing among women with a second birth in the 1930s by using the total number of mothers with a transition between the dates of their first and second children. With adjustments for influences on reproductive timing, we find that an average of four years passed before the second birth, until about 1932–33. The timing of the second birth came earlier, not later, if the couple had experienced economic hardship during the early 1930s, at least in the middle class, for which our estimates are reliable. This timing of conception may reflect a desire to have a second child as soon as possible in view of the uncertain circumstances. Deprived couples in the middle class averaged thirty-four months between births, compared with fifty-two months for the nondeprived in the middle class. Only four months separate the deprived and nondeprived groups in the working class (48.7 versus 53.4).

The decision not to have more children during the Depression may have been a permanent commitment or a temporary postponement. In either case, our attention is drawn to contraception in family planning. How did couples avoid an untimely or unwanted birth? We cannot answer this question with quantitative data, but qualitative data from less structured interviews with the Berkeley women provided valuable insights into their thinking and life situation from 1930–31 up to the mid-1930s.

FAMILY REALITIES AND BIRTH CONTROL

In the records of the intensively studied families, three modes of birth control appear with some frequency: voluntary and involuntary reduction in the frequency of sexual intercourse; use of contraceptive techniques—rhythm or safe period, coitus interruptus, condom, or douche; and control after conception—induced abortion.[3]

Infrequent sexual intercourse stands out as a relatively common adaptation to economic deprivation and marital discord. Interview references to this change mention the wife's intense fear of pregnancy and the adverse effect of unemployment and financial stress on emotional health, especially the husband's. During periods of extreme economic distress, it is not uncommon to find interviewer reports of diminished sexual interest and no sexual activity for as long as six months. In some cases the wife's fear of pregnancy and marital divisiveness led to a modification of sleeping arrangements—to separate beds, rooms, and even residences. Contraceptive methods and abortion were clearly the most elusive aspect of fertility control for data collection, though we do know that staff workers at the Institute served as counselors and referral agents on birth control information. The interview notes refer to women who consulted a local birth control clinic.

Two factors have well-established relevance to effective family planning: the quality of the marriage and childbearing intentions or plans. Couples with incompatible marriages before the economic crisis were unlikely to share cultural and social interests and rarely agreed on finance, child care, and family size. Without a shared understanding of whether and when to have another child, either spouse could take action that would frustrate or defeat the other, such as a woman's getting pregnant against her partner's wishes. Marital discord reduced marital communication and the frequency of intercourse.

Relevant data on the Berkeley couples are based on a small sample, and the timing of measurements did not provide a clear sequence of births. For this reason we use the case histories of families with Depression births (1931–35) that have a reference to marital quality and preference for children. All couples in this analysis were economically deprived and had one or two children as of 1929. As expected, Depression births were typically to those who wanted more children and to couples that were close and supportive. Marital discord and the wife's insistence on not having more children clearly distinguished couples who did not have Depression births from those who did. In addition, some Berkeley women did not have a child they wanted, while others gave birth to a child who was not wanted, at least from their perspective in 1930–31.

To explore these disparities, we examined the case records of women for whom the birth of another child was very important and of women opposed to having another child (the lowest and uppermost quintiles on a five-point scale). Each group was then divided according to reproductive outcome: one birth or more in the 1930s versus no birth. This classification let us assess responses to pregnancy, including abortion. Reports of abortion typically appear among women who expressed strong feelings about not having another child.

We found that half a dozen women in the sample wanted more children but had none. Seventeen reported wanting more children and had at least one. Our interest in this group centers especially on the several deprived women who followed this course. Fifteen women did not want more offspring and succeeded in not having more. Eight of these women were randomly selected for study. Six women did not want more children but had a child nonetheless. Three of these cases with adequate information, all from deprived families, were included in our analysis.

Desired another child but did not have one.   Whether deprived or not (most were not), these women put off another child largely in response to economic uncertainty. As mothers of a single child before the 1930s, they faced anticipated and actual economic pressures that favored delaying subsequent childbearing, which continued throughout the decade. Age, health, and marital strains were other factors in this decision. Three of the mothers had reached age forty by the late 1930s, while the other two experienced the insecurity of an unstable marriage and deteriorating health.

Wanted another child and had one.   The three economically deprived women in this group realized their ambitions despite adverse economic circumstances. But closer examination of family records yields the important distinction between intention and timing. One spouse or both expressed a desire for more children, though the timing was qualified. Husbands uniformly preferred later timing, but only one case met this preference—a Catholic middle-class family that suffered heavy income losses before 1933. The mother in this family was thirty at the time of her first birth in 1929. Both husband and wife said they wanted a larger family, though with births two or more years apart. Records describe the couple as "believing in birth control" with no mention of technique. Large salary cuts and an unsuccessful business venture plunged their family income to a low of $380 in 1932, less than a fifth of their 1929 income. Spring and summer 1933 produced a significant upswing in economic well-being, and in line with the couple's plan, their second child was born during the later stage of family recovery, in late 1934.

An "untimely pregnancy" occurred in the Depression experience of each of the other two deprived families. One of the women, the wife of an engineer, expressed some guilt over having insisted on a Depression child against her husband's wishes. Some years later he looked back on this event with resentment: "One thing that is very hard for me to forgive is that she had the child without my consent." In the other case the wife cheerfully acknowledged that she had become pregnant in 1931, just after agreeing with her husband that at present "it would be unwise" to have more children. We do not know whether she planned to go ahead on having a child or whether a contraceptive measure failed. The worst year for this middle-class family was 1933, when family income dropped to half its 1929 figure.

Wanted no more children.   Fifteen women stand out in what they were willing to do to avoid more children during the 1930s. For the total sample, it is primarily in this group that we find references to induced abortion. Of our subsample of eight cases, four women (two in each social class) are recorded as having had an abortion in the early 1930s, and three of them are in this subgroup. The fourth woman obtained an abortion after discovering she was pregnant for the second time during the Depression. Despite legal constraints and social disapproval, other women in the subgroup are on record as having thought about an abortion and exploring ways of securing one. Two women, for example, discovered they were not pregnant after requesting an abortion. The intense fear of pregnancy and having another child is most often associated with reference to abortion, as fact or intention, among women who were caught between the pressures of two or more children and severe economic deprivation. Marital strains intensified these pressures.

Wanted no more children but had one.   Six economically deprived women resemble the previous group in contraceptive failure and the painful dilemmas it posed, but to our knowledge they did not consider abortion. Though distressed by an unwanted pregnancy, they appear more resigned to the reality. Just after her husband had lost his job, one of the women in the working class realized she was pregnant for the third time. When asked about her situation, she replied, "It's too bad about the coming baby, but that's just one of those things." Another woman focused her anger on a local birth control clinic: "I just have no faith in them anymore." The baby's arrival was accepted, however, and two years later the mother chided herself for being unwilling to "give away the baby clothes," then observed, "You can never tell." These women best illustrate the unpredictable and ambivalent nature of family planning, and all were members of deprived working-class families who entered the 1930s with two or more children. Sociologist Lee Rainwater documented the forces at work in these families in his powerful 1965 book *And the Poor Get Children*.[4]

Though many Berkeley mothers and fathers succeeded in avoiding a Depression birth when misfortune occurred, the pain, sorrow, and uncertainty in doing so are deeply etched in their lives. For other families, childbearing issues and the results of unreliable contraceptive measures pitted husbands against wives and parents against each other and the young. Family conflicts centered on finances, child care, and sex before the Depression, and hard times enhanced their contribution to an unstable, divisive home environment. Postponing a desired second child may have enabled families to make ends meet, but the sacrifice also was said to have diminished lives. One of the Berkeley fathers looked back upon his life and saw a child postponed forever. "The only thing I regret is that we had only one youngster. I know this was the greatest disappointment in my wife's life."

Though economic misfortune questioned the wisdom of having more children, it also made the household assistance of older children more valuable. This dual image of Depression children as burden and as resource characterized family life in a good many Berkeley families with at least two children in 1929. By the later 1930s this dual perspective applied to most hard-pressed families, even those with only a single child. By following the Berkeley families from 1929 to the war years, we see the economic and child care burden of children born in 1928 replaced by helpfulness as they mature.

THE HELPFULNESS OF OLDER CHILDREN

Unfortunately, the Berkeley study did not systematically gather information from the study members and older siblings on household tasks and paid jobs in the community. However, we can obtain a glimpse of this helping role of older children through the observations and home interviews with two lower-status families that experienced a drastic economic decline in the 1930s. Both depended on public assistance at points across the decade. The Horton family was headed by a machine operator in 1929, and the Allen family was headed by a boat builder in the 1920s.

The Horton family. Robert Horton (pseudonym) and his wife entered the Depression with a young daughter and a baby boy born in 1929. They had another child in the mid-1930s. Hard times came early for the family when Robert lost his job at the end of 1930. Their annual income dropped below $400 by the end of 1931 and was supplemented by clothes and food from associated charities. Despite being eager to find work, Robert remained unemployed (except for exchanging occasional work at the Berkeley Welfare Society for groceries through 1933), and a fieldworker found the family trying to live on $6 a week. Gas and lights had been turned off, and the family gathered wood for cooking, raised rabbits and chickens for food, and grew produce in the yard. The Berkeley Welfare Society provided clothing. A study fieldworker noted that every family member had a role in keeping the household running. The older daughter helped her mother and father with household tasks such as washing and ironing, preparing meals, and caring for the younger children.

By 1934 the family's living circumstances had improved when Robert got work as a laborer in the California WPA. A fieldworker found the household cheerful and even-tempered in the midst of hard times and judged the parents firm but loving. But misfortune returned in 1937, when Horton became disabled by his worsening heart condition and his wife got a paid job. In a home visit, one of the study's fieldworkers noted how well the children had kept the household operating. They "come home after school, clean up the house, and often have dinner ready when mother comes home. They have done most of the shopping for the family and have learned all of the thrifty habits of the mother."

The extraordinary hardship of this household may have had developmental value for a teenage child, as shown in Elder's *Children of the Great Depression,* but its heavy toll on their youngest child, born during the Depression, was evident through his much older appearance. One of the study interviewers described the boy at eight years old: "[He] resembles an old man overburdened with cares. In his life, spontaneity and playful spirit are almost a thing of the past. Seems to accept his work-a-day adult role willingly. Gives the impression of a child who has had to skip from infancy into adult life." A year later she observed, "He takes financial problems heavily, as if he were the head of the family. Appeared rather strained and worried looking. But apparently feels little or no conscious rebellion at the amount of work asked of him."

The Allen family.   The second illustration of children's helping roles comes from a Berkeley family with two children whose adaptation illustrates the "back to the land movement" in the Depression.[5] Mike Allen (pseudonym), a boat builder, earned $1,200 in 1929 but faced unemployment a year later. Nevertheless, the family had a larger plan for adapting—in line with their long-held ambition "to move to the country and live off the land." In the summer of 1932 the Allen family was able to trade their house for a small farm in the Sierras, aiming to become self-supporting as soon as possible. Shortly after the family moved to the farm, a fieldworker filed notes on the new rural setting. Pieced together, these notes provide a picture of the new home place:

> It is a 160 acre farm, beautifully situated in a small valley, encircled by hills with excellent timber, oak, pine, cedar; some trees are up to three or four feet in diameter. A several-acre field of oats is being enlarged. A small creek runs through the place which almost dries up in the summer. A large vegetable garden, untended at present, is near the creek and could be irrigated by water from it. A neglected fruit orchard of ten peach and apple trees has possibilities. . . . The couple is very proud of the place and enjoy[s] its many beautiful spots. The house is very old and in need of repairs, but as the roof does not leak too much and the rooms can be kept warm in winter, they let it go as it is for the time being.

A letter from the mother, Nora, to project staff in late November 1932 reported, "We have two goats, two horses, and a good many hens and rabbits." She goes on to say that the children enjoy the animals and take care of them, also helping their father "bring in wood." She observes, "One can never be idle on a farm and we all seem to be well and happy here. If we can make a living, we surely want to stay." A year later another letter from Nora continues to be upbeat, though she acknowledges that "we are not very good farmers yet, but it takes time to learn." She reports that Mike's brother and his wife have moved in and will care for the farm while he works for cash at the National Recovery Camp thirteen miles away. As an aside, she suggests that his NRC work is easier than farmwork. The farm produced a small crop of peaches and a few apples that year, and the number of goats (for milk and meat) doubled, as did the chickens and rabbits.

By 1936 the family reports that they now have 102 goats and sell the milk and meat. Nora notes, "This is sort of a rough life and we all wear jeans or overalls most of the time, live in the open, eat and sleep well, and work hard. The ranch does not make our living yet. But we hope that someday it will." She notes that the children walk to school and back each day—a total of three miles. A fieldworker reported that the study child has many daily chores both in the household and on the farm, "more than any other child in the study." But this farm experiment in family survival ended in summer 1937 when Mike was offered a job in a Bay Area radio shop.

These two families, whose children's help with chores was vital to the family's well-being, present striking contrasts in the life of a child of the Great Depression. Robert Horton's family lived out its hardship within the severe terms of urban public assistance, whereas Mike Allen moved his family from Berkeley to a small farm in the Sierras for most of the Depression. We have little information on the Allens' marriage and the development of their children, but what we do know suggests that the emotional climate of both families was supportive of the children. However, it is apparent that the Horton family lived nearer the edge of survival, and this undoubtedly accounts for the accelerated aging of the study child, a youngster who appeared to a staff member to have skipped the years of development between infancy and adulthood.

Parental Influence in Families under Stress

The Depression created dilemmas for some Berkeley couples about whether to have more children, and it frequently exposed their children to considerable stress. We now ask whether hard times led parents to behave in ways that adversely affected their young children. The Berkeley fathers were typically the sole breadwinners and thus had much to do with whether job and income loss placed children at high risk. As we noted in chapter 7, this level of risk was most likely when fathers were emotionally unstable before the hard times.[6]

Marriages became more conflicted and dysfunctional as couples tried to cope with the harsh realities of income loss. In large part this discord reflected the acute meaning of the loss to the husbands as breadwinners and its dire consequences for their standard of living. Increasing disputes about money significantly weakened the marital bond, especially in families headed by men who became more worried, tense, and explosive. Notably, we find that this path to shattered marital relations did not apply to wives—income loss did not increase marital discord by increasing their emotional instability.

When men's economic misfortune and personal limitations strained family life, their wives typically countered by attempting to shore them up and care for the young. Consider an earlier study of the young Berkeley children conducted by Elder and colleagues during the worst years of the Depression before 1935.[7] Most were three to six years old, a time of primary dependence on their mothers. The 1930 interview shows that some women were affectionate toward their children while others were much less so. We expected mothers who were above average on affection to be protective of their children when there was family conflict. Their love and nurture most likely established a culture that regulated the fathers' actions. But did the mothers' affection curb men's inclination to be arbitrary in disciplining children in hard-pressed families?

The evidence shows that a substantial loss of family income, coupled with a father's emotional instability, dramatically increased the likelihood of a child having temper outbursts in response to the father's arbitrary discipline. Erratic discipline tended to express the mood of the parent so that the child never knew what to expect. The child's emotional outbursts were measured by severity and frequency. To determine whether the mother's affection protected the study child from the father's mistreatment, we divided the families at the median on the mother's affection for the child and compared the two subgroups on the effect that the father's instability and income loss, as expressed through his arbitrary actions (1933–35), had on the child's outbursts.

Consistent with expectations, the emotional instability men brought to the Depression, their heavy income loss, and their arbitrary discipline were most likely to generate bad-tempered outbursts by the study children—especially when they were not protected by an affectionate mother.[8] The total effect of these factors is three times their effect when children were protected by the mother's affection. This contrast applies to both boys and girls at this age. The father's arbitrary discipline is a primary link between his pre-Depression emotional instability and income loss and the child's outbursts—but it is consequential only when children lacked their mothers' protection.

The mother's initial attachment to the study child thus identifies contrasting family trajectories under the economic pressures of the early 1930s. One path led toward the child's mistreatment and subsequent problem behavior, the other led toward a more benign outcome where the child was protected from the adverse influence of Depression hardship and the father's punitiveness. The contrasting dynamics of these pathways highlight the value of comparing family processes in different circumstances. Doing so provides a conditional answer to how children from economically deprived families fared during the early years of the 1930s. The child's gender did not make a reliable difference in any of these outcomes.

The mistreatment the Berkeley children in deprived families experienced may be associated with personal characteristics that placed them at greater risk. The best measure of such early child behavior in the Berkeley archive is an index of problem behavior that would elicit a harsh response by parents at age eighteen months. The mothers were asked about the study child during this initial interview. The index calculates the percentage of thirty-five items that together reflect the degree of problem behavior.

As with children's bad-tempered outbursts, the most notable contrast on the continuity of problem behavior operates in tandem with the affection the mother expressed for the study child.[9] Among mothers who were above average on affection, the child's problem behavior at eighteen months of age did not persist up to 1933–35. But among the least affectionate mothers, children with high scores on problem behavior at eighteen months were likely to continue such conduct up to the mid-1930s. The mothers of problem children were also likely to have difficult spouses who responded to their troubled children in arbitrary and punitive ways.

Substantial differences between girls and boys were observed only during the later years of grade school. We see this expressed in family configurations by deprivation and class origin. The data come from annual interviews with the Berkeley children in grade school. A staff member assessed children's warmth toward their mothers and fathers on scales from 1 to 5, from least to most positive.[10] Scores were averaged across ages eight to ten. Consistent with observations of parents' behavior, the effects of economic deprivation were expressed in girls' greater warmth toward their mothers and boys' diminished warmth toward their fathers, with adjustments for social class in 1929. The affectional status of mothers relative to fathers was especially prominent in deprived families with weak marital ties.

Children's sense of family security provides additional insight into the developmental implications of these gender differences.[11] Boys in deprived families were rated less secure and more hostile toward fathers than boys in families spared such hardship. Girls in economically deprived households, by contrast, experienced greater family security than girls in nondeprived families, reflecting the warmth of mother-daughter relations under extreme hardship. This female bond stands out as the strongest intergenerational tie among deprived families in the Great Depression and represents a general theme of kinship when male support is absent or precarious.[12]

With these observations in mind, we see that under hardship the social configuration of households appears to have shifted toward the emotional centrality and power of the mother, coupled with the father's more estranged, marginal status, a family structure with significant developmental consequences for both sons and daughters. When hard times came to families, boys

tended to lose more than girls in parental affection. Boys became more periph-
eral and girls more central to parents and to family affairs.

The marriage between a boy's mother and father can reveal more about
his family experience in the Depression than his feelings for either parent. A
mother's prominence during her son's early years would let her control the
meaning of the father's behavior through her own attitudes and interpretation, an account that would be least charitable in a conflicted marriage. This
suggests that marital compatibility in 1930–31 was highly consequential in determining boys' experience of the Depression.

When parents did not get along (below average), we find that economic
deprivation most notably impaired the family security of boys during the later
years of grade school (ages eight to ten). Weaker marital bonds are strongly
correlated with economic deprivation and a lack of family security. But this
does not apply to girls. Strong marital ties did not give girls a more secure
sense of family. They were likely to have a more positive sense of family security when mothers did not get along with fathers than when parents had
positive relationships. This finding reflects our point about strong intergenerational ties among women—that they tend to flourish when men lack family
authority.

How were these influences and outcomes expressed in the personalities of
boys and girls? In families marked by marital conflict and violence, boys in
deprived households were less productive in goal orientation and less ambitious than those in nondeprived households. These boys also stand out on
submissiveness. They were least prepared to cope with adversity. Noted psychologist M. Brewster Smith states that this behavior pattern suggests a circle
of causation in which setbacks, imagined and actual, make one "hesitant to
try."[13] On the other hand, we observe little evidence of this syndrome among
boys from deprived families that benefited from the good fortune of supportive marital relations. Assertiveness and self-adequacy represent the principal
advantage these young people have over the economically deprived whose
problems were exacerbated by marital divisiveness.

Elements of "learned helplessness" (depressed feelings, withdrawal, and
passivity) distinguish boys who experienced both the pressures of economic
deprivation and marital conflict during the early 1930s, and in some ways their
family life consisted of the uncontrollable, aversive outcomes that are known
to play a major role in the development of this pattern of behavior.[14] Where
there was marital strife, economic deprivation markedly increased parents'
negative responses to boys, parents' unpredictable behavior, and the prospect
of fathers' impairment in family roles. Men who suffered heavy income loss

and unemployment without the affirmation of close ties to a spouse were more indifferent and punitive toward their sons that those who had their spouses' support.

Parental deprivation involving the father and the unpredictable world of a disorganized family mark a plausible link between Depression hardship in the 1930s and the problem behavior of boys who lacked support from loving parents when times became difficult. Painful memories of interactions with their fathers were among the most vivid childhood recollections of the Berkeley men's sons.[15] As one recalled, "I don't think he ever really heard me, really understood me . . . usually I related to him as a scared, worried, frightened child."

Having Children and Failing to Nurture Them

Looking back on the Depression decade, we can better appreciate what a challenging time it was for men and women of the 1900 generation to start and grow a family and to give children the care and nurture they needed. This was certainly the case for couples who lost heavily in the economic collapse, but we need to remember the many couples who were spared such hardship. Their losses were no greater than the decline in the cost of living, but they lived with the fear that calamity could come their way. The misfortune of friends, relatives, and families in the neighborhood kept alive their apprehension about having another child.

Among families that suffered economic reverses, life became harder if they also carried problems into this situation, whether economic, mental, or marital. Some of the men had to move back in with parents who were skeptical of their ability to support themselves, confirming that judgment. Men who were tense and irritable before the economic collapse became explosive when faced with ever more adversity in financial problems and disputes with wife and in-laws. The more frequent such occasions, the less couples shared, and the weaker the marriage became. Emotionally broken marriages fueled dysfunction with more adversity in children's lives, younger or older. Though affectionate mothers tended to shield daughters from this adversity, their sons were not as fortunate.

The developmental meaning of this gender difference depended in large part on how young the Berkeley study children were in 1932–34 when the full impact of the economic depression occurred. They were heavily dependent on parental care at this time, yet the Berkeley boys were less likely than the girls to receive care from both mother and father. The boys who grew up in economically deprived families were more apt to be psychologically disadvantaged by such adversity than the girls were. This disadvantage was revealed by a comparative study of children from Oakland, California, who were seven to eight years older than the Berkeley children (the Oakland children were born in 1920–21).[16] This birth cohort of boys was old enough to carry responsibilities in both their households and the community. They were less at risk of parents' quarrels than the Berkeley boys and ended up more independent and self-confident.

By contrast, the Oakland girls from deprived families were drawn into household responsibilities at a time of physical and sociosexual maturation, and they often lacked attractive clothes for social activities with peers. Consequently, they were more adversely affected by Depression hardship than the Berkeley girls, who benefited from their mothers' love and support during their critical early years of maturation. By taking gendered expectations into account, these cohort differences (Oakland versus Berkeley) are consistent with Norman Ryder's observation that as each cohort encounters historical change, "it is distinctively marked by the career stage it occupies."[17]

As we have seen, evidence on the fathers and the mothers in economically deprived families tells very different stories about how they influenced their children during hard times. As the primary or sole earners, fathers were expected to be the socioeconomic backbone of their families. However, their widespread losses in the Great Depression brought family hardships that damaged their emotional health and that of the family. Their instability in the 1920s generated marital conflict and mistreatment of children. Young children in these families depended most heavily on the nurture and emotional shelter mothers provided. But a good many children, especially boys, lacked such support and protection and ended up carrying this legacy into their adolescent and adult years.

9

In the Midst of Kin

We did it [helped kin] before, when we had even less than we have now.
BERKELEY WOMAN

Economic hardship marked the beginning of extraordinary efforts by kin to support and share with one another, efforts involving individuals of widely varying means and situations, from grandparents to siblings on both sides of the family. Few Berkeley households emerged from the Depression decade untouched by the claims and resources of kin: four out of five participated in some form of material exchange or transfer over this period.

Kinship ties are known to wax and wane with the economic circumstances of families and generations.[1] Referring to a tailspin in the cotton industry of mid-nineteenth-century Lancashire, England, Michael Anderson writes, "As the crisis worsened and involved more and more of the population, 'huddling' increased. More and more houses became empty, and more and more had two families sharing the rent and fuel and pooling their resources."[2] Many years after the Great Depression, a Berkeley woman described a similar pattern, remembering that "it seemed as if every third house was empty."

In this chapter, we view two forms of kin assistance among the Berkeley families and generations across the Depression decade: the general giving and receiving of material aid (money, goods), and pooling or saving resources through shared living quarters, either by moving in with relatives (as a guest) or by accepting relatives into the household (as a host).

Each form of dependence involves strategies of adaptation that we have examined in earlier chapters: borrowing from relatives, cutting back on expenditures by pooling resources in a shared living arrangement, and mothers' entering the labor force. The kin network expands our perspective on the family economy by centering on the reciprocal roles of recipient and provider and on the distinctive qualities of kinship that made giving possible even at a time of great scarcity. Within the kinship system, the drama of survival in the Depression involved both the deprived households as likely recipients of aid and the helping role of families that somehow managed to escape heavy losses.

We begin with the route of material aid across the Depression decade and its relation to the social standing of families before hard times. The pressures to give and receive aid were structured by the interplay of Depression hardship and the position and resources of families before the 1930s, as indexed by social class and family stage. This dynamic also applies to household composition in the 1930s, as relatives were added and departed.

The doubled-up household, a common if temporary living arrangement among the Berkeley families, represents a strategic context in which to explore both the benefits and the costs of kinship. As Rosser and Harris note in their study of family and social change in South Wales, it is "the stress and strains within the household group rather than the wider family group that are most acutely felt."[3] These implications appear in the concluding section of the chapter as we examine the specific relatives who lived with the Berkeley families, their significance in family life, and the strain associated with their presence.

Configurations of Kin Assistance

With records from 1929 to the end of the 1930s, we can observe patterns of giving and receiving money and goods, as well as whether the Berkeley families were living with relatives as hosts or guests, in three important periods—before, during, and after the Depression, and especially in relation to the second economic downturn of 1937–38.[4] Whether a resource or a burden, the relatives who appear regularly in this history are generally those who made a difference in family life. As such, we are dealing with what anthropologist Raymond Firth and his colleagues have called the "effective set" of kin.[5]

Kinship assistance and dependence most likely entailed a sequence of fluctuations in response to changing economic conditions: a sharp rise in assistance from 1929 to a peak in the Depression's trough, followed by a downward trend until the second economic downturn at the end of the 1930s. This "Depression model" depicts how the Berkeley families interacted with aid and economic hardship, each family occupying a different position before hard times—in social class and in family stage (as indexed by age of household head).[6] Families in the working class and with younger heads were likely to depend on kin in some way before the economic downturn and thus may have continued in this dependent state with the onset of income loss after 1929.

Within each family, kinship supply and demand hinged on the number of relatives nearby and their economic standing during the Depression. In theory, having more extensive networks of nearby relatives with stronger material well-being would lessen the burden of having to support kin who had heavy income losses and unemployment. Slightly more than four out of five couples in the Berkeley sample reported at least one surviving parent on either side of the family, and two-thirds of these parents were living in the Greater Bay Region as of 1931. In lieu of economic data on kin during the 1930s, we use the class position of families (1929) to estimate economic need among relatives—the lower the class position, the greater the likelihood of substantial kin demands.

Especially in the context of kin, "helping" may entail sacrifices that jeopardize one's own welfare.[7] Why are hard-pressed families willing to assist relatives in need? Such actions go beyond self-interest to the moral character of kin ties. According to anthropologist Meyer Fortes, the essential feature of kinship morality is "prescriptive altruism," in which "sharing occurs without reckoning."[8] Long-term reciprocity is possible "because it is not reciprocity that is the motive but morality."[9] This perspective is based on the generalized motivation, and expectation, of sacrificing self for the welfare of others.

With so many Depression families in acute need, those who were spared hardship may have felt stronger obligations to help, especially when hard-pressed families were preoccupied with their own survival.[10] In the absence of a moral motive, uncertain reciprocation would favor a more calculated choice, both in the form and amount of aid and for impoverished and fortunate families alike. Such a decision would take account of the perceived need and worthiness of the party, the obligation to help as judged by the resources of other relatives, and the history of reciprocity between parties.[11]

In Berkeley, middle-class families—particularly the nondeprived—struggled to respond appropriately to the needs of hard-pressed relatives. Several factors complicated decisions about assistance. First, these families had little experience with recurring crises (e.g., disabling illness, unemployment) that necessitate help from relatives, which occur more frequently in the working class. Choices about whether, who, and how to help—and how to ask for it—were relatively unfamiliar to middle-class families. Second, their values (e.g., related to privacy or autonomy) increased the bothersomeness of relatives in need when their needs were perceived as a threat to one's autonomy and financial security.[12] Third, requests for assistance from multiple family members often pitted the needs of relatives against each other, or the demands of the wife's family against those of the husband's, which we discuss in greater detail below. All these factors combined to induce a great deal of what sociologists

Robert Merton and Elinor Barber called "sociological ambivalence" around providing assistance.[13] On one hand, families want to fulfill their obligations to kin and provide help. On the other hand, they want to protect their own livelihoods and not risk tensions in selecting to whom, what, and how to give. For example, based on contact with one of the middle-class families in the study, an Institute staff member noted that the husband, who maintained his professional job and owned three homes throughout the Depression, worried a great deal about family members in need of financial assistance. He gave his sisters and parents monthly sums for some years. His wife, however, referred to his family members as "parasites."

The full story of kinship politics in the Depression entails the joining of families through marriage, for the husband's and wife's relatives emerge as potential and actual competitors in the tug-of-war over scarce resources. Such competition threatens marital stability when pressures shift primary allegiance from spouse to parents, especially in the husband's case. His primary allegiance to his wife means that he will take her side if his parents criticize her and that he will reject their attempts to weaken her position as wife and homemaker by intruding. For the husband's relatives, it is likely to mean that they suspect his wife of trying to alienate him from them, of showing preferences for her side of the family over his, of failing to take proper care of him, and the like. His wife may resent their hold on him, because in effect it "reaffirms his status as a child in his parents' house instead of a man in hers."[14]

The challenge of reconciling ties of blood with those of marriage bears most directly on decisions regarding what might be termed the "last resort" of kin assistance—sharing living quarters with members of the parent generation, especially the husband's mother. Whether as host or guest, this option has consistently ranked at the bottom of preferred alternatives of kin assistance among American families, though unbearable hardship in the 1930s frequently left families with no choice.[15] Judging from the literature on multigeneration households, doubling up with parents in the 1930s should be associated with more conflict, emotional ambivalence, and tension than the nuclear household, given similar economic conditions.[16]

The wife's central role in the household, her greater compatibility with her own kin than with her husband's family, and the marital threat of the husband's allegiance to his parents tended to favor living with the wife's family when doubling up was necessary. This bias appears more generally in surveys of American families and undoubtedly reflects the assumed challenges in women's relationships with their mothers-in-law. Accordingly, we expect to find that a substantial majority of the relatives living in the Berkeley households over the Depression years were members of the wife's family.

However, there are good reasons to expect greater prominence of the husband's family in giving aid. One of the best options deprived men had was falling back on their fathers' resources, and they could do so with less risk to self-esteem than in seeking aid from the wife's parents or her side of the family.

Material assistance across a broad range of household needs reached a high during 1932 and 1933. The proportion of families involved in giving or receiving increased sharply between 1929 and the valley of the Depression, from 23 to 41 percent, declining slowly thereafter to approximately one-fourth of households by the end of 1936. Considering the various forms of help and their often subtle expression in family life, these estimates of prevalence are undoubtedly conservative. The convention of helping relatives almost ensures some degree of under-enumeration.

In each period, families were just as likely to be recipients as providers of aid, but they seldom performed both roles in the same year (3 percent or less). Even within a four-year span of the Depression (1932–35), most families that were helped by relatives did not reciprocate by providing economic assistance to any member of the kin network. Hardship and ability to help are important factors in the timing of reciprocation, as well as the extent of kin needs. Only among families that received aid in just one year do we observe a modest level of reciprocation: half of these families did help others in this period. We do not know what agreements and expectations accompanied material aid, or the precise economic circumstances of relatives who provided such help. One might expect greater reciprocation, and a shorter time limit on it, when money was lent—though even in this case such limits would depend on the relative's well-being and other less tangible considerations.

Giving and receiving assistance in the 1930s roughly correspond to the economic conditions of family life in the middle class and working class. For families in the working class hardship came earlier, was more severe in absolute terms, and tended to persist longer, partly owing to a brief economic downswing that came again in the late 1930s. From the beginning to the end of the decade, it was working-class families who were most likely to be on either the giving or the receiving end of kin support.

The prevalence of giving and receiving among these families increased most abruptly during the early 1930s and reached a peak in the latter half of the decade after a decline during 1934–35 (see fig. 9.1). By comparison, kin

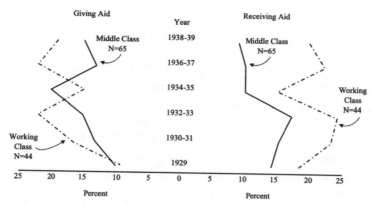

FIGURE 9.1. Giving and receiving aid among middle-class and working-class families by year (percentages). *Note*: Annual percentages were averaged to obtain values for each two-year period.

support in the middle class generally reflects the effect of deprivation during the early 1930s and the subsequent path to economic recovery. In this stratum the Depression slowly increased the burden of helping needy relatives up to 1934–35.

Staff members at the Institute were puzzled by the responsiveness of working-class families to relatives in need and by their accepting such burdens even in the most trying circumstances. The extent of sacrificial giving seemed contrary to their best interests. A foreman at a local machine shop and his wife provide a vivid illustration. Although reduced to half of his 1929 earnings by the middle of 1931, this couple continued to give a small monthly sum to the husband's parents, who were believed to be in desperate straits. Extraordinary reductions in consumption enabled the family to manage this support, but they had to discontinue it by the end of 1932. An Institute staff member at the time noted the couple's genuine concern over "[the] fact that they cannot help." Two years later the family resumed their support despite minimal improvement in their own economic situation. When questioned about the wisdom of this action, the wife replied that "we did it before when we had even less than we have now."

This case may not be representative of working-class families, but it is only among middle-class families that we find outspoken resistance to this practice, along with expressions of resentment and hostility. For example, a family is described as "disgusted with the father's brother, they think he will simply be back for more if they meet his request." In another case a staff visitor notes that "the husband resents his wife's gifts to family, he believes others could help." Though such emotions were in some cases shared by husband and wife, they were most likely to appear when each spouse took a different position on the matter.

Helping patterns suggest that, unlike middle-class families, working-class families considered kin more important than neighbors and friends. Class differences of this sort were observed in San Francisco after World War II, and they have been reported by other researchers as well.[17] Using case materials from 1930–35, we identified a subgroup of families whose social involvement with relatives at least matched their involvement with friends and neighbors. This pattern was most common in the working class, as expected, and among families of foreign parentage or Catholic affiliation. Even with statistical adjustments for ethnicity and religion, half of the working-class families ranked high on kin involvement compared with 21 percent of the middle-class families.

Who were the most prominent in helping families through the economic crisis? Were the husband's parents a standout in this respect, as we have suggested, or were the wife's parents the more important? We find two patterns for 1930–35. First, middle-class and working-class families interacted more frequently with the wife's kin than with members of the husband's family. Second, there is the primacy of hierarchy over "other" ties in the middle class. On each side of the family, middle-class families were more likely to interact frequently with parents than with other relatives, mainly brothers or sisters.

This pattern applies to the husband's family in the working class, but not to the wife's family, where parents were evenly matched with siblings. The overall configuration generally agrees with the historical record on women doing the bulk of the work to maintain family ties (by letter writing, phone calls, or visiting); on the relative strength of parent-child ties over ties to siblings or aunts and uncles in the status-conscious middle class; and on the greater solidarity of siblings in the working class.[18]

The predominant form of kin interaction differs between families that primarily gave or received aid during the Depression, and in ways that conform to expectations. From 1932 to 1934, the husband's kin were most likely to stand out when working-class families *received* help. The wife's relatives are more prominent among middle-class families that *gave* assistance. Whatever the pattern of aid, family interaction was slanted toward the wife's relatives for the middle class and the husband's kin for the working class. On each side of the family, middle class giving and receiving are linked to interaction with parents, not with brothers, sisters, or grandparents. These other (nonparental) family members are more important in the social world of working-class families who provided assistance.

If we interpret interactions as evidence of kin exchange, the data suggest that men were most likely to maintain contact with their own relatives in times of economic need, and that middle-class men were especially inclined to turn to their fathers rather than to a brother or sister. Among families that provided help it is the wife's kin, for the most part, who benefited. Material aid generally flowed toward the wife's parents in the middle class and toward the wife's siblings or other kin in the working class.

Up to this point we have viewed class patterns of material assistance for kin without considering family stage, defined by having an older or younger male head of household, during the Great Depression. The small size of the Berkeley sample requires a stepwise approach, beginning with class differences and followed by economic deprivation and family stage. Deprivation and life stage suggest very different models of kin support and need across the 1930s.

What we earlier called the "Depression model" suggests a peak level of giving and receiving during the worst years of the Depression. By contrast, a "life course model" identifies two different trends, a decline in dependence on kin among younger families over time and an increase in the prevalence of providing kin assistance for families headed by older men. The interaction of hardship and family stage points to three hypothetical patterns: providing temporary aid to nondeprived younger families; increased kin dependence among deprived older families; and the persistence of kin dependence among the families of younger men who experienced heavy income losses.

As a first step toward evaluating trends in giving and receiving aid, we examine patterns in material support over the 1930s by economic deprivation within the kin networks of middle-class and working-class families. Then we introduce family stage as a potential source of variation in helping relatives and receiving aid.

VARIATIONS BY SOCIAL CLASS AND FAMILY STAGE

Berkeley families that managed to avoid heavy economic losses were seldom in debt to relatives. Whether middle class or working class, less than a sixth of these nondeprived families ever received help from 1930 to 1936, a figure not significantly higher than the dependency level of 1929. All the action occurred among hard-pressed families, with the prevalence of aid increasing sharply during the early 1930s and then declining. Viewing the entire decade, class differences in receiving assistance are dramatic: less than 15 percent of the nondeprived middle class ever received aid from kin during the 1930s, compared with 80 percent for families in the impoverished working class.

Social class, in combination with deprivation status, provides essential information for understanding the economic needs of relatives and the culture of sharing resources. Class differences in dependency existed only for deprived families. Nearly two-thirds of deprived working-class families received aid from kin during the first half of the 1930s, compared with less than half of the deprived middle-class families. By the late 1930s, over half of the deprived working-class families were still in that position, whereas in deprived middle-class families aid had tapered off to little more than one-third.

Both economic need and a pattern of sharing were most fully expressed within the working class. The highest level of giving appears in the nondeprived working class, with over 40 percent of these families in this position during the second half of the decade. Both continuing hardship and the norm of reciprocity are reflected in the rising level of giving (from 1929 to the late 1930s) among deprived families in the working class. Reciprocating earlier aid is more common in the working class than among higher-status families (42 percent versus 21 percent).

A family's life stage also affected its propensity to give or receive assistance. Figure 9.2 shows the percentage of families receiving and giving help by year and stage. Before the Depression, families headed by young men occupied an early phase of worklife and earning potential. Consequently their assets and income were frequently insufficient to meet the demands of a growing family. More than 20 percent were getting help from relatives at the time, twice as many as families headed by older men. Depression hardship seems to have postponed the usual age-graded decline in such aid.

Kin dependence turns out to be consistently higher across the decade among younger families, apart from class and deprivation. Ordinarily one might have more evidence of sharing than of dependence among older families, but the Depression made dependence a necessity for some. The career of this group is best described by a Depression trajectory—a peak during the worst years of the 1930s followed by decline and then a modest rise during the second economic collapse of the decade. The imprint of hard times thus assumes different forms in the two age groups, and each departs from predictions based on the "normative" life course.

Giving aid also varies from the life course norm. As the economy turned downward, younger families had fewer resources to offer kin than older families did. By comparison, the older group's career path approximates expectations based on the life course—its level of giving increased from 1929 to the late 1930s. This path may seem surprising in view of family needs during the early 1930s, but it reflects different trends in the two social classes. Among older families, middle-class giving rose slowly to a peak in the late 1930s,

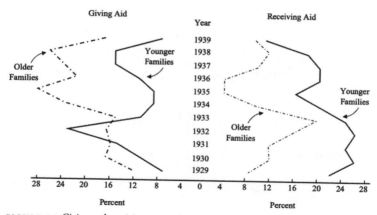

FIGURE 9.2. Giving and receiving economic assistance among older and younger families, by year (percentages).

whereas assistance from working-class families reached a high point from 1932 to 1933. The difference largely reflects the stronger cumulative pressure of kin needs within the working class.

We achieve greater clarity on the helping behavior of older and younger families by turning to the working class and precise measures of deprivation experience. In figure 9.3 we see that, for both age groups, material assistance is concentrated among nondeprived households, but a family's life stage makes a difference in the pattern over time. Among younger nondeprived families, level of giving peaked at slightly more than 30 percent in 1932–33, then dropped steadily to little more than 10 percent by the end of the decade. In the older nondeprived group, helping increased to 50 percent in 1934–35 then declined only slightly to 1938–39. Throughout the decade, this small group of older nondeprived families carried a heavy burden in helping relatives, a pattern that differs most sharply from the low rate of support among older deprived families.

The good fortune of families who were spared hardship altogether represents the most important determinant of resource sharing during the 1930s, but not all such families took part. Kinship needs, values, and resource position—as indexed by social class, deprivation status, and family stage—appear to account for much of this variation. The greater prevalence of assistance among working-class families is consistent with both needs and culture in this stratum.

Older nondeprived families occupied a more favorable position to share than their younger counterparts, and they were more likely to do so. Younger

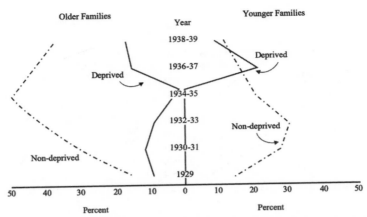

FIGURE 9.3. Giving economic aid to kin among working-class families by career stage, economic deprivation, and year (percentages). *Note:* The younger group includes thirteen nondeprived and eleven deprived families. The older category includes thirteen deprived and seven nondeprived families.

families in the deprived group entered the Depression at a high level of dependency and generally maintained a high level through most of the decade. Two-thirds of the families on public assistance in 1932–33 also received such help in 1929, and deprivation had the effect of prolonging dependency for this group.

The subtle dynamics of kin assistance largely escape our records, but we occasionally see the pressures, expectations, and priorities that made life for the older, deprived men especially trying, even unbearable. The misfortune of job loss, even after a stable worklife of twenty years or more, became a weapon in the hands of some thoughtless family members who questioned the character of a man who could not find a job. A middle-aged craftsman, for example, faced such accusations from his mother, who gave monthly sums to help tide the family over his unemployment. After two years of fruitless searching, he complained bitterly to a staff visitor in 1933, "My mother thinks I'm the biggest boob in the country because I can't find anything. I wish she would try and get something."

Living Together and Apart

Considering flows of kinship assistance across the Depression decade brings us to their most intimate and potentially consequential form, sharing a household. A National Health Survey in 1935–36 referred to sharing households as well as resources as an "adaptive response to economic pressures."[19] This feature, along with the greater frequency of multiple earners, accounts for the more favorable per capita income of multifamily households at this time. Of the Berkeley families that ever gave or received aid in the 1930s, 80 percent also shared living quarters with one or more relatives at some point.

WHEN RELATIVES ENTER HOUSEHOLDS

To generate income in the Depression era, many families took in boarders and lodgers.[20] These might be not only strangers but also family members. Living with relatives ranged from caring for an elderly mother who paid the market value for her board and room to providing room and board for no payment of any kind. In other situations an equitable payment might be made in labor, as when a live-in grandmother managed the household and cared for the children so the mother could take paid employment. Relatives might also pay monthly sums, like boarders or lodgers, a family strategy for making money rather than sharing resources.

Across the Depression decade, the general flow of assistance and doubling up identifies three modes of family functioning and kin support: living with relatives at some point in the decade and either receiving or giving money or goods (52 percent) or, if not, exchanging services or intangible resources (11 percent); maintaining independent households but exchanging material resources (15 percent); or never sharing living quarters with kin or giving or receiving material assistance (21 percent).

Over half of all Berkeley families hosted relatives at some point in the 1930s, in contrast to little more than 10 percent who ever were guests of relatives. Most of the hosts and guests lived with relatives for three years or more. Deprived circumstances had little effect on the prevalence of hosting except in the working class, where nondeprived families were most likely to take in relatives as household members, especially during the worst years of the Depression. Economic troubles tended to prolong residential dependence, especially among the younger, working-class families. Eight working-class families were living with relatives in 1932, and six of them were forced by economic hardship, illness, and marital troubles to remain in this position from 1929 to 1933.

A family's transition from nuclear status to that of host or guest changed its identity and its dynamics. Hosts tended to retain their authority over household affairs, though perhaps challenged at times by a mother or mother-in-law accustomed to managing both her own household and the lives of her offspring. The wife's domestic obligations were also likely to increase, even with help from guests. For guests, prolonged residence in the household of a family member, especially a parent, generally indicated a state of dependence.

Whatever the contrasts between the social and emotional reality of these living arrangements, hosting relatives or being hosted by them may have made the difference between family survival and the "poorhouse," symbolized by dependence on the public treasury. Social agencies and New Deal programs carried a heavy burden of family support during the 1930s, but our data suggest that the burden would have been much greater without the sharing of households and resources among members of the Berkeley area kinship system. However, the Depression's enduring legacy of shared households in the twentieth century is likely to include a "renewed appreciation of living apart in nuclear families" through memories of the time when so many families had to live together.

THE EXPERIENCE OF DOUBLING UP

Beyond its intended consequences of assisting relatives, co-residence produced a range of unintended consequences, from cultural and authority conflicts and overcrowding to frayed nerves and explosive tempers. The pace of such change was bound to be extraordinary for the elderly parents of the Berkeley 1900 generation who came from a world of small towns and agriculture, a third being born in Europe.

Adding relatives to the household increased the social density of living space, often producing more household stress.[21] With a higher number of persons per room, residents are more likely to experience excessive social demands and a lack of privacy. Over the decades these factors have been associated with a host of negative psychological and relationship outcomes.[22] However, the issue extends beyond household size to the particular people living there. Depending on health, personality, and adaptive skills, adding just one relative in a large home might make all members feel crowded. A grandmother's presence sometimes made for a crowded household.

Two general status distinctions apply to members of households that became complex by adding one relative or more: adding the husband's or wife's parents/grandparents, which "extended" the household upward in the family structure; and adding the husband's or wife's siblings, which "expanded" the household outward. Overall, 23 percent of the complex households were "extended," 36 percent were "expanded," and the most complex had relatives from both categories. Over the decade 1930–41, the most common additions were the mother of one of the spouses and a brother or sister. Among the households with kin during the decade, 55 percent included the widowed mother of one of the spouses, with most coming from the wife's side of the family. Only 17 percent of the households hosted a father of either spouse.

A family's social class and life stage (defined by the husband's age) before the economic collapse had much to do with what relative entered its household during the 1930s. The older middle-class families led all subgroups on the percentage of extended households (48 percent) and ranked lowest on expanded households (10 percent). Of these latter families, 43 percent had a residential history that included relatives from both categories. By comparison, older families in the working class were most likely to live with brothers or sisters (59 percent), and seldom lived with parents (12 percent). This composition also described the residential history of young families regardless of social class. When younger couples moved in with a parent, the household typically included younger brothers or sisters. As one Berkeley woman recalled years later, "There seemed to be quite a few people who were moving in with parents and children, with the older families."

Distinctive class values regarding privacy and space emerged from family observations and interviews on sharing households. In the records of middle-class families, we found clear markers about the prospect of sharing one's household with a parent or an in-law. The boundary between the nuclear family space and kin was much firmer in middle-class families than in the working class. Records on middle-class families often included a note that a relative might have to move in—phrased in terms of "worry" or the "hope that another way might be found" or references to the entry of kin and frequent expressions of relief when the relative left. For example, the wife of an accountant said in 1933 that she was "afraid" they might have to take in her husband's mother and that "the children are very fond of her, but grandmother drives me crazy because she makes me feel uncomfortable." A year later an observer's note quotes her as saying, "I'm terribly glad I didn't weaken and let my mother-in-law live with us."

GENERATIONAL TENSIONS

Social class as well as generational identity, family affiliation, and gender had much to do with the emotional chemistry in Depression households. From annual household records in 1930–39, we find that most of the Berkeley families with relatives in their households lived with members of only one side of the family (82 percent). Approximately two-thirds of these asymmetrical households included only the wife's relatives, a figure that generally corresponds with the results of cross-sectional surveys and with a "matrilateral" bias in family life that results in stronger relationships and interaction with the wife's kin.[23]

Twenty-five of the thirty-nine households with a mother in residence at some point included the wife's mother, who stayed for an average of three years. The wife's mother typically remained as long as the husband's mother, but her presence made less of a difference in structuring interaction with her side of the family. Virtually all the households that included the wife's mother had more interaction with kin, especially on her side of the family. When the husband's mother lived in the household, contact with kin was notably less.

In the middle class, a live-in mother was more apt to be a source of tension than in the working class. Gifts from the wife's side of the family threatened the husband's status as provider. The presence of a mother from either side often led to conflicts over control in child rearing and dependence. Personality complaints appear more often in the records of middle-class families than working-class families. Class differences in generational tensions had to do with values, such as privacy or freedom of action, as well as with the type of household. Extended households provided shelter for older parents in the middle class, while expanded households sheltered siblings and other kin. Nevertheless, tensions in middle-class households often reflected the complaints of old-age infirmities and the unacceptable claims of a senior family member who had no role.

One picture of what the presence of an older mother meant in middle-class households can be pieced together from the case materials. In one family, a husband's mother entered the household in 1933 to help care for the children during his lengthy illness. Soon the grandmother became a more permanent resident with the authority to run the household, owing largely to the husband's unwillingness to set limits on her actions. When an Institute staff member asked about the family several years later, the wife burst out, "Well, as a matter of fact, our household would run nicely if it were not for grandmother."

Records describe a pervasive undercurrent of hostility and irritation in the home, with incidents so unpleasant that at times the wife chose to spend at least part of the day out with her children. The husband noted that on several mornings, he had come downstairs feeling grand then almost decided to not wait for breakfast because of things his mother said. As the wife put it, "Grandmother can throw a wet blanket over the group faster than anyone I have ever seen." The family had a maid, but grandmother, according to a staff visitor, "insists on doing things the maid could do and then acts like a martyr. She pays no heed to the rules laid down by the husband, who hesitates to countermand her orders when she gives them. If he does, she immediately starts wailing, 'Oh nobody wants me here. I'm just in the way, an old person.'"

As in any conflict, there is more than one side to the story, and we have only the couple's account as reported by the Institute staff. Whatever the personal history of this grandparent, her experience of being unappreciated can be understood in the rapidly changing world she is experiencing. When an elderly middle-class mother became a member of a son's or daughter's household, her generational difference from the others was accentuated by the intensity of social change from the late nineteenth century into the twentieth century.

This was most striking in the new middle class, with its expansion of higher education. Lacking a social role or function in the household, older mothers were likely to feel out of place, useless, unwanted, or misunderstood. They were not equipped to appreciate the emerging social roles of women in the community and workplace or to value more contemporary views of young children and their rearing. The aged mother of a middle-class son might well usurp household authority on issues that conflicted with his college-educated wife's customary decisions and actions.

Generational differences became especially troublesome when the aged parents, especially mothers, acted on values and beliefs not shared by her daughter-in-law and son. One mother who fits this description grew up in rural England and vigorously took issue with her daughter-in-law's lax views on child rearing. She advocated harsher discipline whenever possible. Her daughter-in-law asked her not to discipline the children, but she continued to impose her values. Typically the mother-in-law would react badly to any reproach, often not speaking to anyone in the family for days at a time.

Other mothers became "cranky" when the household was not run as they thought it should be. They wanted the world they once knew and still preferred instead of the world they experienced in the home of their adult daughter or son. Their critical outlook, irritability, and unsolicited advice or demands were symptomatic of life in a world made alien and irreversible by a rapidly changing world. In a reflective mood, a daughter hoped she would "not be like this when I grow old. I know she is that way and can't help it, so I try to leave her alone when she fusses."

Battles between the husband's mother and wife over household authority most directly involved the dependence of wives in the middle class. Mounting tensions inevitably brought unwilling husbands into the fray. One Berkeley man observed that he never stepped into the door at night without saying to himself, "Well, I wonder what the atmosphere will be when I get inside?" Several years later he returned from a business trip to Los Angeles to find that his mother had ordered his wife out of their house. Though he was furious and "humiliated" by this event, the man's genuine fondness for his mother, who had no housing alternative, ensured this situation would continue despite the wife's resentment and despair. In households that included the husband's mother, complaints over a deteriorating marriage and criticism from in-laws appear together in family records that extend back to the pre-Depression era.

Linked Lives in Kinship

Earlier chapters show that all members of the Berkeley generation were influenced in some way by their variable exposure to family hardship. This influence had consequences for their lives and for their children's development, but the picture is incomplete without considering the role of other relatives living nearby—their own parents, for example, or aunts and uncles, adult brothers and sisters. These members of the kin network appear throughout the decade in family records, observations, and interviews. In this chapter we report what we have learned about these relatives and their role in both giving and receiving assistance, including sharing households.

Whether or not the Berkeley families were spared economic hardship, four out of five helped or were helped by relatives at some point. One of the most striking features of this exchange is that later in the decade many of the assisted families were also providing support in a web of interdependent lives. Moreover, as in the working class, the most economically strapped families stood out in contributions to relatives and even family friends. In three out of four families, these contributions consisted of giving a parent or child a place to live. This assistance enabled many families to avoid the humiliation of applying for public welfare.

The Berkeley families were not systematically asked about the specific amounts or types of assistance received from or given to kin, but they talked about them at length. When the Depression decade ended, virtually all deprived families from the upper middle class had recovered from their economic loss. However, these Berkeley families were likely to object to helping their needy relatives and frequently noted their reluctance to take in an older relative, such as the wife's or husband's mother.

By contrast, the working class entered the Great Depression with much less in material and social resources than the middle class, and half of these families lost most of their 1929 income. For them the heavy hand of prolonged hardship persisted into the 1940s and industrial mobilization for World War II. Most of the families that were spared unemployment and major income loss were actively assisting their less fortunate relatives, such as older siblings and a parent. They made economic sacrifices for their relatives as they were about to enter the war years, which also entailed sacrifices at home and abroad.

The scarcity of family income in the Depression decade led to a doubling up of the generations, with its household stresses, perhaps giving more priority to family life in a "nuclear" household. This outcome represents a plausible effect of "huddling" during the Great Depression. The growth of war industries in the Bay Area also made housing for war workers both scarce and costly and soon led to an increase of lodgers in Berkeley households. War-spurred industrial growth supplied the work sought by the underemployed and jobless during the last years of the 1930s. The long decline of the labor market had finally come to an end.

PART FOUR

War on the Home Front

As the 1930s came to an end, most Berkeley families, along with the community at large, had stories to tell. For the most part those in the middle class had recovered from economic loss, and those in the working class were hoping for better times ahead. But dark clouds had formed over Europe with Germany's invasion of Poland, a development that prompted President Franklin D. Roosevelt to consider a third term so that he could lead the country in Europe's defense. His New Deal for America had preserved democracy during the Great Depression, and he pledged to work for a peaceful world that would not involve America in fighting wars abroad.

But national mobilization was underway in developments that would soon alter the Berkeley community and the lives of its residents. This change sprang from America's response to the urgent pleas for military support from Great Britain's Winston Churchill, prompted by Germany's conquest of European countries. Under mounting pressure, in 1940 Congress finally modified the Neutrality Act and passed critical legislation to establish Lend-Lease. Both actions enabled the United States to begin sending war matériel to Britain. But the nation's survival required transforming America into a major wartime economy and military power.

At a meeting of Roosevelt and his White House advisers, Army Chief of Staff George C. Marshall conferred privately with Roosevelt to emphasize how critical it was to "get serious about arming America for war."[1] He concluded, "If you don't do something and do it right away, I don't know what's going to happen to the country." Roosevelt not only accepted his advisers' recommendations but promptly sent Congress a proposal that called for a stunning increase in the army's appropriation from $24 million to $700 million, along with an appropriation for some fifty thousand planes.

To head the country's industrial war mobilization, Roosevelt selected William Knudsen of General Motors, a proven leader of the American automobile industry. Despite Britain's critical state, Knudsen had difficulty convincing industry leaders of the "transformation" that full-scale mobilization required. And he continued to face a Congress that stubbornly resisted a future with the country at war in Europe. But everywhere he traveled he encountered the need to revitalize an aging industrial base so it could meet the extraordinary scale of forthcoming war demands. To underscore this enormous challenge, he told a stunned audience of business and government representatives that "the war effort was going to require a complete retooling of nearly every American factory over the next eighteen months."[2] This would be necessary if America were to become "the arsenal of democracy."

The initial effect of mobilization on Berkeley and the Bay Area before the Japanese attack on Pearl Harbor stemmed from an urgency to build merchant ships for Britain, spurred in large measure by the enormous shipping losses that threatened to cut off all supplies to the island nation. Henry Kaiser and his Six Companies, Inc., came up with a solution. Kaiser had an unparalleled record for completing huge construction projects such as Boulder Dam, and he had recently turned to building shipyards and cargo ships. With the financial support to Britain of Lend-Lease, Kaiser agreed to build the first shipyard on the Richmond, California, mudflats in the rainy winter of 1941. In record time, the keel of the first British ship was laid by early March.

The shipyard produced what became known as the Liberty Ship. A single design was mass-produced in a weld shop, then major sections (e.g., the bow) were transferred by giant cranes to shipways at the yard. The operation simplified construction and thereby markedly expanded the pool of potential workers. Instead of searching for scarce skilled workers, this mass-production innovation enabled shipyards to hire the unskilled. Across the war years, the Kaiser shipbuilding empire in the Bay Area increased to four shipyards, producing more than seven hundred ships for the Allied and American merchant fleets. By summer 1941, war production had taken off to the point where defense spending was three times its level at the end of 1940. And in the next six months it soared more than twelvefold in response to the ever-growing needs of Great Britain for food as well as war matériel. The high wages paid to shipyard workers and those in other war industries dramatically improved their families' income.

During the winter of 1941, the Japanese military threat in Asia, along with the danger to Great Britain's survival, added to the pressing military concerns of the Roosevelt administration.[3] Developments in Asia were far removed from the everyday world of families living in Berkeley and the San

Francisco–Oakland region. Many elements of a war-mobilized society were along the coast, including major naval stations from San Francisco to San Diego. The navy's Mare Island, between Berkeley and San Francisco, provided a ship repair facility and drydocks unmatched at the time. The army made its presence known through the Fifth Army Command of General John L. DeWitt at the Presidio in San Francisco and nearby army camps. In addition, key defense industries, from oil refineries to bomber plants and shipyards, were constant reminders of California's vulnerability to hostile action from across the Pacific.

Such action came without warning on December 7, 1941, when waves of Japanese planes attacked Pearl Harbor, Hawaii, drawing America into a two-front war across the Atlantic and Pacific Oceans. Japan's declaration of war on the United States was followed by that of Nazi Germany and Italy—the Axis powers. In California the emotional shock of the Pearl Harbor attack had much to do with the loss of battleship crews who had been stationed at the state's major naval stations. They had been redeployed in 1940 as a defensive measure against Japanese aggression in the Pacific region, and now these capital ships of the Pacific were sunk or severely damaged, lying side by side in Pearl Harbor. It would take some time for our Berkeley families to grasp the enormity of this military assault and its devastation.

The Pearl Harbor attack was part of a long historical decline of relations between America and the Empire of Japan, and the same could be said for relations between first- and second-generation Japanese residents and sectors of California's white population—what Kevin Starr describes as the Far Right movement of white Californians and an extremist labor movement.[4] The Chinese Must Go! movement of the 1870s had evolved into the anti-Japanese agitation of the early twentieth century, with its discriminatory legislation, leading some Japanese leaders to regard war with the United States as an inevitable response to blatant racial discrimination and insults.

The perceived Japanese threat following Pearl Harbor was reinforced by reports of Japanese submarines along the California coast that sank cargo ships and shelled oil storage tanks in the Santa Barbara region of Southern California.[5] These threats fueled the state of mind that led to President Roosevelt's tragic executive order in March 1941 for the roundup and incarceration of all Japanese on the Pacific Coast, citizens or not.

California's transition to war preparedness on the home front was swift, as historian Arthur Verge has noted.[6] The windows of factories producing war matériel were soon painted over, and work shifts were established around the clock. Civil defense established a policy of blackouts and then dimouts for communities and residences. As Verge notes, "Anti-aircraft gun emplacements quickly sprang up among the coastal cities and towns, especially around defense plants and military bases. Miles of barbed wire fences were laid along the coast shores to slow any enemy invasion."[7] Planners set up a civil defense system along the California coast so volunteers could contribute to the war effort on the home front. Thousands of residents signed up as first aid providers, air raid and neighborhood wardens, and plane spotters.

It is in this aftermath of Pearl Harbor that we turn to our Berkeley families on the home front of World War II. The women and men of this generation were now in their forties and fifties, and most of their children were between ten and twenty. The younger children, born in 1928–29, were passing through early adolescence and were generally too young to be drafted during World War II. But they were at an impressionable age and living on the very edge of war in the Pacific. Some had older brothers who would serve.

In chapter 10 we observe the Berkeley families as they adapted to life in a war-mobilized town after a long decade of doing without for many and a life of privilege for others. We begin with their exposure to a community completely transformed in size, composition, and safety by shortages of workers, certain foods and commodities, and access to transportation. After years when employment was hard to find, Berkeley adults faced more work than they could handle on many days. Institute interviews during the war years document families' feelings and actions. They address how the long workdays and the acceleration of life during the urgency of war mobilization affected the daily lives of parents and youth and the well-being of household heads. Oral histories from the 1970s provide accounts of memorable personal events and family scenes.

One of the distinctive features of home front mobilization is its tendency to involve all members of families. In chapter 10 we see many older fathers working long hours replacing men recruited for military service and filling critical roles in the domestic economy, such as transporting war-relevant goods. Children in grade school delivered newspapers or merchandise on their bicycles, and women of all ages worked in war production. In chapter 11 we follow a good many of the Berkeley women into wartime employment. Though many of these women had worked during the Great Depression, how important was this experience to their worklife during the war?

The war generated many questions about the future for the Berkeley parents and their children, from teenagers to young adults. Chapter 12 explores such questions within an intergenerational framework. The acceleration of personal and family life in this war-mobilized society was challenging for the Berkeley parents. Their children were growing up in a new world that in many aspects clashed with the parents' experience in childhood and beyond. Moreover, members of the 1900 generation were exposed to a more scientific model of child rearing that conflicted with memories of their own childhoods when children "just grew up."

At war's end, many of the older daughters of the Berkeley generation were thinking about college, but they encountered resistance from fathers who expected they would simply marry. With demobilization of the armed forces underway, returning veterans increased the pressure on them to marry. Among the sons of the Berkeley generation, exposure to the military model in older brothers and friends no doubt made the option of "joining up" more attractive than college and employment, though most were too young to follow this course. Nevertheless, the GI Bill of 1944 made military service a doubly attractive route to both higher education and job training. The military option once again became mandatory through the draft when America entered the Korean War in 1950. Three out of four Berkeley sons had served in the military by the end of this conflict.

10

War's Impact at Home

> When I heard the news about Pearl Harbor I said, Oh my goodness, it can't be true!
> I just bawled. It affected me so bad.
>
> BERKELEY WOMAN

As the Great Depression came to an end, some families were still mired in poverty, but in a few years the country's mobilization for World War II would significantly improve their economic well-being. The war years produced more abundance at home and pulled the country out of its isolation. The Depression created private suffering and turned the Berkeley families inward; the war turned them outward as people banded together against a common enemy. The assault on Pearl Harbor dramatically altered the collective social experience and psyche of the Bay Area and the Berkeley families.

Governor Earl Warren and the California legislature designated a major portion of the state a combat zone in 1942.[1] California was the "arsenal of democracy" for the country,[2] and the Bay Area in particular became a kind of "waiting room" with military recruits coming in, waiting to ship out, and leaving.[3] The cyclone created by what has been called California's second gold rush of shipyards and wartime industry left residents reeling. "Everything happened so fast" is a sentiment repeated among the families as residents felt they were living on the edge in a community undergoing so much change and confronting so many new opportunities and risks.

In this chapter we view the Berkeley families as many adapted to life in an era of prosperity after a decade of doing without. What happened to them had much to do with war mobilization within the San Francisco Bay region and the state at large. We turn first to community change and adaptation in the presence of danger, massive population growth, an influx of strangers, and the excitement of living in a region mobilized for war. We then turn to family change and adaptation, including the costs and benefits of men's accelerated wartime work and higher wages, the ways youth assisted the war effort, the misconduct of unsupervised adolescents, and the crisis of finding child care for working mothers.

Community Change and Adaptation

DIM THE LIGHTS: DANGER!

The Berkeley and Oakland newspapers and City Council minutes discussed the need to extinguish or soften "every light visible from the Golden Gate or from the sea," and told how to paint overhead lights for blackouts and dimouts.[4] Newspaper articles and notices warned against wandering out by car or bike or on foot during these times, as residents were urged to "take our lives into our hands" and assume a much "greater degree of responsibility" for personal safety and for preventing accidents, injuries, and fatalities.[5] The possibility of Pacific Coast bombing prompted Berkeley's city manager to regularly instruct citizens on how to cope with bomb threats and other assaults on the city and to sponsor citywide defense drills.[6] From the shore and from the hills, one could see each day what one observer called the many "Ships of Promise" in the harbor and the Bay.[7]

The thick "apprehension" and "fear in the air" were daily reminders of danger to the Berkeley families. "We had our blackouts," one woman said, "and you weren't supposed to play your radio or have your lights on and things. If you did, they'd haul the men in, because they'd think you were trying to get messages places or doing things you weren't supposed to do. It was terrible." Another couple told a humorous story that conveyed the danger at hand:

> We were driving down the coast and we had a blackout. You weren't supposed to have your headlights on, and I was trying to drive with my fog lights. But I was having a little trouble with the push buttons, and I'd inadvertently turn my lights on and off. Apparently there was a lookout on the hill, and the next thing we knew we were threatened by two armed men who thought we were signaling to somebody off the coast. They told us to douse our lights NOW, and I drove on in the dark.

The shared sense of danger led the State War Council to set up a civil defense system across coastal regions of California, including the Bay Area: city councils of defense nested within county councils that nested within a regional civilian protection agency.[8] These organizations spurred a volunteer ethic as thousands of residents joined together in civil defense roles as a way to contribute to the home front war effort: they became air raid and neighborhood wardens, blackout enforcers, plane spotters, beach patrollers, and first aid providers and took on many other roles and responsibilities. In April 1943 the Berkeley volunteer office had a list of fifteen thousand registered volunteers, filed by name and skill.[9] Window cards in homes identified block lieutenants, wardens, and Gold Star Mothers whose sons had died in the war. These roles were important points of personal pride and gateways to shared solidarity and social activity.

BOOMTOWN: GROWTH AND THE DECLINE OF SOCIAL ORDER

The California Gold Rush (1848–55) had created many "boomtowns"—settlements that sprang up suddenly and expanded rapidly in gold-mining country as people sought their fortunes. These sites of economic hope and prosperity also brought social disruption and poor quality of life because the infrastructure for housing, health, schooling, and goods and supplies could not support the needs of all the people who flooded in. A century later the East Bay would have similar characteristics as a wartime boomtown.

Newspaper accounts noted the dramatic increase in the populations of the Pacific Coast, San Francisco, and East Bay amid a decline in the general US civilian population. Between 1940 and 1943, for example, the US civilian population was down over 2 percent, but the Pacific Coast civilian population rose over 8 percent and the California civilian population increased 13 percent.[10] The East Bay saw an increase of 100,000 people during this time, and Berkeley and Oakland saw a 20 percent gain.[11] The Kaiser shipyard in nearby Richmond employed more than 100,000 people by 1944,[12] and it was just one of thirty shipyards in the Bay Area.[13] The "mystery," as one *Berkeley Gazette* reader wrote, "is: Where have we put all these people? Frankly, we haven't."[14] Thus a major public concern emerged: How to handle the unprecedented increase and new density of the population with no infrastructure to support them. Public controversy also erupted over Berkeley's trailer parks and tent camps of "stationary migrants," one with over 1,300 residents.[15]

The housing shortage created by the dramatic influx threatened to throttle the operations of vital war industries. The dominance of the mobilization also meant that Berkeley residents not working in the war industry lived in fear that they might be displaced, acutely aware that they could not control their lives. This fear was not unfounded, for the city was considering the possibility that residents and families "not considered essential for war work or maintenance of the city government may be removed entirely from this war industry area for the duration."[16] Indeed, the city of Berkeley encouraged all homeowners who could to move to "other sections of the state where the housing shortage is less acute," making their homes available to war workers, or else to "make minor interior alterations to permit other families to live under the same roof" with them.[17]

Although housing codes made it difficult to take boarders,[18] as did the city policy requiring private homeowners to register as landlords,[19] World War II brought an upsurge in the number of Berkeley households with boarders.[20] The tidal wave of new defense workers and their families arrived just as the Berkeley families' older sons and daughters were leaving home. We don't know how many made room for a boarder or another family because that type of data was not systematically collected during the war. Occasional references to these arrangements do appear in the archives, however. One parent whose eldest son was serving in the war described spending Christmas 1942 with three young defense workers who lived in the downstairs bedroom and utility room.

Overcrowded neighborhoods prompted concerns about juvenile delinquency, adult crime, squalor, disease, and air and water pollution. Densely populated neighborhoods heightened the problem of daytime noise, exacerbated by youth loitering. With so many people working nights, the "racket" became a nuisance for wartime workers who needed to sleep during the day. Letters to newspapers address the "thousands of people who are on the night shifts in defense plants of all kinds" and are subjected to "blaring radios, shouting and other disturbances [horn-honking, squealing tires], which in their small way do much to hamper the war effort."[21] One letter begs readers to abide by a new "Golden Rule": to be "quiet through the day, that night workmen may get some rest."[22]

Newspaper accounts described the changing smells and sights of the community caused by patriotic collecting of old newspapers, tires, oil, cans, and other supplies—and the resulting public hazards. One letter writer sneered, "At last the pigs who formerly dumped their garbage and refuse alongside the roadways now have a perfectly legal way to dump their unholy, smelly messes on other people: They now take it to their gas station, in the name of patriotism. Many stations have the appearance and odor of the Berkeley waterfront when the tide is out. Rat traps are slopped all over our fair city."[23]

Berkeley families experienced the erosion of social order: witnessing or being victims of assault and violence, house robberies, street muggings, prostitution, and a variety of public disturbances. Similarly, a "worried homemaker" described the deterioration of civility in her daily rounds with "street car men, laundry men, store clerks, and butchers" who now "treat us as though we were garbage under their feet."[24] Another man wrote of "war psychosis" as people in town have become so "touchy" due to "wartime jitters."[25] "It's so easy," he said, "to offend a friend and still easier for a friend to offend you. Husbands bark at wives, and wives snap back at husbands."

LIVING AMONG STRANGERS

Sociologist Willard Waller, writing in 1940 just at the start of large-scale mobilization in World War II, observed the social flux wrought by mobilization: "War takes large sections of the population away from their homes and their local communities; it stirs up populations as one stirs soup; people are thrown together who have never seen one another before and will never see one another again; regions, culture groups, religious groups, and classes are all mixed as they are at no other period in life."[26]

Waller's observation foreshadowed war as a sort of experiment in racial integration, as black men and white men served together but not always with each other. But Waller's observation would also come to be true of daily life in the East Bay and Berkeley, as "everyone, it seemed, had come from somewhere else."[27] This "stirring up" of populations generated social distrust and exclusion, and the war became a justification for doing unusual, even awful, things to other people. Key targets were poor southerners, who came to the area during mobilization, and the Japanese, who were long-standing members of the community but were targeted after Pearl Harbor.

Poor southerners. The lure of wartime jobs brought a large influx of southerners—a new wave of white "Okies" to follow Dust Bowl migration a decade earlier,[28] and a large wave of black migrants. The presence of these groups would do much to affect the cultural ethos of the place. One newspaper letter sounded an alarm that an "Okie atmosphere" had "engulfed" the Bay Area and eroded "civilized living for the duration" and that "if it is permitted to go unchecked, it will continue after the war."[29] One of the Berkeley men sums it up: "You could sense a different class of people coming into Berkeley." Another man offered an explanation related to selective migration: "The good Okies are still back in Oklahoma making good, and the ones that came out here are those who didn't have anything to leave back where they came from and hoped to better themselves." The result, one woman said, was that what was once perceived as a community of people "living together in perfect friendliness" had turned into "ghettos."

The influx of black migrants into the Bay Area triggered racial tensions that had not been part of the community before then. In Berkeley proper the black population tripled over the 1940s, from 4 percent to 12 percent, with some communities in the East Bay and Bay Area seeing even greater increases. In the Institute archives we are able to hear only the voices of white families and their language about race and poverty. Black families would have seen things differently.

Before wartime mobilization the Berkeley parents reported positive relations, or at least peaceful coexistence, between longtime black and white community members. One Berkeley man observed that "there wasn't any friction. There weren't enough blacks in evidence. During that time, you know, if you walked into I. Magnin's, you'd see these colored people in there trying on hats, you know. They had the money." That "new blacks" were poor and "old blacks" were not was key to understanding the change. In this way the new arrivals were no different from the Okies. They had in common that they were poor.

Not only were the "types" of people moving in different, the racial composition of some neighborhoods and districts had flipped from predominantly white to predominantly black. To use one woman's words, "Now the neighborhood I lived in is all colored." Another woman offered an explanation: "White people didn't like it when blacks moved in, so they left."

One woman noted that when her family moved into the neighborhood, she recalled only one black customer at their corner store. She recalled being startled when that customer showed up when she was minding the store at dinnertime. When her family left the area in 1948, only three white families remained. She said, "Whites and blacks got along well when blacks first moved into Berkeley. But it got rough when *southern* blacks moved in during the war. Black fellows would pester us at the bus stop. My poor daughter was scared to death. She had to take the bus to work in San Francisco. They were fresh. They said things that made me sick. Up to that time, I had no trouble with them." Another woman said, "These new people were *southern* blacks—Louisiana, Alabama, Arkansas, and Texas. They were a different kind of black, the kind that had never had anything, just poverty-stricken blacks. They got an old hack and came out here, camped, threw up a cardboard house or a few sticks of lumber, and made do."

Some in the 1900 generation described a new kind of "turmoil" *between* longtime black residents and the black residents who were now coming in, as "the war brought the wrong kind, people they did not like." One woman described a black woman as saying that the shipyard workers made her "ashamed to be black." Increased "lawlessness" in the community was attributed to the appearance and demeanor of new blacks who had moved to the Bay Area to work in the shipyards. But these perceptions of lawlessness also stemmed from the legitimate frustrations of black workers, who were excluded from unions and subjected to worse working conditions than whites. For example, a series of race riots followed black shipyard workers' being fired (though ultimately rehired) because they were denied the right to become union members.[30] The *Oakland Tribune* reported that Mills College students were told, "More race riots can be expected because Negroes no longer consider themselves inferior and are ready to strike out for their belief."[31]

Some anger was aimed at Henry Kaiser, the American industrialist who established the shipyards that produced the Liberty Ships. One man complained that "Kaiser and his shipyards brought the blacks. Then, we became the highest paid welfare state. And it didn't bring in the best group of the black people either." Then he softened his tone, adding, "I've never had one be rude to me, and I've worked with a lot of them. I couldn't say that about all the white kids." Another man said there were few blacks in the area until "Henry Kaiser went down South and brought trainloads of those guys out here and put them to work in the shipyards."

Others blamed the bleeding heart of Eleanor Roosevelt, who "brought out all the black people from the south. They did nothing for their $55 dollars a week, really, but hand tools to other people. Of course, they're doing better for themselves. There are black people who are very fine people and really make things of themselves, and there are the others who just don't want to work." As in the earlier case, this man then admits, "Well, we have that with whites also."

Thus we can hear members of the 1900 generation sorting out feelings about race and socioeconomic status as the presence of these groups grew amid wartime mobilization. They point to the difference between the "good" black and white people that used to be present and the new—poor—kinds now among them, whom they saw as compromising the social fabric of the community.

The Japanese.   The Japanese invasion of Pearl Harbor on December 7, 1941, was a turning point in the history of the Bay Area and of these families, in that Hawaii's relative proximity to the West Coast sparked fear that the same type of attack could happen to them. One Berkeley man said, "They could have captured Pearl Harbor, could have captured Hawaii, and by golly, if they had, I don't know what would have stopped them from coming on over here."

After Pearl Harbor, "security" in the San Francisco Harbor was what James Hamilton and William Bolce called a "byword of the greatest significance."[32] To use their imagery, the harbor, which was "nestled below high hills and towering skyscrapers, made shipping and waterfront activities extremely vulnerable to the prowling eyes of enemy agents and potential saboteurs. Soldiers and civilians were cautioned to keep all troop and cargo ship movements a secret. Everyone was admonished to 'Zip Your Lip.'"[33]

As a result, there was much fear of the Japanese, especially in places like the Bay Area, which were densely populated with Japanese people. The month of the Pearl Harbor invasion, *Life Magazine* ran its lead article, with photos, titled "How to Tell Japs from the Chinese." The words used in newspaper letters reflect the sentiments Japanese people were often subjected to: "disloyal," "treason," "espionage," "treachery," and with an "unassimilable" and "acquisitive" nature.[34] This was not the first time strong anti-Japanese sentiment had been apparent in California, however. The state already had a history of anti-Japanese organizations, state authorities, and legislation, including the Board of Education's 1906 decision to require children of Japanese descent to attend separate, racially segregated schools, and the Alien Land Law of 1913, which was explicitly created to prevent landownership among Japanese citizens residing in the state.[35]

March 1942, following President Roosevelt's order, marked the start of large-scale evacuation and internment of "Japanese aliens" and their "American-born children" from "strategic Pacific Coast military and industrial areas," including the Bay Area. Many of the Berkeley families described seeing the Japanese among them vanish—individuals and families they had relationships with. Many of these people were interned at Tule Lake, a northern California camp about five hours away. Some were business owners and workers—beauticians and barbers, grocers, laundry proprietors, restaurant owners—or homeowners in their communities. Some of the Berkeley families felt betrayed by the university as professors, students, and alumni they knew were abruptly removed from their positions and interned. "They were all born here. They were all UC students and graduates!" one man exclaimed. Another said, "Most of them were more patriotic than the native-born Americans!" Others were even like family—caretakers, maids, gardeners, and landscapers who had been coming to their homes for years: "We knew them, we knew their family, we knew everything. And they were so faithful. We couldn't even think of them in that category as being a menace in any way."

The Berkeley families spoke of a surge of fear and hysteria and of how quickly it happened—virtually overnight. One man said, "It all went too fast. One morning everything was normal and tranquil here. And in the afternoon, the FBI was over here and moved them out, just like that. They gave them a time limit to get their things together. And the next thing, a truck pulled up. They didn't hardly have time to lock the door." Another man reported that what made it difficult was that there was no ability to protest: one just had to live "with how things were and accepting when things came." A major problem, another woman said, was that "you couldn't speak against anything to do with the war" or you would be suspected too.

And yet the Berkeley families also conveyed how complicated it was emotionally, not knowing whether someone could be trusted. Some high-profile community cases related to spying and propaganda reinforced the need to be both cautious and suspicious. Like it or not, it was no time for "bleeding hearts," one woman said, and internment was "the right thing to do, because it probably protected Japanese Americans from mob violence, since they're so easily seen." Roosevelt had made this same claim when he ordered the internment.

Some of the families tried but failed to relocate interned people, and they had a hard time explaining to their children why these special people had disappeared. Others made successful relocation efforts and even helped Japanese families find homes or start their businesses again. But on their return the Japanese naturally had "bitter feelings"—a phrase used by several study participants—because they were Americans: many had never even been to Japan.

The tension surrounding local people who might be associated with enemy powers was not restricted to the Japanese. To a lesser extent, Germans and Italians were also under watchful eyes. The Berkeley families described how German and Italian relatives, friends, or neighbors were removed or forced to move out of the Bay Area for from weeks to a year as questions about people's "papers" got sorted out or as they were monitored by the US military to make sure they did not pose a risk. One woman mentioned that a neighbor who had a photo of Mussolini in the house was the source of much gossip. Some thought that, ideologically, the situations of Germans and Italians were not so different from those of the Japanese. But the attack on Pearl Harbor changed everything, and the density of Japanese people in the Bay Area, and their identifiability, meant they were easily targeted.

HOME FRONT EXCITEMENT

War brought many challenges to the community, but the Berkeley families also described the excitement of the time—crowds, vibrant nightlife, romance in the air, living for the moment. As historian Arthur Verge noted, "Despite the exigencies of war, fun was not rationed."[36] People had money but limited ways to spend it, so entertainment became a focus: movie houses, dance halls, and drinking and socializing in neighborhood taverns. There was a strong solidarity with others, a sense that "we're all in this together."

Some families continually entertained servicemen in their homes. One woman described their house as a hub of social activity for soldiers: "They called our place the 68th Avenue USO [United Service Organization]. We had soldiers and sailors and marines, in and out. We started out, another neighbor and I, entertaining every Wednesday." People picked up "our boys" from the airport and from train and bus stations. They provided "a home away from home for them," cooking them warm meals, hosting parties and sightseeing tours, and making good friends.

Families said it was exciting to watch the trains, ships, and military personnel and to participate in parades and see well-known people come through town. The owner of a store on Market Street said, "We had windows on both sides. We could see everything from Market and Montgomery. Oh, the parades were fantastic! They were something else. And watching all the celebrities go in the Palace Hotel right from our window, oh goodness. When the United Nations meeting was in San Francisco, we saw presidents! President Roosevelt and President Taft too. All these dignitaries! The cabs coming and going. Oh dear, there were lots of people standing around to see everything. And the city was full of soldiers and sailors."

In the previous section we said that the Japanese and poor whites and blacks from the South were seen as people to fear. Those strangers looked and sounded different and threatened the well-being of family, community, and country. Sailors and soldiers were also strangers, but they wore the halo of serving the country and were seen as outsiders to be welcomed and protected. Patriotism brought like people together, sharpened common values and purpose, and got them aligned around common enemies.

This sentiment is nicely reflected in Jon Meacham's discussion of the British people's psyche during the summer of 1940 as Germany threatened to invade: "Common dangers bind people together, if only for a short while."[37] Meacham quotes C. P. Snow that there was

> a kind of collective euphoria over the whole country. I don't know what we were thinking about. We were very busy. We had a purpose. We were living in constant excitement, usually, if we examined the true position, of an unpromising kind. In one's realistic moments, it was difficult to see what chance we had. But I doubt if most of us had many realistic moments, or thought much at all. We were working like mad. We were sustained by a surge of national emotion.

This applies rather well to what was going on in the Bay Area, especially as people worked extraordinarily long hours, often in the name of victory, and as children and adolescents took part in the wartime effort.

Family Change in Wartime

MEN'S WAR WORK: COSTS AND BENEFITS

In 1944 family sociologist James Bossard remarked, "So comprehensive and fundamental are the changes wrought by war, and so closely is the family interrelated with the larger society, that there is perhaps no aspect of family life unaffected by war."[38] Men's work was no exception. The rapid acceleration of work schedules, with no leeway for failing to meet the nation's goals, created extraordinary pressure during the initial years of building a world war arsenal from the ground up.

The breathtaking pace of war mobilization exacted a terrible price, taking a large but invisible toll on the home front: during 1942–43, American workers in war-related industries died or were injured at twenty times the rate of American servicemen.[39] In Andrew E. Kersten's words, "Quite literally during the first few years of the Second World War, it was safer for Americans to be on the battlefront than it was for them to work on the home front of the arsenal of democracy."[40] Short deadlines became hazardous and even deadly, most notably in shipyards, where the work was dirty and dangerous: in the peak year of 1943, a new ship was launched every thirty hours.[41] But it was not just hands-on work that was stressful: the death rate was high among shipyard executives, who were tasked with getting the yards up and running and were responsible for their effectiveness and output.[42]

Many injuries and deaths also resulted when workers entered positions they were ill-equipped for and unskilled workers were suddenly doing skilled work. The Kaiser shipyards, which were producing Liberty Ships around the clock, had difficulty recruiting skilled people, so jobs were broken down in ways that could be managed by workers with no shipbuilding experience. As one skilled man said, "We're getting so many workers from the south that got into carpentry work during the war but have no training or education, and they just aren't any good at it at all."

Public frustration also mounted because unskilled workers' doing higher-level jobs pulled down the pay of experienced workers. One local newspaper article argued that "inexperienced labor is costing Uncle Sam plenty and may be upsetting the economic platform too" by violating a principled link between pay, training and experience, and seniority.[43] The high employment rate of unskilled workers led to factories' hiring teenagers, even those still in school, for unskilled but lucrative jobs. One Berkeley man remembered "a bunch of kids" at his shop, "earning $1.50 an hour, and they really weren't worth 25 cents. They'd spend it up as fast as they got it and figured life was pretty easy. I used to tell them, 'someday they'll pull the plug out of the bottom of the boat and then where will you be? It won't be so easy to get a job as it is right now.'"

This quotation reflects an important perspective: the Berkeley men and women had known scarcity firsthand and, after enduring a decade of hard times, war mobilization on the home front brought them the chance to make up for lost opportunities and achieve a much better material life. Because pay continued to increase and hours were plentiful, the war elevated the life stations of most of the Berkeley families—especially those from the working class. In fact, from 1940 to 1944 California's per capita income rose over 95 percent: from $803 in 1940 to $1,570 in 1944.[44] Most families described or recalled the prosperity of the war years. As one woman reported, "Those were better years, much better years, when the war came along. Better money, more to spend. We had a few new things in the house." But they also recalled a darker side—the guilt over making good money when "our boys are over there fighting."

Men's worklives from the Great Depression through the war displayed sharp contrasts: from labor scarcity to surplus and from low wages and job insecurity to higher earnings and the chance for advancement. A handful of the Berkeley men were in the armed forces as military engineers, carpenters, and draftsmen, and one was a psychotherapist. More worked in the shipyards as foremen, welders, machinists, patternmakers, architects, guards, or clerks handling contracts and shipments. Others worked outside the shipyards but in jobs that were affected by the local war industry: in print shops, public utilities, and oil and chemical research labs or as truck drivers or police officers.

Vivid memories of wartime employment centered on the long hours—shifts of twelve hours or more, seven days a week, even at times adding a "victory" shift in the name of patriotism. A supervisor for a local oil refinery got up at five in the morning and returned home about nine at night: "They'd work us straight through." A chemist reported that people in his firm who "normally worked forty-eight hours were all working sixty hours a week." Some men noted the health strain of long hours. In the words of a truck driver, "The war almost put an end of me. I had a job running from San Francisco to Oakland, and it was pretty rough. I'd run and run, day and night." The wife of a long-distance trucker attributed her husband's heart condition to his long workday: "He was working just too, too many hours, sometimes for 24 hours straight." A draftsman asked his wife "if the sun ever shone here," because "it was dark when I left and dark when I got home."

Higher wages put more money in pockets and brought a higher potential standard of living and an eagerness to consume. Yet there was less time for leisure and there were fewer places to go because transportation was constrained: automobile travel was limited to conserve resources and avoid noise, and railway travel was limited to transporting freight and troops. Many desirable commodities were rationed (such as meat, butter, sugar, and gas) or prohibited (such as products made of silk or metal), and Berkeley families describe difficulty in meeting their daily needs. The war opened personal possibilities at the same time that it closed them.

TWO WORLDS OF YOUTH

The children in the Berkeley study were too young to serve during the peak years of mobilization. They were aged thirteen to fourteen and in school during the acceleration years. Still, they too were swept up in the war, which permeated schooling and political socialization. Students' learning was disrupted by anxieties about danger, death, and dying. As historian William Tuttle has noted, "Some [children] believed that they were living on the front lines; these boys and girls feared that the next air raid siren might not be another drill, but the real thing."[45] The ideology taught in schools stressed that this was a "'people's war,' a battle for democracy against dictatorship and brutality."[46]

At the same time, educators worried about the "exploitation" of youth by the war industry. This led the Berkeley Board of Education to enact "more stringent legislation" to "prevent non-essential industries from 'exploiting' high school students during the school week for the war effort."[47] Still, educators felt strong pressure to "gear the educational process to war" because of the strong pro-war public sentiment, the many ways high schoolers were being organized to help, and the prospect of early or eventual wartime service for many high school students.[48] This included pressure to increase their proficiency in mechanical production. To help students "face present and future uncertainties of life with courage and fortitude," schools introduced courses in morale, which incorporated material on "war mental hygiene," not only in psychology, but in English, history, physical education, sociology, and civics.[49]

The changing aspects of community we described earlier affected friendships and peer groups. For example, the Japanese internment meant that Berkeley children lost important peers and didn't know where they were or whether they were safe. Parents worried about their students' communicating with Japanese friends because, in the words of one mother, "One can't be too careful about one's associations these days." Another mother was concerned about the "kinds of children who have come into the child's school in recent months." She thought her son had picked up "off-color" talk from incoming defense workers' children, who had overcrowded classrooms. She, like several other parents, moved her children to other schools, even private schools that strained their family resources, so they would have smaller classes and not be exposed to these newcomers.

Outside school, there were two worlds of youth, with both sometimes existing for individual boys and girls: exemplary displays of discipline and a willingness to sacrifice through contributions to the war effort, and worrisome displays of misconduct and delinquency amid limited supervision and the enticements of a fully mobilized war environment.

Exemplary: Assisting in the war effort. The children of the Berkeley parents were surrounded by many signs of war: a local radio series, *My War*, dramatized "the wartime contributions of every man, woman, and child on the home front." Saturday movies exposed children to the reality of war through newsreels. Nearby army bases and warships brought a constant flow of troops in and out of the Bay Area. Families worked in community "victory" gardens on vacant lots—over forty thousand in the East Bay area during 1943—to increase the supply of vegetables, fruits, and herbs in the face of rationing.[50] Young people's active role in the war effort was most strikingly documented through family accounts of the seemingly endless round of scrap drives (such as the monthly collection of fat, waste paper, and scrap metal), the selling of war stamps and bonds, and the distribution of war-related posters and flyers. Boy Scouts and Girl Scouts were active in these drives. The city of Berkeley granted their Junior Chamber of Commerce permission to set up a "Victory House" for selling war bonds.[51]

As military events began to shift in favor of the United States and the Allies, the sons of the Berkeley 1900 generation were asked what they most often talked about with friends. The list included popular culture (movies, radio programs, hit songs), relationships with girls, family and school affairs, and war items— the war in general, which armed service one would choose, the new defense workers and their families, and postwar planning. In fact, "the war" became the most popular topic of conversation among the Berkeley boys and their peers, outranking girls, school, and "things I want." Over half the boys claimed they often talked about the war with other boys, and discussing their preferred branch of military service was only slightly less popular (41 percent versus 53 percent).

For many boys a primary preoccupation was how to get into the armed services while they were still underage. Amid the hardships of wartime, some public commentators argued that the war had transformed a generation of immature youth: "Almost overnight they seemed to grow up to become responsible men and women. The boys throng to join the Army by hundreds of thousands, before they're called. The girls eagerly grasp at every opportunity for war work."[52] In 1942 teenage boys and girls were increasingly recruited into the military and war efforts. In early October, Major General James A. Ulio twice called for the immediate enlistment of eighteen- to nineteen-year-old boys in "this young man's war."[53] In November the Labor Department "opened the gates of war plants . . . to girls 16 and 17 years old."[54] Aimed at youth still in school and not quite old enough to serve, the emerging climate sent the message that education was "secondary to victory."[55]

Problematic: Misconduct and delinquency.   As fathers and mothers worked, older children were left to their own devices, bringing a rise in misconduct. Unsupervised "latchkey children"[56] in a war-mobilized community and nation brought a dramatic increase in delinquency, imposing another strain on Berkeley parents who worried about their children while they were working. Governor Warren rallied a statewide conference to discuss how to address growing juvenile delinquency.[57] The increase in teenage delinquency created the need for a legal and an institutional response: the legal one was a 10:00 p.m. curfew, and the institutional one was youth centers. The Berkeley community created "Teen Age Centers" to provide structured and monitored activities and sports to prevent delinquency and to inform parents about the facilities and services available for children and youth.[58]

The "misconduct" problem was particularly troubling. Arrests of boys in Berkeley more than doubled from 1941 to 1943. Although the increase in boys' arrests was a problem, it was the sharp increase in misconduct by Berkeley girls that captured public attention: up 52 percent in the first seven months of 1942, compared with just 15 percent for boys.[59] The major national government report on crime statistics from this era notes the same "alarming upswing" in crime among girls and young women, but it gives little detail.[60] In examining specific offenses, however, the categories for which there were steep hikes included "prostitution" and "other sex offenses" and "disorderly conduct" and "vagrancy." In retrospect it is clear that the arrest and prosecution of females was meant to restrain "problem girls" whose behavior was "incorrigible" and "ungovernable" and therefore not consistent with the standards of their era.[61] It became a way to "punish precocious female sexuality" and to "act as a guardian of female virtue,"[62] even though girls were more often the victims than the offenders and the men (including soldiers) and boys with them were not similarly held accountable.[63]

Otherwise the emphasis was largely on the surge in youth delinquency, not specific to gender, from the teenage years through age twenty-one, underscoring the "need to keep the home front clean, wholesome, and strong." The report hinted that war was the ultimate culprit, since "boom conditions and 'easy money' in the hands of youthful persons, together with a possible let-down in the influence of the home are factors which must be offset in designing programs to combat [this problem]." Juvenile delinquency, the report further declared, "is an inexcusable waste of manpower during a period of crisis when every available person is needed for essential services to the Nation." Local law enforcement agencies were "confronted with many additional duties in wartime," complicated by their having "lost many of their most capable and experienced personnel to the armed services and to national defense industries."[64]

The Berkeley interviews provide a limited but important glimpse into the concerns of parents—for whom a major explanation was "the movies." In the golden era of Hollywood, movies were a major source of entertainment for everyone. But during the war years, parents repeatedly cited movies as a source of tension with their teenagers, suggesting that films had a negative influence by encouraging immoral or risky behavior, especially sexual activity. In the words of one father, movies "attract kids' attention to things that they shouldn't be doing." Another father complained that his son has "seen more movies than you'd believe, and I can only hope the kid will swing back into line."

"The movies" was a destination for groups of unsupervised teens and a place for taking and finding dates—and therefore a place where teenagers, especially girls, could get into trouble. For example, one mother worried about her daughter, who was just beginning to go out unchaperoned. One day the daughter picked up a sailor at a movie and brought him home. Another day she picked up a soldier on the street, an Italian Catholic boy, and for three or four weeks she went to church with him every Sunday. Her daughter had also begun corresponding with two boys in the service. The mother, who was working, said, "I hate to have her go to the movies alone, but I'm not home to go with her and she has sneaked off several times to go down to movies in Oakland."

What "the movies" ultimately symbolize is parents' growing inability to control and protect their children: the coupling of the early teenage years, when they naturally wanted more autonomy, with the reality that parents' wartime work schedules granted youth greater freedom and the Bay Area offered many enticements, including many young servicemen coming and going.

Parents seemed especially worried about daughters' drinking, smoking, and sexual activity. Several said they feared girls' tendencies to "go boy crazy," wanting to get into romantic relationships at "earlier ages, and often with older boys they don't know." Girls gathered at train stations and in the port as troops came in. In a serious incident, a father reported that his daughter got "into one adolescent scrape for which she got hell. She went out on a date with a serviceman and practiced deception on the family. She and another girl, whom I didn't trust anyhow, went to the movies with a couple of Marines. She didn't like the way the evening was going and phoned in, and I could tell what was happening from the sound of her voice. I ordered her to come home immediately, so she left and came right home. Later that night, the other child was raped."

Another father shared the need to talk to his daughter about sex "because she was hanging around army camps, and it was necessary for her to know what might happen. I believe completely in telling youngsters all the biological facts, and I always intended to tell her before then but never got around to it until it was too late. Because of the army camps, she already knew lots of things."

Raising teenagers during wartime clearly heightened the challenges their parents already faced. One Berkeley man spoke of the "unsettledness of things," the "stresses of the present time," and "how confusing modern life is to children." One woman emphasized that before the war life was "simpler and less complex" and that "it is harder now for parents to provide the sort of simple, natural home life that was possible before the change in morals" that came with the war. Another woman added, "Youngsters would have had an easier time had it not been for the war. It has added so many complications and strains to their lives that I think, for both the boys and girls, it's always hanging over their heads. I think this whole uncertainty has been harder on them than grown-ups realize."

CARING FOR WAR WORKERS' CHILDREN

The social history of women often points to World War II as a pivotal moment in opening women's pathways into the labor force. Chapter 11 examines women's worklives during wartime. Consistent with the narrative of women's history, many of the middle-class Berkeley women in our study did indeed begin to work during the war and said they did so not out of economic need but out of patriotism. For some women, though, work brought new life options.

What is surprising—and something our study is uniquely positioned to reveal, given its long historical view—is that for working-class women World War II was not a sudden gateway into paid work. For these women, wartime work was a continuation of significant work histories that were started during or before the Great Depression and had always been a necessity. Many of the middle-class women had also worked before marriage and childbearing. In both cases their work experience made working during wartime easier.

Working mothers and overtime or absent fathers inevitably raised serious questions about the care and supervision of children. What to do with the children of working mothers became a major issue among local residents and city leaders during the summer and fall of 1942. Child care was "California's pressing No. 1 war problem," and locally the Berkeley Defense Council formed a Child Care Committee in 1942 to get "all agencies concerned with the care of children of working mothers" to find solutions to the child care crisis.[65]

By the close of 1942, shipyards were sponsoring child care centers. Augmented by federal emergency funds directed to states to provide day care programs for the children of working mothers, the Berkeley Board of Education developed a comprehensive plan to create ten centers to care for these children: community child care centers, public preschools, and after-school care. The belief that working women were among the "real winners of this war" was coupled with the fear that their young children would be among the losers if child care arrangements were not forthcoming. After the war, however, these federal and local supports were withdrawn, reinforcing the push for women to quit working and return to domestic and civic pursuits.

Conclusion

World War II marked the end of "old Berkeley" as the 1900 generation had known it, prompting much community change and adaptation. But the war also marked the end of a decade of hardship, not only creating conditions for economic recovery but generating abundance unlike anything people could have imagined and elevating their life stations beyond where they had been during the Great Depression. The war opened their worlds and turned them outward.

The social fabric of the Berkeley families' community changed overnight. There were daily reminders that the personal safety they once took for granted had vanished. In a war-mobilized community, it was clear that they were in the presence of danger. Fear was in the air amid blackouts, bomb threats, and defense drills. Community members volunteered in a civil defense system spread across the Bay Area and the California coast. Boomtown conditions associated with wartime opportunity, especially in the shipyards, led to the unprecedented increase and density of the population: housing shortages brought boarders and tent and trailer parks, overcrowded neighborhoods and schools, squalor and disease, air and water pollution, crime and delinquency.

The lure of wartime jobs also brought an influx of strangers, poor white and black laborers from the South, which triggered tensions in the community and unrest in schools. After Pearl Harbor there was also great fear of the Japanese. The Bay Area was densely populated with Japanese, and the state of California already had a long history of anti-Japanese sentiment. The large-scale evacuation and internment of Japanese families, some of whom were friends of the Berkeley families, brought complicated emotions. To a lesser extent, so did associating with persons having immediate links to Germany and Italy.

Despite these many threats, wartime also brought great pleasures—watching trains and ships, soldiers and sailors, being in crowds and participating in parades, seeing celebrities and dignitaries, entertaining servicemen, absorbing nightlife, living in the moment. The constant excitement and shared purpose of life in a war-mobilized community stimulated a kind of euphoria in its population.

World War II also prompted significant family change and adaptation. It opened up the family and made it less of a sanctuary as it was subjected to the influence of the outside world. This demanded that parents implement new "fortifications" to protect their families.[66] The claims on men grew as work hours got longer and production quotas rose during the peak years of mobilization. The dizzying pace of work was hazardous and even deadly. Injuries and deaths also resulted when workers took on jobs beyond their skill levels. High wages and plentiful hours meant that families had a higher potential standard of living and wanted to consume—but there was less time for leisure, and travel and consumption were limited. Of course, for many families in the community fathers were completely absent in military service.

As women entered the labor force, households were emptied out, leaving children unsupervised. Aged thirteen to fourteen during the peak of mobilization, the Berkeley children were still in school, where war permeated learning and social experience. They were too young to do war work or be called up for service, but they could actively volunteer for the war effort. At the same time, they were old enough for parents to leave them on their own but also to be vulnerable to the enticements of a wartime hub and inclined to misconduct and delinquency. For working mothers with younger children, and for the Berkeley community as well as for California, the problem of child care had become a crisis.

The dramatic increase of married women in the Bay Area labor force was heralded by the local newspaper as "one of the most notable movements of this war, a development that perhaps not one American in a hundred would have thought possible. . . . Already there are thousands of women working in factories which formerly confined their employment to men."[67] Although many working women shifted their employment to war-related industries, gainful employment was not foreign to most study mothers who helped fill labor needs. Approximately half of the Berkeley mothers were employed at some point during the war, and most of them had also worked in the 1930s. Yet the emptying out of the household made domesticity more attractive after the war, as did the retreat from community and the corresponding rise in privatism. We now look more closely into the Berkeley women's work experiences from the 1920s through World War II.

Women at Work

I did secretarial work during the war. That's what I had done before having kids. I could help a little and earn some money. It felt kind of patriotic.

BERKELEY WOMAN

Amid wartime mobilization in the Bay Area, the demand for skilled and semi-skilled workers soared as waves of younger men were recruited to military service. The expanding labor market dramatically increased job openings for women as well as men, along with the need for volunteers. As employed men left for the military, subordinates were promoted to fill their jobs, creating vacancies for others—known as a "vacancy chain."[1] Vacancy chains especially created new openings in the wartime labor market for qualified women, and the Berkeley women often filled them.[2] One woman recalled being promoted from assistant librarian to manager in an armed forces library when the man who held that position left for active military duty. This left her former position to be filled by another woman.

Rosie the Riveter is a symbol of women's changing role in the workforce brought on by World War II. Historical accounts often emphasize that this period was pivotal in the dramatic long-term increase in married women's moving into predominantly male occupations.[3] Many claim that the change in married women's work preferences during World War II and their acceptance into jobs previously reserved for men stemmed from patriotism.[4] There were far more jobs open than men could fill, and many believed the future of the country depended on both women and men on the home front, doing what was necessary to keep the country working.[5] Yet others have downplayed the influence of World War II by asserting that women's role in the workforce had been steadily growing before the war and that the massive expansion in women's employment during World War II receded significantly as many of these women returned to homemaking after the war.[6] We ask, then, How did the Berkeley women respond to, understand, and experience the wartime expansion of job availability, and why?

Much of what is known about women's employment during World War II comes from three kinds of data: national census or labor bureau data on women's jobs by year or decade, grouped by marital status and occupational category;[7] oral histories from women who worked in war industry jobs typically held by men;[8] and archival materials such as classified ads, magazine articles, images, or advertisements, novels, and war propaganda.[9] These types of evidence shed light on women's work at discrete points in time or give an in-depth understanding of certain types of war work and various aspects of social, cultural, or economic climates of the time. However, they have limited ability to represent a general population of women and show how their work during World War II fit into their lives across time. Here we present the Berkeley women's work experiences during World War II in the context of their experiences up to that point, revealing which aspects of a woman's past and present might define her response to war mobilization.[10]

Just over half of the Berkeley women graduated from high school (54 percent) and 38 percent had at least some college, so many had the education to prepare them for occupations outside the home. In fact, at least two-thirds of the women reported doing paid work before the birth of their first child, usually in female-typical occupations such as nursing, teaching, or secretarial work, but nearly all quit once they became pregnant. While these women and their husbands were having their children and raising them, the economy collapsed, and many of the women helped make ends meet by working part-time or full-time outside the home or in family businesses. Before World War II, married women almost never considered outside work for any reason other than family financial hardship.[11] Their work experience before childbearing and marriage brought them into the World War II era with individual expertise, personal preferences, and family realities. How would this cohort of women respond to the greatly expanding labor market of World War II?

World War II was definitely a unique moment in history, a time of rapidly expanding economic opportunity, social diversity, and national unity. But women's work was not entirely new. For many it grew out of past experiences and existing skills. Moreover, women's wartime employment was not motivated only by patriotism but still required negotiating personal, family, and social preferences and needs. We find some unique aspects of work for women in World War II, but to a much greater degree we can see it as a continuation of circumstances earlier in their lives.

Wartime Work for Women

Although the economic situation of the Berkeley families improved with men's employment and compensation during wartime mobilization, paid employment was compelling to many women: they were helping to meet the country's need for workers, and they could contribute toward their children's education expenses.[12] Wartime mobilization radically altered the labor market for women after the years of Depression scarcity when workers often had to settle for any job in an economy where jobs outnumbered workers. Nationwide estimates place more than 37 percent of all married women in the labor force at some point during 1944.[13] For the Berkeley women, employment rose to a new high of 45 percent during 1943, up from 32 percent in 1940, and by the end of the war more women were working full-time than part-time (see appendix figure A11.1).

Much had changed for the Berkeley women between the Great Depression and World War II, but there were also noteworthy continuities in their family roles and economic situations. Both historical periods expanded the household demands and time pressures on married women. They coped with income loss during the Depression by "making do" with family labor, and they practiced conservation to deal with the shortage of goods and services in wartime. Despite the contrast in situations, women who learned to cope with hard times in the 1930s were well equipped to run a household amid wartime shortages.

Perhaps the greatest adjustment to wartime circumstances was made by women who were spared misfortune during the 1930s. The privileged middle-class woman did not "have to" work then, nor was she forced to get by on less and conserve. Though ample resources ensured maximum control over lifestyles in the 1930s, during the war external regulations directly undermined such control. Gas and food rationing, clothing shortages, and other constraints applied to the privileged as well as the less fortunate. No matter how much money a family had, some goods and services simply could not be found, except perhaps on the black market. A Berkeley woman who had a live-in maid throughout the 1930s recalled how difficult it was to find domestic help during the war: "Because women could find better paying jobs in the shipyards, it was almost impossible to get even day help to come in and clean up the house once a week, or once a month, or at all. I suppose I didn't need help really. In any case, I took over as the person who did everything. I remember putting butter in a water glass, putting eggs down,[14] and buying big crocks and filling them. You looked ahead." So, even for women who did not join the labor force during World War II, daily routines were altered.

The war brought much less change to the lives of working-class women. Economic needs were intense in the Depression, and they remained pressing during the war, in part because no matter where a family stood socially and financially, members set their aspirations beyond their means. As we discussed

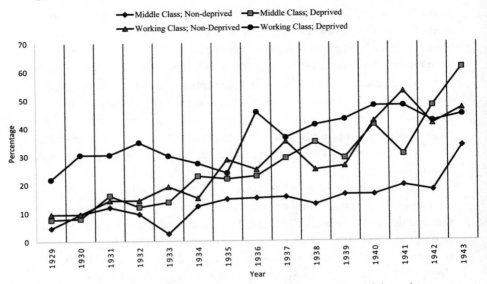

FIGURE 11.1. Berkeley 1900 generation women working 1929–43, by social class and economic deprivation (annual percentages). $N = 113$.

in chapter 7, a family defined its standard of living in terms of an income that it hoped to achieve rather than by the reality of the paycheck.[15] Rising wages during the war spurred the appetite for goods after many years of denial and getting by. Berkeley mothers from the working class were more than twice as likely as higher-status women to have worked in 1932–33 when their children were very young (25 percent versus 9 percent), and they maintained this disparity (50 versus 24 percent) up to 1941 when the booming wartime economy began drawing more middle-class mothers into the labor force, closing the social class gap.

These variations in wartime experience by social class and by economic deprivation during the Great Depression are evident in figure 11.1, which graphs annual percentages of female employment for four groups: women whose families are categorized as middle class and nondeprived in the Great Depression; middle class and deprived; working class and nondeprived; and working class and deprived. Toward the end of World War II, the most dramatic increase in paid work was for middle-class women, especially those whose families had faced deprivation during the Great Depression. Working-class women's rates were already relatively high coming out of the Depression decades, suggesting a certain path dependence in working outside the home. Historical accounts of World War II as a time when many women were new to working outside the home do not square with the experience of this cohort. Many of these women returned to or continued previous employment.

Worklife Pathways

Much is made of the effect of World War II in attracting women to the workplace, especially married women, who made up 72 percent of the total increase in American women working between April 1940 and March 1944 and outnumbered single women in the labor force for the first time in recorded history.[16] But nearly nine in ten of the Berkeley women who worked during World War II had held paid jobs earlier in their lives. Figure 11.2 shows the distribution of Berkeley women across eight pathways of work from the roaring 1920s, when many were still single, through the 1930s and the Great Depression, when they were at least a few years into marriage and childbearing, and into the 1940s and the home front of World War II. The two most common pathways, each representing 30 percent of the Berkeley women, were having worked in all three eras and having worked only before having children (and not during either the Great Depression or World War II). Only 7 percent of the Berkeley women did not work in any of the three eras. However, it is noteworthy that 37 percent of them remained housewives through both the Great Depression and World War II.

A third of Berkeley women who worked for at least one year in three time periods—in the years before having children, in the Great Depression, and during World War II—are an interesting group. Typically they had husbands who struggled to provide for the family. In almost half these cases (41 percent), the husband was impaired (e.g., physical or mental illness or alcoholism), which interfered with his ability to provide adequate economic or social support for the family in the 1930s.[17] Throughout these women's lives, the only socially acceptable reason for married women to hold jobs outside the home was to help meet the family's financial needs.[18] Having worked between the end of their schooling and marriage, they had built useful skills in jobs typically held by women, for example, as nurses, teachers, and secretaries. These service industry occupations continued to expand during the Great Depression, creating promising ways for these women to supplement the family income or in some cases to provide the only support.[19]

A handful of the Berkeley women who received postsecondary degrees and worked during all three eras did so to maintain a career, despite their husbands' having salaries that could easily cover the families' needs. One of these women described how much she enjoyed her work as secretary for an academic department at UC Berkeley. Her husband, who was being interviewed

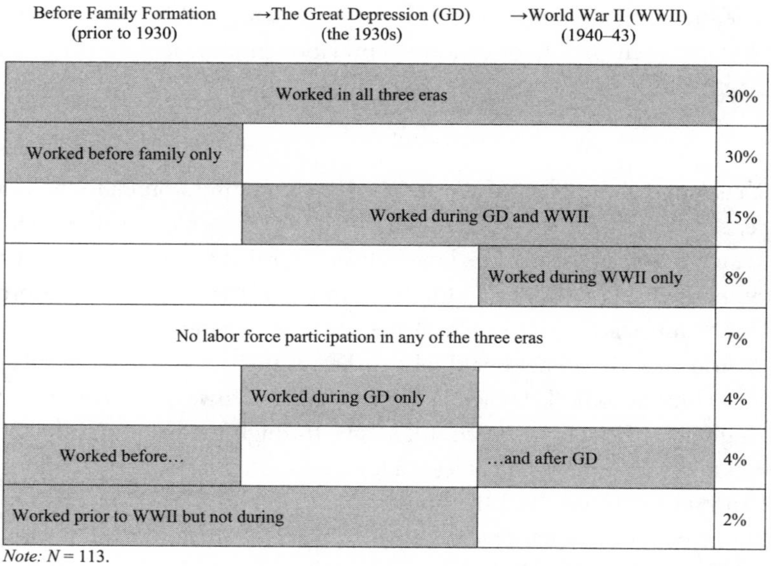

Before Family Formation (prior to 1930)	→The Great Depression (GD) (the 1930s)	→World War II (WWII) (1940–43)	
Worked in all three eras			30%
Worked before family only			30%
	Worked during GD and WWII		15%
		Worked during WWII only	8%
No labor force participation in any of the three eras			7%
	Worked during GD only		4%
Worked before...		...and after GD	4%
Worked prior to WWII but not during			2%

Note: $N = 113$.

FIGURE 11.2. Berkeley 1900 generation women's work pathways through three eras: before family formation, during the Great Depression, and during World War II.

at the same time, interrupted to proudly say that she was far more than a secretary, proficiently running every aspect of the department. His mother was "tickled" to care for their young children because they "could all use the extra money." This Berkeley woman continued to work after marriage, through the Great Depression, and through World War II. For the most part, however, the Berkeley women who consistently worked were doing so to meet family financial need. When employment and advancement expanded in World War II, they either returned to the workforce or kept working. Work was not a new experience for them.

Another third of the Berkeley women worked before marriage or childbearing but did not return to the labor force in either the Great Depression or World War II. In addition to the handful of women who never worked, these were primarily middle-class women with husbands in very stable or advancing careers across all three eras. They tended to be older, born before 1900. This concentration may reflect two factors. They may have been brought up to be even less accepting of married women's work than the younger women. And their older husbands were more established in their careers when the Great Depression hit and therefore better able to weather economic deprivation than younger men. Women who never worked again after marriage were also much less likely to have experienced a divorce or any kind of physical or mental impairment, their own or their husbands'. They had the means and family stability to achieve what was a strong public ideal for women—continuing to be full-time housewives and mothers.

Yet another set of the Berkeley women (15 percent) had work pathways that did not start until the Great Depression. Of these women 42 percent had some college, likely dropping out to marry and having little time to accrue work experience before marriage and the Great Depression that followed. However, their families were likely to have experienced the financial hardship and deprivation that so often required women to help support their families. In addition, whether as a cause or an effect of their families' economic struggles, 36 percent of these women and 42 percent of their husbands reportedly had some type of impairment that kept them from fulfilling their family roles. Two out of five of the women were divorced at some point and needed to support themselves and their children with stable employment.

Note that marital stability is the key difference between the women who worked in all three eras and the women who worked only in the Depression or the war era or both. Both groups faced economic deprivation, but the women who had worked before marriage and childbearing were less likely to divorce. Perhaps they had an easier time finding jobs, or had better jobs, to stabilize the family economy in light of their previous work experience. Perhaps they and their husbands were more accustomed to the idea of a woman's working, reducing marital stress. Cause and effect are impossible to disentangle here. But the women who worked only after marrying and having children were more likely to have experienced some impairment in family roles (whether their husbands' or their own) and to divorce.

Another distinctive pathway for the Berkeley women was to work for the first time during World War II. These women tended to be older and to have less education, but their husbands were more educated than other husbands. These women had married up the social ladder and were less likely to have been economically deprived during the Great Depression. Their husbands were more likely than other husbands to have had stable work or advancement in their careers, but the women were more likely than others to have experienced some family impairment or divorce. Given this, most of these women presumably saw wartime employment as the chance to become financially independent after or in anticipation of divorce.

There were too few cases in the other three work pathways to obtain a reliable sense of what factors contributed to the women's evolving worklives. What we see in five of the work pathways, however, makes clear the importance in family functioning of economic deprivation and stability, which are highly correlated. Also, there is clear momentum in the likelihood of working, especially from the Great Depression to World War II. Women who had worked before were the most likely to return to work or continue working.

Types of Work

Pathways of women's work also varied according to the kinds of work they did. Field notes and interviews with the Berkeley women provide more detailed insights into the positions they held over the years. From the intensive sample, we have extensive notes and records collected by study staff from 1929 through the mid-1940s. In addition, a subset of the women and their husbands participated in oral history interviews in 1976 and were asked to specifically reflect on their life and the times during World War II. Together these in-depth narratives provide a rich account of the types of jobs women held during World War II and how they compared with work they did before and during the Great Depression.

Of the 125 women for whom we have the most detailed records, about half (62) report being in the wartime labor force, 1941–45. Of the sixty-two women who worked during World War II, only three did manual labor typically reserved for men: one in the shipyards, one full-time in a semiskilled position manufacturing radio tubes, and one in a quartermaster salvage depot in Oakland, driving trucks and operating forklifts in addition to helping to repair large batches of used uniforms and coats so they could be reissued to soldiers on the front lines.

This information corroborates research showing that most positions advertised to and filled by women during World War II were female-typical jobs in the service sector.[20] Many of these jobs opened within the armed services, in war industry corporations, or in response to a rapidly growing Bay Area population with high demand for cooking, cleaning, child care or education, and health care. Thus the stereotypical "Rosie the Riveter" image of women taking on new, previously male lines of work during World War II likely best fits younger, unmarried women. Older cohorts, such as these Berkeley women, had a different experience.

Not only did most Berkeley women work in typically female jobs, the thirty-six in our intensive sample who had worked during marriage before World War II held wartime jobs in the fields they had been trained for, worked in before, or both. This reinforces the notion that older women's work during the war was not always as pathbreaking as it is often portrayed. The Berkeley women's histories rarely contain radical shifts in occupation.

Women who had worked in schools as teachers, cafeteria workers, or nurses had greater job security during the wars years when the population expanded and schools grew. Store clerks and cashiers continued their work as well. What did sometimes change was the type of employer. For example, one woman who had been divorced several times and had worked on and off as a teacher and a photographer through the 1920s and 1930s landed a job as a badge photographer in the shipyards. Women with secretarial credentials often took those skills to a military base or a factory in the war industry.

Several women were promoted within the fields they had worked in earlier, probably in some part because of the turnover as some women moved into higher-paying positions or male superiors left for military service. For example, one woman began working as a bookkeeper in the late 1930s to support her family when her husband died, and she was then promoted during World War II to managing the library at Standard Oil's Analytical Laboratory. Another woman, after working several years as a saleswoman and cashier in the same department store, was promoted to a bookkeeping position during the war.

Several of the Berkeley women continued to work in family businesses, tending to see an increase in hours and opportunity as well as in compensation. One woman whose family ran a gas station started helping with bookkeeping on and off during the Great Depression but then worked there full-time during the war as her husband spent more time managing a walnut ranch they inherited from her family. Another woman worked periodically in her father's photography studio through the 1930s, and when he died in 1939 she took it over and worked full-time through World War II. Yet another woman helped her father in his drugstore, then took it over when he died during World War II.

Wartime prosperity and opportunities seem to have increased women's involvement in family businesses when elders died, husbands expanded into other work, or sons left for active military duty. A couple of these women said they could spend more time on the family business because their children were older, in school longer, and finding their own work. As their children needed less supervision, it was easier to take advantage of employment opportunities.

Seventeen of the sixty-two women in the intensive sample who reported working during World War II had not worked between marriage and the war. These women were more likely to be employed in war-related workplaces, but most were nonetheless in jobs such as timekeepers in shipyards or were clerical workers in the navy, army, or war industries. A couple of women who had obtained postgraduate degrees but had not worked since marriage returned to the fields their degrees had prepared them for. One woman with a PhD in astrophysics worked in a statistical lab in the physics division at Los

Alamos National Laboratory. Another, with a master's degree in education, supervised a Great Books program in San Francisco during the war.

As a cohort of married mothers with some work experience, the Berkeley women generally held jobs that capitalized on skills they had learned in school or in previous jobs. They were predominantly lines of work that were service-oriented, and thus typically female. That they did not move into the types of jobs portrayed in images like Rosie the Riveter had much to do with their life stage: such jobs were predominantly filled by young, unmarried women.[21] However, it is also likely that older women were drawn to positions that involved skills they had used in earlier periods of employment.

Framing Women's Work

To further understand the work of the Berkeley women, it is essential to understand how the motivations for, restrictions against, and experiences of women's work changed across eras. These women lived through major economic and social transitions accompanied by changing expectations for women and their roles, including whether and when it was considered acceptable to work outside the home. These aspects of social history and the women's personal and family biographies interacted to frame and reframe the desirability, acceptability, and experience of work in women's lives. Very little is known about the aspirations and experiences of women working in the 1920s, 1930s, and 1940s, so interviews with the Berkeley women and their husbands shed unusual light on these issues.

DEFINING BOUNDARIES

Consistent with other descriptions of the time, the qualitative data we use contain little evidence of disapproval of the Berkeley women's having worked before marriage and childbearing. It was not uncommon for single women to work either to support their family of origin or to support themselves until they married.[22] On marriage or shortly thereafter, most women stopped working and became housewives and mothers for at least some time.

One exception was a very small but interesting group of women who insisted on cultivating a career after they married. One of these women was an education scholar who founded and ran a private school. Another, as noted earlier, was for years a secretary in an academic department at UC Berkeley; she and her husband joked in an interview that it was a good thing her husband had understood her desire to work from the start of their marriage or he wouldn't have lasted long. He chuckled and replied that her work never bothered him: "Money is money." Another woman, who waited tables, worked for a catering company, and later started a rose-growing business with her husband, said she never felt uneasy trying to both work and be a mother: "I don't think I had time to think about such things." Her husband added that he did not mind her working as much as she did. "We had a common goal and . . . I didn't resent her working. I felt that she enjoyed it, as I enjoyed what I was doing. She was always a healthy, energetic individual, and I too." Although these were a minority, it is important to note that some women openly discussed their work as personally satisfying and had supportive husbands.

As we showed earlier, the most important factor determining the Berkeley women's returning to or entering the workforce after marriage was economic deprivation during the Great Depression or later. This demonstrates the power of the norm that married women should not work unless it was economically necessary. Interviews with the women and their husbands reveal the underpinnings of this norm. For the most part, husbands felt it was their job to provide economically for their families, so if a wife worked it signaled that her husband could not meet this expectation. Many of the women who did not work after marriage cited their husbands' objections as the main reason. They described their husbands as "narrow-minded," "old-fashioned," and "domineering" regarding married women's working. When men whose wives never worked after marriage were asked why, they simply replied that "it just wasn't necessary."

Another component of this issue was the pervasive view that women's most essential role was raising children. Women who did not work in the 1930s or 1940s often explained that they needed to be home with their young children. Those who did work after marriage occasionally said they regretted not being fully present for their children in those years. One woman who worked as a controller during the Great Depression and World War II because her family needed the money said: "I regret that I had to work because I think a mother with young children should be home. I guess I'm old fashioned in that respect, I think that children need a mother's constant care when they are young. But I couldn't help myself, I had to go to work. I had to leave them."

The strong opinion that men should be breadwinners and women primary caretakers underscored the persistent norm that married women stay out of the labor force.[23] Even when married women needed to help meet a family's economic needs, some disapproval existed—and it grew worse during the Great Depression, when married women who worked were disparaged in the media, charged with taking jobs from married men who were trying to support their families.[24] In reality, most jobs that disappeared in the Depression were in production and manufacturing or entailed heavy labor, whereas the service sector was growing and jobs typically held by women, such as teach-ers, nurses, and stenographers, still had high demand for workers.[25] Men's un-employment was higher than women's, but it had much to do with a heavily sex-segregated job market in which traditionally female jobs remained avail-able while traditionally male jobs were disappearing. Yet women were still blamed for taking jobs from men.[26] They also had the burden of gender dis-crimination. Because wives were often assumed to be working for unneces-sary luxuries, or "pin money," men were often hired over women, and women were paid less than men.[27] Some employers instituted "marriage bars" against hiring married women, and once a woman married, she was expected to quit her job.[28] Even parts of the New Deal pressured women to stay home. For example, men could not qualify for WPA work if family income was above a certain threshold, so some wives refrained from working to give their hus-bands a chance at these jobs.[29]

STRETCHING BOUNDARIES

In contrast, when the World War II era arrived, Berkeley women uniformly reported that jobs were everywhere. The local press praised the sacrifice of women workers and helped mobilize community resources to provide ad-equate day care—unthinkable ten years earlier.[30] At least temporarily, the na-tional interest in "winning the war" partly overruled social opinion, norms, and stereotypes of married women workers.[31] Though women still faced dis-crimination in pay and treatment, they were part of a national cause whose success would ensure the safety of home and the common way of life.[32]

Many historical accounts emphasize how patriotism encouraged married women to join the labor force, and there is no doubt it must have played some role. However, in the voices of the Berkeley women a few decades after the war, it comes across as secondary, if it's mentioned at all. Patriotism was never cited as the sole motivation for working. Most women paired it with making some money for the family, like the woman quoted in the chapter epigraph. As we showed earlier, a large proportion of the married women in this study who worked in World War II had also worked during the Great Depression and continued to experience family hardship. Some had lost husbands to death or divorce and were the sole breadwinners for their households. For them em-ployment during World War II brought very welcome promotions and pay in-creases, not to mention the social camaraderie and respect that is missing from their reports of work during the Great Depression.

In both eras, women's earnings played an important role in the family economy. Thus their employment in these times did not pose a fundamental departure from the concept of women's proper place in the home. But the wartime economy loosened the tie between extreme family need and women's employment, giving room for the expression of personal and social values. Compared with the 1930s, during the war Berkeley women were more likely to take jobs for reasons beyond the household, and these jobs provided some of their most gratifying moments in the labor force.

Unlike men who described work during World War II as frenetic and exhausting, women who were interviewed in 1976 tended to look back on their work during the war years with nostalgia. When the woman who drove a forklift at the quartermaster salvage depot was asked about living through World War II, she replied, "I should be ashamed for saying this, but I had a ball during that time. It was work, but there was so much compensation." Her use of the word "compensation" seemed to mean more than just good pay. She was paid well—twice the salary she had made as a nurse in the few years before, a job she had taken when her husband contracted tuberculosis. At the salvage depot, a few blocks from her house, she reported that there were ten female workers to every male employee and "no tensions in the workplace." When asked if there was a union at work, she replied, "Oh no, nobody worried about a union during the war." She said she never experienced any kind of discrimination but rather felt a deep solidarity among the hundreds of women sewing and repairing defense supplies, loading and unloading train cars and trucks. They could work as much overtime as they wanted, but she could also set her hours to get off at 3:30 each day and be home when her children returned from school. She also fondly described donating blood along with her coworkers and organizing USO events. The ability to earn more money, be appreciated for their contributions, and connect with other women in the workplace recalls the way women spoke of their employment just after completing their education and before marriage.

Several women who worked during World War II reported a lack of prejudice against working women: three explicitly mentioned that all the women in their neighborhoods were working. One senses a certain diffusion of women's work through social networks, not just in working-class social circles. A couple of middle-class women report that friends encouraged them to take jobs so they could all work together. They repeatedly mention that no one was thinking about whether married women should work. But this contrasts with reports by several upper-middle-class women whose husbands made lucrative salaries throughout the Great Depression and World War II. Most of them said they themselves did not know any women who worked during the war.

One concern was the welfare of working women's children. Some women, like one quoted earlier, regretted having worked when they could have been home caring for their children. However, the main strategy for dealing with this pervasive ideology was to arrange their work schedules so they could see their children off to school and be home when they came back. Several women talk about how easy it was to ask their employers for these hours and to win over their husbands because they could be there when the children got home and have dinner on the table in the evening. One woman described enlisting her ten-year-old daughter and fourteen-year-old son in household tasks: "Someone would shop, someone would clean. They were good. They never resented it, and I paid them a little." If women could convince others that they could keep up with their domestic responsibilities, their employment was more acceptable.

Social strictures on the employment of married women loosened in wartime, but in a way that considered their paid work temporary, supplemental to men's incomes, and they were still expected to do their work at home. Even the women whose husbands were completely unemployed reported having to do all the housework alongside their employment. A few women who chose not to work during World War II said it was because they couldn't handle the two shifts. One woman said, "I was not strong enough to work all day and then have to manage the home at night."

Across the decades of the Berkeley women's lives—before marriage, through the Great Depression, and in World War II—we see a common set of explanations or motivations for women's employment, with different ones taking precedence depending on the era. The belief that a man should be the main, if not the sole, economic provider was strong but was challenged in hard economic times and when male workers were scarce during war. But the breadwinner/housewife model remained strong and was partly why so many married women left the workforce after World War II. This ideology goes hand in hand with the evolution of "intensive mothering," the idea that children need their mothers' constant attention, another value that encouraged married women to stay home when possible.[33]

Patriotism also enters the scene in the 1940s (having been instrumental during World War I as well) and somewhat overrides, albeit temporarily, the power of the breadwinner/housewife norm. It also may be that some women began wanting to work for personal satisfaction and accomplishment. When asked why they worked during World War II, a few women said it was because "all the women were." Some mentioned that all the women on their street worked at the same place and that they enjoyed the social time when they all took a bus together to and from work. They sounded delighted when they discussed working before marriage or during World War II, times when social approval rose. Thus pride and enjoyment might have motivated their return to work when it was more socially acceptable.

Yet it was not acceptable to say or to think that women might want to work for their own benefit. Even today, sociologist Sarah Damaske finds that mothers—whether they work or not—overwhelmingly describe their choice to work as a decision made in the best interests of their family.[34] However, this does not mean personal preferences were not in play. In fact, economists T. Aldrich Finegan and Robert Margo present evidence that married women's entering the labor market was less related to their husband's employment status in 1940 than it was in 1930.[35]

In one anomalous case, a woman did directly demonstrate her strong personal desire to work. Her family had immigrated to the United States from Greece when she was young. She said, "It's been a long and difficult life for me. Very difficult. I never had any kind of life before. Just raising babies. For a lot of women that's okay. But I felt cheated." Without telling her husband, who was very opposed to her working outside the home, she took typing classes and hid the typewriter she practiced on at home. They had a family store that went bankrupt at the end of the Great Depression. To help make ends meet, she applied for a job at a department store: "I went in on a Saturday just to apply. I was dressed in sports clothes, and they asked 'How would you like to work in sports clothes? Go to Department 54, second floor, and start working.'" It was 11:00 a.m. The other girls were from all over; their husbands were in the navy like mine. He didn't know about my job."

She doesn't say how she kept the job a secret for long, but her insistence on pursuing work secretly, despite her husband's opposition, suggests a strong personal desire not be "cheated" of that experience.

The Berkeley women's desire to work for reasons other than saving the family economically rose over their lifetimes. Their reflections on the personal and social benefits of working foreshadow the coming revolution in women's careers and their roles in the household economy.

Women's Work in Context

Women's work during World War II is often studied for its uniqueness and for its relation to women's work patterns in the decades to follow. For the Berkeley women, however, it was a link in an existing chain of work experiences, heavily shaped by what came before (e.g., job skills gained before marriage or during the Great Depression, continuing household deprivation). This is an important broadening of how we understand women who worked, when they did so, and what types of jobs they held in World War II. Work was not new for all these women, especially those who had ample opportunity to work before marriage or who needed to help make ends meet for their young families during the Great Depression.

Earlier examinations of women's work during World War II have understandably highlighted the patriotism of the time as driving women's entry into the labor force, and it surely is a part of what motivated them. It also served as a highly acceptable public narrative justifying women's working. But the voices of the Berkeley women reveal more complex motivations, some more directly expressed than others. Supporting the family when necessary or even earning extra funds to meet rising material aspirations, wanting to join in what their female friends and neighbors were doing, and even liking the work—all of these helped motivate women's labor force participation. We must keep in mind this complex set of motivations for women's working and examine how they alternate in dominance or become hidden under acceptable narratives across time.

In fact, after the war American women largely retreated to the home. The boundaries of women's work that had been stretched were coming back into place. Government-funded child care centers, which were never very popular, were defunded.[36] The breadwinner/housewife model of family organization, with its emphasis on women's belonging in the home, not in the workforce, reemerged as the guiding framework for life.

Our unique longitudinal data provide an unparalleled view into continuity and change in women's work. This view challenges popular conceptions of World War II as a turning point that exclusively prompted women's entry into the labor force. It underscores the need to understand women's work at any point within the context of their earlier experience and of personal, family, societal, and historical circumstances.

From Generation to Generation

Previously, parents just let children grow up and hope they turned out for the best.
Parents of our generation worry over what we have done wrong.

BERKELEY WOMAN

The lives of the Berkeley 1900 generation unfolded alongside the scientific study of children and families. In the space of one generation, these parents, who were having children in the 1920s, benefited from more knowledge about child and family development than their parents had. This information would continue to grow as quickly as their children did. What was this new information? How had parenting changed? How were new ideas about gender altering what it meant to be a husband or wife, father or mother or changing what parents wanted for sons or daughters? How were these parents managing a new generation of youth in a rapidly changing world?

The archives of the Berkeley study—especially interviews conducted with parents at the close of World War II when the study children were about seventeen years old—permit us to examine how the experiences of the Berkeley parents differed from those of their own parents, how their youth differed from their children's, the virtues and faults they ascribed to modern men and women, and their aspirations for their sons and daughters. These observations provide a powerful lens for understanding historical change from generation to generation. Our story repeatedly, and surprisingly, reveals just how pivotal the 1900 generation was in shaping or foreshadowing many of the perspectives, strategies, and struggles of parents today.

The Long Arc toward Modern Parenting

Before 1820, any professional advice related to child rearing in the United States was imported from England.[1] After the 1820s some American literature began asserting that mothers could improve, and even save, the nation through child rearing—and that it was the mother's responsibility to foster her children's moral development.[2] This was consistent with the eighteenth-century notion of "republican motherhood" that emerged as part of the American Revolution: that women should be the "custodians of civic virtue" and train each generation of daughters to uphold the morality of their husbands and children.[3] This responsibility reinforced the idea that the domestic sphere belonged to women, and in carrying this responsibility, mothers relied on religious and cultural traditions to guide their parenting.

ENTER SCIENTISTS AND SPECIALISTS

It was not until around the births of the 1900 generation that more scientific approaches to parenting began to emerge, challenging long-held cultural norms. L. Emmett Holt's *Care and Feeding of Children*, which saw multiple editions from 1894 to 1910, encouraged parents to look to specialists for knowledge about caring for children. As one of these specialists, Holt largely dismissed the notion of "maternal instinct" and instead gave mothers clear directives that allowed little room for misinterpretation. Holt emphasized the rigid scheduling of feeding, bathing, sleeping, and bowel movements and advised mothers to guard vigilantly against germs and avoid undue stimulation of infants. He discouraged mothers from kissing their babies and told them to ignore crying and to break habits like thumb sucking. Upper-class and middle-class mothers were much more likely to adopt Holt's advice than were working-class mothers.

About the same time, psychologist G. Stanley Hall ushered in the child study movement, particularly with the growing visibility of his 1893 book *The Contents of Children's Minds upon Entering School* and, in 1907, *Adolescence*.[4] Hall advocated somewhat more progressive and flexible views of parenting than Holt did—for example, that parents should respect children—although he still emphasized the necessity for physical discipline. Hall raised awareness of distinct stages in children's development that demanded different approaches to parenting. Hall also viewed mothers, at least educated mothers, as more capable than Holt did. Still, in this era, homemaking and motherhood were increasingly depicted as professions that required training and expert guidance.

It was during the 1910s—when the youngest of our Berkeley parents were children or adolescents and the eldest were a handful of years from forming their own families—that revolutionary advances occurred in the amount and quality of child care information available to parents. The establishment of the US Children's Bureau in 1912 was particularly influential in this regard. It was the first government agency in the world to focus solely on the problems of children and the first in the United States to be headed by a woman, Julia Lathrop.[5]

The Children's Bureau launched a set of publications that, by the late 1920s, benefited about half of American babies.[6] Before then parenting information was mostly shared informally by women across generations. With the Bureau's publications, not only was advice conveyed in a printed and accessible form, it became more prescriptive. The Bureau's initial focus was how to reduce infant mortality through research, outreach, intervention, and political advocacy. Its social surveys pointed to several factors that heightened infant mortality: poverty, low income, immigrant status, and working mothers. The Bureau's first modest pamphlet, "Prenatal Care," published in 1913, was designed to reduce infant mortality, and its "Baby-Saving Campaigns" that same year focused on prenatal care, sanitation, and maternal education.

"Prenatal Care" was the precursor to a longer booklet, "Infant Care," released in 1914.[7] It gave mothers information on a wide range of topics: bathing and sleeping, breast-feeding and solid foods, immunizations and injury prevention, and oral health, sun protection, and exercise.[8] Another Bureau booklet, "Your Child from One to Six," which arrived in 1918, provided advice from pediatricians and obstetricians on the years immediately following infancy.[9]

PARENTING SCIENCE AND EXPERTISE COME OF AGE

It was not until the 1920s—the decade when our Berkeley parents would be fully involved in family formation and would have a newborn child enter the Guidance Study in 1928—that the scientific study of children and the professionalizing of child-rearing experts had come of age. This was reinforced by federal funds through the Sheppard-Towner Act passed by Congress in 1921, more formally known as the Promotion of the Welfare and Hygiene of Maternity and Infancy Act. These funds led states, including California, and local areas like Berkeley to expand public health programming for women and children—such as maternal and child health clinics, midwife programs, traveling demonstrations and centers, and parenting literature—and to gather statistical information on mortality and morbidity.

The Society for Research in Child Development (SRCD) pinpoints 1922 as the moment when the field of child development was first formally recognized, with the creation of a subcommittee on child development within the National Research Council. In 1925 the committee was formally recognized as the "Committee in Child Development," with offices and staff in the National Academy of Sciences. In 1933 this committee was incorporated into the newly formed Society for Research in Child Development.

The science of child development and parenting was advanced in the late 1920s by funds from the Laura Spelman Rockefeller Memorial to create a handful of university-based child institutes across the nation. These included the Institute of Human Development (then Child Welfare) at UC Berkeley in 1927, which would become a powerhouse of scientific studies as well as a treasured resource for the community, providing families with information in the service of child and family development.[10] The Berkeley Guidance Study was aptly named as an experiment meant to provide parents with that very kind of information.[11] *Parents* magazine—the first major and widely read periodical devoted to parenting—was established at the same time (1926),[12] and the popular NBC radio series *Your Child*, hosted by the Children's Bureau chief, began about then as well (1929). In 1936 SRCD began to publish its highly influential Child Development Monographs, which fostered both professional and public discussion about child development.

It is noteworthy that these developments began to raise questions about the role of fathers, at least in the middle class. The lives of the Berkeley 1900 fathers, when they were boys and young men, unfolded amid these changing ideas. Although the norms of breadwinning and patriarchal authority remained intact, a more companionate family ideal began to emerge, one that emphasized the importance of fathers' care and their relationships with their children.[13]

The 1930s continued this trend, especially with the Bureau's publication of a new periodical, *The Child*, which ran from 1936 to 1953 and was meant to reach people in states and communities "striving to establish a more adequate basis for child life."[14] Four sections of the Social Security Act of 1935 brought landmark protections to mothers and children: Aid to Dependent Children, Maternal and Child Health Care, Crippled Children's Services, and Child Welfare Services.[15] About 1930, the minimum age for full-time employment was raised to sixteen; teens fourteen and fifteen were permitted to work only when school was not in session.[16]

It is no surprise, then, that in the 1920s and 1930s the burgeoning field of child development introduced new language that permeated everyday vocabulary—such as "sibling rivalry," "phobia," "maladjustment," "inferiority," and "Oedipus complex." It also offered important insights into types of parenting such as "demandingness" or "permissiveness" and into the stages and milestones of children's development and their characteristics at particular ages, such as the "terrible twos." Some of these phrases reflected how far Sigmund Freud's ideas had, in the two decades before his death in 1939, also captured the public imagination.

Middle-class parents in particular began to turn to psychologists for help with a variety of concerns and became consumers of parenting information.[17] Advice in newspaper columns and magazines emphasized that children's emotional needs must be met, that parenting was a skill to be learned, and that poor parenting could lead to disastrous outcomes for children.[18] The premium on emotions also extended to parents: all of this attention to doing the right thing for children heightened parents' anxieties. In the span of a few decades, children, who had once been viewed as economically valuable, were now "economically worthless" but "emotionally priceless" to parents.[19]

As we showed in chapters 10 and 11, women's work during wartime mobilization in the early 1940s prompted the need for affordable, high-quality day care. Given the Children's Bureau's emphasis on mothers' presence in ensuring children's welfare, it took a defensive stance, reinforcing the need for women to safeguard their roles as mothers. The Bureau recommended that day care services be developed only in communities where economic necessity required mothers to work, and only for children over age two. They also recommended "foster family" day care—home-based care provided by another mother who was staying home. This was viewed as superior to group care for children younger than three.[20] At the peak of mobilization in 1942–43, the Bureau also launched *Children in Wartime*, a series of radio broadcasts accompanied by magazine and newspaper campaigns, booklets, and pamphlets about the physical and emotional needs of children during the war. After the war, federal and local supports for child care were withdrawn, encouraging working women to return to their primary responsibility as full-time mothers.

GENERATIONAL CHANGES IN PARENTING

Immediately after the war, the best-selling 1946 book *The Common Sense Book of Baby and Child Care*, by Benjamin McLane Spock ("Dr. Spock"), symbolized the culmination of decades of parenting advice based on scientific evidence and clinical expertise.[21] By 1946, when a set of Guidance Study interviews were conducted, the 1900 generation had witnessed firsthand the evolution of this knowledge. In comparing her experiences with her mother's, one Berkeley mother noted, "Parents have much more training and much more information now. When I think how useful the federal bulletins [of the Children's Bureau] were, and how much more information I had than my mother about children growing up and the problems at various ages, I can see that, although the problems are more complex, the modern parent is better equipped to handle them."

A father similarly explained, "More of the parents of today have read and thought and heard about psychology, just as kids are getting better food than they did a generation ago. For the little time parents are in contact with their children, they're more understanding of them and better able to help them."

Parents' greater knowledge prompted a shift from what we might call "natural" systems of child rearing—children simply grow up—to more "scientific" child rearing, as expressed through education and training in college and in popular periodicals. The Berkeley parents seem to be early carriers of what sociologist Annette Lareau calls the "concerted cultivation" of children's development today—the intentional fostering of children's talents, achievements, and individuality through organized activities.[22] For the 1900 generation, these strategies departed significantly from those of their parents. Children stepped onto center stage in family life. In the words of one father: "Parents used to have an easier time raising children because they didn't pay so much attention to them and just let them grow up. They didn't have all these inhibitions about having to take them to nursery school and give them all kinds of special lessons and worry over their adjustments, etc. Our children have been tied up in one thing or another—either nursery school, this study, or something like that—ever since they were born. And all of that takes up the parents' time." Another father put it more bluntly: "In my parents' generation, children were supposed to be seen and not heard. The family didn't just revolve around the children as it does now."

Parents repeatedly cited a litany of opportunities that they provided to their own children but didn't have themselves: music, art, and dancing lessons; clothes, toys, and material things; plenty of food; better education and health care; a "good home" with more involved parents, less troubled family relationships, and greater economic security. Several parents said that members of their generation had actively decided to have fewer children than their own parents, precisely so they could make these greater investments in them. One father succinctly summarized this position: "We have had to restrict our family so that we would be sure that each child could get the help he needed."

Despite its many advantages, "scientific" child rearing also had a dark side. As parents became better schooled in child psychology, that knowledge also created pressure, anxiety, and even a sense of incompetence. One middle-class mother poignantly summarized this predicament: "There has been so much propaganda on parents, to point out their psychological responsibilities, that we are always overanxious, afraid we will create fixations. Previously, parents just let children grow up and hoped they turned out for the best; and if they didn't, that was due to perverseness in the child. Whereas parents of our generation worry over what we have done wrong."

It is important to remember, however, that the very study the Berkeley parents participated in with their child—the Guidance Study—was meant to provide them with information on how to raise children, gleaned from child psychology. It had, by design, equipped them with greater knowledge, so that is likely why we do not see major differences in how middle-class and working-class parents describe generational changes in parenting. Middle-class parents might otherwise have been the primary consumers of literature on child rearing, but these working-class parents, benefiting from the study, are somewhat more selective than their peers in their exposure to this literature.

Equipped with this scientific knowledge, the 1900 generation realized that approaches to parenting were not nearly as certain or as universal as their own parents had assumed. They noted that the role of parent was inherently ambiguous and uncertain, heightened because American life, even at that time, involved much more interaction with diverse people and ideas than in the past. Previous generations, they said, were sure what was "right" and consequently trained youngsters early to fit in with the parents' demands. This might not have been good for children's development, but it was easier for adults and, to some extent, for children. In the words of one mother, "Everybody was more comfortable in knowing precisely where the lines were drawn, and now [in 1946] neither the parents nor the children know." And yet, as another mother acknowledged, "The torture of doing the 'right thing' [in my parents' generation] must have been terrible, when all of your good sense as a parent said it was ridiculous." In the end there is a contradiction in the 1900 generation's having learned so much more about parenting, yet feeling they knew less because standards were less well defined and therefore led to inconsistent child rearing.

Shifting Gender Ideologies

Not only was parenting changing across the generations, gender ideologies were changing too, affecting what it meant to be a man, husband, and father or a woman, wife, and mother. As we will see, in the Berkeley archives these shifting ideas are powerfully reflected in discussions of the virtues and faults of modern men and women and in parents' aspirations for their sons and daughters.

There is a widespread positive hope that men might, in the words of some of the Berkeley wives, become "less restrictive" of their wives, "less domineering" toward their children, and generally "less old-fashioned." For another mother, the advantage of a modern man is that "he's given up the old patriarchal demand for obedience, is better rounded and educated, and has wider interests than when he just lived to work from dawn to dusk and had no energy for anything else."

At the same time, as we saw in chapter 10, a persistent theme during the war and the postwar period was that economic pressure made it difficult for men to be different kinds of husbands and fathers even if they wanted to. The stresses of work and financial responsibility piled up, and long hours meant less time with family. As one mother observed, "The problem of the modern man is the heavy financial load he has to carry with everything costing so much. Many men have to go on doing things they don't want to do that are dull and uninteresting because they have the financial responsibility and don't dare give up their job to look for something that would be better." These trends only compounded the psychological toll that many men had felt in the face of chronic unemployment during the Great Depression. In times of prosperity as in hard times, the role of breadwinner itself created significant strain and pain in men's lives.

Still, the loosening expectations of patriarchal dominance in families, coupled with higher aspirations for women's education and work, made possible greater equality in marriage. Parents repeatedly emphasized that marriage should be seen as a partnership characterized by give and take and by greater expressiveness and companionship. Equality in marriage was especially symbolized in the way finances were handled—not only what women knew about family finances, but especially their helping to make decisions about spending or saving.

It is important to keep in mind that the interviews we have been drawing on were mostly conducted in 1946, immediately after World War II. This was an important historical moment when women's participation in the labor force brought major changes in the care of children and management of households—role changes that would also be contested after the war. But women's work outside the home during World War II was framed as very much a temporary situation, a help to the country, that would not continue once the war was over.[23]

It is no surprise, then, that we hear tensions in these parents' expectations for their daughters' futures. On one hand, new pathways were opening for daughters, who were perceived, to use one father's summation, as "having better education and work experience, and providing better care for their children, and more intelligently than they used to." Many parents thought their daughters should not invest in education and work to become "career women," which would compromise their role as wives and mothers. This worry seemed to stem partly from parents' thinking women could not raise a family and invest in a continuing career at the same time. Their daughters straddled two groups that economist Claudia Goldin calls the "job then family" and the "family then job" cohorts, both expected to sideline their careers for marriage and child rearing, taking jobs outside the home only before having children or when the children were grown.[24] Although women's education and work were laudable, there was nonetheless little social support for women to develop families and careers concurrently.

Parents' worries about their daughters' becoming "career women" seemed to stem from perceptions that the emergent "modern woman" was challenging gender conventions. Beginning in the 1920s this was reflected in public controversies about women's behavior, such as smoking, drinking, and dancing at jazz clubs, as well as women's fashion, which promoted androgynous or boyish hairstyles and clothing. It was also reflected in the dramatic growth of women's political and civic clubs, initially in response to Prohibition and the women's suffrage movement, as well as social clubs related to literature, the arts, children's education, and the like. Berkeley had popular chapters of the YWCA and the League of Women Voters, but it was the Berkeley Women's City Club (now the Berkeley City Club) that became one of the most pivotal women's clubs in the Bay Area. The Berkeley Women's City Club had designed and built a clubhouse and hotel that included reception and assembly rooms for education and recreation, ballrooms for dances and performances, public and private dining space, a library, swimming pool, beauty parlor, and tearoom. The expansion of clubs like this seems innocuous from today's vantage point, but they were pivotal in the social history of women. They contributed to controversies about the "faults" of modern women because they threatened long-standing gender ideologies and created spaces for women to gather and engage in pursuits outside the home and unrelated to employment.

Having witnessed these changes, the 1900 generation seemed to want more for women beyond the domestic sphere. Yet they simultaneously viewed outward-looking or work-focused mothers as being away from home too much, as expecting too much of their husbands, and as materialistic, selfish, and "overstimulated by [their] new freedoms." This was especially likely in the middle class and upper middle class. In the words of one mother, young women "now want to be equal, but are at the same time dissatisfied and mad if they don't get a lot of chivalrous attention. They want to have equal rights and special privileges and pampering." Another mother observed that young women "say they want to be independent, and that only means that they want to be taken care of physically and not asked questions. They want so much. And the way they treat their husbands is a disgrace." A father expressed concern that "because women are much too involved with their clubs and social activities, they risk losing contact with their children."

Parenting Youth in a New World

Perhaps the heaviest weight on parents' minds was that young people faced a world filled with new "temptations," a word used so regularly it seems scripted: automobiles and streetcars, alcohol, sex, the influence of radio and movies. Youth had more opportunities to get into mischief, and the war-mobilized Bay Area heightened those opportunities.

At the same time, youth had "more opportunity to be better informed about all manner of things," to use the words of one middle-class mother, which left them "both wiser and more stimulated," in the words of another. The pace of such exposure was also quick: as one middle-class mother noted, "Adolescents now have things thrown at them with such speed that they can't digest them." Another said, "When you're kept ignorant," as were children of the past, "you don't have so many things to worry about."

As youth grew more mobile, they were harder to supervise. Parents knew less about where their children were, who they were with, and what they were doing. Large high schools, with their many social clubs and activities, created more reference groups and became more important in socializing youth. Much as Robert and Helen Lynd described in their Middletown study of the 1920s, and as other social scientists pictured more thoroughly thereafter, the American high school had grown so dramatically in size and composition as to be "a fairly complete social cosmos in itself—a city within a city."[25] As schools became the locus of youth activity and peer association, parents faced greater competition from these and other "agents of socialization," reducing their influence over their children.

Because the world was becoming more competitive economically, there was a growing premium on parents' investments in their children. Yet parents were keenly aware that they could not control the choices of their offspring, who had more opportunity to reject their parents' wishes about conduct, education, jobs, or mates. People worried that their children would suffer from their mistakes. As one mother said, "The children have this terrible problem of making their own decisions. I don't think it's right to put that burden on them."

And yet, as another mother pointed out, when youth "have more choices this creates more strain—but they may also gain more strength on account of it." In line with this more positive view, another middle-class mother offered a unique perspective on youth independence: "The trouble with the modern parent is that they say 'no' too much to a child. I think this is because the average child is superior to its parents. This is a speedier age, and the parents are trying to put brakes on their children. But I am a great believer in modern youth. They know what they want, they go full speed ahead and go after it. That's different from the way I was brought up. I think adolescents now have fewer problems than their parents did because they are freer and mature much earlier."

Along with the sense that youth were maturing faster, there was a sense that they were *less* involved in adult tasks and did not have as much "real" responsibility. One problem was that labor-saving devices had replaced some of the chores that children (and women) did in the home. Similarly, the shift from agriculture to city life released children from the intense demands of farmwork. But the biggest factor cushioning them from responsibility was that families had far more money. In providing so much more, parents worried that they had made their children unmotivated and lazy. As one mother explained: "My daughter has had more material advantages than either parent. She just lives in a better age, and while we've had our periods of low income and anxiety, she nonetheless hasn't lived in the acute poverty that both of us did when we were growing up. The interesting thing is that, at the time, I didn't realize we lived in acute poverty. But when I look back, and I think of how little we had in comparison to what our children have had, I realize what a meager material existence I had. It may have been an asset; who knows? But I had to live on inner resources rather than external ones."

Not only was it a different historical time, the place was different too. Many of the Berkeley parents grew up in rural environments. The urban spaces their children were navigating looked nothing like the small communities they knew as youngsters. Parents lamented that some important things had been lost in raising children in the city—the sense of belonging, the closeness to nature, the responsibility of farm chores, and an appreciation for a slower, purer, and more protected life. The city was a hard place to raise children and a dangerous place to grow up.

The very nature of parent-child relationships was also being transformed as the "generation gap" got smaller. Modern parents were seen as less authoritarian and more "authoritative." This concept, which for decades has been considered an optimal style of parenting, was based in part on early research on the Berkeley parents and their children.[26] Parents had greater regard for their children and were more interested in their lives, and parents and children alike were more open and willing to share with one another. Ratings on the relationships between the Berkeley parents and their children from early childhood to late adolescence showed that high levels of parental affection and involvement, especially from mothers, led directly to strong involvement with parents, especially mothers, and between fathers and their daughters.[27]

As one mother put it, "There's a free flow of communication with both of us that neither of us had with our own parents." Another said, "There's more frankness and more willingness for mutual understanding, even about things that in previous times were undiscussable." A father noted that, compared with his own upbringing, "we are a much closer family. Sometimes the children say I'm short with them, but they don't realize that they are 500 percent freer to talk with me than I was with my father."

The desire to parent in these ways was often attributed to the widespread availability of parenting information described earlier. As one mother said, "It is modern parent education that has made parents more understanding. They can discuss with their children many things that were tabooed by the older generations, and it has resulted from women, especially, having better education for child training." Of course, greater equality in the parent-child relationship also brought new challenges, primarily that children were more critical of their parents and might become too confident and less submissive. And yet, as one parent noted, this could also be good for children, even if it was hard for parents: "Today's children may openly criticize their parents, but they don't pile up their resentments!"

Aspirations for Sons and Daughters

PARENTS' ASPIRATIONS FOR SONS AND YOUNG MEN'S OUTCOMES

Given the more precarious early life circumstances of the 1900 generation, it is no surprise that parents place a premium on economic stability.[28] For sons, not a single parent referred to marriage and family as the central desire. They took it for granted that their sons would form families. What mattered most for them was that "my son make something of himself," as one mother put it, in order to be a good man, husband, and father. Parents wanted sons to secure decent-paying jobs, and for most this included pursuing higher education or postsecondary training. These achievements would ensure that they would be good providers with financial stability and upward mobility. And, in fact, over 80 percent of Berkeley sons reached educational or occupational levels well above their fathers', fueled by postwar opportunity.

Aspirations for sons centered on training for established male-dominated occupations such as medicine, science, engineering, farming, and the trades. Middle-class parents more often assumed that sons would go to college and pursue professional careers. Berkeley working-class parents ranked well below middle-class parents in the educational achievement they expected and encouraged in their children.[29] Working-class parents, especially fathers who had done heavy manual labor, nonetheless hoped their sons might have less grueling and better-paid work than they had known. As one said, "Hard work don't hurt nobody if you're grown and have some time for play too. But it's wrong to do that to a child. I've worked hard all my life—hard physical labor—and I don't like it. I don't want my son to have to do it. I think he should work some while he's in school so he appreciates school more. But I want him to get the schooling so he can get a better job and not have to do the heavy work for long hours I had to do. I had a chance to get an education and I let it slip through my fingers. I don't want my son to lose out on it."

Although early marriage and work were a common alternative to higher education in the transition to adulthood, in California higher education was available even to the economically disadvantaged. The state offered free tuition to high school graduates through an extensive system of four-year universities and junior colleges. A large proportion of the Berkeley sons— 79 percent—enrolled in higher education, three-fourths of them in four-year institutions (one-third at UC Berkeley). Approximately 30 percent of the sons completed one to three years of higher education, 29 percent stopped with a bachelor's degree, and 9 percent pursued some type of postgraduate work, usually a master's degree.

Even though qualified youth could enter a state college or university at minimal cost, inadequate economic support from a hard-pressed family made full-time study toward a four-year degree challenging. Our evidence suggests that deprived sons were just as capable on measured intelligence as the sons of nondeprived parents. But many of those with an economically disadvantaged family origin ended their formal education with high school or junior college: 56 percent of working-class sons followed this course, compared with only 8 percent from the middle class. (Those who enrolled in junior college were exclusively from the working class, and none of them later transferred to a four-year college or university.) Sons with just some college or none were also more likely to marry before completing school or before entering the labor market.

Although parents did not seem to aspire to military service for their sons, many nonetheless saw their sons inducted. Fully 73 percent of the sons would eventually see wartime service. But because the Berkeley study sons were teens at the close of World War II, most served thereafter and during the Korean War, at a median age of 22.3. Still, the Berkeley families were no strangers to sending boys to war, or to losing them, as older sons and their friends were of prime age for service in World War II.

The imprint of wartime can be seen in the early adult lives of the Berkeley

sons, who were young adolescents in a war-mobilized community and forged
pathways to adulthood during a prosperous postwar period when, for those
who served, the GI Bill brought generous benefits. This climate fostered the
fast path into adult life that would become a hallmark of postwar America.
The Berkeley sons finished their education at the median age of 21.6, began
full-time employment at 21.1, entered first marriages at 22.2, and became fathers at 24.6.

PARENTS' ASPIRATIONS FOR DAUGHTERS AND YOUNG WOMEN'S OUTCOMES

Many parents said they hoped their daughters would receive education beyond high school, but their aspirations for girls differed considerably from
those for boys.[30] Parents wanted their daughters trained for traditional female
occupations such as teaching, secretarial work, dress designing, and the arts.
Support for a daughter's nontraditional aspirations was qualified, as the following quotation from a father illustrates: "I think it would be fine for her to
go into lab work or become a physician, but I really don't expect her to do
much of anything. . . . I expect she will be married."

One reason for educating daughters was so they could gain work experience until marriage or, at the latest, until motherhood. Many parents mentioned that having training and holding a job would boost a daughter's self-
assurance and teach her how to value and manage money. As a mother put
it, a daughter "should have had an opportunity to try her hand at something,
which will give her confidence in herself." Another said, "Working is insurance that she won't just grab a man for a free meal ticket."

Having some education and work experiences was also "insurance for the
future," to use another mother's phrase. That is, daughters needed to have a
"backup" plan and be "prepared in some line of work so that if anything goes
wrong in her life, she can be self-supporting." Education and a work history
were viewed as protection for women in the face of life's unexpected turns:
divorce, widowhood, a husband's unemployment, or hard economic times
when wives might need to work to keep the family afloat. Keep in mind that
these interviews were conducted in the 1940s, amid both newfound prosperity and a dramatic increase in American divorce that may have sensitized
parents to the risks.[31] We should also remember that the 1900 generation had
experienced firsthand just how crucial women's work was during the hard
times of the Great Depression.

In contrast to mothers' aspirations for their daughters, fathers more often
emphasized that higher education would prepare them to manage a house-

hold. This perspective was not exclusive to fathers; mothers too saw education as valuable in this regard. College was perceived as making daughters more intelligent wives and mothers. In the words of one mother, daughters "can make home life much more interesting with more education, more reading, and more opportunity for discussion of child training. They can do a better job of raising their children because they are better informed. Also, they are better companions to their husbands because they can be more interesting."

Parents also saw college as generating "suitable" social contacts and ultimately increasing their daughters' chances of finding good husbands, as implied by one mother who wanted "college, social popularity, and an early marriage" for her daughter. Another said, "I want her to get a good education, choose a good occupation, and then [focus on] a home and family of her own." This was the default life course that parents saw for their daughters, and it was reflected in daughters' actual pathways into early adulthood.

In a few short years—by age twenty-four or twenty-five—most daughters had completed their schooling, entered the labor market, married, and given birth to a first child. Two out of three daughters (64 percent) began higher education, typically at a state college or university. Approximately 28 percent completed one to three years of higher education, the same percentage ended their educational careers with a bachelor's degree, and 9 percent pursued some type of postgraduate work. Half were out of school and employed full-time by age twenty-one, and they generally left school and started working within the same year. Most daughters became wives within a year or so of finishing school or starting work (average age of 22.2) and had their first child two years later (average age of 24.6). Except for the extraordinary level of college attainment, these skeletal features of the life course generally resemble those observed in a national cohort of American women born during 1925–29.[32]

Despite parents' desire for daughters' postsecondary education, they assumed that a continuing occupation would not be central in their daughters' lives. Each rung on the educational ladder increased the chances that daughters would be employed in professional, managerial, or lower-level administrative jobs and would attain career advancement into the childbearing years. And yet each rung also meant that economic need would not be a major factor in a woman's decision to work. Daughters who married well (in terms of the husband's socioeconomic status) were least likely to be in the labor force after childbearing, and higher-status women also gave birth to more children on average that women of lower standing (3.2 versus 2.6). By midlife, three out of five daughters had some experience with gainful employment, but only one-fifth had a stable work pattern that was not significantly interrupted by motherhood.

As with the Berkeley sons, that daughters came of age in the immediate prosperity of the post–World War II period left an indelible mark on their lives: the daughters entered domestic roles more quickly than their mothers had. Marriage became more a mandate than an option for everyone, and couples married and had children more quickly. In this way, postwar prosperity collided with a set of ideas (such as the rising importance of women's education and the acceptability of women's employment) that should otherwise have slowed family scripts, fostered education, and secured women's attachment to the labor market.

Conclusion

The lives of the Berkeley 1900 generation unfolded in synchrony with revolutionary advances in the amount and quality of child care information available to parents. By the late 1920s, when the Berkeley couples had begun their families, the scientific study of children and the professionalizing of child-rearing experts had come of age. Even more, the Guidance Study their children were part of was meant to equip their families with information to promote child and family development—and the Institute of Child Welfare at UC Berkeley that housed it conducted scientific studies to yield that information.

Parents of this generation were the first to recognize that parenting was a skill to be learned. They were the first to have at their disposal a growing arsenal of information to help them—from government reports, public health interventions, newspaper columns, magazines, radio and television programs, and the efforts of newly formed professional organizations. They were harbingers of a dramatically revised view of children: as human beings who needed careful tending and intentional fostering, who were emotionally priceless, and who would move to center stage in family life. They were also the first to provide a dramatically better standard of living than earlier generations. Parents were able to supply many material things, and children had many more opportunities and choices.

This generation of parents would also be the first to feel the downside of being better schooled in the science of parenting: knowledge brought new worries, anxiety, even feelings of incompetence. It also brought the realization that approaches to parenting were not nearly as clear-cut or universal as their own parents, and generations before them, had conveyed in being so certain about what was "right." Parenting now seemed uncertain and ambiguous, and this sense would be accentuated as the diversity of people and ideas grew. Indeed, this indecision continues to be a major source of tension today as America struggles with the social, ethical, and legal implications of diversity in family structures, parenting practices and resources, and child outcomes.

This appears to be the first generation of parents to wrestle with traditional gender ideologies. It is easy to observe tensions with respect to opportunities for women, equality in marriage, and the problems of men, masculinity, and power in society and social relationships. Notions of what it meant to be a man or woman, husband or wife, and father or mother were being contested and revised in new ways. These changes were playing out in the way they raised children and what they wanted for their sons and daughters. And they are still being worked out today.

There were widespread hopes that men would become more emotionally expressive, more companionate, and less restrictive toward their wives and less domineering and more nurturing with their children. These transformations would especially be driven by men's wives—in demanding new things and in coaching them. And yet, in both good and hard economic times, there was a persistent sense that the expectations and strains of the provider role interfered with men's ability to be better husbands and fathers.

This generation of women began to find greater engagement in life outside the home, but not necessarily in work unless in case of family need or, in wartime, national necessity. Parents saw new options opening up for women's education and work, options that would increase their daughters' self-confidence, experience, and success as wives and mothers. But many also thought daughters' focus on careers would threaten these roles. This group of women seems to have wanted more for themselves and their daughters but feared that too large a deviation from conventional gender roles would compromise their lives.

This generation also faced the challenges of parenting youth in a world full of many new "temptations"—temptations of the city relative to the country or small towns, temptations created by automobiles, movies, television and radio, and temptations of a war-mobilized city alive with the rhythm of production, a vibrant social life, and the steady flow of service personnel arriving or leaving by ship or rail. Youth had more opportunities to get into mischief, even risking adult-sized troubles that might alter their futures. These young people were also among the first American cohorts to attend large high schools, which created more reference groups and played bigger roles in socializing youth. These things eroded parents' influence over their children. Perhaps most important, this was the first generation to seriously change the nature of parent-child relationships. They were less authoritarian and more authoritative. They had greater regard for and interest in their children, and parents and children alike were more open to sharing with one another. The desire to parent in these ways was often attributed to growing information from the science of child development and parenting that had evolved as they formed their families and as their children grew. The Berkeley parents exemplified—and also unknowingly championed—a larger change in parenting that disrupted the styles of generations of parents before them and set the stage for much of what we know today.

PART FIVE

Transforming Times and Lives

In later years members of the Berkeley 1900 generation often talked about the past, especially the 1930s. Coming between eras of prosperity, the Great Depression shook the very essence of life for men and women and their children. Looking back on her life forty years later, one older woman from the lower middle class shared a vivid memory of a devastating loss of family income:

> My memory of the Depression is one of humiliation and frustration. It all started in 1931 when my husband returned home from a successful business trip only to find a telegram stating that he no longer had a job—no explanation.
>
> We had two young children, the youngest but a few months old. Soon all our savings were gone. I remember the day when the last can was gone from the shelf and the last bit of flour—to make biscuits. . . . Mother gave us money each week until I was able to get a typing position with the WPA [Works Progress Administration]. My husband did very little until he got into the shipyards sometime later. . . . It humbled me considerably.

The determination to be self-supporting motivated her drive for economic security and gave her a sense of accomplishment throughout her life. These and other major turning points marked the lives of the 1900 generation. How were such experiences expressed in personal continuity or change into their later years? What did they see as their best and worst periods? What had they learned about life?

13

The Past in Later Life

The past is never dead. It's not even past.
WILLIAM FAULKNER[1]

We have followed members of the Berkeley 1900 generation from their so-cial origins in Europe and America across the turbulence of the first half of the twentieth century to their middle age in postwar California. By this time in life, their children had left for college, taken jobs, and started families. Some older sons were serving in the armed forces as World War II ended and American troops entered the Korean War in the 1950s. As veterans, these sons had access to financial support through the GI Bill for job training, higher ed-ucation, and even housing loans. In many cases daughters enrolled in college or professional schools such as nurses' training, despite skepticism from par-ents, especially fathers, who insisted that they "will just get married." Some did just that, leaving college after a year or so to marry.

In their lifetime the 1900 generation experienced a uniquely disruptive sequence of social change, from the soaring urban prosperity of the 1920s to the unparalleled collapse of the economy in the 1930s, then to a massive reindustrialization to equip American and Allied forces in World War II, fol-lowed by twenty years of postwar affluence. What was the historical imprint of this extraordinary era of change on the lives of this generation? With one step at a time, we have traced their life journey.

From their vantage point in the 1920s, this generation could not have imagined the future that lay before them, a life course that would turn out to be anything but a customary path with familiar signposts. Earlier chapters told how this change influenced the kind of people they became in marriage, parenthood, and worklife. Yet no one in the 1920s could have imagined that they would live through the Great Depression and bring up their children in such a time, or experience the emotional shock of the Empire of Japan's attack on Pearl Harbor. Mobilization for World War II eventually set in motion decades of postwar affluence during their later years.

In this concluding chapter we ask how the Berkeley men and women fared in health and well-being along the path to old age, shaped as it was by their history and the inevitable loss of friends and family. Data on these years come from the 1969–70 follow-up as well as from another round of data collection in the 1980s. Philosopher Søren Kierkegaard once observed that we live our life forward from childhood to old age, but we understand it by looking backward. With this in mind, we turn next to the Berkeley generation's reflections on the life they lived.

In their late thirties to fifties, what had men learned from their work or women learned about the need for more education and the time to pursue a postponed career? And in their sixties and seventies, as they remembered the Great Depression and World War II, what stages of life did they regard as their best and worst years? What insights did they have about the turning points that placed them on a more rewarding path, or what changes would they make if they had the chance to do so?

Last, in an ever-changing world, how is this generation distinct from others, and what might it have in common with them? In chapter 1 we framed the life span of this generation in terms of Robert Gordon's documented assertion that the years from 1870 to 1970 constitute an unparalleled revolutionary century of economic growth in America's standard of living.[2] The oldest members of the Berkeley generation were born in the 1880s and the youngest during the first decade of a new era, the twentieth century with its years of even more accelerated change. This generation thus becomes a hinge between very different historical times and includes markers of a new life course that vividly reveal how lives are shaped by the eras, places, and social ties of a world in transformation.

Life Transitions into a Transformed World

The lives of the Berkeley 1900 men and women extend across most of the twentieth century's dramatic cyclical economic changes, from the urban prosperity of the 1920s to the Great Depression of the 1930s and the extraordinary economic boom of World War II, which brought their generation years of later prosperity. But were the health benefits of this much better time undermined by the wear and tear of a stress-ridden decade in America's greatest economic valley? We address this question by looking at the Depression experience of unemployment and heavy income loss as a decade-long stressor wedged between historical times that both were prosperous, but in very different ways: the 1920s and the war-mobilized 1940s.

The class position of the Berkeley men and their families led most directly to well-being or deprivation during the Depression. Advantaged men were those who achieved the education and employment that placed them in the middle class before the economic collapse of the 1930s. This stratum was less likely to experience unemployment and a heavy loss of income than were blue-collar workers and semiskilled or unskilled workers. However, middle-class men's elevated socioeconomic position in the community made them uniquely vulnerable if they did face notable income loss during the Depression.

By the mid-1940s they may have experienced worsening health caused by Depression hardship or wartime experiences. For men, health issues such as hypertension were aggravated by pressure to meet urgent production targets by working long hours. Women who worked during the war, by contrast, earned the nation's gratitude for their contribution to its defense and thus were likely to feel a sense of accomplishment despite any sexism of male co-workers.[3] Their experience enhanced competence acquired in the 1920s before marriage or in the 1930s both from working and from managing hard-pressed families.

We turn now to an account of the Berkeley couples' lives across three decades, from the 1920s into the 1940s, experiences relevant for understanding the Depression's enduring effect on their health and well-being by the turn of the 1970s.

FROM THE PROSPEROUS 1920S TO DEPRESSION HARDSHIP

The prosperity of the 1920s was especially beneficial for couples who had made it into the middle class by the end of the decade, despite the stock market crash of 1929. This prosperity was especially evident among older couples. They tended to own the houses they were living in, and husbands were well along in their careers. Younger couples were most often living with their parents as the 1920s ended. Whether older or younger, household heads in the working class faced a future with more job changes, dislocations, and periods of unemployment and underemployment across the 1930s.

Family transitions from the prosperous 1920s to the economic collapse of the 1930s usually occurred across many months, from 1929 to the depth of the Depression in 1933. In this first year of Franklin D. Roosevelt's presidency, the economy in California plummeted to its lowest point, and most families in the working class would not return to their pre-Depression level until World War II ended in the mid-1940s.

As the economy bottomed out in the early 1930s, the psychological impact of status loss hit the middle class particularly hard, making life especially difficult for women who had married men of lower status—the presumed public perception of a downwardly mobile daughter. Parents expected the new son-in-law to provide the living standard their daughter was accustomed to. When he did not, some parents threatened to undermine his self-worth and the marriage itself, for example, by giving their daughter money or paying the rent for a time.[4]

Even young husbands from the upper middle class, with modest salaries in new careers, experienced the economic anxieties of the 1930s if their wives were accustomed to a high standard of living. However, as shown in chapter 7, a third of the wives in the lower middle class held standards higher than their husbands. They aspired to an upper-middle-class lifestyle while unhappily managing households at a lower economic level. Nearly 70 percent of these women were inflexibly committed to high standards, a stance that left both husband and wife unhappy and stressed when they had to deal with a heavy income loss. Some of these women were openly critical of their husbands and compared them unfavorably with their fathers.

Berkeley couples, regardless of social class, also brought to their marriages other differences (such as age and foreign birth) that became a source of conflict during the Depression and led to a lack of shared activities and interests (chapter 5). For example, appreciably older husbands preferred markedly different social activities than their wives. Some of these couples did not have a single friend or activity in common. Cultural differences also were divisive, as when the modern beliefs of a native-born woman angered her husband, an immigrant from a middle-class Greek family.

The stress and conflict stemming from age differences were magnified for these couples by broad generational differences involving elderly parents who had emigrated from rural villages in eastern Europe. When the economy hit bottom, some couples could not afford to pay their rent or the mortgage on their home and had to move in with in-laws. Strained relations were common. This became more of an issue later in the decade, when families needed to bring an irritable elderly mother into their household. These women frequently tried to discipline the children in unacceptable ways or simply became very disruptive in temperament and beliefs.[5]

The adverse effects of income and job loss during the Depression were most evident among men who were below average on emotional health in 1930 (chapter 7). Vulnerability to economic and social stresses increased significantly for working-class men or those who experienced marital discord. A strong marriage enhanced the emotional health of men and women who were initially healthy. Even wives who ranked below average on emotional health in 1930 did not become less healthy in deprived families with supportive marriages.[6] Instead, as they had to assume a more prominent managerial role in the household, both that and their paid work fueled a resilient adaptation.

However, no social factor was more predictive of hard times across the 1930s and the Great Depression than membership in the working class in 1929. This status generally foreshadowed a Depression history of unstable work and unemployment, low earnings, and income losses into the 1940s and the country's rush to mobilize for World War II. Deprived families in the working class frequently had to turn to a last resort—welfare support from the community and state. In the middle class, the more deprived families faced changes in their accustomed way of life and became acutely sensitive to what neighbors might think. In all these ways, the stress of lost status in the eyes of friends and neighbors undermined marriages and harmed the mental health of men across social classes.

Many women in the hard-pressed middle class and working class entered the labor force during the late 1930s when their children were old enough to care for themselves and handle essential household chores. Their husbands were most likely to be the casualties of hard times, especially when they entered the 1930s with health problems.

FROM HARD TIMES TO THE ECONOMIC BOOM OF WORLD WAR II

The outbreak of war in Europe during the last months of the 1930s spurred the economy's resurgence as it responded to the critical needs of Great Britain for war matériel and civilian supplies. By this time capital investments and new housing in the United States had surpassed their level in 1929–30. The revival of the war industry mobilized greater local employment that turned sharply upward after Pearl Harbor.

Skilled and semiskilled workers were vigorously recruited by the newly established shipyards around San Francisco Bay and for civilian jobs on military bases and factories in the region. Accelerated production demands to meet military needs in the Atlantic and Pacific led to longer workdays and workweeks for men, and older men were pressured to work past retirement age. This pressure extended to some Berkeley men. As a result, health problems and death rates increased significantly among men in their forties, fifties, and sixties. Fatalities from accidents in the shipyards and other war industries also increased sharply—in 1942–43 the home front death toll of civilian employees exceeded that of the military.[7]

In 1942 the *Berkeley Gazette* heralded an influx of married women into the labor force of the Bay Area as "one of the most notable movements of this war, a development that perhaps not one American in a hundred would have thought possible. . . . Already there are thousands of women working in factories which formerly confined their employment to men."[8] As we said in chapter 11, approximately half of the Berkeley women worked during World War II, though most had worked during the Great Depression and before marriage and children in the 1920s.

The war workers with no such experience in the 1930s tended to come from middle-class families that were largely untouched by hard times. Women generally remembered wartime employment as having special significance compared with their stigmatized work that was done "out of necessity" in the Depression years when so many men were unemployed. A woman who worked in the 1930s observed that it was not enjoyable to remember a time when women were publicly criticized for taking jobs away from unemployed men when they were only trying to support their families. But they cherished the companionship of other women at work during the anxious moments of World War II and felt proud that they were contributing to the war effort.

Older sons of the Berkeley families frequently joined the armed forces after Pearl Harbor and served in marine, navy, and army units in the Pacific. The pain of economic losses and the stress of the Depression added to the worry of having one's own sons in harm's way along with the sons of close friends. Notes by a Berkeley study visitor to families reported that one of the women with sons in the war nodded toward her husband sitting in the living room and said that he had never gotten over "the shame of his joblessness" and now fretted about his sons' risky service in the military. Another Berkeley father with a history of unemployment in the 1930s took his own life in despair when his eldest son died in the South Pacific.

The war's end brought relief to many Berkeley families, along with enhanced economic well-being in the middle class and working class. Family income in the San Francisco region had grown threefold. Consumer goods were still in short supply as industrial plants began converting to peacetime production of automobiles, household goods, and foods. The coming years would bring war home again for the younger Berkeley sons, this time on the Korean peninsula, but it would also usher in decades of abundance.

As we follow the Berkeley women and men into their later years, cumulative evidence of hardship and adaptation during the Depression suggests that their life course will have much to say about how women survived this challenging time and about the substantial costs to their husbands in health and longevity.

The Legacy of Hard Times in Later Life

Immediately after World War II, the men and women of the Berkeley 1900 generation were interviewed about their life and family. Fifteen years would pass before they were contacted again for a major follow-up (1969–70), this time on their aging, health, and social ties.[9] Eighty-two women in the 1900 generation were interviewed both in 1929–30 and again in the 1969–70 follow-up, at the average age of seventy. By contrast, only thirty-nine men participated in the interview and general data collection, and all were still married to women in the Berkeley sample. (The survival rate of the Berkeley women by their seventies surpassed that of men.)[10] Some widowers and divorcees also ended up in the follow-up, but there were too few for analysis. In the Great Depression, family hardship affected men more adversely than their wives (see chapter 7).

At the time of the follow-up, the Berkeley women had at least two children and several nearby grandchildren as part of their social support, as well as close friends. Nearly half reported seeing at least one of their children every month. Family members and close friends were especially important to women with a past of Depression hardship. The Berkeley children had established families and careers and were part of another Institute follow-up (about 1970–72), along with grandchildren, most of whom lived close enough for occasional visits with grandparents.

In following the Berkeley generation up to the 1970s, we could not identify a single decade that had a greater impact on the health and well-being of its members and their families than the 1930s, with the Great Depression. Although this event did not expose all families to hardship, its effects seem to have lasted interminably, especially among the working class. The prevalence of loss in one's life and in the lives of significant others represents a central theme of this generation's life course as its members moved from the 1920s into the Great Depression and then to World War II.[11] From the vantage point of 1969–70, we view their well-being in later life as partly a function of adaptation to the stressful problems of human and material loss they encountered during the 1930s. Their adaptations to loss also depended on the social and psychological resources they brought to the Depression from the 1920s. Although the middle class had significantly greater personal and social resources, economic deprivation also exposed these families to loss of status.

With sample limitations in mind, we begin by noting the economic well-being of the Berkeley women as well as their housing, then explore the lasting effect of their Depression experience. When asked whether they were still dealing with hardship, fewer women from the middle class than from the lower strata reported such times (29 percent versus 50 percent). The middle-class advantage reflected both their status and economic resources during the Great Depression and their employment history. Supporting themselves was essential after the heavy loss of income, since they were also more likely to lose the support of their husbands through death, illness, and divorce—three-fourths did so by 1969–70.

During the late 1930s, when their children were older, 40 percent of women in the hard-pressed middle class had a paid job, compared with only a tenth of the nondeprived middle class. In the working class, the same percentage held jobs whether deprived or not. Virtually all of their employment was part-time during these years. By the 1970 follow-up, three out of four middle-class women with a background of Depression hardship were in the labor force and self-supporting. Over half are known to have been employed during all the postwar years up to 1970. By comparison, women in the privileged middle class (no economic deprivation) typically had intact marriages and were homemakers during these years. They lacked the economic incentive for employment, though some did hold jobs for other reasons. Women from the working class typically were dissatisfied with their economic situations, and two out of five held jobs but made only meager earnings during the post-war years.

In the middle class and to a lesser extent the working class, the Berkeley women were less likely to live in their own homes in 1969–70. Moreover, those who still lived in their homes had become less satisfied with them. For many the home had become a repository of unwanted memories of dependence during the Depression years. Evidence suggested that much of their discontent had to do with the need to be "independent" or in control. One of the women who lived through Depression hard times in the deprived middle class emphasized independence: "I do not ever want to become dependent upon anyone, which may partially explain the fact that I am working full-time at age seventy-five and travel a total of three hours a day."

Some women, especially in the middle class, gained inner strength from their expanding roles as their unemployed or economically deprived husbands withdrew. When men lost jobs, income, and meaning in life, their wives had to take on more obligations and tasks, from home production and management to caring for relatives and children and even as breadwinners and heads of households. Survival needs pushed women into more demanding managerial roles, such as borrowing money from banks and relatives. They got along on less by reducing purchases to the barest minimum and entered the labor force despite the adverse public opinion of women who worked while men were unemployed. Necessity encouraged perseverance.

These adaptations to family hardship bring to mind the personal qualities of women who have acquired a conscientious lifestyle, one that is planned and disciplined. Studies have repeatedly shown this pattern to be associated with good health throughout life, even during the later years.[12] The challenges the women faced tested their coping skills. By contrast, smooth sailing in adulthood, like that experienced by the nondeprived middle class, did not promote such personal growth.

Consistent with their education and economic level, middle-class women brought greater coping resources to hard times in the 1930s than did women from the working class.[13] Interviewers rated them as more intelligent and articulate in a pre-Depression interview, as well as more stable on emotional health. Having faced less deprivation previously and having on average more education and other privileges, middle-class women had greater reserves for adapting to economic hardship. Moreover, these pre-Depression personal characteristics did not vary by subsequent economic hardship within the middle class and working class of 1929.

To assess the enduring effects of Depression hardship on women's emotional health in later life, we used a three-dimensional model of health in 1929–30 and in 1969–70, with identical interviewer ratings on being self-assured, cheerful, and worrisome. Other factors in the analysis include economic deprivation and an index of socioeconomic variation in each social class. These analyses show a lasting effect of Depression hardship, both positive and negative, in women's emotional health in later life (1969).[14]

Middle-class women, whether subsequently deprived or not, entered the 1930s with similar resources. However, the wives of economically deprived men became more self-assured and cheerful in later life than the nondeprived wives. They were also less bothered by the limitations and demands of living. Remarkably, hard times left them more rather than less resourceful and thus less vulnerable to the inevitable problems and setbacks of the later years. It is noteworthy that neither economic resources nor emotional health during the early years of adulthood tell us as much as does exposure to Depression hardship about the vitality and self-confidence of these women in later life.

In contrast, these developmental benefits from family hardship are not evident in the lives of women from the working class. Considering all factors, the toll of economic loss on their physical health was insignificant, but there were long-term negative effects on their mental health. Income losses lowered working-class women's self-esteem while increasing their feelings of insecurity and dissatisfaction with life. However, only women in the deprived working class actually lost mental acuity by their later years, a result that corresponds with the findings of a larger study.[15]

Another way of thinking about loss and health looks at the relation between assertiveness and a sense of helplessness. In theory, the good results
of self-assertion diminish feelings of helplessness, in turn strengthening assertiveness.[16] Using ratings from the 1969–70 follow-up as measures of assertiveness, mastery, and helplessness, we found that Depression hardship
enhanced the assertiveness and mastery of elderly women from the deprived
middle class, whereas lower-status women who underwent hardship showed
more passivity and helplessness in later life. Their passivity reflected personal
vulnerability, concern about adequacy, and anxiety as opposed to feelings of
self-efficacy and confidence. These concerns clearly have roots in the harshness of working-class life.

Wives and husbands among the Berkeley couples experienced the same
level of Depression hardship, but as "breadwinners" men were held accountable for this misfortune. The psychological effects of this difference emerged
clearly from the thirty-nine couples who participated in the 1969–70 follow-
up.[17] Ratings on assertiveness depict a "strong woman/defeated man" theme
among couples who experienced significant income loss. Assertiveness is
based on three ratings: "behaves in an assertive fashion in interpersonal
situations," does not "give up and withdraw where possible in the face of
frustration," and does not "delay or avoid action." Nearly twenty-five years
after the Great Depression, these women clearly stand out as more agentic
than their husbands in families that were economically deprived in the Great
Depression.

How did the overall lives of these women change as they moved into the
1970s and 1980s? We do not have life records that relate the 1980s to their
early experiences in the Great Depression and the war years. Nevertheless, an
Older Generation Study of the 1900 generation in 1982–83 provides some insight on how they experienced aging.[18] The Older Generation Study included
fifty-three interviews with women from the Berkeley Guidance Study, which
is the basis of this book, and the Berkeley Growth Study, which contained
the same birth cohorts.[19] Despite the small sample size, data on these women
provide an informative account of their health and social relationships with
family, friends, and caregivers in their later years. At the follow-up in 1982,
they were generally in their late seventies to nineties.

To identify women who were receiving significant care from their family,
the investigators used multiple measures of health that were relevant to the
later years: self-reported health, judgments of health by the interviewer rat-
ers, frequency of doctor visits in the past year, difficulty with self-care, and interviewer assessments of reliance on help from others.[20] Physician visits and
self-reported health were the strongest measures of health in both 1969 and

1983, with emphasis on physical well-being. The study found that women in poor health at follow-up were receiving the most support and assistance from family members. However, this observation applied only to the one-third of the women who reliably reported a decline in health. Most of the Berkeley women were still living independently in their eighth and ninth decades.

During the 1960s, children and grandchildren were an important part of these women's lives, whatever their distance from them, and emotional ties to their adult children did not decline into their eighties.[21] In fact, their connections to their children grew stronger over the years despite little change in actual contact. However, their family worlds had become smaller as they lost husbands and elderly siblings. Contact with grandchildren had also declined with the transition to college, employment, and marriage, but the women's feelings of being close remained unchanged. In the midst of their shrinking family world, friendship ties remained strong. Most of these connections were with people they described as "old friends," though a similar proportion claimed to have made new friendships over the past decade or so, which were especially important to the widows.[22]

The well-known psychoanalyst Erik Erikson visited the Institute of Human Development in the early 1980s to observe how the Berkeley generations were aging—a project conducted with his wife Joan and clinician Helen Kivnick.[23] Erikson's earlier research at the Institute had included observing a small number of Berkeley study children in the early 1940s. During Erikson's return visit, he and his collaborators met family units that included members of the 1900 generation (who were by then grandparents and even great-grandparents), their middle-aged children, and their grandchildren (who were up to their thirties).

To their pleasure, it was apparent that members of the 1900 generation, as "investigated" and "guided" parents, were taking great pride in their grandchildren and great-grandchildren. Grandparenting had become a major source of meaning for them—a foundation for what Erikson called "vital involvement" during their eighth and ninth decades. They regarded this involvement as essential for creating generational continuity, especially in a world that uproots families for opportunity and creates family disruptions such as divorce.

Looking Back in Life

Members of the Berkeley 1900 generation learned much about their lives, interests, and abilities as they left home, pursued higher education and employment, and formed families in an ever-changing world. This generation married and started families before the massive disruptions and hardships of the Great Depression, followed by the mobilization for World War II.[24] Toward the end of the war or just afterward, they talked to an interviewer about their lives and these historical experiences. Some worried that the Depression might return after the war the way an economic recession occurred after World War I. The boom times of home front mobilization also brought memories of the prosperity of the 1920s and its shocking disappearance in the 1930s.

With lives tested and even pulled apart by the hard times of the Depression, some men in the Berkeley generation were critical of teenagers, with their high wages and carefree actions during the last year of the war. Would they be able to survive if hard times came again? In the middle class, men talked about the strain of long workdays and the urgent war production schedules they faced daily on the home front. They knew about men in high and low places who did not survive these unrelenting pressures, and they vowed to seek a more balanced life in the years ahead.

Aging was an issue as well. A dentist talked about how his career had changed as he grew older. By the postwar years, he claimed, there had been no turning points that would have led him to follow a different career, but by his mid-thirties he did not expect to become a "big success." Nevertheless he found "a lot of satisfaction in feeling established and settled. I can still see a lot of useful years ahead."

Berkeley women also spoke of learning what really mattered on their path to the later years. They saw quality schools and access to higher education as among Berkeley's attractions, and middle-class women were likely to earn degrees. Those who did not go on to college or other training after high school typically lost this option when confronted with the compelling needs of marriage, motherhood, and family. These circumstances were typical of the life story of noncollege women from the middle class. Life in a university community had made them keenly aware of this loss. When asked if they would like to change anything in their lives, they typically named going to or staying in college.

Two other themes were important to the Berkeley women in the interviews: resuming creative interests they had set aside to have and care for children, and taking more time to appreciate relationships and life's daily pleasures. One of the women had given up teaching art when she married and had children during the Depression years. But times changed. Her husband served as a naval officer during World War II, and as her children grew up she was able to return to teaching art. She soon became head of the art department at a local women's school. "I feel that many children in school have their art interest stifled by people who have no talent and are coercive, so that was a wonderful experience for me." Another woman wanted to travel with her husband, an interest she'd had to put aside during hard times in the 1930s because of the cost and because she had young children. Then came rationing during the war. Once her children were following their own careers, she was eager to make a space in her life for travel.

Women's lifelong education also expanded their range of interests. A Berkeley woman noted that her "points of view have been changing all my life. The shift to college changed my attitudes on a great number of things as I spread out and got wider values." Leaving behind her family's wealth and her father's preoccupation with what the neighbors thought placed her in a very different world by the 1950s. As time passed, she acquired "more concern with ways to be intelligently kind and helpful and appreciative of the needs of others." Married life brought a similar change to a woman who discovered that the important things in life were "everyday experiences." In her words, "The romance of daily reality is more meaningful to me and my husband than the straining fret over distant goals."

THE MOST AND LEAST SATISFYING YEARS

One might expect that when the Berkeley generation looked back on their lives, the Depression years would be an unchallenged "worst time of life." However, this decade was also a time of building families and the pleasures that accompanied it. The experience of any particular era invariably brings to mind the dualities of experience, the sentiment Charles Dickens observed in *A Tale of Two Cities*: "It was the best of times, it was the worst of times." Robert and Helen Lynd also made note of dualities in their study of "Middletown," Indiana, during the Great Depression. Hard times brought families together and also pulled them apart.

Such dualities exist in the recollections of the Berkeley men and women. After a series of life review questions in 1969–70 and 1982–83, the study members were asked open-ended questions about the periods that had brought them the most and least satisfaction.[25] They had the option of mentioning one or two of these best and worst periods, which coincided with specific decades, such as the 1920s and 1950s. Berkeley researcher Dorothy Field, who had analyzed these data earlier, did not link these judgments about periods of life satisfaction to their particular historical experiences, such as Depression hardship or wartime employment, or to actual family events such as the birth of a child. We focused on data from the first follow-up (1969–70) because its larger sample of men made it possible to compare women and men. We assumed that reports of the most and least satisfying periods of life reflect what was most memorable personally or most valued socially.[26]

From 14 to 18 percent of the men and women mentioned various decades between the 1920s and the 1960s as the most satisfying times in their lives. No other decade came closer than 12 percent. As one might expect, women were over three times as likely as men to report "having children" as a reason for satisfaction at this time (38 versus 12 percent). The most satisfying time of women's child-rearing was when children were small and mothers played a major role in their lives, whereas men were more likely to report the satisfaction of seeing children complete their education, marry, and enter rewarding careers. These differences clearly reflect the social-historical context of the 1900 generation, with its gender norms strongly emphasizing men as bread-winners and women as focused on domestic responsibilities. This rigid role division changed dramatically across the Great Depression and war years.

Most of the Berkeley women worked at some point, whether before mar-riage, during the Great Depression, or on the home front of World War II— but only 5 percent reported a job as one of the most satisfying times of life. What many women accomplished in finding work in dire circumstances in the 1930s was heroic, but the Great Depression was generally not a time they wished to remember or regarded as satisfying, since they were blamed for taking jobs away from unemployed men. Likewise, women's work was cru-cial during World War II, as they acknowledged, yet they rarely reported this period as satisfying. However, interviews tell us that war work had special significance because they and other women were making a contribution to winning the war. It is also noteworthy that only one out of five *men* consid-ered their work as most satisfying, and nearly 30 percent remembered it as one of their least satisfying times in life. As one man put it, men of this gen-eration had either too little work, as in the 1930s, or too much, as during the accelerated mass-production pressure of World War II.

A revealing portrait of a best time in life involves marriage. The Berkeley marriages typically occurred after World War I and well before the economic collapse of the 1930s. Not surprisingly, the 1920s emerged as the most satisfy-ing years of marriage for both wives and husbands, with dissatisfaction tend-ing to peak during the stressful years of the 1930s and 1940s. Berkeley wom-en's responses about marital satisfaction underscore this story by naming the early years of marriage as most satisfying.[27] In chapter 5 we told about mar-riages that were troubled over time by husbands' unwillingness to share their daily experiences and discuss their views with wives, as well as by chronic disagreements over finances and child care. The economic pressures of the Depression years heightened marital tensions, as did the birth of children. As the country mobilized for war after Pearl Harbor, the accelerated pace of life and longer work hours added to marital pressures.

In the early years of Depression hardship and war, the marital bond was clearly a major factor in the health and resilience of the Berkeley families, as described in chapter 7. Hard times frequently became bad times for both parents and children when marital relations dissolved in conflict and violence. Although less than 5 percent of the marriages ended in divorce, a number of conflicted marriages survived only with a live-and-let-live mentality. Only 12 percent of the Berkeley wives and husbands considered their marriage and their spouse among their greatest satisfactions in life, but their children ranked at the very top with 30 percent naming them.

This study asked about people and experiences that the Berkeley men and women considered among "their greatest life satisfactions," but it also asked about people and experiences that were "an important source of life satisfaction." Children are a case in point. Slightly less than one-third include their children among their *greatest* satisfactions, although this figure would be much higher if based simply on whether they are *an* important source of life satisfaction. Similarly, only 3 percent of the Berkeley 1900 generation mention grandchildren as the greatest satisfaction, yet we know from Erik Erikson's interviews with members of the Berkeley families that grandchildren were treasured in their grandparents' later years.[28]

Generational Themes

That we are able to detail the experiences of this generation over most of their life span is due to the inventiveness of Jean Macfarlane, the original architect and director of the Berkeley Guidance Study. At a time when social surveys about people were typically collected at a single point in time, Macfarlane initially recruited parents of newborns in the city during 1928–29 to observe their relationships across the dependency years. Thereafter, data were collected periodically with parents and their study child. Macfarlane broadened her intergenerational framework in 1930–31 by asking the parents about their own family backgrounds. Forty years later, in 1971–72, the Berkeley investigators again extended the intergenerational frame by interviewing grandchildren. In focusing this "longitudinal telescope" on families and individuals, the Berkeley study became a scientific pioneer, unmatched in its time for exploration of human development.[29] Over the years, Berkeley's Institute of Human Development achieved international recognition for the prominence of its affiliated researchers, women and men, as they broke new ground with multiple longitudinal studies of children, adolescents, adults, and eventually into old age.

To accomplish all this without federal support, the investigators had to use economies of scale in determining the sample size and the scope of data collection. Indeed, the National Institutes of Health in Bethesda, Maryland, the major US agency devoted to biomedical and public health research, did not launch such a longitudinal project until the Framingham Cardiovascular Study in Massachusetts in 1948, some twenty years later.[30] Abroad, the first countrywide longitudinal birth cohort study was launched in Great Britain in 1946.[31]

In the early 1970s, Elder began to work with the Berkeley archive, extracting information from the remarkably detailed life records of approximately 211 couples, their parents, and their children. These archival records, which are the foundation of this book, included a wealth of open-ended interviews across the years that we mined for valuable insights into how the participants' changing world influenced their lives, for better or worse. They enable us to capture their own perspectives, in their own words, and to transport readers into this changing world of many decades in the past. Our study of how social change is expressed in the lives of this generation, embedded in a specific time and place, has revealed its distinctiveness relative to generations before and after it as well as its commonalities. We turn to such themes in the lives of men and women in the Berkeley 1900 generation, whose parents were born in the nineteenth century, whose own children were born in the prosperous 1920s and hard times of the 1930s, and whose grandchildren entered their adult years as postwar prosperity slowly dissolved into economic stagnation and growing inequality by the twenty-first century.[32]

THE DISTINCTIVENESS OF THE 1900 GENERATION

Themes that distinguish the Berkeley 1900 generation include their experiencing major lows and highs of history at key junctures in life—World War I as teenagers or young adults, the Great Depression as they were raising young children, and World War II as they were in their prime working years and guiding teenagers or launching youth into adulthood in a war-mobilized community. More broadly, consider that they also experienced much of the revolutionary rise in America's living standard between 1870 and 1970; unimagined advances in travel from the expansion of railroads to the Model T Ford to mass air travel; revolutions in nutrition, public health, and medicine, including dramatic declines in mortality and morbidity and the eradication of diseases like polio and smallpox. These examples vividly illustrate the extraordinary acceleration of scientific and technological development during the Berkeley generation's life span. The son of a study member summarized this succinctly: "Never again will history equal the rate of change of this period: From covered wagon to the moon!"

This generation, like other early Californians, typically had roots in other parts of America or the world far beyond the United States. This too is an important aspect of their distinctiveness. All we have learned about them tells us that their families were attracted to California and to the city of Berkeley for a variety of reasons. They usually made the journey with others to seek greater opportunity or to settle with other family members in the state in what is called chain migration. They also typically left some family members behind. We think of the migrants as adventurous or as free spirits seeking a better life in a healthful climate, with access to higher education for both women and men and attractive economic opportunities.

There can be no doubt that the story of the great migration to California, involving members of the Berkeley 1900 generation as well as the Great Depression emigrants from the Midwest Dust Bowl and the World War II emigrants from the impoverished southern region, reflects selectivity in those who followed the lure of the west and made the journey. These factors pulled them westward just as other forces—the death of a parent or guardian, the loss of homes, family businesses, or workplaces to fire—pushed them from where they were.

The state of California offered great educational opportunity for young people after high school when it established the University of California, Berkeley, in 1868 and opened the doors to young women several years later, many decades before most state universities along the East Coast. Educational opportunity expanded once again when all California students gained free access beginning in the 1920s. Macfarlane herself was a member of the 1900 generation, born in rural California; she took full advantage of this educational opportunity, being among the first women to obtain a doctorate in clinical psychology from the Berkeley Department of Psychology in 1922.

The Berkeley study revealed a distinctive life story of status gain among women who overcame the limitations of the hard-pressed middle class. Gender norms in the 1920s defined women's sphere as the household, regardless of their education, yet most of the Berkeley women took on a community role of some kind, whether in paid employment or as volunteers. They were active, and often successful, in fostering marital communication, even in the most adverse circumstances. Before the deprivation of the 1930s and the stresses of wartime, men had the upper hand in determining family outcomes. This changed dramatically in deprived middle-class families when wives took on a dominant place with their earnings, family caregiving, and household management. When we observed many of these women again in later life, they ranked among the healthiest and most resilient members of the Berkeley 1900 generation.

By the end of the Depression decade, the husbands of these women had survived some of their worst years and were now entering a dramatic economic upswing. The reindustrialization of World War II fueled a distinctive historical era of prosperity and job security that continued up to the 1970s.[33] Young men prospered during this era, including millions of returning veterans who benefited from the GI Bill. These included the Berkeley sons and sons-in-law who entered military service during the Korean War. However, this uniquely beneficial time for employment came too late to make a notable difference in the careers of the men in the 1900 generation, though it contributed to their well-being in their later years.

A GENERATIONAL BRIDGE TO THE FUTURE

The lives of the 1900 generation exhibited major departures from generations before them, but we also see them as a "hinge" generation, to use Leonard Cain's phrase, between past and present.[34] Members of this generation were poised on the edge of dramatic changes in the life course that would intensify across the twentieth century and persist in contemporary life. Indeed, we have often been struck by how similar the voices of this generation are to voices of today, in a new century.

Some of the most profound examples concern the way men and women negotiate gendered expectations for family and work roles. Men in the 1900 generation shared much with later cohorts. To establish themselves economically, they focused on finding good jobs in growing cities, and they commuted to work. For many this was possible because their families had moved to urban California in search of opportunity rather than remaining tied to the land where they were raised.

These men also share with subsequent cohorts a strong focus on education. A bachelor's degree or some form of higher education was a gateway to rewarding jobs and economic security as husbands and fathers. And yet working full-time meant spending long hours at work and in transit. The increased premium on the provider role and on raising the family's standard of living often left men acutely aware of how little time they could spend with their wives and children. Thus job loss was exceedingly painful, especially during the Great Depression—both the material loss of pay and the symbolic loss of their role as family provider. The tensions they experienced are not unlike those of today's unemployed or working fathers.

Women in this generation also share much with later cohorts of women. Unlike their own mothers, many attained higher education and worked before marriage. On meeting their partners, however, they often dropped out of school or quit work to marry, and on marriage or a first birth virtually all of them paused, if not ended, any thought of a career—and had few regrets at the time. This outlook declined significantly in subsequent generations, although society's expectations for women's lives continue to hold powerful sway over their transitions and roles. Many of the 1900 generation women went back to work during the Great Depression, especially if their husbands could not find work or earn enough to make ends meet; and they did so again in World War II, when national demand for workers spiked.

In both cases the need for women's work was framed as being either "for the family" or "for the country." The need for such a frame reflects the default position that for women work, or continuous work, is not a normative behavior. Women's work patterns have changed dramatically since then, yet this framing is evident in the way recent generations of women continue to describe their work as being about family needs rather than self-fulfillment.[35] Still, women of the Berkeley 1900 generation demonstrate that women were employed and played a crucial role in the household economy well before World War II, which is so often heralded as the turning point for women's entering the labor market. The 1900 generation women show us that the Great Depression is also a very important marker in that history.

This is a generation of women for whom social scripts were in flux, and middle-class women were quietly rewriting them. They were pursuing some postsecondary education, though generally in fields like teaching or nursing, and working before marriage. They were claiming significant roles outside the domestic sphere, often in social and civic ventures, that left them more fulfilled and better integrated into their communities. They were seeking more companionate marriages, characterized by greater communication and equality. In all these ways, the behaviors and choices of the 1900 generation women were harbingers of what was to come in women's lives as the century unfolded—certainly for the middle class.

What is perhaps even more profound is that the 1900 men and women in the middle class foreshadowed—and, we might argue, were leading—a deep cultural turn in their commitments and approaches to parenting. In these families we can see the roots of the intensive parenting we know today. They were the first generation of parents to see revolutionary advances in the amount and quality of child care information. They absorbed a sense that parenting is a skill to be mastered. Their greater knowledge meant they worried about their children's futures. They were conscious of fathers' important role in children's development, and of modeling intimate relationships and gender roles for their sons and daughters. They struggled with raising children in a new world that offered greater mobility, plentiful temptations, the erosion of tradition, and diminished parental influence.

The lives of the 1900 generation remind us of the experiences they have in common with generations born later in the twentieth century. Social origins and resources are important in determining life's directions and outcomes, alongside choices and actions. Our lives are not our own but are embedded in family relationships and interactions that shape us. And all lives carry the imprint of their times, distinguished by changes that punctuate an era. Most of all, they remind us that human beings are extraordinarily resilient in the face of unexpected and often dramatic alterations in life circumstances. Moreover, every generation since 1900 has experienced a rapid, even accelerating social change that may seem beyond its control, leaving members feeling unsettled, standing as they are on the edge of change.

Acknowledgments

This book, cultivated over four decades, has benefited from the wisdom, generosity, and support of a great number of people. Here we endeavor to acknowledge those who have been a central part of the journey.

As detailed in appendix C, this project was ultimately made possible more than ninety years ago by the pioneering vision of Harold E. Jones and Herbert R. Stolz, then research director and director of the Institute of Child Welfare (now the Institute of Human Development, or IHD) at the University of California, Berkeley. In 1927 Jones and Stolz invited Jean Walker Macfarlane to direct a study that would follow children born in 1928–29 through preschool and across the transition into elementary school. The parents of these children are the subjects of this book, whom we call the Berkeley 1900 generation. We owe a great debt to these early investigators, especially Macfarlane for her rigorous attention to the family backgrounds of these parents, their coming of age, and the interactions of the families over the course of the study.

The initial stage of data preparation and analysis for this project was completed at the IHD during Elder's sabbatical year in 1972–73 with support from the National Science Foundation (NSF). By the end of the academic year at the Institute, Elder had drafted his concept of a book with chapters dealing with social change in the family and individual lives. We are grateful to IHD and NSF for supporting his vision and helping to launch this project.

Motivated by the book's core themes, in the decades that followed Elder began developing appropriate measures and chapter drafts, as well as publications on the parents' child rearing, the sons' and daughters' transition to adulthood, and the parents' aging and health. During those years, he benefited from the exceptional support of graduate students, postdoctoral fellows, staff, and other collaborators at his multiple institutional homes. These included the Odum Institute for Research in the Social Sciences at the University of North Carolina at Chapel Hill (UNC-CH) in the early 1970s, the Boys Town Research Center during the late 1970s, the Cornell University Department of Human Development during the early 1980s, and the Carolina Population Center at UNC-CH from 1984 to the present. Other projects slowed his progress until he recognized about 2010 that the time had come to make the book a priority.

Elder invited Richard Settersten and Lisa Pearce to join the project, and in 2012 they embarked on a journey that initially reviewed drafted chapters and developed a book outline that addressed additional topics and incorporated new chapters. With their involvement and leadership, a book on the changing lives of the 1900 generation began to emerge. During the next seven years, the authors took turns developing and revising new and old chapters, with frequent communications by phone, by mail, and at conferences. The book project benefited tremendously from the ongoing support of staff, colleagues, and students at our two institutions: the University of North Carolina at Chapel Hill and Oregon State University.

The Carolina Population Center (CPC) provided space for Elder and Pearce to work as well as to meet with Settersten remotely and in person. The CPC staff, especially members from the Information Technology, Graphics, and Library groups, have been invaluable in supporting this project. We greatly appreciate the seed grant CPC provided in 2013 to enable very helpful assistance from Joyce Tabor, Karam Hwang, and Rachel Rowe to digitize, clean, and organize study documents and data. When we first came together, Terry Poythress identified and shared core study documents from Elder's files. We thank the students of Pearce's first-year seminar in the spring of 2014 for helping to code and analyze interview data used in chapter 4. We are grateful to Renee Ryberg for assistance with analyses used in chapter 11. And we are grateful to Karolyn Tyson and Michele Berger for providing helpful comments on chapter drafts.

At Oregon State University (OSU), people and centers have been similarly generous in their support. The Hallie Ford Center for Healthy Children and Families, which Settersten directed, was the site of significant support, both through his endowed directorship and from the College of Public Health and Human Sciences. Over the years, multiyear graduate research assistantships were provided to Bethany Godlewski, Asia Thogmartin, and Corine Tyler, who all played important roles along the way—scanning and cleaning archival documents; analyzing quantitative or qualitative data; conducting literature searches; and generating an extensive collection of meeting notes that have become an archive in their own right. Bethany was especially helpful with chapters 2 and 10 and Corine, with chapter 12. Settersten was supported by a Library Research Travel Grant from OSU's Valley Library, which funded one trip for him to obtain data at UNC-CH and another for Bethany and Terese Jones to gather documents from UC Berkeley's Bancroft Library and the Berkeley Historical Society. Patty Jackson and Laura Arreola helped with formatting chapters and generating tables and figures. The OSU Center for the Humanities, then directed by David Robinson, provided space for Settersten to focus on the book during his sabbatical year, where he also received helpful feedback on an early draft of chapter 10. The Hallie Ford Center also provided support for Elder to visit Oregon when he was selected to give the Campbell Lecture on Childhood Relationships, Risk, and Resilience.

We are grateful for the support and guidance of the superb staff of the University of Chicago Press—Elizabeth Branch Dyson, executive editor, who saw the great promise of this book early on and waited patiently for many years as we crafted it; Alice Bennett, longtime copyeditor, who helped the prose sing more beautifully; and Erin DeWitt, Rian Lussier, and Mollie McFee in their respective roles as senior manuscript editor, promotions coordinator, and editorial associate.

We also wish to thank Kevin Grimm, now at Arizona State University, and Keith Widaman, of the University of California, Riverside, for their assistance in securing additional Berkeley Guidance Study data.

Finally, across the years of this collaborative project we have been ever grateful to each other and to our partners for their love, support, and understanding. This most remarkable journey has brought its challenges, but it has above all been deeply rewarding and left an indelible bond between us.

Addendum

In the first decade of this century, I viewed two scholars, Rick Settersten and Lisa Pearce, as an ideal match for collaboration on the Berkeley book project. They have indeed been that and much more. In every respect their distinguished literary contributions and hard logistical labors have brought our book to life. I am most fortunate and grateful for the privilege and pleasure of working with them on this unique enterprise.

Glen H. Elder Jr.

Appendix A: Additional Tables and Figures

TABLE A5.1. Aspects of the marital bond in relation to areas of marital conflict and differences (average scores and correlations)

Areas	M (SD)	Aspects of the marital bond[a]		
		Adjusted to each other[k]	Wife close to husband	Husband close to wife
Conflict over:				
Finances[b]	6.2 (1.67)	−.70	−.34	−.39
Sex[c]	3.3 (1.17)	−.69	−.59	−.60
Child discipline[d]	3.3 (0.88)	−.66	−.31	−.40
Neatness[e]	2.6 (1.06)	−.29	−.09	−.28
Culture (nationality)[f]	1.7 (0.90)	−.27	−.18	−.11
Kin[g]	2.9 (1.22)	−.24	−.23	−.12
Religion[h]	1.8 (0.93)	−.17	.07	−.10
Differences in:				
Education standards[i]	2.6 (1.06)	−.39	−.31	−.18
General interests (social, recreational)[j]	3.0 (1.04)	−.53	−.34	−.45

[a] These columns reflect correlations between husbands and wives. All ratings in this correlational analysis range from scores of 1 to 5 (except conflict over finances, which ranges from 1 to 10). Correlations above .20 are statistically significant at the .05 level. Minimum $N = 105$.

[b] Scores on finances reflect a sum of scores on two five-point ratings: conflict over expenditures (from no friction [1] to acute disagreement [5]) and conflict over the size or management of income (from no friction, completely satisfying [1] to much friction over management [5]).

[c] Scores on sex range from exceptionally well adjusted (1) to mutual hostility, discrepancy in attitude and drive (5).

[d] Scores on child discipline range from practically complete agreement (1) to marked differences with real conflict (5).

[e] Scores on neatness conflict range from no difference in standards (1) to real conflict over differing standards (5).

[f] Scores for culture, which refers to cultural patterns associated with nationality, range from no conflict (1) to severe conflict (5).

[g] Scores for kin range from great companionability (1) to serious conflict and open hostility (5).

[h] Scores on religion range from no conflict and the same attitude (1) to severe conflict (5).

[i] Scores on similarity of educational standards range from very similar (1) to very discrepant standards (5).

[j] Scores on general interests range from all interests in common (1) to no interests in common (5).

[k] The general rating on adjustment between husband and wife varies from exceptionally happy adjustment (1) to extreme incompatibility and conflict (5). These scores were reverse-coded to make a higher score to mean better compatibility.

TABLE A5.2. Marital compatibility, by family type and social class (average scores)

| Family type | Social class | | Class comparison |
	Middle class	Working class	
Toward symmetry	53.1 (28)	56.5 (5)	$t = 0.71$, ns
Transitional	49.3 (31)	55.2 (11)	$t = 1.73$, $p < .10$
Asymmetric	40.2 (6)	47.8 (24)	$t = 1.78$, $p < .10$
F	4.21, $p < .01$	3.69, $p < .05$	

Note: Ns in parentheses. Scores on marital compatibility index were subtracted from 100 to make high values equal to compatibility.

TABLE A5.3. Role preferences by family type (percentages)

| Role preferences | Family type | | |
	Asymmetric relations	Transitional	Toward symmetry
Woman's role as homemaker[a] (N)	(N = 31)	(N = 42)	(N = 22)
Neither spouse prefers	3	17	34
One spouse prefers more than the other	23	19	22
Husband and wife	74	64	44
Mutuality in marriage[b] (N)	(N = 31)	(N = 41)	(N = 33)
Both spouses value	26	32	55
One spouse values more than the other	43	44	33
Neither	32	24	12

Note: Interviews with both parents and records of home contacts during the 1930s provided the information for coding these items.

[a] Woman's role as homemaker was assessed by the following question: "To what extent do mother and father believe that a woman's central role is that of a homemaker?" This item and the code categories were designed to measure sentiment regarding the idea that a "woman's place is in the home."

[b] Mutuality in marriage was assessed by the following item: "To what extent are mother and father inclined toward the ideal of mutuality in marriage: in affection, shared communication, decision making, companionship?"

TABLE A6.1. Economic deprivation among middle-class men, by antecedent factors (regression coefficients)

| Antecedent factors | Economic deprivation | | | |
| | Without unemployment | | With unemployment | |
	r	beta	r	beta
Unemployed 1930–35				
(1 = unemployed; 0 = other)	—	—	.39	.33
Socioeconomic dependence, 1929				
(1 = dependent; 0 = other)	.33	.28	.33	.27
Industry of 1929 occupation				
(1 = high risk; 0 = other)	.25	.20	.25	.17
Education of family head				
(1 = less than college; 0 = college)	.25	.11	.25	.08
	$R^2 = .17$		$R^2 = .28$	

Note: Regression coefficients in standard form, intensive sample ($N = 59$). Men in the economically deprived category were given a score of 1, the nondeprived men a score of 0. Owing to the variance limitations of the dependent variable in this analysis (economic deprivation), we restrict our interpretation of the effects of the independent variables to their relative position (in contrast to emphasis on the absolute value of each beta coefficient). By focusing on how well antecedent variables predict membership in the deprived versus nondeprived groups, our use of multiple regression analysis parallels a discriminant function analysis.

TABLE A6.2. Economic deprivation among working-class men, by antecedent factors (regression coefficients)

| Antecedent factors | Economic deprivation | | | |
| | Without unemployment | | With unemployment | |
	r	beta	r	beta
Unemployed 1930–35				
(1 = unemployed; 0 = other)	—	—	.54	.50
Occupation of family head, 1929				
(1 = semiskilled, unskilled; 0 = other)	.07	−.04	.07	−.13
Socioeconomic dependence, 1929				
(1 = dependent; 0 = other)	.20	.24	.20	.12
Age of family head				
(older = higher value)	.32	.33	.32	.23
	$R^2 = .15$		$R^2 = .36$	

Note: Regression coefficients in standard form, intensive sample ($N = 41$). See note, Table A6.1.

TABLE A6.3. Worklife instability of men, by social class, economic deprivation, and birth cohort (percentages)

	Older men		Younger men	
	Nondeprived	Deprived	Nondeprived	Deprived
Middle class				
Stable	90	50	69	35
Mixed	10	21	19	41
Unstable	—	29	13	24
	100 (41)	100 (24)	100 (32)	100 (17)
Working class				
Stable	92	26	64	19
Mixed	8	32	23	25
Unstable	—	42	14	56
	100 (13)	100 (19)	100 (22)	100 (16)

Note: Worklife instability was coded on a four-point scale, with 0 being stable, 2 to 3 being unstable, and 1 being mixed. *N*s in parentheses.

TABLE A7.1. Economic standards of middle-class women, by economic deprivation and time period (partial correlations)

Economic standard	Wife unhappy with own lot[a] 1931–32	Rating of financial security 1932–34	Rating of marital consensus 1932–34
Level of standard[b]			
Nondeprived (*N* = 40)	.14*	−.17	−.15
Deprived (*N* = 23)	.44	−.22	−.21
Inflexible standard[c]			
Nondeprived (*N* = 20)	.11*	−.42*	−.57**
Deprived (*N* = 16)	.48	−.20	.05

Note: Analyses control for annual family income. Total annual family income in 1931 was used for wife's dissatisfaction with her own lot. In the case of financial security and consensus, we used an average of the yearly income for 1932–34.

*<.05, **<.01 for comparison of averages between deprived and nondeprived.

[a] Scale ratings: A seven-point scale, obtained in 1931–32, with a higher score representing greater dissatisfaction.

[b] Level of economic standards was coded from early 1930 case materials as follows: 1 = plain standards, 2 = average, 3 = above-average, and 4 = high economic standards.

[c] Only cases with above average economic standards were coded on flexibility of commitment; the four working-class women with above-average standards were omitted from the analysis. Evidence of inflexibility was coded 1; flexibility as 0.

TABLE A8.1. Depression fertility of Berkeley women, by economic deprivation in the 1930s and number of children in 1929, adjusted for selected antecedent factors

| Parity in 1929 | Depression fertility (1930–39) | |
	Nondeprived adjusted percentage	Deprived adjusted percentage
One child	58 (63)[a]	44 (35)
Two or more children	27 (56)	27 (57)
Percent difference	31[b]	17

[a] Adjusted percentages of women who gave birth to at least one child. *Ns* in parentheses. This table presents the results of multiple classification analyses by 1929 parity. Four variables were controlled: woman's education, age, and ethnicity (in each case, 1 = Catholic; foreign-born; or black; 0 = other), and social class in 1929.

[b] Percentage difference between those with one child and those with two or more children.

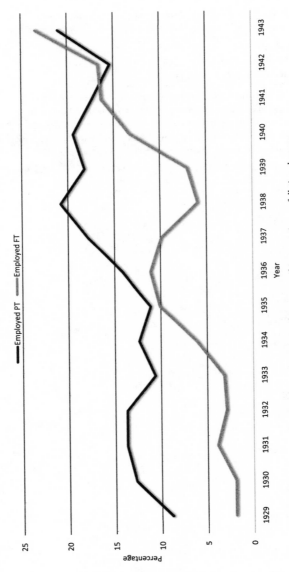

FIGURE A11.1. Percentage of women working part-time or full-time, by year.

Appendix B: The Sample, Data Sources, and Methods

Here we give readers essential information about the intergenerational and longitudinal study that is at the heart of our book, offering a glimpse into our primary sources of archival data rather than an exhaustive compendium of methodological strategies or measures.

Archival longitudinal data are often collected for purposes that differ from those of the contemporary investigator. As a result, they are at best an approximation of the data researchers would gather had they been able to design the original data collection. The availability of the Berkeley archive of longitudinal data made the present study possible because it met certain standards. The data's suitability for the research is the essential requirement.

An archive with substantial qualitative data based on observational methods and open-ended interviews is a treasure for exploratory, inductive, and interpretive forms of analysis. Transforming these qualitative data into systematically developed quantitative measures enhances their value for testing hypotheses, yet at no small cost. Early on, Elder saw great opportunity in these data for a wealth of systematically applied codes and measurements (see appendix C). However, he could not foresee the substantial cost in time and labor, as the project's evolution over four decades makes clear.

The Berkeley Sample and Its Community

The University of California at Berkeley launched the Institute of Child Welfare in 1928 to conduct research on child development under the direction of Herbert R. Stolz, MD, with Harold Jones as the research director. They invited Jean Macfarlane, a recent PhD from the university's psychology program, to direct a preschool study with funds from the Laura Spelman Rockefeller

Memorial. The initial question centered on the developmental value of giving parents opportunities to discuss child behavior with staff members.

The study included every third child born in Berkeley during an eighteen-month period (January 1928 through June 1929), using the birth certificate registry. Of the 405 families, a final sample of 244 couples was available to participate with the study child. The loss was accounted for by stillbirth or death of the child, moving away, refusing to participate, or a language barrier. When the focal children were twenty-one months old, the sample was divided into two subsamples matched on socioeconomic and family variables: an experimental subsample of 124 subjects who received staff guidance and were involved in an intensive program of data collection and a control subsample of roughly equal size that had a less intensive program of data collection. In the decades that followed, the distinction between "experimental" and "control" groups shifted to "intensive" and "less intensive" samples, terms we adopt in this book. In 1929, 60 percent of the families were in the middle class and 40 percent were in the working class.

Comparing the groups at the end of the five-year study revealed no significant difference in child outcomes owing to differences between the two samples in intensity of staff-family interaction. Because there was much more data on the intensively studied sample, it became the core of this long-term longitudinal study. Macfarlane and her staff had begun to shift their focus from a short-term assessment to one focused on developmental change across the life span: understanding how and why children develop as they do. Accordingly, the project moved to collecting data on children through a series of follow-ups interviews, from birth into adolescence and then into the adult years. Data were also collected from their parents over the years. By the 1960s, with life span development established as a framework, the Institute of Child Welfare had become the Institute of Human Development.

DATA COLLECTION IN THE 1930S AND 1940S

The Berkeley Guidance Study has always been distinguished by an intergenerational framework of data collection and research that includes the grandparents and parents of the study children, who were born in 1928–29. Another generation was later added to this framework in the follow-up of 1972: a child of each member of the study children—the grandchildren of the 1900 generation.

When the Berkeley children were twenty-one months old, the mothers and frequently the fathers in the intensive sample were interviewed at the Institute by Jean Macfarlane, with a focus on individual attributes and family relationships (marital and parent-child) as well as the parents' own family backgrounds (socioeconomic and cultural).[1] This first major data collection on the Berkeley families was extensive in breadth and depth and included follow-up interviews as well as observations. At the same time, and on other occasions, social workers at the Institute visited the homes to interview the mothers concerning child care and to make observations.

Important by-products of these and related interviews were detailed work and family histories of the men and women. These interviews provided rich contextual ratings concerning the financial stresses the parents and their children experienced each year during the 1930s. In addition, the Berkeley archives included lists of births, annual household rosters, and records of whether the family served as hosts or guests of relatives. Last, the archives contained detailed information on nationality and religion across the generations.

Some notable aspects of family life were not addressed by quantitative measures in the Berkeley archive, but we were able to generate such measures by applying codes developed through an in-depth reading of selected case assemblies for each of the families in the intensive subsample. During a year at the Berkeley Institute (1972–73), Elder constructed codes on aspects of family life after a thorough reading of the temporal records and qualitative materials on a sample of thirty families in the intensive subgroup ($N = 111$).

Two advanced graduate students were trained to apply these codes to the case assemblies on the remaining families in this subsample. These materials cover the period 1928–29 to 1945. Because most of the code categories per item were categorical, coder agreement was indicated by the percentage of cases on which the coders agreed perfectly. When coders failed to agree because there was a lack of clarity, code categories were combined if possible. Differences were also reviewed in case discussions.

Most of the Berkeley couples married between World War I and the Depression, a time of great change for young couples and families. With this in mind, we focused on how the partners viewed their roles and their relationship. We developed measures of how they viewed a woman's role and how far husbands and wives regarded "homemaking as a wife's central role." We also focused on mutuality. Was it an important ingredient of a satisfying marital relationship? We designed a question about equality. Was it important in marriage? Men and women in the 1900 generation talked about other marriages as well as their own in terms of "being modern" or not. Mutuality and equality were recurring elements of such a relationship. In addition to these aspects of the marriage, interviews included descriptions of the couple's relationships with the parents of each spouse. Codes were also constructed to address perceptions of whether one's spouse acted or failed to act properly as husband and father, wife and mother. This matter is related to the issue of attachment to parents.

Another concept that could be assessed only with the open-ended interviews involved the standards each husband and wife embraced. Following Joseph Kahl's thoughtful book on social stratification, we refer to economic, cultural, and moral standards.[2] For economic standards, we focused both on their level and on one's commitment to them. For example, how do husbands and wives evaluate themselves and others in terms of their standard of living? Are they above average, average, or below average in this regard? Flexibility was assessed in terms of matching standards to the reality of the situation. For cultural standards, we asked whether individuals seemed to regard themselves as superior to the average person in culture and background—manners, tastes, interests. For moral standards, we focused on respectability. Did the husband and wife give the impression that they valued moral character—integrity, trustworthiness, respectability?

The Berkeley couples were interviewed in a major follow-up when their study child was seventeen years old. The years were 1945 and 1946, when World War II had ended, with overseas military units beginning to make the long trip home to the United States. In many ways this interview focused on the relationship between the parent and child generations and on their changing life patterns. The interviewer began by asking the Berkeley men and women a series of retrospective questions about their early lives, focusing on childhood family experiences at the end of the nineteenth century and the early years of the twentieth, then turning to views of their own parents—their education, worklife, and migration experience.

They were then asked about their study child's experience "growing up in a very different time and place." What were the differences and similarities? Did they think the role of parents had changed and, if so, how? We address such issues in chapter 12, "From Generation to Generation," which moves from World War II to the postwar era that was soon to shift back to international conflict with the Korean War in 1950. Most of the sons of the Berkeley families served in this conflict.

This section of the interview established a context in which the parents were asked what they thought about their sons' or daughters' futures. The outbreak of war on the Korean peninsula played an important part in the timing of children's post–high school education, entry into a desired line of work, and marriage. We explored whether the Bay Area's World War II culture influenced the scheduling of these events and whether it made the parents' role difficult. If it did, we took note of how they dealt with these issues.

Many of the difficulties came from study children who had older brothers in the armed forces, especially in combat zones overseas. We learned of some cases where the loss of an older son proved overwhelming to fathers who had endured years of hardship during the 1930s.

Data Collection and Measures, 1969–82

By the end of the 1960s, plans had been made at the IHD for an intergenerational follow-up of its longitudinal samples—Macfarlane's Guidance Study sample and the one taken by Nancy Bayley, director of the Growth Study, as well as the Oakland Growth sample. Two UC Berkeley faculty members affiliated with the IHD, Henry Maas and Joe Kuypers, followed up on the parents in both the Macfarlane and Bayley samples of Berkeley parents, who were by then grandparents with a median age of seventy.

They completed lengthy interviews with 142 men and women. Eighty-one of the women and thirty-eight of the men were members of Macfarlane's study and these men were still married to women in the study. Few men were widowers, but a third of the women were widows. The investigators compared the seventy-year-olds in the follow-up to the original sample of parents in 1929 and found them, as expected, to be better educated and more accomplished in their careers, although the difference was not pronounced. Mean differences in education were little more than a year. Data collection centered on an extensive interview conducted by staff members with clinical expertise. The interview was audio-recorded and transcribed verbatim for Q-sort and other psychological ratings. We draw on these data in exploring the later years of the Berkeley 1900 generation.

The last two follow-ups occurred during the early 1980s, and both provide insights concerning late life. One is known as the Berkeley Older Generation Study, directed by Dorothy Field from the Gerontology Center of the University of Georgia. Field's 1983 sample included the surviving members of the Maas-Kuypers 1969 follow-up. Field and her research team obtained complete interviews in 1983 from forty-two women and twenty men, aged seventy-four to ninety-three. We also draw on Erik and Joan Erikson's project (with Helen Kivnick), which investigated the "vital involvement" of these men and women in old age.[3] They managed to interview only twenty-eight of the parents, but the project generated rich accounts of life-cycle dynamics that connected the generations across their life stages. One of its treasures is the documented conversation between the investigators and the Berkeley parents about the many rewards of grandparenting. To a significant extent, Erik and Joan Erikson, who were born in 1902 and 1903, shared the same

historical position as the Berkeley 1900 generation and could relate personally to their lives and to the dramatic social and economic changes this generation had seen.

A Rich and Flexible Abundance

It is unlikely that anyone could have foreseen how powerful these data and
their many pieces and transformations would be for understanding the lives
of the focal children's parents—the Berkeley 1900 generation. In completing
this book, we have benefited greatly from the thorough and open-ended nature of many of the study's interviews and case notes. We have been able to
examine topics not explicitly addressed by the study's originators. For example, for chapter 9 the study had no systematic measures of the residential
doubling up of families during the Great Depression, but the open-ended
staff interviews with families and the oral histories conducted in the 1970s
produced ample discussion of this key adaptation, with its benefits and its
drawbacks. In chapter 7 we drew on the interviews regarding standards of living to situate experiences of income deprivation within couples' understanding about their quality of life.

The work pathways of these men and women, and how they felt about
them, were revealed in detailed, systematic employment and income records
as well as in the open-ended interviews. They let us compile rich quantitative
and qualitative assessments of the ups and downs, the consistencies and the
inconsistencies, of men's and women's employment that contribute greatly to
understanding this generation, especially in chapters 3, 4, and 11.

Our repeated reading of the qualitative materials, sorting of excerpts on
particular topics, and creation of matrixes regarding experiences before marriage, during the Great Depression, and in World War II let us expand topi-
cally far beyond what the original investigators likely imagined for the study.
The value of this type of sample, with intensive and far-reaching longitudinal
and intergenerational data collection, is immeasurable. In the face of continued trends toward larger and more representative samples, we highly encourage the continued use of this type of design alongside others. There is no
substitute for the richness with which lives are documented in these intensive
efforts, leaving the door open for future generations of scholars to distill new
knowledge about human experience.

Appendix C: The Story of the Project, 1962–2019

Glen Elder's appointment to the Institute of Human Development at the University of California, Berkeley, in 1962 eventually led to his collaboration over the past decade with Rick Settersten and Lisa Pearce on a longitudinal study of American lives across the twentieth century that has resulted in this book. Out of the 1960s came *Children of the Great Depression* (1974) with its life course perspective, followed by studies of cohort comparisons (Oakland and Berkeley) of people born at opposite ends of the 1920s, and now a major project based on members of the 1900 generation—the parents of the Berkeley study children—that extends across the twentieth century. Elder's discovery over four decades ago of the remarkably rich data archive on this generation (birth dates 1885–1908) led to a series of chapter drafts on social change in the family and now to a book on the men and women who married and then lived through the tumultuous decades of the Great Depression, World War II, and the extraordinary prosperity of the postwar years and beyond.

The Beginning

The seeds of this long-term project were sown in 1962 when John Clausen, the new director of the famous Berkeley Institute of Human Development, invited Elder, a recent PhD graduate in sociology and social psychology from the University of North Carolina at Chapel Hill, to become his research associate on a longitudinal study of Oakland children born in 1920–21. By the 1930s, the Institute (then called the Institute of Child Welfare) had become a pioneer in studying children over time, adding two studies drawn from a cohort of Berkeley infants born in 1928–29. They were henceforth known as the Berkeley Guidance Study and the Berkeley Growth Study. Jean Macfarlane directed the Guidance Study, and Nancy Bayley was director of the Growth Study. Several members of the Growth Study were also members of the Guidance Study. The entire membership of the Guidance Study is referred to in this project as the Berkeley cohort of 1928–29.

By the time Elder arrived in Berkeley in 1962, the children in both the Oakland and Berkeley studies had been followed across multiple waves of data collection. They were now middle-aged adults with brothers and sisters and with children of their own. Many of the younger members of the Berkeley study had living parents as well. Longitudinal studies were still exceedingly rare, but Elder's unique experience as a researcher with the Oakland study project had given him invaluable exposure to rich longitudinal data and helped him develop ways of thinking about how people's lives changed as they aged. It also exposed him to detailed records on family and socioeconomic change in the Great Depression. He could see that not all families suffered a significant income loss in 1929–33. He was able to identify Oakland families in the middle class and working class who lost heavily during the worst years of the 1930s and others who avoided such losses. Analysis of these cases became the foundation for his 1974 book *Children of the Great Depression*, which documented the biographical effects of historical change and generated a conceptual perspective on the life course.

The diverse Depression experiences of the Oakland families were well represented in that study, though it could not address the generality of the findings. Would the effects of the Depression differ significantly for an older or younger cohort? The developmental (or career stage) hypothesis suggested that younger children from deprived families would be more vulnerable to heavy income loss than older children. In many respects the Berkeley cohort, with birthdates in 1928–29, was an ideal group for this comparison, since the Institute held data archives for both cohorts.

As Institute director, John Clausen gave Elder access to the Berkeley data archive, and he quickly checked whether its income data would let him assess family income in 1929 and also in 1933, the worst year of the Depression. For the intensively studied Berkeley families ($N = 111$), it did have such data, and for the less intensively studied families ($N = 103$), it included a mix of socioeconomic data (e.g., income, dependence on welfare) that enabled estimates of nondeprived and deprived status roughly matching findings on the intensively studied Berkeley families.

With these data in hand, in the summer of 1971 Elder began work on a two-year research proposal for the National Science Foundation. He proposed a year of data collection and coding at the Berkeley Institute, then a year of data analysis at the Institute for Research in Social Science at the University of North Carolina at Chapel Hill (UNC-CH). The proposed study, "Economic Deprivation in Personality and Achievement," was approved in the summer of 1972, and Elder prepared to establish a research team.

A Plan and Serendipity

In exploring any large data archive, serendipity may intervene, as in starting to develop one thing and ending up with another. An exploration's purpose can be transformed by unexpected discoveries even after the archivist and staff have done much preparation and orientation. Such discoveries need not lead them to discard the original plan. Instead, they might expand the project and change the timetable. This is exactly what happened during Elder's year in the archive (1971–72). Elder's primary objective that year was to develop measures that would permit a systematic comparison of the Oakland and Berkeley cohorts, 1920–21 and 1928–29. This required surveying the early childhood data obtained from interviews and ratings on the parents and study members, then surveying the adult years of the study children and their parents. Elder initially reviewed the parent interview data with the project coders to ensure sound measurements for the cohort comparisons. He was surprised to find that the amount of archival data on the 111 parents in the intensive sample was immense compared with the limited data on the 100 less intensively studied families and the dearth of information on the Oakland parents. Much of the data had been filed uncoded. The project's sole director, Jean Macfarlane, was trained as a clinician with a focus on children in families, and the uncoded data reflected this orientation. The case assemblies were meant to be used to understand the individual child in a family.

In the Oakland study, by the end of the Depression decade parents were no longer being tracked. The Berkeley parents were interviewed periodically across the 1930s and also followed across the 1940s up to a major intergenerational interview in 1946–47. This interview focused on the parents' life experience until the end of World War II and on the relationships of surviving parents and their children, who were in transition to the adult years. This included the military service of sons in the study. At the end of the 1960s, the surviving parents were interviewed about themselves, their children, and their spouses. This trove of parent data went far beyond what was needed for a comparative study of the Oakland and Berkeley cohorts, and Elder realized the extraordinary possibilities of studying the parents' lives as a project on the 1900 generation.

The remarkable depth of data on the parents, much of it uncoded, called for a major unplanned commitment of project resources. The research team organized the essential information by study members' identification numbers, prepared codebooks, then applied the codes, leading to decisions that broadened the scope of the archival work well beyond what was needed for the cohort comparison study.

Four complex data sets were generated from the coded data, focused on the family and on individual lives. The young ages of the Berkeley study children when the economy collapsed (two to three years old) added to the value of our efforts to code all qualitative information that depicted family life from 1929 through the 1930s. One data set focused on family relationships across the 1930s, and another covered relations with kin, marital interaction, and changing household composition. Developing coding manuals and coding the data became especially demanding conceptually. Life record data on the parents' early years, their experiences across the 1930s and 1940s, and the adult lives of the Berkeley study children were transferred to magnetic tape files for transport back to UNC-CH and the Institute for Research in Social Science (now called the Odum Institute).

By the end of the Berkeley project year (summer 1972), data files had been prepared with two analytic themes: one as planned for the comparative cohort study of Oakland and Berkeley, and one focused on the 1900 generation of parents, with emphasis on social change in the family.

THE COMPARATIVE COHORT STUDY

The Comparative Cohort Study required developing measures to compare Depression hardship in the lives of the Oakland and Berkeley study members up to middle age. In theory, because the Berkeley study children were so young, the boys in particular were at greater risk of Depression hardship than the older Oakland adolescents. Understanding the full meaning of drastic income loss required measurements of family patterns before income losses and unemployment. This pre-Depression information was available on the Berkeley families (though not on the Oakland parents) and was added to the data files in Chapel Hill.

SOCIAL CHANGE AND THE 1900 PARENT GENERATION—BERKELEY STUDY

This project was designed to investigate the effects of socioeconomic change in the Great Depression and World War II on family adaptation and the life course. Having family and life history data before the Depression enabled the proposed study to assess continuity and change into the Depression years.[1]

Data were also available on income loss and unemployment across the 1930s. In addition, the Berkeley data archive included socioeconomic records for mothers and fathers that covered the war years.

During the NSF-funded year back at UNC (1973–74), the project staff viewed research on the Berkeley families as a first step toward comparing the Oakland and Berkeley study members. Data on Berkeley family life before the Depression enabled an examination of continuities and discontinuities into the 1930s. As a whole, this work provided essential insight on the Depression's effects. Were they concentrated among families with distinctive vulnerabilities, such as economic dependence, or did they extend across the adaptive and maladaptive families in the 1920s?

During the second year, chapter-length manuscripts were developed on family migration and settlement in the city of Berkeley, on the education and worklife of mothers and fathers, and on the stability or instability of their marriages up to the 1930s. Most of the men and women in the 1900 generation settled in Berkeley after migrating from other countries and the eastern United States. Last, men played the more important role in determining the harmony and stability of their marriages. These chapters were the basis of the project's final report to the National Science Foundation.[2]

The 1973–74 year of research was carried out at the Institute for Research in Social Science where the project was housed. Two major phases of the project's history emerged from the transformative experience of the National Science Foundation study. The first phase centered on the Depression's family impact in the Berkeley study and its relevance for understanding the differential effect of hard times on children of different ages—the younger Berkeley children and the older Oakland youth. The second phase extended this work across the lives of the Berkeley parents and children. Using the panel study, the parents were followed into old age and their children into their middle years.

Phase 1: The Depression's effect on families and cohorts of older and younger children.   Project research launched with the NSF grant was extended three more years by a grant from the National Institute of Mental Health (NIMH, 1974–79) and by Elder's appointment as visiting senior research fellow at the new Boys Town Research Center in Omaha, Nebraska.[3] Charles Morrissey, an oral historian of distinction, agreed to work on interviews with key staff at the Berkeley Institute and with members of the 1900 generation who were living in the greater San Francisco area. All staff interviews aimed at understanding the early years of the Institute.

Resources and risk factors that the Berkeley families carried into the Great Depression (e.g., dependence on relatives) proved very consequential for their experience of hardship. Working-class families and those who depended on other support before the 1930s were most at risk. Job loss was clearly the most potent source of prolonged deprivation for men in the working class. By the end of the Boys Town affiliation, we had produced chapter-length manuscripts on the consequences of Depression losses. One investigated the key determinants of the two faces of the 1930s, misfortune and prosperity. Not all hard times became "bad times" for families, and a chapter explored this effect among economically deprived families. A third chapter reported how families coped with scarcity across the 1930s.

Elder then turned to how the Depression affected the study children and shaped their adult lives. As noted earlier, the children were of preschool age when the economy collapsed. This led to the hypothesis that the younger Berkeley children were at greater risk than the older Oakland children because they were more sensitive to abrupt changes in family relations and the household economy. The Berkeley boys followed this expectation, but not the girls, who were protected by their mothers. In deprived families especially, boys did not do as well in school as girls and were less confident and self-directed during adolescence. The Berkeley girls benefited from their mothers' emotional support in hard-pressed families, whereas the boys typically lacked a caring, involved father.

By contrast, the older Oakland boys in deprived families were resourceful and were old enough to play an important economic role in the community, but the teenage girls were engaged with their mothers in household duties and frequently felt excluded from social affairs by their lack of attractive clothes. Some of these cohort and gender variations were reported in a chapter for the twenty-fifth anniversary edition of *Children of the Great Depression* in 1999.

Phase 2: Studying lives and the generations (1979–99).   At the end of the 1970s, Elder concluded his Boys Town appointment and become professor of human development at Cornell University.[4] The Cornell research phase focused on the Depression and wartime experiences of the Berkeley parents, with emphasis on their relationships with kin during the 1930s. Most parents lived near kin and thus could help and be helped by them. We gave special attention to living in the home of relatives and accepting relatives into one's own household. The three-generation households often brought together conflicting cultures. This research established a context for investigating life trajectories from the 1930s into old age.

As the project turned to the later years, it focused on the emotional health and well-being of the Berkeley mothers in old age and then on their husbands' well-being about 1969. The adverse effect of economic deprivation during the 1930s was most pronounced among women in the working class, and corresponding results were obtained for them in late life. The Berkeley men were less likely to survive into old age, and among couples in late life, the men were less efficacious, active, and outgoing than their wives, as had been true during the 1930s in hard-pressed families.

The project returned to the University of North Carolina at Chapel Hill in the summer of 1984 when Elder was appointed Howard W. Odum Professor. During the fall of 1985 he received an NIMH Senior Scientist award (NIMH00567) that continued up to 2000 and let him revise chapter drafts. It also enabled him to launch new data collection on the military service of the sons of the Berkeley and Oakland parent generations. The Berkeley parents were involved in World War II, but almost exclusively through home front mobilization. War mobilization in the Bay Area drew a significant number of the Berkeley women into the labor force, especially to the booming shipyards around San Francisco. Most of their husbands who had spells of unemployment across the 1930s returned to full-time work and even overtime. Mounting labor needs also pulled teenagers into the workforce, at much higher pay than their parents had received during the 1930s.

Working on the home front was thus an important theme for a chapter-length manuscript on the Berkeley generation. We know, for example, which women worked because of economic hardship across the 1930s and whether they continued working during the war years. We can also identify the women who worked only during the war. The oral histories obtained by Charles Morrissey are especially relevant to this period. Published research papers provide accounts of the sons' military service in their later years.

Working toward a Book

A decade ago, Elder recognized that the time had come to wrap up the project he had nourished and produce a book. Nearly four decades had passed since he launched this innovative project with a remarkable data archive. Over this time five research grants provided support, and the rewarding stimulus of the project itself ensured its continuity. To pass the longitudinal data archive on to the next generation, in 2011 he began to collaborate with two younger colleagues, Richard Settersten of Oregon State University and Lisa Pearce of the University of North Carolina's Department of Sociology at Chapel Hill.

Settersten, a senior figure in human development, aging, and life course studies whom Elder had known since his graduate student days at Northwestern University, had firsthand knowledge of the Berkeley Institute of Human Development and had worked with data from the Oakland and Berkeley archives. Pearce, a colleague of Elder's at UNC-CH and an expert in the sociology of family, gender and religion, had a strong reputation in mixed-methods research, the type Elder employed in the Oakland and Berkeley studies.

Joining a project with a forty-year history brings major challenges of understanding how it evolved with the materials at hand. We began by discussing the drafts of early chapters in sequence within the original framework, staying open to modifying those drafts, adding new chapters, and aware of the need for more data. After a first review, during the 2012 annual meeting of the American Sociological Association at Denver we met for two days to develop a complete chapter outline of the proposed volume.

Since then we have continued to write new chapters and rewrite old ones, taking turns revising each draft. We met regularly by phone and in person to discuss the book's architecture and story lines, chapter revisions, the data archives, qualitative and quantitative analyses, and future tasks. The resulting manuscript has its foundation in the early history of the project, and we are grateful to all those who made it possible. Yet our own deep and persistent collaboration over more than nine years has made use of our particular strengths and expertise, resulting in a book that is uniquely ours—one that illuminates how the revolutionary changes of the twentieth century affected the 1900 generation of American men, women, and their families.

Notes

Part One

1. Robert J. Gordon, *The Rise and Fall of American Growth: The U.S. Standard of Living since the Civil War* (Princeton, NJ: Princeton University Press, 2016), 61.

Chapter One

1. Robert S. Lynd and Helen Merrell Lynd, *Middletown: A Study in Modern American Culture* (1929; repr., New York: Harcourt Brace Jovanovich, 1957), 5; Walter Lippmann, *Drift and Mastery: An Attempt to Diagnose the Current Unrest*, revised introduction and notes by William E. Leuchtenburg (1914; repr., Madison: University of Wisconsin Press, 1985), 92. At the end of the 1920s, a study by William I. Thomas and Dorothy Swaine Thomas documented Lippmann's observation that "we have changed our environment more quickly than we know how to change ourselves." The Thomases concluded from their nationwide survey that the pace of change in children's lives far exceeded society's ability to effectively care for them. In their introduction to *The Child in America*, they note that "it is widely felt that the demoralization of young persons, the prevalence of delinquency, crime, and profound mental disturbances are very serious problems, and that the situation is growing worse instead of better." William I. Thomas and Dorothy Swaine Thomas, *The Child in America: Behavior Problems and Programs* (New York: Alfred A. Knopf, 1928).

2. Members of the Berkeley 1900 generation lived most of their adult life span within a century of unparalleled advances in the American standard of living, from 1870 to 1970, as documented by Robert Gordon's magisterial study of economic growth during this historic time, *The Rise and Fall of American Growth: The U.S. Standard of Living since the Civil War*. The Lynds' comparison of Middletown in 1890 and the 1920s vividly documented such change in the midwestern community of Muncie, Indiana. Lynd and Lynd, *Middletown*.

3. In his commencement address to the graduating class of Milton Academy in the mid-1920s, Franklin Delano Roosevelt focused on the rapid pace of change that was continuing to widen the gap in cultural experience between the generations. David M. Kennedy, *Freedom from Fear: The American People in Depression and War* (London: Oxford University Press, 1999), 100.

4. Kennedy, *Freedom from Fear*, 13.

5. Kennedy.

6. Gordon, *The Rise and Fall of American Growth*, 535–65.

7. Carey McWilliams, *California: The Great Exception* (Berkeley: University of California Press, 1948), chap. 8, "'The Fabulous Boom' in the 40s," 233–348. McWilliams notes that "unlike other areas, the West did not *convert* to production for there was nothing much to 'convert'; what happened was that *new* industries and *new* plants were built overnight. It is most significant, therefore, that the expansion in industry was in new lines of industrial production, notably in the production of durable goods" (234).

8. Gordon, *Rise and Fall of American Growth*, chap. 16, "The Great Leap Forward from the 1920s to the 1950s: What Set of Miracles Created It?" (535–65). According to Gordon, the evidence is compelling that World War II "represented the economic miracle that rescued the American economy from the secular stagnation of the late 1930s" (536). The dramatic rate of change in twentieth-century America contributed to the emergence of a lively community of futurists, featuring especially Ray Kurzweil's books and articles. Especially relevant is his "Law of Accelerating Returns," where he documents the way the "rate of change itself is accelerating." See http://www.kurzweilai.net/the-law-of-accelerating-returns. This line of thinking can be found in *Thank You for Being Late*, in which Thomas Friedman claims that the "age of accelerations" emerged around 2007 with the digital revolution and opened up "a wide gap between the pace of technological change, globalization, and environmental stresses and the ability of people and governing systems to adapt to and manage them" (212). In words that bring to mind Walter Lippmann's observation that the rate of change around the turn of the century exceeded Americans' ability to adapt themselves to this new world, Friedman asserts that "many people seem to be feeling a loss of control and are desperate for navigational help and sense-making" (212). Thomas Friedman, *Thank You for Being Late: An Optimist's Guide to Thriving in the Age of Accelerations* (New York: Farrar, Straus and Giroux, 2017).

9. Suzanne Mettler, *Soldiers to Citizens: The G.I. Bill and the Making of the Greatest Generation* (London: Oxford University Press, 2015).

10. Gordon, *Rise and Fall of American Growth*, chap. 1, "The Ascent and Descent of Growth," 1–23.

11. See Glen H. Elder Jr., *Children of the Great Depression: Social Change in Life Experience* (Chicago: University of Chicago Press, 1974) and the twenty-fifth anniversary edition, enlarged (Boulder, CO: Westview Press, 1999).

12. Born in 1894 and reared in California's San Joaquin Valley, Jean Walker Macfarlane received her doctoral degree in 1922 in the Department of Psychology at the University of California, Berkeley. Before the establishment of the Berkeley Institute of Child Welfare (later named the Institute of Human Development) in 1927, Macfarlane carried out research and lectured at the UC Pediatrics Department on the Medical School campus in San Francisco, taught half-time in UC Berkeley's Department of Psychology, devoted two years to lecturing at Harvard University's Medical School and Department of Psychology, and had a research appointment at the Boston Psychopathic Hospital. During this time she developed a supportive relationship with Lawrence Frank, administrator of the Laura Spellman Rockefeller Memorial, who was instrumental in UC Berkeley's success in achieving a five-year Rockefeller grant that established the Institute of Child Welfare and provided funds to launch Macfarlane's Berkeley longitudinal study with newborn children in 1928–29. The Foundation continued to provide essential funding for the Institute and Macfarlane's pioneering longitudinal study across the 1930s. See Jean Walker Macfarlane, *Studies in Child Guidance: I. Methodology of Data Collection and Organization*, Monographs of the Society for Research in Child Development 3 (Washington, DC: Society for Research in Child Development, 1938).

13. For more information on Jean Macfarlane's life and career, see Vicki Green's 1982 interview, Institute of Human Development Oral History Project, deposited in the Bancroft Library, University of California, Berkeley.

14. Appendix B provides an overview of the data in the Berkeley archive and its coding.

15. See Glen H. Elder Jr., Michael J. Shanahan, and Julia A. Jennings, "Human Development in Time and Place," in *Ecological Settings and Processes in Developmental Systems*, vol. 4 of *Handbook of Child Psychology and Developmental Science*, 7th ed., ed. Michael Bornstein and Tama Leventhal (New York: John Wiley, 2015), 6–54. For a brief account of the paradigmatic life course principles, see Glen H. Elder Jr., "The Life Course as Developmental Theory," *Child Development* 69 (1998): 1–12.

16. Craig Calhoun, ed., *Sociology in America* (Chicago: University of Chicago Press, 2007), 16.

17. Edmund H. Volkart, ed., *Social Behavior and Personality: Contributions of W. I. Thomas to Theory and Social Research* (New York: Social Science Research Council, 1951), 93.

18. Life course dynamics can result in the accumulation of disadvantage or advantage—what sociologist Robert Merton once dubbed the "Matthew effect" when he first applied the principle to scientific careers. Robert K. Merton, "The Matthew Effect in Science," *Science* 159 (1968): 56–63. This principle, named for a passage in the book of Matthew *and* reflected in the adage that the "rich get richer and the poor get poorer," can be extended to life course dynamics in which inequalities among individuals grow over time owing to social processes. See Dale Dannefer, "Cumulative Advantage/Disadvantage and the Life Course: Cross-Fertilizing Age and Social Science Theory," *Journals of Gerontology: Social Sciences* 58 (2003): 327–37.

19. The classic essay on cohort and social change was written by Norman Ryder, "The Cohort as a Concept in the Study of Social Change," *American Sociological Review* 30 (1965): 843–61. For a review of research in this tradition, see Glen H. Elder Jr. and Linda K. George, "Age, Cohorts, and the Life Course," in *Handbook of the Life Course*, vol. 2, ed. Michael J. Shanahan et al. (New York: Springer, 2015), 59–85.

20. Leonard Cain, "Age Status and Generational Phenomena: The New Old People in Contemporary America," *Gerontologist* 7 (1967): 83–92.

21. Elder, *Children of the Great Depression*.

22. Elder.

23. "History of the University of California, Berkeley," http://berkeley.edu/about/hist/foun dations.shtml.

24. Glen H. Elder Jr., "Social History and Life Experience," in *Present and Past in Middle Life*, ed. Dorothy H. Eichorn et al. (New York: Academic Press, 1981), 3–31.

25. Charles Wollenburg, *Berkeley: A City in History* (Berkeley: University of California Press, 2008).

26. Elder, *Children of the Great Depression*, 18–20.

27. These trends are based on data from the Berkeley Welfare Society and can be found in *Report and Recommendations of the California Unemployment Commission* (San Francisco: Unemployment Commission, 1932), 384–85.

28. "History of the University of California, Berkeley," 1930s.

29. Arthur Herman, "Master Builder," in *Freedom's Forge: How American Business Produced Victory in World War II* (New York: Random House, 2013), 37–57, a vivid account of Henry Kaiser's role in developing the shipbuilding industry in the San Francisco region during World War II.

30. Lewis M. Terman, with the assistance of others, *Genetic Studies of Genius*, vol. 1, *Mental and Physical Traits of a Thousand Gifted Children* (Palo Alto, CA: Stanford University Press, 1925).

31. The Depression left families in such difficult positions that the control group parents also asked staff members for advice even though they were controls.

32. Herbert H. Hyman, *Secondary Analysis of Sample Surveys: Principles, Procedures, and Potentialities* (New York: John Wiley, 1972).

33. In the mid-1970s, Charles T. Morrissey had just launched a career as a self-employed oral historian. Elder was fortunate to hire him to conduct oral history interviews with the Berkeley parents who lived within sixty miles of the city of Berkeley. Morrissey was asked to focus on the decades from the 1920s through the 1960s, with emphasis on the 1930s and 1940s. Over the years, Morrissey served as director of the John F. Kennedy Library of Oral History and as president of the Oral History Association. See Tracy E. K. Meyer and Charles T. Morrissey, "Living Independently: The Oral History Career of Charles T. Morrissey: Part II," *Oral History Review* 26 (1999): 85–104.

Part Two

1. C. Wright Mills, *White Collar: The American Middle Classes* (Oxford: Oxford University Press, 1951).

Chapter Two

1. Carey McWilliams, *California: The Great Exception* (Berkeley: University of California Press, 1999).

2. Margaret S. Gordon, *Employment Expansion and Population Growth: The California Experience, 1900–1950* (Berkeley: University of California Press, 1954), 1.

3. McWilliams, *California*, 73. For example, 90 percent of people born in California from 1860 to 1930 stayed there most of their lives.

4. The San Francisco earthquake was the most expensive disaster—in terms of relief efforts and insurance losses—before the 9/11 terrorist attacks and required an even larger relief effort than Hurricane Katrina. See also the History Channel's "Mega Disasters: San Francisco Earthquake," broadcast in 2009, https://www.history.com/topics/natural-disasters-and-environment/1906-san-francisco-earthquake.

5. National Board of Fire Underwriters' Committee on Fire Prevention and Engineering Standards, *Report on the Berkeley, California Conflagration of September 17, 1923* (New York: National Board of Fire Underwriters, 1923).

6. Life course scholars often speak of distinct "trajectories" punctuated by states and transitions in education, work, family, health, and other life domains. Residential trajectories are composed of states and transitions in living arrangements and places, whether the view is of local households or addresses or of broader cities, states, regions, or countries. Residential transitions are often interwoven with transitions in other domains, particularly family (like marriage or divorce), work (unemployment or new employment, retirement), or health (assisted living), which may trigger or prevent migration.

7. Brinley Thomas, *Migration and Economic Growth* (Cambridge: Cambridge University Press, 1954); Stanley Lebergott, *Manpower in Economic Growth* (New York: McGraw-Hill, 1964); Richard Easterlin, *Population, Labor Force, and Long Swings in Economic Growth: The American Experience* (New York: Columbia University Press, 1968).

8. Though socioeconomic and skill distinctions have been made between the "old" and "new" waves of immigration, between northwestern and southern Europeans, the great majority

of migrants throughout the period of unrestricted immigration were "people without acceptable economic opportunities in their own countries who came here relatively untrained and socially disadvantaged to secure jobs at the bottom of the hierarchy of urban occupations and incomes." Conrad Taeuber and Irene Taeuber, *The Changing Population of the United States* (New York: John Wiley, 1958), 67.

9. McWilliams, *California*, 234.

10. Gordon, *Employment Expansion and Population Growth*, 91–102.

11. Thomas, *Migration and Economic Growth*; Lebergott, *Manpower in Economic Growth*; Easterlin, *Population, Labor Force, and Long Swings in Economic Growth*.

12. Walter Nugent, *Into the West: The Story of Its People* (New York: Alfred A. Knopf, 1999).

13. Margaret Gordon concludes that the "periods of heaviest migration have been those in which employment opportunities have expanded most rapidly and have attracted in-migrants of working age." Gordon, *Employment Expansion and Population Growth*, 13; see also 91.

14. Kevin Starr, *Americans and the California Dream, 1850–1915* (Oxford: Oxford University Press, 1986), 137.

15. Gordon, *Employment Expansion and Population Growth*, 162.

16. Marcus Hansen, *The Immigrant in American History* (Cambridge, MA: Harvard University Press, 1940), 193.

17. Danielle Moon, "Educational Housekeepers: Female Reformers in the California Americanization Program, 1900–1927," in *California History: A Topical Approach*, ed. Gordon Morris Bakken (New York: John Wiley, 2003), 108–25. School systems relied on help from women's clubs (for volunteers and money) to keep schools open and staffed. On the expansion of higher education in California, see McWilliams, *California*.

18. John S. MacDonald and Leatrice D. MacDonald, "Chain Migration Ethnic Neighborhood Formation and Social Networks," *Milbank Memorial Fund Quarterly* 42, no. 1 (1964): 82–97.

19. Cohort comparisons of birthplace origins cannot be derived directly from the decade comparisons given by Gordon, *Employment Expansion and Population Growth*, for region of birth of California residents born outside the state is based on census records (1954, 162, table A.2). But the aggregate distribution of the Berkeley parents by birthplace compares well with that for the population of the state as a whole for the year 1930. Gordon's percentages are based on the native-born population of the state and exclude the foreign-born.

20. The comparable figure for the state as a whole in 1930, for the native-born population, is 65 percent born west of the Mississippi (inclusive of those born in California). Computed from Gordon, *Employment Expansion and Population Growth*, 161–62, tables A.1 and A.2.

21. Background material available for the Berkeley parents suggests considerable regional homogamy in marriage patterns in the parent generation. Where cell sizes are large enough to allow reasonable comparisons, the young men appear to have married either women native to California or (when born outside the state themselves) women from their region of origin.

22. Stephan Thernstrom, *The Other Bostonians: Poverty and Progress in the American Metropolis, 1880–1970* (Cambridge, MA: Harvard University Press, 1973), 170.

23. Barbara Solomon, *Ancestors and Immigrants: A Changing New England Tradition* (Chicago: University of Chicago Press, 1956).

24. E. P. Hutchinson, *Immigrants and Their Children* (New York: John Wiley, 1956), 23.

25. Hutchinson.

26. Cf. Thernstrom, *Other Bostonians*, 209–56.

27. Peter Blau and Otis Duncan, *The American Occupational Structure* (New York: John Wiley, 1967), 363.

28. The dominant feature of change in the occupational structure through this period (approximately the late 1840s through the mid-1880s) was the increase (relative to that in agriculture) of opportunity in industrial, service, and construction sectors (all non-agricultural jobs connected with industrialization and the rapid expansion of transport, regional and urban). Agricultural opportunity in itself did not contract significantly until late in the century, but the increasing demand for unskilled and industrial labor was almost insatiable except in periods of depression. Hansen, *Immigrant in American History*, among others, has pointed out that "even agricultural immigrants came to America in greatest numbers at times when industrial activity was at its height: their westward movement was always strongest in periods of depression" (69). Thus the occupational composition of immigrant nationality groups varied over the long period represented by the parental generation, perhaps considerably weakening patterns that might be observed if specific cohort comparisons were possible.

29. For example, see Charlotte Erickson, *Invisible Immigrants: The Adaptation of English and Scottish Immigrants in Nineteenth-Century America* (London: Widenfeld and Nicolson, 1972).

30. The self-reported reflections on childhood hardship are best viewed with caution, especially given the advanced age of the Berkeley 1900 generation in 1973. The perception of hardship may to some degree be a question of social definition and social comparison as well as of the later experience of hardship or comfort.

31. This outcome, however, may well reflect our inability to adequately capture family situations that occurred many years before our first encounter with the Berkeley generation in 1928–29. A single staff member rated families based on interviews with parents in 1930–31. Retrospective ratings that summarize family experience over the preadult years may obscure more than they clarify.

Chapter Three

1. In this context Leuchtenburg also notes the "disturbing amount of unemployment." Willian Leuchtenburg, *The Perils of Prosperity, 1914–32* (Chicago: University of Chicago Press, 1958), 193. Between 1900 and 1930, the quantity volume of manufactures increased by more than two times the growth of population. Lynd, "People as Consumers," 857–911.

2. Embedded in social Darwinism and voluntarist associations for benevolent ends, the ideology of self-sufficiency "became a regressive force in the early twentieth century, as conditions demanded new forms of social security. Voluntarism became, in the words of I. M. Rubinow, the great American substitute for social action and policy. . . . What occurred was the creation of a socio-economic no-man's land; voluntary institutions failed to respond to mass needs, but thwarted governmental efforts to do so." Roy Lubove, *The Struggle for Security: 1900–1935* (Cambridge, MA: Harvard University Press, 1968), 2. See also Kirsten Grønjberg, David Street, and Gerald Suttles, *Poverty and Social Change* (Chicago: University of Chicago Press, 1978). Rubinow's eloquent case for social insurance draws on a large number of American studies that document the lack of an economic surplus in the working class. Isaac Rubinow, *Social Insurance, with Special Reference to American Conditions* (New York: Henry Holt, 1916). Efforts to promote more humane work were frustrated by the persistence of preindustrial ideologies about work and why men work: it is "hunger or fear of hunger" that drives men to labor, and the new industrial realities of that time. Dorothy Kahn, "Problems in the Administration of Relief," *Annals*

176 (1934): 140–48. See also Daniel T. Rodgers, *The Work Ethic in Industrial America, 1850–1920* (Chicago: University of Chicago Press, 1978).

3. Thomas Cochran, *The Great Depression and World War II* (San Francisco: Scott, Foresman, 1968), 2.

4. Richard Hofstadter, *Social Darwinism in American Thought* (Boston: Beacon Press, 1955).

5. Seymour Martin Lipset, "A Changing American Character?," in *The First New Nation: The United States in Historical and Comparative Perspective* (New York: Basic Books, 1963). With the coming of hard times in the 1930s, inequality and the excesses of achievement striving became targets of a vigorous critique. Lipset writes, "Analysts of the thirties, like Robert S. Lynd, Harold Laski, and W. Lloyd Warner, all agreed that the egalitarian emphasis in American democracy was declining sharply under the growth of the large-scale corporation, monopoly capitalism, and economic competition. They asserted categorically that mobility had decreased, and Warner predicted the development of rigid status lines based on family background. Twenty years later, these interpretations are almost unanimously rejected" (322). Lipset notes that prosperous times have tended to shift the criticism of intellectuals toward the decline of competition, achievement, and excellence in work, as in the immediate postwar era and the writings of David Riesman and William Whyte.

6. Leuchtenburg, *Perils of Prosperity*.

7. Winifred D. Wandersee Bolin, "The Economics of Middle-Income Family Life: Working Women during the Great Depression," *Journal of American History* 65, no. 1 (1978): 60–74.

8. M. E. Tyler, "The Pursuit of Domestic Perfection: Marriage and Divorce in Los Angeles, 1890–1920" (PhD diss., University of California, Los Angeles, 1975).

9. Otis Dudley Duncan, David Featherman, and Beverly Duncan, *Socioeconomic Background and Achievement* (New York: Seminar Press, 1972); Dennis Hogan, *Transitions and Social Change: The Early Lives of American Men* (New York: Academic Press, 1981).

10. Guy Benveniste, Charles Benson, José Luis Aranguren, and Ladislav Cerych, *From Mass to Universal Education: The Experience of the State of California and Its Relevance to European Education in the Year 2000* (The Hague: European Cultural Foundation, 1976).

11. Michael Haines, "Industrial Work and the Family Life Cycle, 1889–90," in *Research in Economic History*, ed. Paul Uselding (Greenwich, CT: JAI Press, 1979), 289–356. From the late nineteenth century to the generalization of child labor laws and the decades following the 1930s, historical records suggest that the economic contributions of older children and mothers to family income were inversely related. Among urban working-class families during the late 1800s, the contributions of older children, especially boys, were substantial, many times that of married women and mothers at any age. Using Carroll Wright's unparalleled labor survey of 1889–90, Haines concludes from a secondary analysis that, when the male head entered his forties and fifties, the percentage contributions of older boys ranged from a fourth to a third of total family income. This compares with the married woman's share, which never exceeded 5 percent at any stage of the family life course. "Children were more likely to go to work where the need was greater, that is where the relative income of the household head was lower (especially as the head grew older), where the mother wasn't working, or where other sources of income (from boarding or from wealth) were deficient" (48–49). Older children were more often employed in communities with textile mills and in labor markets that had few constraints on child labor and school attendance.

12. Leuchtenburg, *Perils of Prosperity*, 174.

13. Thernstrom, *Poverty and Progress*, 136.

14. Claudia Goldin and Lawrence Katz, *The Race between Education and Technology* (Boston: Belknap Press, 2008).

15. Claude S. Fischer and Michael Hout, *Century of Difference: How America Changed in the Last One Hundred Years* (New York: Russell Sage Foundation, 2006).

16. Wilbur Fisk Henning and William Harvey Hyatt, *Henning's General Laws of California: As Amended and in Force at the Close of the Forty-Third Session of the Legislature, 1919, Including Initiative and Referendum Acts Adopted at the General Election of 1920* (San Francisco: Bender-Moss, 1921).

17. Leonard D. Cain, "Age Status and Generational Phenomena: The New Old People in Contemporary America," *Gerontologist* 7 (1967): 83–92.

18. These estimates are based on a 1985 survey with children of these men, who reported whether their fathers did military service. We do not know dates of service. Given the birth years of the Berkeley fathers, we assume that most of the older men who served in World War I were likely to have come from the nineteenth-century birth cohort. Most of these men would have been too old to be mobilized for World War II, except perhaps the very youngest at the beginning of the war.

19. For example, the educational disadvantage of Catholics during the first half of this century has been partly attributed to anti-intellectual and low achievement orientations of the Catholic home and its traditional culture. Andrew M. Greeley and Peter Henry Rossi, *The Education of Catholic Americans* (Chicago: Aldine, 1966).

20. The educational handicap of having foreign-born parents reflects in part the cultural history of Catholic families, the limitations of a large family, and relatively low income. All three factors are associated with the lives of adults who were born outside the United States. A substantial number of Catholic families in the backgrounds of the Berkeley men traced their descent to relatively disadvantaged regions (southern Italy, rural Poland). These regions differed sharply in cultural priorities from the New World and its middle class: individualism, competitive achievement, social mobility through education, and household economies that did not subordinate the interests of offspring to family welfare. Indeed, men whose parents were born in southern and eastern Europe were less apt to finish high school or enter college than sons of other immigrants, but where they were from is so entwined with religion that we cannot disentangle the effects. Regardless, the educational disadvantage of a first-generation Catholic home has much to do with its cultural background.

21. Herbert Hiram Hyman and Charles Robert Wright, *Education's Lasting Influence on Values* (Chicago: University of Chicago Press, 1979).

22. The other factors that negatively predicted educational attainment of men—family economic strain, family size, having Catholic parents, or being foreign-born of foreign-born parents—did not directly predict marital timing, but they may have some influence on marital timing through education.

23. There is another side to the picture of a man's assets, which can be traced through marriage to his wife's side of the family. Marriage to the daughter of a wealthy family might bring economic assistance at various points along a man's career in connections for a lucrative or rewarding job, in loans or outright gifts for acquiring a home, business, or work equipment, and of course through inheritance. Balanced against this are the social and psychic costs of marriage to a woman who shared her family's narcissistic aspirations and rigid claims regarding a materialistic lifestyle. As we shall see in subsequent chapters, these costs are substantial and not matched by the economic returns of such a marriage, at least as we can measure them through

the Berkeley Social Rating—a summation of six four-point ratings on quality of house exterior, neighborhood, yard, living room, family accommodations, and special equipment. One of the highest scores was assigned to the residence of a business executive: a nine-room, two-story home in the Berkeley hills. Field notes describe the home as "attractive, beautifully furnished, much outdoor space for children, and separate sleeping rooms." At the other end of the continuum is the "tiny shingled cottage" of a young carpenter, situated on a small lot in the Berkeley Flats below San Pablo Avenue. The family had just moved in at the time of the fieldworker's visit and was "busily engaged in fixing the place up." Nearly half of the variation in such conditions is accounted for by total family income, and men's occupation and socioeconomic background increases this figure to about 56 percent. Wives' education and background add little more than 1 percent to this figure. The only factor that makes a reliable, independent difference in a man's living conditions is the economic status of the wife's family. Men who married the daughters of well-to-do families were slightly better off on quality of home and neighborhood than the husbands of women from lower-status families.

24. Two staff members at the Institute used the interview to rate men on five-point scales. Their ratings were averaged to produce single measures. Both scales are strongly related to men's occupational status and their actual standard of living and the quality of home and neighborhood.

25. Robert Ferber, "Consumer Economics, a Survey," *Journal of Economic Literature* 11, no. 4 (1973): 1303–42.

26. Cecile Tipton Lafollette, *A Study of the Problems of 652 Gainfully Employed Women Homemakers* (New York: Bureau of Publications, Teachers College, Columbia University, 1934), 79.

27. Of the younger men from the managerial class, 43 percent had assumed a mortgage or owned a home, versus 14, 24, 24, and 11 percent in the professional, white-collar, skilled, and unskilled classes, respectively.

28. Of the older men from the professional and skilled classes, 68 and 79 percent, respectively, assumed a mortgage or owned a home, versus 57, 56, and 36 percent for the managerial, white-collar, and unskilled classes.

29. In the younger age group, families in the managerial class led the way on standard of living (an average of 13.6 out of 24) as indexed by the Berkeley Social Rating described above. They were followed by the professional and white-collar groups (an average of 11.8 and 11.1, respectively) and then the skilled and unskilled (9.8 and 7.9). According to age comparisons, families headed by professionals gained the most on living standards and were evenly matched in the older category with the managerial group (an average of 14.7). The lower three classes followed in order: white collar, 12.0; skilled, 10.8; and unskilled, 8.0.

30. These more complex analyses are available to readers on request.

31. Constance Perin, *Everything in Its Place: Social Order and Land Use in America* (Princeton, NJ: Princeton University Press, 1977), 69.

32. Peter H. Rossi, *Why Families Move: A Study in the Social Psychology of Urban Residential Mobility* (Glencoe, IL: Free Press), 1955. Daniel R. Fredland, *Residential Mobility and Home Purchase: A Longitudinal Perspective on the Family Life Cycle and the Housing Market* (Lanham, MD: Lexington Books, 1974).

33. James Flink, *The Car Culture* (Cambridge, MA: MIT Press, 1975). In a thoughtful historical assessment of the automobile in American life, Flink notes that "individualism defined in terms of privatism, freedom of choice, and the opportunity to extend one's control over his physical and social environment was one of the important American core values that automobility promised to

preserve and enhance in a changing urban industrial society. Mobility was another" (38). Reflecting on such issues and the nearly five million automobiles that had come off assembly lines by the end of the 1920s, Flink concludes that "it is no wonder that automobility, for two generations after Henry Ford initiated the volume production of the Model T at his Highland Park plant in 1910, became the most important force for change in American civilization" (40–41).

34. Burkhard Strumpel, "Economic Behavior and Economic Welfare: Models and Interdisciplinary Approaches," in *Human Behavior in Economic Affairs: Essays in Honor of George Katana* (Amsterdam: Elsevier, 1972).

35. See Reuben Hill, *Family Development in Three Generations: A Longitudinal Study of Changing Family Patterns of Planning and Achievement* (Cambridge, MA: Schenkman, 1970).

36. Hill.

Chapter Four

1. Self-reports of highest level of education attained were collected in 1929.

2. Data extracted from IPUMS-USA, 1940 Census of Population Data, https://usa.ipums.org/usa/.

3. Specific information on educational institutions the women attended and types of jobs they held are compiled from multiple interviews and interviewer notes in a file called "Women's SES Histories."

4. Carl Degler, "Revolution without Ideology: The Changing Place of Women in America," *Daedalus* 93, no. 2 (1964): 657.

5. Paula S. Fass, *The Damned and the Beautiful: American Youth in the 1920s* (Oxford: Oxford University Press, 1977).

6. Thomas Snyder, ed., *120 Years of American Education: A Statistical Portrait* (Washington, DC: Center for Education Statistics, 1993).

7. The patterns discussed here come from an ordered logit regression model predicting women's educational attainment (using seven categories of educational attainment: less than seventh grade, seventh to ninth grade, some high school, a high school degree, some college, a college degree, or a postgraduate or professional degree). Measures of the women's family socioeconomic backgrounds were coded from interviews with the women in the early 1930s concerning their family and childhood experiences. Socioeconomic background was assessed on a five-point scale from extreme poverty to affluence. Family size ranged from one to more than nine. In terms of cultural origin, we measured religious affiliation as being Catholic or not (a category including Protestants, Jews, and those with no reported affiliation). Religious affiliation has special cultural relevance, since 30 percent of the foreign-born parents came from traditionally Catholic regions of eastern and southern Europe. Immigrant status includes three groups: native-born with foreign-born parents, foreign-born with foreign-born parents, and native-born with native-born parents (the comparison group). To rule out variations in age as a factor, we adjust for whether a woman was born in 1890 to 1899 or in the first decade of the twentieth century. Results are available from the authors on request.

8. Fass, *Damned and the Beautiful*.

9. Most likely these women truly did not work before marriage, but it is also possible that they did and it never came up in any of the interviews.

10. William Chafe, *The American Woman: Her Changing Social, Economic, and Political Roles* (New York: Oxford University Press, 1972), 54.

11. Reuben Hill, *Family Development in Three Generations: A Longitudinal Study of Changing Family Patterns of Planning and Achievement* (Cambridge, MA: Schenkman, 1970), 29–42.

12. John Modell, *Into One's Own: From Youth to Adulthood in the United States, 1920–1975* (Berkeley: University of California Press, 1991), 44.

13. Ernest W. Burgess and Paul Wallin, *Engagement and Marriage* (Philadelphia: J. B. Lippincott, 1953).

14. Glen H. Elder Jr., "The Social Context of Youth Groups," *International Social Science Journal* 24, no. 2 (1972): 271–89.

15. These results come from a comparison of means demonstrating that women who married before age twenty-two averaged a value of 8 out of 10 on a measure of father's lack of interest (as reported by their mothers in a 1930–31 survey) compared with an average value of 6.8 for women who married after age twenty-five.

16. Viktor Gecas, "Parental Behavior and Contextual Variations in Adolescent Self-Esteem," *Sociometry* 35, no. 2 (1972): 332–45.

17. Burgess and Wallin, *Engagement and Marriage*.

18. Burgess and Wallin. See also Andrew Cherlin, *The Marriage Go-Round: The State of Marriage and the Family in America Today* (New York: Vintage Books, 2010). Stephanie Coontz, *Marriage, a History: From Obedience to Intimacy, or How Love Conquered Marriage* (New York: Viking, 2005). John Modell, *Into One's Own: From Youth to Adulthood in the United States, 1920–1975* (Berkeley: University of California Press, 1991).

19. Ernest R. Groves, "Social Influences Affecting Home Life," *American Journal of Sociology* 31, no. 2 (1925): 227–40.

20. The findings reported here are not presented in a table but are based on the statistically significant results of an ordinary least squares (OLS) regression model in which the women's subjective report of satisfaction with the family home is regressed on women's education, standard of living in 1929 (based on an index summing scores from five interviewer ratings—house exterior, living room, family accommodations, household appliances and other equipment, and socioeconomic status and quality of neighborhood), homeownership, husband's occupational status in 1929, total family income in 1929, and woman's age.

21. This finding comes from a comparison of average values of dissatisfaction with one's home and one's husband's job in 1930–31. Women who had less than a high school education and whose 1929 per capita household income was *over* $1,000 (the highest category) averaged 1.9 and 1.7 on the five-point scales of dissatisfaction with home and husband's job, respectively. By comparison, the other groups of women averaged from 2.3 to 2.9 and 2.3 to 3.3, respectively, on these scales.

22. Burgess and Wallin, *Engagement and Marriage*; Groves, "Social Influences."

23. Christina Simmons, *Making Marriage Modern: Women's Sexuality from the Progressive Era to World War II* (Oxford: Oxford University Press, 2013).

24. Cherlin, *Marriage Go-Round*.

25. Sharon E. Kirmeyer and Brady E. Hamilton, "Transitions between Childlessness and First Birth: Three Generations of U.S. Women," *Vital Health Statistics* 153, ser. 2 (2011): 1–18.

26. Edward A. Ross, *The Social Trend* (New York: Century, 1922), 91.

27. William F. Ogburn, "The Changing Family," *Family* 19, no. 5 (1938): 139–43.

28. Ernest Watson Burgess and Harvey James Locke, *The Family: From Institution to Companionship* (New York: American Book Company, 1945); Cherlin, *Marriage Go-Round*; Coontz, *Marriage*.

29. Arthur A. Campbell, "Family Planning and the Five Million," *Family Planning Perspectives* 1, no. 2 (1969): 33–36.

30. Robert Heuser, *Fertility Tables for Birth Cohorts by Color*, publication 76-1152 (Rockville, MD: US Department of Health, Education, and Welfare, 1976), table 2.A.

31. Chafe, *American Woman*, 92, 100–104; Degler, "Revolution without Ideology," 666–67.

32. Coontz, *Marriage, a History*; Groves, "Social Influences Affecting Home Life."

33. Burgess and Wallin, *Engagement and Marriage*.

34. Claudia Goldin, "The Changing Economic Role of Women: A Quantitative Approach," *Journal of Interdisciplinary History* 13, no. 4 (1983): 707–33.

35. Carolyn Moehling, "Women's Work and Men's Unemployment," *Journal of Economic History* 61, no. 4 (2001): 926–49.

36. This is consistent with Cecile Tipton La Follette, *A Study of the Problems of 652 Gainfully Employed Married Women Homemakers* (New York: Bureau of Publications, Teachers College, Columbia University, 1934), 29.

37. Degler, "Revolution without Ideology," 669.

38. Latent class analysis (LCA) is a person-centered analysis or data reduction technique; the focus is on identifying subgroups of individuals in a population based on the most common configurations of values obtained through a set of measures. By drawing on a set of indicators, LCA produces better estimates of the size of the subgroups of individuals and more accurate representations of their composition than would a single indicator. The seven indicators of women's identification with various roles that we used come from a rigorous and intensive coding exercise in which all records and materials collected from the core guidance sample from 1929 to 1931 (e.g., recorded interview responses or field notes written by staff about interactions of conversations with family members) were coded based on a scheme developed and tested for reliability. The seven dichotomous indicators we use from this coding exercise are evidence (1) that a woman viewed marriage as a main source of her personal gratification, (2) that she was inclined toward mutuality in marriage, (3) that children were a main source of personal gratification for her, (4) that she liked homemaking, (5) that she viewed homemaking as women's central role, (6) that she was interested in gainful employment, and (7) that she was interested in community involvement.

39. Based on two fit statistics, the Bayesian information criterion (BIC) and the Akaike information criterion (AIC) indicators, the best-fitting model was that with four latent classes. This model had an entropy score of .94, suggesting a clear delineation of classes.

40. Alice S. Rossi, *Feminists in Politics: A Panel Analysis of the First National Women's Conference* (New York: Academic Press, 1982), 13.

41. Simmons, *Making Marriage Modern*, 8.

42. Simmons, 8.

43. Floyd Dell, *Janet March* (New York: Alfred A. Knopf, 1923), 53.

Chapter Five

1. Stacey J. Oliker, "The Modernisation of Friendship: Individualism, Intimacy, and Gender in the Nineteenth Century," in *Placing Friendship in Context*, ed. Rebecca G. Adams and Graham Allan (Cambridge: Cambridge University Press, 1999), 18–42.

2. Ernest Groves discusses the rapid rise in education for women and its effect on their relationships with men as well as on their own activities in and outside the home. See Ernest Groves, "Social Influences Affecting Home Life," *American Journal of Sociology* 31, no. 2 (1925): 230–36.

3. Michael Young and Peter Wilmott, *Family and Kinship in East London* (London: Routledge and Kegan Paul, 1957), 30.

4. Michael Young and Peter Wilmott, *The Symmetrical Family* (New York: Pantheon Books, 1973).

5. Ernest W. Burgess and Leonard S. Cottrell, *Predicting Success and Failure in Marriage* (New York: Prentice-Hall, 1939), 15. From their study of middle-class couples during the early 1930s, Burgess and Cottrell identified the greater potency of the husband's background for marital adjustment as the outstanding finding of their research. See also William A. Barry, "Marriage Research and Conflict: An Integrative Review," *Psychological Bulletin* 73, no. 1 (1970): 41–47.

6. This parallels nicely the ideas of Berger and Kellner in defining marriage as a social construction in which husband and wife are, through their interactions, constantly redefining themselves and their relationship in order to make sense of life and the world they live in. Peter L. Berger and Hansfried Kellner, "Marriage and the Construction of Reality—an Exercise in the Microsociology of Knowledge," *Diogenes* 12, no. 46 (1964): 4–17.

7. For a detailed historical analysis of changes in household composition and male and female occupations, see Steven Ruggles, "Patriarchy, Power, and Pay: The Transformation of American Families, 1800–2015," *Demography* 53, no. 6 (2015): 1797–823. Other scholars point to the changes in social life brought by the rural to urban shift in the population. Wirth highlights how city living leads to later marriage and fewer children, shrinking the social significance of family life, but he also notes how interpersonal interactions become more anonymous and superficial, often existing as transactions necessary for individual social mobility rather than for the good of a social collective. Louis Wirth, "Urbanism as a Way of Life," *American Journal of Sociology* 44, no. 1 (1938): 1–24. Testing Wirth's ideas, in his subcultural theory of urbanism Claude Fischer suggests that urban life is not always destructive of social ties. He argues that urban life is different from rural life, but that depending on its context and available subcultures, individuals can adapt in ways that promote social connection. See Claude Fischer, "The Subcultural Theory of Urbanism: A Twentieth-Year Assessment," *American Journal of Sociology* 101, no. 3 (1995): 544–46. In another article Fischer shows evidence that individuals who live in cities have less "traditional" values (including ideas regarding teenagers' using birth control and patriarchal family organization), which suggests that this occurs through the development of unconventional subculture groups whose members share ideas (rather than through a loss of family values, as Wirth argued). See Claude Fischer, "The Effect of Urban Life on Traditional Values," *Social Forces* 53, no. 3 (1975): 430–31. Fischer's ideas are very much in line with Groves's assertion that families change, but not always in negative ways—some adaptations make them stronger. See Groves, "Social Influences," 228–29. Gail Bederman traces shifts in the definition of manliness over time, pointing to the rural to urban shift as a time when men transitioned from expectations of physical strength to a need for mental acumen and when homogenization of work roles and marketplace competition (and longer hours farther from home) favored rational, restrained behavior over expressive or emotional styles. All of this likely contributed to changes in men's interactions with their wives and children. Gail Bederman, *Madness and Civilization: A Cultural History of Gender and Race in the United States, 1880–1917* (Chicago: University of Chicago Press, 1995).

8. Oliker, "Modernisation of Friendship."

9. George Levinger and David J. Senn, "Disclosure of Feelings in Marriage," *Merrill-Palmer Quarterly* 13, no. 3 (1967): 237–49. For a review of sex differences in self-disclosure, see Paul C. Cozby, "Self-Disclosure: A Literature Review," *Psychological Bulletin* 79, no. 2 (1973): 73–91.

10. Jessi Streib, *The Power of the Past: Understanding Cross-Class Marriages* (New York: Oxford University Press, 2015).

11. Burgess and Cottrell, *Predicting Success and Failure in Marriage.*

12. Burgess and Cottrell write that of the 526 completed questionnaires in their study, only 30 were filled out by the couple together, and on a handful an interviewer assisted one or both spouses; most were completed by one spouse (in 153 cases it was a husband and in 317 cases a wife). Burgess and Cottrell, *Predicting Success and Failure in Marriage,* 18.

13. A total of 244 families were recruited for the Berkeley Guidance Study and randomly assigned to two subsamples: one with an intensive regime of data collection featuring parent interviews and observations, and one with a less intensive regime. The intensive regime was designed to provide ongoing guidance to parents as they encountered the challenges of rearing children. From here on we refer to this intervention arm of the sample as the "intensively studied families," the "intensive sample," or the "intensive group." For further details, see Jean Walker Macfarlane, *Studies in Child Guidance: I. Methodology of Data Collection and Organization,* Monographs of the Society for Research in Child Development 3 (Washington, DC: Society for Research in Child Development, 1938).

14. Each five-point scale represents the weighted average of ratings made by two staff members of the Institute. One rater, Jean Macfarlane, saw the parents in interview situations; the other rater used both interviews and observational materials obtained from home visits. The weights assigned to each rating were determined according to the rater's familiarity with those particular areas of marital relations. Thus Macfarlane's ratings were weighted most heavily on internal aspects of the marriage, social and emotional. By using the judgments of skilled clinicians, we have access to measures of marriage that are not likely to emerge from the individual reports of husband and wife. Using an array of interview and observational reports, a clinician can view the marriage as a whole, in all its surface and underlying complexities, and assess aspects a partner would be unaware of.

15. For example, the average correlation coefficient for husband-wife pairs is .55.

16. Sigmund Freud, *Group Psychology and the Analysis of the Ego,* trans. James Strachey (London: International Psychoanalytical Press, 1922), 54.

17. Burgess and Cottrell, *Predicting Success and Failure in Marriage.*

18. Berger and Kellner, "Marriage and the Construction of Reality," 14.

19. See note 7 above.

20. Andrew J. Cherlin, *The Marriage-Go-Round: The State of Marriage and the Family in America Today* (New York: Alfred A. Knopf, 2009).

21. Mirra Komarovsky, *Blue-Collar Marriage* (New York: Random House, 1964), 197.

22. W. Bradford Wilcox and Steven L. Nock, "What's Love Got to Do with It? Equality, Equity, Commitment and Women's Marital Quality," *Social Forces* 84, no. 3 (2006): 1321–45.

23. For a critical evaluation of the empirical evidence on the effects of class heterogamy, see Norval D. Glenn, Sue Keir Hoppe, and David Weiner, "Social Class Heterogamy and Marital Success: A Study of the Empirical Adequacy of a Textbook Generalization," *Social Problems* 21, no. 4 (1974): 539–50. As the authors point out, any attempt to assess the effect of a life or historical difference must include the status of each spouse and their current social positions. Such research faces an "identification problem" because one independent variable is determined by the other two (see Hubert M. Blalock Jr., "The Identification Problem and Theory Building: The Case of Inconsistency," *American Sociological Review* 31, no. 1 [1966]: 52–61). The literature on both differences in SES origin and age differences shows inclusive results. See J. Richard Udry, *The Social Context of Marriage* (Philadelphia: Lippincott, 1966).

24. See Felix M. Berardo, Jeffrey Appel, and Donna H. Berardo, "Age Dissimilar Marriages: Review and Assessment," *Journal of Aging Studies* 7, no. 1 (1993): 93–106.

25. Larry L. Bumpass and James A. Sweet, "Differentials in Marital Instability: 1970," *American Sociological Review* 37, no. 6 (1972): 754–66.

26. To account for the effect of age differences in marriage, we constructed an index of marital differences by summing scores in the areas of general interests, finances, and child discipline. This index was then entered into a stepwise regression equation after the age difference, the age of husband, and class position.

27. Using intensive interviews with 409 husbands and wives, Rainwater conducted an in-depth examination of couples' childbearing desires, contraceptive use, and fertility, and of how that varies across type of marital relationships as well as other social categories. Lee Rainwater, *Family Design: Marital Sexuality, Family Size, and Contraception* (Chicago: Aldine, 1965).

28. Rainwater, *Family Design*, 30.

29. Rainwater, 72.

30. Groves, "Social Influences," 227–40.

31. Burgess and Cottrell, *Predicting Success and Failure in Marriage*, 343.

32. Many of these same gender dynamics and resulting levels of marital quality are reflected in contemporary studies of marriage preferences and behaviors. Wilcox and Nock find that wives' marital satisfaction is higher when men do more emotion work and, interestingly, that tends to happen more often in asymmetric, husband-dominant households than in more egalitarian couples. Wilcox and Nock, "What's Love," 1321–45. Gerson finds that young men and women aspire to companionate, egalitarian marriages but find them challenging to implement. While women tend to plan for self-sufficiency as an alternative, men plan to fall back on an asymmetric family organization, prioritizing men as providers and women as caregivers. Men's preferences most often win out, and couples default to more asymmetric forms. See Kathleen Gerson, *The Unfinished Revolution: How a New Generation Is Reshaping Family, Work, and Gender in America* (New York: Oxford University Press, 2010). Across the decades, marriage as an interactive institution has involved tensions between individual accomplishments outside the home and emotional bonding between the couple, as well as between models of gender-differentiated work and family practices and commitments to equality and mutuality.

33. William J. Goode, *World Revolution and Family Patterns* (New York: Free Press, 1963), 55.

34. Émile Durkheim, *Suicide: A Study in Sociology*, trans. John A. Spaulding and George Simpson, ed. George Simpson (New York: Free Press, 1966).

35. For an exception, see Tamara Hareven, *Family Time and Industrial Time: The Relationship between the Family and Work in a New England Industrial Community* (Cambridge: Cambridge University Press, 1982).

Chapter Six

1. Glen H. Elder Jr., *Children of the Great Depression* (Chicago: University of Chicago Press, 1974), chap. 3.

2. A total of 244 families were recruited for the Berkeley Guidance Study and randomly assigned to two subsamples: one subject to intensive data collection featuring parent interviews and observations, and one less intensive. The intensive group was designed to provide ongoing guidance to parents as they encountered the challenges of rearing children. From here on we refer to

this intervention arm of the sample as the "intensively studied families," the "intensive sample," or the "intensive group." For further details, see Jean Walker Macfarlane, *Studies in Child Guidance: I. Methodology of Data Collection and Organization*, Monographs of the Society for Research in Child Development 3 (Washington, DC: Society for Research in Child Development, 1938).

3. E. Wight Bakke, *Citizens without Work* (New Haven, CT: Yale University Press, 1940), 237. See also Donald A. Hansen and Reuben Hill, "Families under Stress," in *The Handbook of Marriage and the Family*, ed. Harold T. Christensen (Chicago: Rand McNally, 1964), 803.

4. Paul Woolf, *Economic Trends in California, 1929−1934* (Sacramento: California Emergency Relief Administration, 1934), 22.

5. *Berkeley Gazette*, March 21, 1933.

6. Elder, *Children of the Great Depression*, 145.

7. The Berkeley Welfare Society was described in chapter 1. It handled all welfare cases in the city of Berkeley up to May 1935, when it reached its resource limit. Alameda County, where Berkeley is located, assumed the public task of handling the city's relief cases, but county welfare covered only what were considered to be the survival needs, such as rent, food, water, heating, some clothing, and medical care. Family allocations varied by need and household size. When the Berkeley Welfare Society became a private agency dependent on the Community Chest and other funds, it began to address supplementary family needs—those not met by the county, such as medical emergencies and assistance through personal contact with children and adults in need of emotional assistance and guidance.

8. Elder, *Children of the Great Depression*, 45.

9. Of some 1,500 manufacturing concerns that were canvassed in 1932 by the National Industrial Conference Board, slightly more than 15 percent were operating on a five-day schedule— most of these firms claimed they had adopted this schedule since the Depression in order to "spread the work." This altruistic interpretation (*Berkeley Gazette*, October 22, 1932) is interesting for what it does not say about the manufacturers' motives. The concept of "spreading the work" was far superior in public relations to describing the reduction as what it actually was—an attempt to cut labor costs.

10. Robert Lynd and Helen Merritt Lynd, *Middletown in Transition: A Study in Cultural Conflicts* (New York: Harcourt, Brace, 1937), 474.

11. Both structural and personal characteristics are expressed as the market value of the worker. See Robert Hodge, "Toward a Theory of Racial Differences in Employment," *Social Forces* 52 (973): 16−31.

12. Joan Huber and William Form, *Income and Ideology: An Analysis of the American Political Formula* (New York: Free Press, 1973).

13. As Beveridge put it, "The problem of industry is the problem of unemployment." William H. Beveridge, *Unemployment: A Problem of Industry* (London: Longmans, Green, 1930). Industrial sectors or status categories represent a horizontal form of occupational differentiation as distinguished from a prestige-based occupational hierarchy. For a discussion of occupational hierarchies and status categories, see Richard T. Morris and Raymond J. Murphy, "The Situs Dimension in Occupational Structure," *American Sociological Review* 24 (1959): 231−39.

14. Paul H. Douglas, *The Problem of Unemployment* (New York: Macmillan, 1934).

15. Broadus Mitchell, *Depression Decade: From New Era through New Deal, 1929−1941* (New York: Rinehart, 1947), 97.

16. Robert W. Hodge, "Toward a Theory of Racial Differences in Employment," *Social Forces* 52 (1973): 16−31.

17. John D. Durand, *The Labor Force in the United States* (New York: Social Science Research Council, 1948), 113–14.

18. On age as a factor in obtaining a new job after loss of employment, see Michael Aiken, Louis A. Ferman, and Harold L. Sheppard, *Economic Failure, Alienation, and Extremism* (Ann Arbor: University of Michigan Press, 1968), 36. See also a study of unemployed workers in three English cities: M. J. Hill, R. M. Harrison, A. V. Sargeant, and V. Talbot, *Men Out of Work: A Study of Unemployment in Three English Towns* (Cambridge: Cambridge University Press, 1973). The workers were assigned to nine age groups and then compared on mean length of unemployment. In all three cities, duration of unemployment increased with age.

19. Durand, *Labor Force in the United States*, 114–15.

20. Mitchell, *Depression Decade*, 98.

21. Robert W. Hodge, "Toward a Theory of Racial Differences in Employment," *Social Forces* 52 (1973): 16–31; Rueben Hill, *Family Development in Three Generations* (Cambridge, MA: Schenkman, 1973).

22. Mitchell, *Depression Decade*, 97–98.

23. Stephan Thernstrom, *The Other Bostonians* (Cambridge, MA: Harvard University Press, 1973), 58–68.

24. Lynd and Lynd, *Middletown in Transition*, 295.

25. Elizabeth W. Gilboy, *Applicants for Work Relief: A Study of Massachusetts Families under the FERA and WPA* (Cambridge, MA: Harvard University Press, 1940), 176.

Chapter Seven

1. Robert S. Lynd and Helen Merrell Lynd, *Middletown: A Study in Modern American Culture* (1929; repr., New York: Harcourt Brace Jovanovich, 1957), 145.

2. Donald A. Hansen and Reuben Hill, "Families under Stress," in *The Handbook of Marriage and the Family*, ed. Harold T. Christensen (Chicago: Rand McNally, 1964), 803.

3. E. Wight Bakke, *Citizens without Work* (New Haven, CT: Yale University Press, 1940), 237.

4. Joseph Kahl, *The American Class Structure* (New York: Rinehart, 1957), chap. 7.

5. The social class index is described in depth in chapter 3.

6. We constructed the codebook on social standards from a thorough reading of longitudinal records and materials on a one-fifth sample of family units in the intensive subgroup of the Berkeley study ($N = 111$). Two advanced graduate students were trained to apply the resulting codes on social standards to case assembly materials on all families. These materials cover the period 1928–29 to 1945 or departure from the study. One-third of the intensive cases were selected for an assessment of coder reliability. The codes on social standards were reduced to dichotomies so that coder agreement represents complete agreement. Responses to economic standards were grouped as "above average" versus "average or lower."

7. For persons with above-average economic standards, coders also noted the flexibility in standards—whether the parent showed some evidence of flexibility (to gear standards to the reality of the situation) or showed evidence of inflexibility (rigid adherence to standards).

8. Social standards were indexed by a dichotomous variable "moral standards on respectability" to indicate whether there was evidence of these values. With two independent coders, differences were resolved by case review in conference. Additional funds at the end of this work enabled one of the coders to reread the case assemblies and code each case without referring to the previous coding. When this coder completed the second set of codes, she compared them

with her original set and resolved the differences. A similar code, "relative moral standards," was developed to note whether there were differences between wives and husbands in the salience of these standards as a basis for self- and social evaluations.

9. We see this difference clearly in connection with similar measures of value orientations of the Berkeley men and women in an earlier unpublished study at the Institute of their "values and interests." Trained judges rated the individuals on a set of value themes after reading the abstracts on case assemblies of the families. Their ratings on valuing "economic status" and "moralistic perspective" came closest to our measures of social standards of economics and respectability. Economic status indicates valuing upward mobility, social prestige, and material possessions, and moralistic refers to valuing rigid standards and rules. Men's economic standards were strongly associated with valuing economic status, whereas a standard of respectability among men is positively related to a moralistic value orientation. The correlation between our measure of economic standards and the rating of economic status (with its focus on upward mobility and material possession) is strong for both men and women. The standard of respectability is positively correlated with a moralistic value orientation. By contrast, an economic status orientation is negatively correlated with a standard of respectability.

10. Joseph Kahl, *The American Class Structure* (New York: Rinehart, 1957), 193–205. Susan Fiske explores the human obsession with status and social comparisons, both up and down: Susan Fiske, *Envy Up, Scorn Down* (New York: Russell Sage, 2012).

11. Studies of family life during the Depression generally document the adaptational significance of marital solidarity before the economic decline and unemployment. In their extensive review of the literature, Eisenberg and Lazarsfeld concluded that "where there was a good home the depression tended to bring the family together, and where the home was ready to break, the unemployment was the last straw." Philip Eisenberg and Paul Lazarsfeld, "The Psychological Effects of Unemployment," *Psychological Bulletin* 35, no. 6 (1938): 384. The integrative effect of hardship among "good homes" before the Depression remains an open question, since family studies in the 1930s generally lacked adequate measurements of family patterns before, during, and after.

12. Jane Addams, "Social Consequences of Business Depression," in *Aspects of the Depression*, ed. Felix Morley (Chicago: University of Chicago Press, 1932), 13.

13. Economic security is frequently associated in the public mind with economic abundance, and insecurity is linked with poverty or want. But the evidence shows no one-to-one between these emotional states and economic conditions. Writing in the mid-1930s, Kardiner provides a definition of economic security that corresponds with our usage and with that based on contemporary reference group theory. As an emotional state, economic security "is relative and cannot be standardized in terms of physiological or economic units; and, although purely subjectively perceived, it is singularly dependent upon socially determined stimuli and goals. It has a different meaning to the same person at different epochs in his life, varies among different individuals in the same group, and varies widely in different groups as compared with each other." Abram Kardiner, "The Role of Economic Security in the Adaptation of the Individual," *Family* 17, no. 6 (1936): 187–97).

14. The correlation between financial security and marital consensus for 1932–34 is .70. Among nondeprived families, both middle class and working class, financial security is correlated .56 with consensus on spending issues. In the deprived group, the correlation is .48.

15. For the middle-class comparison, the averages for the nondeprived versus deprived groups are significantly different at 3.78 and 4.71, respectively. Dissatisfaction with their husbands' jobs extends to the working-class women as well.

16. Glen H. Elder Jr., *Children of the Great Depression: Social Change in Life Experience* (Chicago: University of Chicago Press, 1974).

17. Robert S. Lynd and Helen Merrell Lynd, *Middletown: A Study in Modern American Culture* (1929; repr., New York: Harcourt Brace Jovanovich, 1957), 179.

18. Jack Weller, *Yesterday's People: Life in Contemporary Appalachia* (Lexington: University of Kentucky Press, 1965), 242.

19. This part of the chapter is inspired by text, tables, and figures in Glen H. Elder Jr., Jeffrey K. Liker, and Bernard J. Jaworski, "Hardship in Lives: Depression Influences from the 1930s to Old Age in Postwar America," in *Life-Span Developmental Psychology: Historical and Generational Effects*, ed. Kathleen McCluskey and Hayne Reese (New York: Academic Press, 1984), 161–201.

20. Jeanne H. Block and Jack Block, "The Role of Ego-Control and Ego-Resiliency in the Organization of Behavior," in *Minnesota Symposium on Child Psychology*, ed. W. A. Collins (Hillsdale, NJ: Erlbaum, 1980), vol. 13, 39–102. C. B. Thomas, "Stamina: The Thread of Life," *Journal of Chronic Disease* 34 (1981): 41–44. Definition of "stamina" provided by Thomas is informed by an earlier edition of the *Merriam-Webster* dictionary.

21. C. Schaeffer, J. C. Coyne, and R. S. Lazarus, "The Health-Related Functions of Social Support," *Journal of Behavioral Medicine* 4 (1981): 381–406.

22. See also Thomas J. Cottle, *Hardest Times: The Trauma of Long Term Unemployment* (New York: Praeger, 2000).

Chapter Eight

1. This historical sequence applies to the United States up to the 1960s. See Dorothy S. Thomas, *Social Aspects of Business Cycles* (New York: Alfred A. Knopf, 1927); Richard A. Easterlin, "Relative Economic Status and the American Fertility Swing," in *Family Economic Behavior*, ed. E. B. Sheldon (Philadelphia: J. B. Lippincott, 1973), 170–223; and Morris Silver, "Births, Marriages, and Business Cycles in the United States," *Journal of Political Economy* 237 (1965): 237–55. Ryder has described the event sequence as a decision strategy: Norman B. Ryder, "The Emergence of a Modern Fertility Pattern: The United States, 1917–66," in *Fertility and Family Planning*, ed. S. J. Behrman, L. Corsa Jr., and B. Freedman (Ann Arbor: University of Michigan Press, 1969), 99–123. The event sequence in Middletown is reported in Robert S. Lynd and Helen M. Lynd, *Middletown in Transition: A Study in Cultural Conflicts* (New York: Harcourt, Brace, 1937), 166.

2. Frank W. Notestein, "The Fertility of Populations Supported by Public Relief," *Milbank Memorial Fund Quarterly* 114 (January 1936): 37–49.

3. When we encountered some reference to a couple employing birth control, it was frequently no more specific than that. Information on methods of contraception in the upper middle class between 1890 and the mid-1920s is reported from a compilation of clinical records by Robert Latou Dickinson and Laura Beam, *A Thousand Marriages: A Medical Study of Sex Adjustment* (Westport, CT: Greenwood, 1931). See also Katharine Bement Davis, *Factors in the Sex Life of Twenty-Two Hundred Women* (New York: Harper, 1929).

4. Lee Rainwater, *And the Poor Get Children* (Chicago: Quadrangle Books, 1960).

5. In the New Deal social programs, the Subsistence Homestead division and the Resettlement Administration attempted to settle urban slum dwellers in garden cities and farm villages. See Jim F. Couch, "The Back-to-the-Land Movement during the Great Depression," *Southern Social Studies Journal* 23 (Fall 1997): 60–67. Moving to the farm and ranch country around San Francisco was an option for economically deprived families, who could supplement their

earnings by bartering their labor for food, clothing, and even medical care. One of the Berkeley families moved to a fruit ranch in the valley, where the head of the household worked as a ranch hand; they bartered gardening services for these goods. His wife described this mode of support as tiring and time consuming.

6. The emotional instability of men before their economic misfortunate undermined their marriages, which in turn intensified the negative effects of economic hardship on all members of the family. See Jeffrey K. Liker and Glen H. Elder Jr., "Economic Hardship and Marital Relations in the 1930s," *American Sociological Review* 48 (June 1983): 343–59. This is a dynamic that has extended across the Berkeley generations, from grandparents to parents and children. See Glen H. Elder Jr., Avshalom Caspi, and Geraldine Downey, "Problem Behavior and Family Relationships: Life Course and Intergenerational Themes," in *Human Development and the Life Course: Multidisciplinary Perspectives*, ed. Aage Sørensen, Franz Weinert, and Lonnie Sherrod (Hillsdale, NJ: Erlbaum, 1986), 293–340.

7. The Berkeley longitudinal study collected observations and behavior ratings on the study children during their first three years, thus enabling an assessment of deprivation effects during a most vulnerable developmental period, as reported in Glen H. Elder Jr., Avshalom Caspi, and Tri Van Nguyen, "Resourceful and Vulnerable Children: Family Influences in Hard Times," in *Development as Action in Context: Problem Behavior and Normal Youth Development*, ed. R. K. Silbereisen, K. Eyferth, and G. Rudinger (New York: Springer, 1986), 167–86.

8. Elder, Caspi, and Van Nguyen, "Resourceful and Vulnerable Children."

9. Elder, Caspi, and Van Nguyen.

10. Glen H. Elder Jr., "Historical Change in Life Patterns and Personality," in *Life-Span Development and Behavior*, vol. 2, ed. P. Baltes and O. Brim Jr. (New York: Academic Press, 1979), 117–59.

11. Elder, "Historical Change," 128–29.

12. This is illustrated in Glen H. Elder Jr., *Children of the Great Depression: Social Change in Life Experience* (Chicago: University of Chicago Press, 1974), as well as in Carol B. Stack, *All Our Kin: Strategies for Survival in a Black Community* (New York: Harper and Row, 1974).

13. M. Brewster Smith, *Social Psychology and Human Values* (Chicago: Aldine, 1969), 215.

14. Martin E. P. Seligman, *Helplessness on Depression, Development, and Death* (San Francisco: W. H. Freeman, 1975).

15. Glen H. Elder Jr. and Richard C. Rockwell, "Economic Depression and Postwar Opportunity in Men's Lives: A Study of Life Patterns and Health," in *Research in Community and Mental Health*, ed. Roberta G. Simmons (Greenwich, CT: JAI Press, 1979), 294.

16. Elder, "Historical Change." For an in-depth examination of this difference in the timing of birth cohort exposure to the Great Depression and subsequent wars, see Glen H. Elder Jr. and Martha J. Cox, "When Societal Events Occur in Lives: Developmental Linkages and Turning Points," in *Children in Changing Worlds: Sociocultural and Temporal Perspectives*, ed. Ross D. Parke and Glen H. Elder Jr. (Cambridge: Cambridge University Press, 2019), 25–56.

17. Norman Ryder, "The Cohort as a Concept in the Study of Social Change," *American Sociological Review* 30, no. 6 (1965): 843–61.

Chapter Nine

1. Lawrence Stone, "The Rise of the Nuclear Family in Early Modern England," in *The Family in History*, ed. Charles E. Rosenberg (Philadelphia: University of Pennsylvania Press, 1975), 13–58.

2. Michael Anderson, *Family Structure in Nineteenth Century Lancashire* (Cambridge: Cambridge University Press, 1971), 150.

3. Colin Rosser and Christopher Harris, *The Family and Social Change: A Study of Family and Kinship in a South Wales Town (Swansea)* (London: Routledge and Kegan Paul, 1965), 259–60.

4. From 1929 to World War II, the Berkeley families were classified each year according to whether they gave or received material assistance of one kind or another and whether they were living with relatives as guests or hosts. The empirical base of these measurements stems from frequent contacts and field notes of Institute workers who visited the families periodically during each year of the 1930s and from annual interviews with the wives. Records are available only on the families from the intensive sample, as is the case for all detailed information on Depression family life. Because kinship was not an explicit target of data collection at the time, we gain a picture of families within the larger kin network only to the extent that relatives entered their interactive world. The archive is thus most satisfactory as a record of kin who impinged on families' daily experience.

We cast a broad net for evidence of giving and receiving aid, from exchanging goods and money to providing temporary shelter. Annual entries on kin assistance usually describe the type of aid in general terms (e.g., blankets, rent, fuel money) and frequently offer no more specific information on the person and family involved than their side of the family (e.g., "the wife's father brought over a check to pay the mortgage"). For the source of aid, we must rely on an overall measure of frequency of contacts with each side of the family. When living quarters were shared, a history of household composition and dynamics recorded the identity and number of resident kin by year, as well as the emotional tone and configuration of relationships.

5. Raymond Firth, Jane Hubert, and Anthony Forge, *Families and Their Relatives: Kinship in a Middle-Class Sector of London* (London: Routledge and Kegan Paul, 1970), 113.

6. The stage of a family might be indexed by the age of the head and children and by size of family. Age of the head is essential in view of our desire to tap the worker's position in his career, and it is so closely linked to number of children that we gained little by developing a composite measure. Only 15 percent of the youngest men had more than one child. All youngest children before the Depression were, in light of the study design, born in 1928–29.

7. E. Wight Bakke, *Citizens without Work* (New Haven, CT: Yale University Press, 1940), 207.

8. Meyer Fortes, *Kinship and the Social Order: The Legacy of Lewis Henry Morgan* (Chicago: Aldine, 1969), 238.

9. Maurice Bloch, "The Long Term and the Short Term: The Economic and Political Significance of the Morality of Kinship," in *The Character of Kinship*, ed. Jack Goody (London: Cambridge University Press, 1973), 76.

10. Anderson, *Family Structure*, 12.

11. Firth, Hubert, and Forge, *Families*, 113.

12. Jack Brehm, *A Theory of Psychological Reactance* (New York: Academic Press, 1966).

13. Robert K. Merton and Elinor Barber, "Sociological Ambivalence," in *"Sociological Ambivalence" and Other Essays*, ed. Robert K. Merton (New York: Free Press, 1976).

14. Hope Jensen Leichter and William E. Mitchell, *Kinship and Casework* (New York: Russell Sage Foundation, 1967), 179.

15. Leichter and Mitchell, *Kinship and Casework*, 179. Bert N. Adams, "Isolation, Function, and Beyond: American Kinship in the 1960s," *Journal of Marriage and the Family* 32 (1970): 575–97; Morris Zelditch Jr., "Doubling Rates and Family Structure in the United States," unpublished manuscript (1956).

16. Peter Townsend, "The Effects of Family Structure on the Likelihood of Admission to an Institution in Old Age: The Application of a General Theory," in *Social Structure and the Family: Generational Relations*, ed. Ethel Shanas and Gordon F. Streib (Englewood Cliffs, NJ: Prentice-Hall, 1965); Rosser and Harris, *Family and Social Change*; Leichter and Mitchell, *Kinship and Casework*.

17. Wendell Bell and Marion D. Boat, "Urban Neighborhoods and Informal Social Relations," *American Journal of Sociology* 62 (1957): 391-98; Adams, "Isolation, Function, and Beyond."

18. Adams, "Isolation, Function, and Beyond."

19. Barkev S. Sanders, Anne G. Kantor, and Doris Carlton, "Income, Children, and Gainful Workers in Urban Multi-family Households," *Social Security Bulletin* 2 (1940): 28.

20. John Modell and Tamara Hareven, "Urbanization and the Malleable Household: An Examination of Boarding and Lodging in American Families," *Journal of Marriage and the Family* 35 (1973): 467-79. We note that the terms "boarder" and "lodger" have been used interchangeably in the literature to refer to nonkin residents of a household, although we use the terms to refer to kin as well, and the terms do have different meanings. Lodging refers merely to co-residence, and boarding to both room and board. We use the term "boarder" without making assumptions regarding the provision of board as well as room. In addition to boarders, some households included a resident domestic. Slightly more than a fifth of the middle-class families had a maid in the household at some point between 1930 and 1941. We have no record of a live-in maid in working-class households.

21. Alan Booth, *Urban Crowding and Its Consequences* (New York: Praeger, 1976); Mark Baldassare, *Residential Crowding in Urban America* (Berkeley: University of California Press, 1978).

22. Walter R. Gove, Michael Hughes, and Omer R. Galle, "Overcrowding in the Home: An Empirical Investigation of Its Possible Pathological Consequences," *American Sociological Review* 44 (1979): 59-80. Excessive social demands, for example, were associated with physical and psychological withdrawal, poor mental health, lack of effective planning, and a general sense of "being washed out." Adults who felt "crowded" were likely to report harassment by children, emotional distance from spouse, lack of marital support, and frequent arguments.

23. Adams, "Isolation, Function, and Beyond." Dorian Apple Sweetser, "Asymmetry in Inter-Generational Family Relationships," *Social Forces* 41 (1963): 346-52.

Part Four

1. Arthur Herman, *Freedom's Forge: How American Business Produced Victory in World War II* (New York: Random House, 2012), 10. This part introduction draws heavily on Herman's vivid account of the mobilization of American business for World War II and on Winik's incomparable history of President Roosevelt's leadership during the war. Jay Winik, *1944: FDR and the Year That Changed History* (New York: Simon and Schuster, 2015).

2. Herman, *Freedom's Forge*, 12.

3. Jean Edward Smith, *FDR* (New York: Random House, 2007); see especially chapter 23, "Day of Infamy."

4. Kevin Starr, *Embattled Dreams: California in War and Peace, 1940-1950* (New York: Oxford University Press, 2002); see especially chapter 2, "Shelling Santa Barbara."

5. Starr.

6. Arthur Verge, "Daily Life in Wartime California," in *The Way We Really Were: The Golden State in the Second Great War*, ed. Roger. W. Lotchin (Urbana: University of Illinois Press, 2000), 15.

7. Verge.

Chapter Ten

1. State of California, *War Council Manual* (Sacramento: California State War Council, Office of State Director of Civilian Defense, 1943).

2. Roger W. Lotchin, "Introduction," in *The Way We Really Were: The Golden State in the Second Great War*, ed. Roger W. Lotchin (Urbana: University of Illinois Press, 2000), 2.

3. Arthur Verge, "Daily Life in Wartime California," in *The Way We Really Were: The Golden State in the Second Great War*, ed. Roger W. Lotchin (Urbana: University of Illinois Press, 2000), 23.

4. Verge, 16. "Blackouts" required extinguishing all lights in the city, while "dimouts," which were implemented later, required extinguishing lights only in areas visible from the ocean and therefore permitted more freedom.

5. For example, "Berkeley 'Dim Out' Deadline Wednesday," *Berkeley Gazette*, May 30, 1942; "Word to Pedestrians," *Oakland Tribune*, September 11, 1942.

6. Berkeley City Council, Regular Meeting, Minutes, December 15, 1942.

7. "In the Puritan Spirit, with Prayers and Confidence, America Today Gives Thanks," *Oakland Tribune*, November 26, 1942 (Thanksgiving Day).

8. State of California, *War Council Manual*.

9. The April 1943 "Messenger" of the Berkeley Defense Council named many local civilian defense volunteer opportunities, including the "Mobilized Women's Army," which asked drivers to share their cars to ease the transportation situation; positions as nurses at local hospitals or as staff at the Southwest Berkeley Hospitality Center; drives for "victory books" for men in the armed forces; tending victory gardens and cooking and canning food (there were 40,000 to 50,000 gardens in the East Bay area); selling war bonds and stamps; collecting salvage; conducting first aid training and block incident drills; providing housing or child care for war workers.

10. [Untitled article], *Berkeley Gazette*, November 18, 1943. From 1940 to 1944, California gained over a million civilians.

11. "Population up 100,000," *Berkeley Gazette*, September 28, 1942.

12. Mark S. Foster, *Henry J. Kaiser: Builder in the Modern American West* (Austin: University of Texas Press, 1989), 71.

13. "During the war, the San Francisco Bay area has become the mightiest concentration of naval ship repair and construction facilities in the world—with 30 separate shipyards under direct control or general supervision of a single naval command." Shipbuilding Review Publishing Administration, *Western Shipbuilding in World War II* (Oakland, CA: Shipbuilding Review, 1945), 21.

14. [Untitled letter], *Berkeley Gazette*, November 18, 1943.

15. Berkeley City Council, Regular Meeting, Minutes, December 8, 1942.

16. "Non-War Workers May Be Moved from City," *Berkeley Gazette*, October 13, 1942.

17. "Local Housing Survey Order," *Berkeley Gazette*, November 21, 1942.

18. "Housing Problem," *Oakland Tribune*, September 22, 1942.

19. "For Private Home Landlords," *Oakland Tribune*, September 7, 1942.

20. For example, the April 1943 "Messenger" of the Berkeley Defense Council reported that 220 property owners in Berkeley had applied to convert buildings into apartments for housing war workers. The rental situation was growing more serious each month. Families with children, in particular, were finding it impossible to secure any accommodations for less than $80 a month, beyond the reach of most renters.

21. [Untitled letter], *Oakland Tribune*, September 2, 1942.

22. "More on Noise," *Oakland Tribune*, September 11, 1942.

23. "Do Some Do This?," *Oakland Tribune*, September 10, 1942.

24. [Untitled letter], *Berkeley Gazette*, November 27, 1942.

25. "War Psychosis," *Berkeley Gazette*, November 16, 1943.

26. Willard Waller, *War and the Family* (New York: Dryden, 1940), 14.

27. Verge, *Way We Really Were*, 20.

28. The first wave occurred in the 1930s as poor farm families from the American prairies were displaced during the Dust Bowl of the 1930s. They were called Okies because so many had come from Oklahoma, but they also hailed from Texas, New Mexico, Colorado, and Kansas. https://en.wikipedia.org/wiki/Dust_Bowl.

29. [Untitled letter], *Berkeley Gazette*, November 16, 1943.

30. "Order Halts Negro Firing at Marinship," *Berkeley Gazette*, November 30, 1943.

31. "More Race Riots Are Predicted," *Oakland Tribune*, November 5, 1943.

32. James W. Hamilton and William J. Bolce, *Gateway to Victory: The Wartime Story of the San Francisco Army Port of Embarkation* (Palo Alto, CA: Stanford University Press, 1946), 37.

33. Hamilton and Bolce.

34. "To Face Problem," *Oakland Tribune*, October 8, 1942; "Return of Japanese," *Berkeley Gazette*, November 13, 1944.

35. https://en.wikipedia.org/wiki/Anti-Japanese_sentiment_in_the_United_States.

36. Verge, *Way We Really Were*, 23.

37. Jon Meacham, *Franklin and Winston: An Intimate Portrait of an Epic Friendship* (New York: Random House, 2004), 71–72.

38. James Bossard, "Family Backgrounds of Wartime Adolescents," *Annals of the American Academy of Political and Social Science* 236 (1944): 33.

39. Arthur Herman, *Freedom's Forge: How American Business Produced Victory in World War II* (New York: Random House, 2012).

40. "High accident rates threatened the allies' ability to win the war." Andrew E. Kersten, *Labor's Home Front: The American Federation of Labor during World War II* (New York: New York University Press, 2006), 167; see especially tables 6.1 and 6.2.

41. Mostly eleven-knot Liberty Ships, followed by a smaller number of faster Victory Ships. Shipbuilding Review Publishing Administration, *Western Shipbuilding in World War II*.

42. Herman, *Freedom's Forge*, x.

43. "Must Get Experience," *Oakland Tribune*, October 5, 1942.

44. California State Chamber of Commerce, "Individual Incomes of Civilian Residents of California by Counties, 1939–1946," Research Department, 1947.

45. William Tuttle, "America's Home Front Children in World War II," in *Children in Time and Place: Developmental and Historical Insights*, ed. Glen H. Elder Jr., John Modell, and Ross D. Parke (New York: Cambridge University Press, 1993), 29.

46. Tuttle.

47. "School Directors Rap 'Exploiting' of Youth," *Berkeley Gazette*, October 1, 1942; "'Exploitation' of Student Hit by Action of Board," *Berkeley Gazette*, October 8, 1942.

48. "Schools and War," *Oakland Tribune*, September 11, 1942.

49. T. L. Engle, "Wartime Mental Hygiene," *Clearing House* 16 (1942): 532–33.

50. Glen H. Elder Jr., "Social History and Life Experience," in *Present and Past in Middle Life*, ed. Dorothy H. Eichorn, John A. Clausen, Norma Haan, Marjorie P. Honzik, and Paul H. Mussen (New York: Academic Press, 1981), 23.

51. Berkeley City Council, Regular Meeting, Minutes, December 1, 1942.

52. "Discipline," *Berkeley Gazette*, October 6, 1942.

53. "Renew Appeal for Youths 18–19 as Army Recruits," *Berkeley Gazette*, October 8, 1942.

54. "Girl Workers' Age Limit Cut," *Oakland Tribune*, November 15, 1942.

55. "Need 18–19 Draftees Now, Says Hershey. Teen Aged Youth Flock to Nation's Recruiting Office," *Berkeley Gazette*, October 15, 1942.

56. The term "latchkey children" seems to have its origin in World War II as children were left at home without supervision while parents worked. https://en.wikipedia.org/wiki /Latchkey_kid.

57. "State and Delinquency," *Oakland Tribune*, November 3, 1943.

58. "Juvenile Centers to Be Considered," *Berkeley Gazette*, November 2, 1944; "Delinquent Parents," *Berkeley Gazette*, November 12, 1943.

59. "Oakland May Have a Curfew," *Berkeley Gazette*, September 30, 1942.

60. United States Department of Justice and the Federal Bureau of Investigation, *Uniform Crime Reports [United States], 1930–1959* [distributed by the Inter-University Consortium for Political and Social Research, University of Michigan, 2003]. See especially parts 2 and 3, 1937–1943 and 1944–59, respectively. https://doi.org/10.3886/ICPSR03666.v1.

61. "Adolescence," in *American Women during World War II: An Encyclopedia*, ed. Doris Weatherford (London: Routledge, 2010), 3–4.

62. Steven Schlossman and Robert Cairns, "Problem Girls: Observations on Past and Present," in *Children in Time and Place: Developmental and Historical Insights*, ed. Glen H. Elder Jr., John Modell, and Ross D. Parke (New York: Cambridge University Press, 1993), 110–30. See also Karen Anderson, *Wartime Women: Sex Roles, Family Relations, and the Status of Women during World War II* (Westport, CT: Greenwood Press, 1981), especially "The Family in Wartime."

63. Weatherford, *American Women during World War II*.

64. United States Department of Justice and the Federal Bureau of Investigation, *Uniform Crime Reports [United States], 1930–1959* [distributed by the Inter-University Consortium for Political and Social Research, University of Michigan, 2003]. See especially parts 2 and 3, 1937–1943 and 1944–59, respectively. https://doi.org/10.3886/ICPSR03666.v1.

65. Berkeley City Council, Regular Meeting [minutes], November 17, 1942; "School Board May Provide Nurseries for War Workers," *Berkeley Gazette*, October 29, 1942.

66. The July 1943 "Messenger" of the Berkeley Defense Council recommended the following six "family fortifications": that parents know where their children are at all times; appoint a responsible person to take charge if they must be away from home; arrange first- and second-choice meeting locations if they are separated during an emergency; obey all orders for civilian defense; have family recreation in the home or on their blocks or in their districts; and cooperate with block and sector wardens to safeguard their families amid this national emergency.

67. "Industrial Amazons," *Berkeley Gazette*, September 11, 1942.

Chapter Eleven

1. Ivan D. Chase, "Vacancy Chains," *Annual Review of Sociology* 17, no. 1 (1991): 133–54.

2. Karen Beck Skold, "The Job He Left Behind: American Women in the Shipyards during World War II," in *Women, War and Revolution*, ed. Carol R. Berkin and Clare M. Lovett (New York: Holmes and Meier, 1980), 55–76; Marc Miller, "Working Women and World War II," *New England Quarterly* 53, no. 1 (1980): 42–61.

3. William Chafe, *The American Woman: Her Changing Social, Economic, and Political Roles* (New York: Oxford University Press, 1972), 54.

4. Maureen Honey, *Creating Rosie the Riveter: Class, Gender, and Propaganda during World War II* (Boston: University of Massachusetts Press, 1985).

5. Chafe, *American Woman*, 54.

6. Karen Anderson, *Wartime Women: Sex Roles, Family Relations, and the Status of Women during World War II*, Contributions in Women's Studies 20 (Westport, CT: Praeger, 1981); Claudia D. Goldin, "The Role of World War II in the Rise of Women's Employment," *American Economic Review* 81, no. 4 (1991): 741–56; Honey, *Creating Rosie the Riveter*.

7. Claudia Goldin, "The Changing Economic Role of Women: A Quantitative Approach," *Journal of Interdisciplinary History* 13, no. 4 (1983): 707–33; Claudia Goldin, "The Quiet Revolution That Transformed Women's Employment, Education, and Family," *American Economic Review* 96, no. 2 (2006): 1–21; Evan W. Roberts, "Her Real Sphere? Married Women's Labor Force Participation in the United States, 1860–1940" (PhD diss., University of Minnesota, 2007), http://econterms.net/pbmeyer/research/occs/morecontent/evan_roberts_dissertation.pdf.

8. Miller, "Working Women and World War II."

9. Andre Alves and Evan Roberts, "Rosie the Riveter's Job Market Advertising for Women Workers in World War II Los Angeles," *Labor: Studies in Working-Class History of the Americas* 9, no. 3 (2012): 53–68; Honey, *Creating Rosie the Riveter*.

10. See also Margaret Mueller, "Work, Family and Well-Being Over the Life Course: Continuities and Discontinuities in the Lives of American Women" (PhD diss., University of North Carolina at Chapel Hill, 2002).

11. W. D. Bolin, "American Women and the Twentieth-Century Work Force: The Depression Experience," in *Woman's Being, Woman's Place: Female Identity and Vocation in American History*, ed. Mary Kelley (Boston: G. K. Hall, 1979), 296–311; Valerie Kincade Oppenheimer, *The Female Labor Force in the United States: Demographic and Economic Factors Governing Its Growth and Changing Composition*, Population Monograph 5 (Berkeley: Institute of International Studies, 1970); Lois Scharf, *To Work and to Wed: Female Employment, Feminism, and the Great Depression* (Westport, CT: Greenwood Press, 1980).

12. Chafe, *American Woman*, 54; Bolin, "American Women."

13. D'Ann Campbell, *Women at War with America: Private Lives in a Patriotic Era* (Cambridge, MA: Harvard University Press, 1984), 32.

14. A method of preserving eggs.

15. Bolin, "American Women."

16. Anderson, *Wartime Women*.

17. These estimates and those that follow come from supplemental analyses not presented here, conducted by the authors and available by request. For this specific result, we use a measure of impairment obtained by coding all family records for any evidence of physical, mental, or alcohol-related issues that interfered with family life from 1932 to 1939.

18. Goldin, "Quiet Revolution," 1–21.

19. Ruth Milkman, "Women's Work and Economic Crisis: Some Lessons of the Great Depression," *Review of Radical Political Economics* 8, no. 1 (1976): 71–97.

20. Alves and Roberts, "Rosie the Riveter's Job Market Advertising."

21. Alves and Roberts.

22. Scharf, *To Work and to Wed*.

23. Mary Frank Fox and Sharlene Nagy Hesse-Biber, *Women at Work* (Palo Alto, CA: Mayfield, 1984).

24. Scharf, *To Work and to Wed*.

25. Milkman, "Women's Work."

26. Scharf, *To Work and to Wed*; Carl N. Degler, *At Odds: Women and the Family in America from the Revolution to the Present* (New York: Oxford University Press, 1980); Mary Kelley, ed., *Woman's Being, Woman's Place: Female Identity and Vocation in American History* (Macmillan Reference USA, 1979); Oppenheimer, *Female Labor Force*; Milkman, "Women's Work."

27. Scharf, *To Work and to Wed*; Winifred D. Wandersee, *Women's Work and Family Values, 1920–1940* (Cambridge, MA: Harvard University Press, 1981).

28. Cecile Tipton La Follette, *A Study of the Problems of 652 Gainfully Employed Married Women Homemakers* (New York: Teachers College, Columbia University, 1934); Scharf, *To Work and to Wed*.

29. Scharf, *To Work and to Wed*; Susan Ware, *Beyond Suffrage: Women in the New Deal* (Cambridge, MA: Harvard University Press, 1981).

30. Anderson, *Wartime Women*.

31. Joan Ellen Trey, "Women in the War Economy—World War II," *Review of Radical Political Economics* 4, no. 3 (1972): 40–57.

32. Campbell, *Women at War*, 32; Chafe, *American Woman*.

33. Sharon Hays, *The Cultural Contradictions of Motherhood* (New Haven, CT: Yale University Press, 1998).

34. Sarah Damaske, *For the Family? How Class and Gender Shape Women's Work* (Oxford: Oxford University Press, 2011).

35. T. Aldrich Finegan and Robert A. Margo, "Work Relief and the Labor Force Participation of Married Women in 1940," *Journal of Economic History* 54, no. 1 (1994): 64–84.

36. Anderson, *Wartime Women*.

Chapter Twelve

1. Alice Smuts, *Science in the Service of Children: 1893–1935* (New Haven, CT: Yale University Press, 2006); see especially chapter 1, "Save the Child and Save the Nation: The Rise of Social Feminism and Social Research."

2. Smuts.

3. See Linda Kerber, "The Republican Mother: Women and the Enlightenment—an American Perspective," *American Quarterly* 28 (1976): 187–205.

4. Smuts, *Science in the Service of Children*; see especially chapter 2, "G. Stanley Hall and the Child Study Movement," and chapter 3, "Scientific Child Rearing, Organized Motherhood, and Parent Education."

5. Nancy S. Dickinson and Richard P. Barth, *The Children's Bureau: Shaping a Century of Child Welfare Practices, Programs, and Policies* (Washington, DC: National Association of Social Workers, 2013); see especially chapter 1, "Lessons Learned and the Way Forward."

6. *The Children's Bureau Legacy: Ensuring the Right to Childhood* (ebook via cb100.acf.hhs. gov); see especially chapter 2, "Saving Babies and Restoring Childhood (1912–1929)." Dickinson and Barth, *Children's Bureau*. From 1914 to 1921, over 1.5 million copies of "Infant Care" had been distributed to American families. By 1940 that count was 12 million.

7. The 1914 "Infant Care" was the first of fourteen editions published through 1989. To this day it is one of the most widely circulated publications in the history of the federal government.

8. "Infant Care" provided very little information on the role of fathers in caring for infants. In the 1935 edition, for example, fathers are mentioned only twice: in the sections on preventing tuberculosis and on training the baby at birth. Kimberly Deavers and Laura Kavanagh, *Caring for Infants Then and Now: 1935 to the Present, a 75th Anniversary Publication* (Rockville, MD: US Department of Health and Human Services, 2014).

9. "Your Child from One to Six" saw editions through the 1970s.

10. The Rockefeller funds were awarded to six university-based research institutes that would "study the factors that affect human development from the earliest stages of life." The intention was that all these centers would "move away from simply providing social welfare and emergency relief and instead advocate for a radically different approach: to invest in scientific research aimed at understanding the roots of poverty, focusing on child development, and emphasizing the practical applications of that research toward the improvement of social problems through early intervention." http://ihd.berkeley.edu/about/history.

11. That is, the experimental group received intensive intervention in child guidance and the control group did not. For more information, see chapter 1 and appendixes B and C.

12. *Ladies' Home Journal* was established over thirty years earlier, in 1882, but in the table of contents from 1890 to 1910 topics related to mothering and parenting do not often appear. Instead, the focus is on tips for homemaking, cleaning, cooking and baking, and recipes.

13. Caroline M. Hinkle, "Child Management in Middle-Class Families in the Early Twentieth Century: Reconsidering Fatherhood in a New Context," Working Paper 42, Center for Working Families, Berkeley, 2002.

14. Archives of *The Child* can be found at http://hearth.library.cornell.edu/h/hearth/browse/title/4732639.html.

15. *Children's Bureau Legacy*, chapter 3, "The Great Depression and Social Security (1930–1939)."

16. *Children's Bureau Legacy*. See also Viviana Zelizer, *Pricing the Priceless Child: The Changing Social Values of Children* (Princeton, NJ: Princeton University Press, 1985).

17. Steven Mintz, *Huck's Raft: A History of American Childhood* (Cambridge, MA: Harvard University Press, 2004).

18. Mintz.

19. Zelizer, *Pricing the Priceless Child*, x.

20. *Children's Bureau Legacy*, chapter 4, "Wartime and Recovery (1940–1956)."

21. The title was shortened to *Baby and Child Care* for the many editions that followed.

22. Annette Lareau, *Unequal Childhoods* (Berkeley: University of California Press, 2003).

23. Karen Anderson, *Wartime Women: Sex Roles, Family Relations, and the Status of Women during World War II* (Westport, CT: Greenwood Press, 1981).

24. Claudia Goldin, "The Long Road to the Fast Track: Career and Family," *Annals of the American Academy of Political and Social Science* 596, no. 1 (2004): 20–35.

25. Robert S. Lynd and Helen M. Lynd, *Middletown: A Study in Contemporary American Culture* (1929; repr., New York: Harcourt, Brace, 1957), 211. The first major assessment of the social world of high school was written by Willard Waller in 1932, followed some ten years later by another classic, August Hollingshead's empirical investigation of high school youth in Elmtown (1949). With the proportion of youth in high school climbing above 80 percent in the 1950s, it is not surprising that the literature of that decade included major studies of adolescent subcultures and peer influence, such as James S. Coleman's *The Adolescent Society* (Glencoe, IL: Free Press, 1961); Willard Waller, *The Sociology of Teaching* (1932; repr., New York: John Wiley, 1965); and

August Hollingshead, *Elmtown's Youth: The Impact of Social Classes on Adolescents* (New York: John Wiley, 1949).

26. The concept of the "authoritative parent"—juxtaposed to "authoritarian" and "permissive" parenting—was developed by Diana Baumrind, professor at the Institute of Human Development at UC Berkeley. For Baumrind, "the authoritative parent attempts to direct the child's activities but in a rational, issue-oriented manner. She [the parent] encourages verbal give and take, shares with the child the reasoning behind her policy, and solicits his objections when he refuses to conform. . . . She enforces her own perspective as an adult, but recognizes the child's individual interests and special ways. The authoritative parent affirms the child's present qualities, but also sets standards for future conduct. She uses reason, power, and shaping by regime and reinforcement to achieve her objectives, and does not base her decisions on group consensus or the individual child's desires" (891). Diana Baumrind, "Effects of Authoritative Parental Control on Child Behavior," *Child Development* 37 (1966): 887–907. An early study of a subset of the Berkeley parents, conducted by Wanda Bronson and her colleagues, demonstrated two modal patterns: one, common to mothers and fathers, is the "highly authoritative and affectionate parent who has a strong emotional investment in the child," and the other is either "a woman who, while clearly assuming responsibility for disciplining the child, gives him little warmth or involvement" or the inverse, "a man who is very warm and involved but unwilling—or unable—to exercise strong parental authority" (151). A danger of the high "permissiveness" and "self-regulation" of child rearing in this era, they noted, was that neither parent would assume "clear responsibility for the socialization of the child" (151). Wanda C. Bronson, Edith S. Katten, and Norman Livson, "Patterns of Authority and Affection in Two Generations," *Journal of Abnormal Psychology* 58 (1959): 143–52. The authoritarian/authoritative/permissive typology has been central to family science in the decades since Baumrind's work, but it is also increasingly criticized for having limited generalizability today outside white middle-class or upper-class families. As an example, see Nadia Sorkhabi and Jelani Mandara, "Are the Effects of Baumrind's Parenting Styles Culturally Specific or Culturally Equivalent?," in *Authoritative Parenting: Synthesizing Nurturance and Discipline for Optimal Child Development*, ed. Robert E. Larzelere, Amanda S. Morris, and Amanda W. Harrist (Washington, DC: American Psychological Association Press, 2012), 113–36.

27. Norman Livson, "Parenting Behavior and Children's Involvement with Their Parents," *Journal of Genetic Psychology* 109 (1966): 173–94.

28. Some of the data in this section on the early adult outcomes of the Berkeley sons were reported in Glen H. Elder Jr. and Richard C. Rockwell, "Economic Depression and Postwar Opportunity in Men's Lives: A Study of Life Patterns and Health," *Research in Community and Mental Health* 1 (1979): 249–303.

29. Jean Walker Macfarlane, *Studies in Child Guidance: I. Methodology of Data Collection and Organization*, Monographs of the Society for Research in Child Development 3 (Washington, DC: Society for Research in Child Development, 1938).

30. Some of the data in this section on the early adult outcomes of the Berkeley daughters were reported in Sheila Kishler Bennett and Glen H. Elder Jr., "Women's Work in the Family Economy: A Study of Depression Hardship in Women's Lives," *Journal of Family History* 4, no. 2 (1979): 153–76.

31. Steven Ruggles, "The Demography of the Unrelated Individual, 1900–1950," *Demography* 25 (1988): 521–36.

32. See Bennett and Elder, "Women's Work in the Family Economy."

Chapter Thirteen

1. The epigraph is from William Faulkner's *Requiem for a Nun* (1951; repr., New York: Random House, 2011), 73.

2. Robert J. Gordon, *The Rise and Fall of American Growth: The U.S. Standard of Living since the Civil War* (Princeton, NJ: Princeton University Press, 2016).

3. Katherine Archibald, *Wartime Shipyard: A Study in Social Disunity* (1947; repr., Champaign: University of Illinois Press, 2006).

4. Within the Berkeley middle class, parents viewed marriages between the upper and lower middle class as marrying beneath one's class. In response, some upper-middle-class fathers whose daughters married into the lower middle class sought to minimize the difference in standard of living by providing substantial material gifts. As conditions became more difficult in the 1930s, the daughters struggled to adapt their consumption to this new reality. For an insightful study of contemporary cross-class marriages see Jessi Streib, *The Power of the Past: Understanding Cross-Class Marriages* (New York: Oxford University Press, 2015).

5. One of the Depression's challenges for the Berkeley couples was deciding about support for their own parents who were not able to care for themselves. As chapter 9 showed, households that took in elderly parents (usually the wife's mother) often had to confront the vastly different worldviews of parents who came from rural small towns in the United States or eastern Europe. Intergenerational conflict was endemic in such middle-class households, especially over child rearing.

6. See chapter 7 on the health consequences of traditional gendered roles in the Berkeley families, with men as breadwinners and wives in family roles.

7. Andrew E. Kersten, *Labor's Home Front: The American Federation of Labor during World War II* (New York: New York University Press, 2006), 166.

8. *Berkeley Gazette*, September 11, 1942.

9. The Institute follow-up in 1969–71 was directed by Henry Maas and Joseph Kuypers. See Henry S. Maas and Joseph A. Kuypers, *From Thirty to Seventy* (San Francisco: Jossey-Bass, 1974).

10. Maas and Kuypers, table 1, p. 8. Their husbands' breadwinner role was too often a no-win option as the strain of finding and keeping work in the Depression, and the long hours and physically grueling work of wartime, took an extraordinary toll on men's psyches and bodies. A similar contrast appears in the lives of women and men in the British national birth cohort of 1946, a uniquely hard time following World War II. Helen Pearson's vivid account of the survival rates of men and women in this cohort shows that women from more privileged backgrounds had death rates about half those of women from poorer backgrounds and also from men with both low- and high-status backgrounds. The proposed explanation centers on the postwar educational and health options available to middle-class women. These options were also available to men, but as breadwinners men also experienced the severe economic hardships of postwar Britain. As we shall see, this finding has relevance to the resilient health in later life of the Berkeley women from the deprived middle class. See Helen Pearson, *The Life Project: The Extraordinary Story of 70,000 Lives* (Berkeley: Soft Skull Press, 2016). Other recent research shows that unemployment has enduring negative effects on men's well-being that persist even when they are employed again. See Cristobal Young, "Losing a Job: The Nonpecuniary Cost of Unemployment in the United States," *Social Forces* 91, no. 2 (2012): 609–34.

11. Maas and Kuypers, *From Thirty to Seventy*.

12. Brent W. Roberts, Kate E. Walton, and Tim Bogg, "Conscientiousness and Health across the Life Course," *Review of General Psychology* 9, no. 2 (2005): 156–68.

13. Glen H. Elder Jr. and Jeffrey K. Liker, "Hard Times in Women's Lives: Historical Influences across Forty Years," *American Journal of Sociology* 88, no. 2 (1982): 241–69, esp. 252.

14. Elder and Liker, 259. The regression coefficient linking economic deprivation and emotional health in 1969–70 is significantly positive for women of middle-class status and negative for working-class women before the Great Depression. For more empirical details on this assessment of Depression hardship in late life, see Glen H. Elder Jr., "Historical Experiences in the Later Years," in *Aging and Life Course Transitions*, ed. Tamara K. Hareven (New York: Guilford, 1982), 75–107. A similar contrast by social class was obtained on the Berkeley women's life satisfaction in later life. Avshalom Caspi and Glen H. Elder Jr., "Life Satisfaction in Old Age: Linking Social Psychology and History," *Journal of Psychology and Aging* 1, no. 1 (1986): 18–26.

15. Elder and Liker. "Hard Times in Women's Lives." The regression coefficient in the Berkeley working class is −.22 versus .14 for middle-class women. Using data from the Health and Retirement Study, Jo Mhairi Hale found evidence from growth curve models that exposure to Depression hardship in early life is negatively associated with fluid cognition. Jo Mhairi Hale, "Cognitive Disparities: The Impact of the Great Depression and Cumulative Inequality on Late-Life Cognitive Function," *Demography* 54 (2017): 2125–58.

16. Elder and Liker, "Hard Times in Women's Lives." esp. 260–64.

17. See Glen H. Elder Jr., Jeffrey K. Liker, and Bernard Jaworski, "Hardship in Lives: Depression Influences from the 1930s to Old Age in Postwar America," in *Life-Span Developmental Psychology: Historical and Generational Effects*, ed. Kathleen McCluskey and Hayne Reese (New York: Academic Press, 1984), 161–201, esp. 179–80.

18. Study directed by Dorothy Field, the Gerontology Center of the University of Georgia, through affiliation with the Berkeley Institute of Human Development.

19. A few Berkeley men provided data for this study in 1982–83, but the subgroup was too small for consideration here.

20. Dorothy Field, Meredith Minkler, R. Frank Falk, and E. Victor Leino, "The Influence of Health on Family Contacts and Family Feelings in Advanced Old Age: A Longitudinal Study," *Journal of Gerontology: Psychological Sciences* 48, no. 1 (1993): 18–28.

21. Dorothy Field and Meredith Minkler, "Continuity and Change in Social Support between Young-Old and Old-Old or Very-Old Age," *Journal of Gerontology: Psychological Sciences* 20, no. 4 (1986): 100–106.

22. The social circle of significant others tends to shrink and becomes more selective, with emphasis on family members. From the evidence presented by Field and Minkler, this selectivity is most evident among friends of the elderly Berkeley women. See Laura L. Carstensen, "Selectivity Theory: Social Activity in Life-Span Context," in *Annual Review of Gerontology and Geriatrics*, ed. K. W. Schaie (New York: Springer, 1991), 195–217.

23. Erik H. Erikson, Joan M. Erikson, and Helen Q. Kivnick, *Vital Involvement in Old Age: The Experience of Old Age in Our Time* (New York: W. W. Norton, 1986).

24. This postwar interview asked how the Berkeley couples viewed their life trajectory to this point and what they thought of their current life situation and their future. In each stage of the time line, they made assessments and expressed dissatisfaction/satisfaction as well as occasionally a plan for a different life in the years to come. In a nationwide survey of life assessments at two points nine years apart, Lachman and her associates conclude that "older adults are more realistic in their retrospective and prospective ratings, a pattern consistent with a focus on accepting the past, maintaining functions, avoiding losses, and coming to terms with one's life course as lived" (896). See Margie E. Lachman, Christina Rocke, Christopher Rosnick, and

Carol D. Ryff, "Realism and Illusion in Americans' Temporal Views of Their Life Satisfaction: Age Differences in Reconstructing the Past and Anticipating the Future," *Psychological Science* 19, no. 9 (2008): 889–97.

25. Dorothy Field, "Looking Back, What Period of Your Life Brought You the Most Satisfaction," *International Journal of Aging and Human Development* 45, no. 3 (1997): 169–94.

26. Allison J. Pugh, "What Good Are Interviews for Thinking About Culture? Demystifying Interpretive Analysis," *American Journal of Cultural Sociology* 1, no. 1 (2013): 42–68; Stephen Vaisey, "Is Interviewing Compatible with the Dual-Process Model of Culture?," *American Journal of Cultural Sociology* 2, no. 1 (2014): 150–58; Michèle Lamont and Ann Swidler, "Methodological Pluralism and the Possibilities and Limits of Interviewing," *Qualitative Sociology* 37, no. 2 (2014): 153–71.

27. Field, "Looking Back," 182.

28. Erikson, Erikson, and Kivnick, *Vital Involvement in Old Age.*

29. The concept of a longitudinal telescope is described in William P. Butz and Barbara Boyle Torrey, "Some Frontiers in Social Science," *Science* 312, no. 5782 (2006): 1898–1900.

30. The Framingham Heart Study began in 1948, after the premature death of President Franklin D. Roosevelt from heart disease and stroke in 1945 and sparked by the growing recognition, codified in the National Heart Act of 1948, that "the Nation's health is seriously threatened by diseases of the heart and circulation, including high blood pressure. . . . These diseases are the main cause of death in the United States and more than one in every three of our people die from them." US Senate Committee on Labor and Public Welfare, 80th U.S. Congr., 2nd sess., Senate Report 2215. The National Heart Act, June 16, 1948, 481, 62 Stat. 464, as reported in Syed S. Mahmood, Daniel Levy, Ramachandran S. Vasan, and Thomas J. Wang, "The Framingham Heart Study and the Epidemiology of Cardiovascular Disease: A Historical Perspective," *Lancet* 383 (March 2014): 999–1008. This article provides a fascinating historical account of how the Framingham Study came about and advanced knowledge of the epidemiology of cardiovascular disease and medical practice.

31. Michael Wadsworth provides a historical account of conditions in Great Britain during Depression hard times and World War II that played a major role in generating support for this pioneering study. See Michael Wadsworth, "The Origins and Innovatory Nature of the 1946 British National Birth Cohort Study," *Longitudinal and Life Course Studies* 1, no. 2 (2010): 121–36.

32. Annette Bernhardt, Martha Morris, Mark S. Handcock, and Marc A. Scott, *Divergent Paths: Economic Mobility in the New American Labor Market* (New York: Russell Sage Foundation, 2001).

33. Arne L. Kalleberg, "Precarious Work, Insecure Workers: Employment Relations in Transition," *American Sociological Review* 74, no. 1 (2009): 1–22.

34. Leonard Cain, "Age Status and Generational Phenomena: The New Old People in Contemporary America," *Gerontologist* 7 (1967): 83–92.

35. Sarah Damaske, *For the Family? How Class and Gender Shape Women's Work* (Oxford: Oxford University Press, 2011).

Appendix B

1. Jean Walker Macfarlane, *Studies in Child Guidance: 1. Methodology of Data Collection and Organization,* Monographs of the Society for Research in Child Development 3 (Washington, DC: Society for Research in Child Development, 1938).

2. Joseph Kahl, *The American Class Structure* (New York: Holt, Rinehart and Winston, 1961).

3. Erik H. Erikson, Joan M. Erikson, and Helen Q. Kivnick, *Vital Involvement in Old Age: The Experience of Old Age in Our Time* (New York: W. W. Norton, 1986).

Appendix C

1. Data preparation at Berkeley included able coding by Stephen Schultz and Jerrold Buerer, with assistance from Natalie Luchese as a half-time administrative member of the staff. Janice Stroud and Elizabeth Wilson helped with coding for most of the year. Marjorie Honzik, a senior member of the Institute staff, provided much valued guidance regarding the Berkeley study, as did Rose Fox, an administrative assistant at the Institute, and Carol Huffine. Barbara Burek, the Institute archivist, played a most important role across the 1970s.

2. The project also received valuable support from Angel Beza, assistant director at the Institute. Tom Hastings and Don Kacher, sociology graduate students with methodological training, gave expert help in data analysis. They continued as research assistants over the next two years in a related National Institute of Mental Health project, along with Howard Sacks and Sheila Bennett, two of Elder's doctoral students in sociology.

3. A UNC colleague, Richard Rockwell, joined the research team at the Boys Town Research Center along with David Ross. Linda Hunt, Jani Morrison, and Susan Paz from Omaha did valuable statistical and clerical work.

4. Elder recruited Jeffrey Liker as a postdoctoral fellow from the Department of Sociology at the University of Massachusetts, along with Bernard Jaworski and Deborah McInnis, two highly regarded research assistants. Cathy Cross, a recent graduate of the Human Development program at Cornell, became a central member of the research staff, and Steve Stewart another Cornell graduate, carried out expert data analyses.

Index

Fortes, Meyer, 144
Framingham Heart Study, 15, 238, 298n30
Frank, Lawrence, 268n12
Freud, Sigmund, 75–76, 206
Friedman, Thomas, 268n8
frontier, closing of, 21–22, 28
futurists, 268n8

gender, 85, 155, 181–82, 203, 266; birth cohort, 10; of children, 137–38, 140; cohort differences, 141; discrimination, 58, 198; division of labor, 72; gender differences, 119–20; gendered expectations, 240; gender ideologies, 209–11, 219; gender norms, 236, 239; gender relations, 86, 119, 281n32; gender roles, 219, 240–41; gender variations, 264; and health, 121; mental health, 125–26; model of adulthood, 63; "modern woman," challenging of, 211; parenting of, 8; separation of work, 62; as status differentiator, 10; unemployment and mental health, 125–26. See also men; women
generation gap, 213. See also age differences; cohort; cohort differences; family
Germany, 10, 15, 22, 28, 161, 163, 176
Gerson, Kathleen, 281n32
GI Bill, 4, 165, 216, 223, 240
Goldin, Claudia, 210–11
Goode, William, 86
Gordon, Margaret, 23, 271n13, 271n19
Gordon, Robert, 1, 4, 224, 267n2, 268n8
grandparenting of 1900 generation, 233, 237, 257
Great Britain, 28, 32, 161–62, 227, 238, 298n31. See also England
Great Crash, 106, 111
Great Depression, 4, 6–7, 9, 13–14, 20, 23, 36–37, 40, 48, 63, 65, 67–68, 71–72, 78, 105, 112, 116, 119–20, 127, 136, 139–41, 161, 164, 167, 178, 183–84, 189, 191–94, 197–98, 200–202, 210, 216, 221, 223–25, 228–29, 231–39, 255, 259–63, 270n31, 282n9, 284n11, 287n6, 296n10, 298n31; back to the land movement, 135; Berkeley children, effect on, 264; Berkeley men, effect on, 91–92, 96–98, 102–3, 108–9, 122, 125, 137, 240; Berkeley women, effect on, 93, 117, 126, 241; births, 131–33; boarders and lodgers, taking on, 153; construction and manufacturing industries, 98–99; "Depression model," 143, 149; deprived families, and female bond, 138; doubling up, of generations, 145–46, 153, 158, 258; emotional health, effect on, 122; fertility, 128–30; hardship, and fluid cognition, 297n15; huddling during, 158; job loss, 10, 89, 100–101, 103–4, 226, 240; kinship, 76, 98, 138, 142–50, 152–55, 158, 264, 287n4; legacy of, 107–9; long hours, 97; long-term unemployment, trauma of, 108; material aid, 143, 146, 149; middle class, effect on,

92, 94, 110, 115, 158, 190, 230; self-employment, 97, 99; shared households, 152–54; social class, and generational identity, 155; status change, 110; unstable worklife, 107; "untimely pregnancy," 132; working class, effect on, 8, 92, 94, 115, 158, 190, 227, 264
Groves, Ernest, 85, 278n2, 279n7

Haines, Michael, 273n11
Hale, Jo Mhairi, 297n15
Hall, G. Stanley, 204
Hamilton, James, 173
Harris, Christopher, 143
Herman, Arthur, 269n29
heterogamy, of marital partners, 81. See also homogamy
Hill, Reuben, 50
hinge generation, historical hinge, 10, 240
Hollingshead, August, 43, 294–95n25
Holt, L. Emmett, 204
homeownership: age differences, 47–48; as core value, 19; home, satisfaction with, 47–48; men, attitudes toward, 19, 46–48, 53, 64; and middle class, 64; respectability, 46, 111–12, 114; stature, reflection on, 47; thrift, association with, 49; women, attitudes toward, 46, 63–64; and working class, 64
Homestead Act (1862), 27–28
homogamy, of marital partners, 29, 79. See also heterogamy
Hoover, Herbert, 3, 46
Hoover Dam, 14. See also Boulder Dam
Hurricane Katrina, 270n4
Hutchinson, E. P., 31

immigration, 11, 21, 32–33, 35, 41–42; foreign born, and factories, 31; mass, 3; second generation, mobility of, 30. See also chain migration; migration
individualism, 23, 98, 275–76n33
inequality, 38, 42, 98, 238, 273n5; asymmetry, 83; marital, 83–85
"Infant Care" (publication), 293n7, 294n8
intergenerational frameworks, 6, 164, 237, 253–54, 257–58, 261; deprived families, 138; households, 8; patterns, 51; transfers, 50, 53; among women, 139
Ireland, 22, 28
Italy, 15, 26–28, 34, 163, 274n20

Janet March (Dell), 70–71
Japan, 15, 23, 162–63, 175, 223–24
Japanese Americans, internment of, 163, 174–75, 179
job loss, 10, 73, 89, 96, 100–101; character, questioning of, 152; emotional health, adverse